AESCHYLUS
AGAMEMNON

EDITED BY THE LATE

JOHN DEWAR DENNISTON
LITT.D., F.B.A.
FELLOW OF HERTFORD COLLEGE, OXFORD

AND

DENYS PAGE
M.A., F.B.A.
REGIUS PROFESSOR OF GREEK, AND
FELLOW OF TRINITY COLLEGE
CAMBRIDGE

OXFORD
AT THE CLARENDON PRESS

Oxford University Press, Amen House, London E.C.4

GLASGOW   NEW YORK   TORONTO   MELBOURNE   WELLINGTON
BOMBAY   CALCUTTA   MADRAS   KARACHI   KUALA LUMPUR
CAPE TOWN   IBADAN   NAIROBI   ACCRA

FIRST PUBLISHED 1957
REPRINTED LITHOGRAPHICALLY IN GREAT BRITAIN
AT THE UNIVERSITY PRESS, OXFORD
FROM SHEETS OF THE FIRST EDITION
1960

PREFACE

AMONG the papers left by the late John Denniston was the draft of a commentary on Aeschylus' *Agamemnon*, written in his own hand and dated at the end 'August 1947'. It was known at that time that Professor Fraenkel's major edition of the play would be published before very long; and Denniston's intention was to wait, and to take Professor Fraenkel's work fully into consideration before making a final version of his own commentary.

This was the position at the time of his death in May 1949. In the autumn of that year Mrs. Denniston suggested to me that I should prepare the edition for publication; and I need say no more about my reasons for agreeing to do so than that Denniston had left me in no doubt that this would be his wish if he should leave the work undone.

There is a special reason why I should have found it a difficult and lengthy task. Professor Fraenkel's edition of the play was published in the summer of 1950; and it was at once obvious that there could be no question of merely making additions and subtractions in Denniston's draft. I do not intend to go into much detail about this. Professor Fraenkel's commentary is very long and very learned: the differences between him and Denniston were very numerous; and there was an immense amount of information and argument to be considered and judged. I had to decide what Denniston himself would have done: and I have never seriously doubted what that would have been. He would have reconsidered everything afresh, from the first line to the last, in the light of the enormously extensive researches embodied in Professor Fraenkel's book; and he would have rewritten his own draft accordingly, of course with fullest acknowledgement of his obligations and candid expression of his disagreements.

My duty, which has taken five years to discharge, was to

undertake that reconsideration and rewriting. It follows that I am responsible for a considerable measure of the form and substance of the completed work. I do not see how it could have been otherwise; and I should find it very distasteful, even if it were possible, to enter upon any more detailed definition of what is Denniston's, what is mine, and what is a blend of the two. I would add this only: it has been a source of constant anxiety to me, that I should have taken upon myself the responsibility of using Denniston's work in this way. Few scholars in our time have been so much at home as Denniston in Greek literature and the Greek language; his reputation does not at all depend on anything I may do or leave undone, but I shall never be quite rid of the feeling that I have given myself too free a hand, and that I may not have completed his work in a way that would have met with his approval.

It was inevitable from the start that the present edition should quite often assail positions held or supported by Professor Fraenkel. I have the strongest personal reasons for regretting this: but a glance at any ten pages of his commentary will show that Professor Fraenkel will be the first to agree that it is not possible to edit this play without taking up arms from time to time against eminent predecessors. There is nothing surprising if 812 pages of commentary provide material for a few dozen instances of strongest disagreement; and I have no doubt, *si parva licet componere magnis*, that the next editor will react in the same way to the present book. δράσαντι παθεῖν, τριγέρων μῦθος τάδε φωνεῖ: and little by little our understanding of the play improves. I am particularly sorry that the severe limitations of space deliberately imposed on this edition preclude the fuller discussion which such differences of judgement usually deserve, and enforce a disagreeably dogmatic-looking brevity; but I reflect that nobody can fail to notice how lightly the disagreements weigh in the scales against the debts.

Since both editors had covered, over a long period of time, a great deal of the same ground, it follows that in a number of places they had drawn similar conclusions or made similar observations or quoted the same evidence. In such cases, wherever an acknowledgement of priority was due to Professor Fraenkel, I have taken much care to make that acknowledgement, as I am sure Denniston would have done; and quite frequently, where the discussion appeared to extend beyond the immediate needs of this edition, I have simply referred the reader to the fuller commentary.

Denniston's work was primarily designed for use by students at Universities; though he hoped (and so of course do I) that it might also meet the requirements of the higher forms in schools. One of the most serious problems which confronted him—a problem still more serious for me, who had Professor Fraenkel's immense commentary to take into account—was the need for compression. It is a task of the utmost difficulty to limit a commentary of this kind on this play to these dimensions without defeating its purpose: let those who have tried, even for fifty lines, be judges in this matter. I ruefully reflect on notes in this edition, extending to half-a-dozen lines of print, which represent the mere summary and conclusion of elaborate essays extending to half as many thousand words. Among many economies I mention one in particular: although Denniston systematically explored all previous editions and all periodicals and the like, he did not as a rule include in his notes references to works generally inaccessible to his potential readers, or written in languages with which they were likely to be unfamiliar.[1] This fact, that so many of the references to modern researches are to works written in English, gives a false impression not only of the amount of work which we have done, but also of the obligation which any editor of this play must owe to Continental scholarship. I have adhered to Denniston's policy in this respect, especially since

[1] He did, however, refer the reader very frequently to the great German work on Greek Grammar, Kühner–Blass and Kühner–Gerth (abbreviated throughout to K.–B. and K.–G.); and in this I have followed him.

the deficiency is so amply supplied by Professor Fraenkel's commentary.

Denniston left no text or introduction of his own: these I have therefore supplied. The introduction is not of a conventional type: it sketches, without elaboration, a portrait of Aeschylus different from that which is apparently popular in this country nowadays; though Walther Kranz and Herbert Weir Smyth would have recognized it quickly enough. There is surely need for a fresh examination of this poet's aims and achievements, and I have long wondered whether I ought to make this short and summary introduction more elaborate and erudite: in refraining from doing so I am guided by the opinion of students in more than one University who have already heard it read.

I have to acknowledge a particular obligation to Professor A. J. Beattie, Mr. P. H. J. Lloyd-Jones, and Mr. G. S. Kirk. For two years we met weekly for two hours or more during term, and studied the play (and also Professor Fraenkel's commentary) from start to finish. I learnt and unlearnt much during those sessions, and I have an uneasy feeling that my friends will recognize property of their own incorporated in this work. I am deeply indebted also to Professor K. J. Dover, who read the commentary in manuscript and made a considerable number of suggestions, none of which I could afford to ignore and most of which I thankfully adopted. Finally, I have been so fortunate as to obtain the advice of Professor Paul Maas on many passages in manuscript; and Mr. Lloyd-Jones has applied great learning and ingenuity to the reading of the first proofs; he has most generously permitted me to incorporate a large number of improvements, most of which could not, at that stage, conveniently be ascribed to their author by name.   D. L. P.

Trinity College
Cambridge

CONTENTS

NOTE ON ABBREVIATIONS

*In general I have followed the example of the
Liddell–Scott–Jones Lexicon; but among the
abbreviations which differ from it there is one
which may prove obscure if not explained,
'E.H.' = 'Euripides' Herakles'*

INTRODUCTION

AESCHYLUS AND *AGAMEMNON*

AESCHYLUS was born in a year not far removed from 525 B.C.,
when Athens was still governed by a Tyrant, an absolute
ruler of a type to which many states in Greece owed much
of their prosperity and progress in the sixth century; but
already old-fashioned, doomed to early extinction in most
of the great cities of Hellas and Asia Minor.

When Aeschylus was about ten years old, the long-awaited
revolution came. During the next six years he witnessed the
greatest social and political upheaval in the history of
Athens: the assassination of the tyrant's brother (514 B.C.);
the expulsion of the tyrant (510 B.C.); the arrival at Athens
of a Spartan king (508 B.C.), with sword in one hand and a
new constitution for Athens in the other; the surrounding
of the Spartan and his soldiers on the Acropolis; their sur-
render and ignominious retreat. And then the social and
political reforms of Cleisthenes, the earliest structure of
Athenian democracy (but not its foundation; that had been
laid by Solon, and by no means dismantled by Peisistratus);
whereby not a person in the state of Attica but was required
to abandon, at a word, his primary allegiance, sanctified by
immemorial time, to the ties of family and clan, and to look
in future, for the centre of his loyalties and the source of his
rights, to an artificial and complicated network of parishes.
Aeschylus grew to manhood in the midst of overthrown
traditions; this was the beginning of a brave new world,
destined to a brief season on the heights of human achieve-
ment.

And this great change, this liberation of the people, came
only just in time. For in 490 B.C., when Aeschylus was about
thirty-five years of age, the King of Kings, Darius, sent a
great expedition from Persia across the sea to destroy the

city of Athens; and then, as later, it was the new-founded spirit and confidence of Athens which saved the day. Aeschylus was one of that devoted band of whom it was long remembered how they charged in full armour down the hill at Marathon; who, through their own valour and the superior tactical skill of their commander, Miltiades, routed the Persians on the shore and drove them back into the sea. Aeschylus' brother was among the heroes of that great victory; his own courage was commemorated in the epitaph on his tomb far away in Sicilian Gela, where he died some thirty-five years later.

But soon there was talk of a much greater Persian host assembling; of a bridge thrown over the Hellespont; of a channel dug through the peninsula of Mount Athos; of two million men in arms advancing by land, and twelve hundred ships at sea. In 480 B.C. (in whatever numbers) they were come: the pass of Thermopylae was turned; the Athenians left their city and lay in their fleet off Salamis, waiting for the dawn that meant destruction—if democracy had not built two hundred ships a few years ago, and if its leader were not the craftiest statesman of his day, Themistocles.

Out of the Persian wars arose the Athenian Empire, the command of a confederation of Hellenic states; and out of her fleet arose the more radical democracy of Aeschylus' later years. The Persian wars proved that the safety of Hellas depended on two things above all: first, the ability of the greatest maritime state to control the rest, so that a large fleet might at any time be assembled and properly commanded; and secondly, on the skill and loyalty of the men who rowed the ships. Now the men who rowed the ships for Athens were (for the most part) *citizens*, of a class lower and more numerous than those hitherto admitted to full rights and powers in the state. An enormous number of able-bodied citizens were henceforth to be employed in the making and maintenance of the fleet, working in the harbours, and rowing the ships on which the safety of the state depended. A new political force had been created, and

Aeschylus lived to see the new school of democratic politicians who controlled and exploited that force: Pericles won his first great triumph a few years before *The Oresteia* was produced at Athens; and *The Eumenides* leaves little room for doubt that its author counted himself in the ranks of the progressive.

In these great events Aeschylus was deeply engaged. And it is by no means enough to say that his tragedies have some relation to contemporary thought and practice. In the history of this great social upheaval there was no more agitated question than that of the principles and administration of Justice; and half a century was to elapse before comfortable (however misleading) answers were found by radical politicians for some of the questions propounded or implicit in Aeschylean plays.

Under the rule of the tyrant the meaning and sanction of justice and the law are not problematic. There is no law but what the tyrant dictates or approves; there is no justice but his verdict; there is no sanction but his power. But now the tyrant has been removed from society: it was like removing the supreme deity from religion. There was no longer an absolute standard or sanction; a new Zeus must be invented, and invested with the authority which the tyrant had exercised.

It is clear that not even liberated democratic man can live without some rule of law. But, in practice, the foundations of law had been subverted together with the abolition of tyranny; and, in theory, what room was left for law in a community of equals? Let the law be freely made by democratic man: is there any reason why democratic man should not freely break or evade it, if he can do so to his advantage and with impunity, perhaps even without harm to others? We have abolished the only sanction of law, the power of an absolute ruler; and we do not yet understand the right of our equals to interfere with us. We need an entirely new philosophy of Justice; and Aeschylus will give us one.

It would be well if the sun did not shine so impartially on

the just and the unjust; if pride always went before a fall, as sometimes it does. Many who saw *Agamemnon* must have called to mind the career of the Spartan general Pausanias some twenty years earlier. He too had led his army to victory; he too was corrupted by pride and oriental pomp; he too came home to ignominious death. But these requirements of the moral sense are not always so simply satisfied. The world has always known the unworthy in high places, and the good man unrewarded or even afflicted with misfortune. It is quite obvious that on earth, here and now, there is no certainty of justice. It seems therefore tenable that the criterion by which we should test our actions is not Justice but Expediency; the question is not whether they conform to law, but whether they are to our advantage. Justice has a strictly limited and practical part to play: it is something which we may be called upon to seek in law courts if our path to prosperity is obstructed by others; it is a grand name for a jury's verdict in our favour, a verdict which we are free to seek to obtain by all means at our disposal, fair and foul.

Aeschylus' answer to this problem emerges clearly, both by statement and by implication, from his plays. The rule of law among men was not made by man: it is a condition imposed upon society by the will of a supreme god; and the sanction of law is his power. And if it is said that the unjust are nevertheless observed to prosper, Aeschylus will answer that this is not ultimately so. He offers two solutions, where one would have sufficed: first, that the unjust will be punished in an afterworld;[1] secondly, that their sins will be visited on the heads of their posterity.[2] Crime is always followed, sooner or later, by punishment; δράσαντι παθεῖν, τριγέρων μῦθος τάδε φωνεῖ. This theory of 'sooner or later' has great advantages: the 'sooner' is exemplified often enough to serve as a powerful deterrent; the 'later' cannot be disproved.

---

[1] *Suppl.* 230 f., 415 f.; *Eum.* 269 ff.

[2] *Suppl.* 433 ff.; *Agam.* 369 ff.; Dodds, *The Greeks and the Irrational* (1951) 33 ff.

Most of this, and more, had been said in Athens by Solon a hundred years before.[1] It is the will of Zeus that justice should govern men in all their dealings. The transgressor goes his way at his peril; retribution will overtake him in the end. The righteous are rewarded with prosperity and happiness: if this should appear not to be so, the theological problem is easily solved. The proposition 'no crime without punishment' is convertible: 'no punishment without crime'. If the righteous man suffers, you may be sure that his ancestors have sinned. Some fault can always be found in every example; for man is prone to error, and the Athenian gods were easily offended. Such in effect was the teaching of Solon.

Both Aeschylus and Solon observed (and their times afforded them abundant proof) that man is never in such danger as when prosperity or success attends him. There is a limit which is easily overstepped; a point at which wealth turns to luxury, pride to arrogance, self-confidence to denial of the divine. And the wages of these is Ruin. There is no escape, no atonement. Mankind is taught in a hard school of experience: he may not even have the opportunity to profit from his lesson. Agamemnon's time for learning was brief enough: 'Clytemnestra's ax gave him no pause to take to himself the lesson that wisdom comes through suffering';[2] but the rest of the world may mark, and stifle its misgivings about the justice of the gods.

Yet this omnipotence is exercised indirectly: the will of Zeus on earth is done through the agency of a numerous and discordant host of angels. Athena and Apollo play important parts in *The Eumenides*; Aphrodite in *The Danaids*. But these, the Olympians, are not the most prominent or effective of the ministers of Zeus. Aeschylean man moves

[1] See especially Solon fr. 1 (Diehl), with Lattimore's comments in *Am. Journ. Phil.* lxviii (1947). The ideas are as old as Hesiod, and had been familiar to the Hittites long before him.

[2] Weir Smyth, *Aeschylean Tragedy* (Sather Classical Lectures, 1924) 164; a very good book, from which I have often borrowed.

bewildered among a multitude of sterner demons—Ruin, Fury, Retribution, Imprecation, Avenger, and their fellows —who are not occasional visitors, seasonal tourists among men, but ever present, ever intervening; the threads of their existence are woven into the fabric of man's life. All deeds are watched, and weighed; and whereas it is doubtful whether recompense awaits the just hereafter, it is certain that punishment awaits the wicked—he will be brought to trial in Hades, and here on earth the hand of heaven will smite his posterity. This demonology is characteristic of common opinion at Athens in the time of Aeschylus.[1] For us, it is hard to imagine, harder to understand:

> In our land there dwell no more immortals, such as were adored on the heights and in the caverns of Aeschylean Attica. Unlike that people to whom the poet belonged, we have no faith in the thousand various phantom powers above and below the earth, gods and goddesses, heroes and demons and holy serpents. We build them no temples to house their images, celebrate no festivals at which they are our invited guests. Their sublime portraits are not everywhere before our eyes in cult-statue or temple-frieze. We do not encounter in the streets their priests and priestesses, processions and sacrificial trains. We have no trust in oracles, mysteries, soothsayings and dreams; we do not pray at sunrise and sunset, before we drink, at departure and home-coming. We make no libation of bread and wine, no sacrifice to the souls of our dead; we do not give the god his share at each success in battle, in the games, in the theatre, in the work of our hands.[2]

Innumerable superstitions darkened and dominated the lives of men, even among the most intelligent; and in this respect Aeschylus was certainly not in advance of his time. For him, the ministers of the divine will are a diverse and

[1] See Dodds, op. cit. 40: 'Aeschylus did not have to revive the world of the daemons: it is the world into which he was born.' In general, it would be hard to show that Aeschylus has advanced appreciably beyond the position reached by Hesiod in the realm of theological speculation. See now Lloyd-Jones in *J.H.S.* lxxvi (1956).

[2] W. Kranz, *Stasimon* (1933) 37 f., translated; this part of the Introduction is much indebted to the second chapter of that remarkable book.

jealous brood, and Zeus appears indifferent to the conflict of their claims. The crime of Orestes was enjoined by Apollo at the command of Zeus; who nevertheless authorized the Furies to exact retribution. Zeus himself commanded Agamemnon to sail to Troy;[1] but looked on with stoical calm while his daughter Artemis prevented Agamemnon from sailing except at the cost of inexpiable crime, the killing of Iphigeneia.

There is much that is crude, and much that is confused, in these conceptions; there is no possibility of deducing a coherent theology, let alone philosophy, from the diversity of demons revealed in only seven plays. There may be light within Aeschylus, and light at the end of the path along which he struggles; but around him still is darkness, or twilight at most. We must be on our guard against the temptation to believe that his gods and demons are represented as being laws or forces of a spiritual kind; in truth he gives them human shape and many human qualities. All, except Zeus, may walk on earth, and all may be manifest to human sight. We are told that they have eyes to see and ears to hear; what clothes they wear, and by what means they travel. Zeus himself has human shape, is seated on a throne in a palace like a mortal tyrant; has bow and arrows, weighs in actual scales. Even he was once a character in an Aeschylean play. Nowhere is there any awareness of what profounder thinkers had been preaching for many years: reading the meagre fragments of Xenophanes and Heracleitus, we should naturally suppose that Aeschylus must have lived long before them, so much more penetrating is their insight into the nature of the world and the mind of man.

Aeschylus is first and foremost a great poet and a most powerful dramatist: the faculty of acute or profound thought is not among his gifts. He takes for granted certain long-established opinions about man's relation to the supernatural

[1] This fact of cardinal importance is often overlooked by those who discuss the conduct of Agamemnon as described in the opening Chorus of our play; Aeschylus repeatedly insists on it (see below, pp. xxiii n. 3).

world; and he is not concerned to criticize doctrines which Solon in his time would have thought conventional. He devoutly believes in the manifold divinities and demons of whom he writes; believes that man is at the mercy of their inscrutable and often uncomfortable dealings; and yet finds therein a pattern of Justice, which is too often also the tragedy of man. He is pious and god-fearing; and indeed there is much room for piety and fear in man's relation to these unmerciful and exacting gods. The will of Zeus be done: it is not always clear how it could possibly be justified by any reasoning acceptable to man;[1] but that is not our concern. Our part is to obey, or to be most grimly punished. Religion advances hardly one step in these pages. Philosophy has no place in them. Morality is simple and practical: its primary lesson is the rule of Justice, imposed by divine will on human society; it is a lesson which was lamentably forgotten, if it was ever learnt, in the generation to come.

Tragedy developed out of a choral song performed as an act of worship. For this development, from narrative to drama, there are two elementary requirements: impersonation, and plurality of characters. The Chorus must begin, instead of narrating, to converse—perhaps with its own leader, perhaps with some other person engaged in the ritual action; and somebody, or some group, must assume a fictitious character, instead of speaking in his own person. According to tradition these steps were taken about the middle of the sixth century B.C., in Attica, by Thespis, at a performance in worship of Dionysus. It is impossible to discover precisely what he did. Perhaps the most primitive form of drama is represented in the XVIIIth Ode of Bacchylides, where the Chorus and its leader both impersonate and converse. Or perhaps the change was more abrupt, the leader

---

[1] For example, it is the will of Zeus that Troy shall be taken (*Agam.* 362 ff.), but also that anybody responsible for many deaths (as the taker of Troy must be) shall be severely punished (461 ff.).

(or some other) making speeches in intervals between choral songs. Whatever the truth about this may be, it is certain that one more step must be taken to reach a form of art which can properly be called Drama. While the Chorus and its leader are the sole performers, there may be both conversation and impersonation; there may even be some conflict of purpose or at least of character. But nothing worthy of the name of *action* is possible until the poet introduces some extraneous person into the scene—until what we may call a *second actor* is brought in, someone who can come and go, out of whose conflict with the Chorus and its leader a developing action can be created. It seems a simple innovation; but, if the tradition is to be trusted, half a century passed before the second actor was introduced. The innovator, we are told, was Aeschylus; and the moment marked the origin of true drama. It was then for the first time possible to develop a story in terms of a conflict of character and purpose between two persons and parties. Indeed, since the second actor might impersonate a number of different characters in successive appearances, some complexity of character and variety of plot might be introduced. And of course the door was then open for the admission of a third actor; it is not certain that a fourth was ever employed.

Between the remotest origins of drama and the highly developed form of the earliest extant tragedies the space of time is long—about eighty years—and the darkness profound, thinly populated by shadowy figures, of whom Phrynichus is the least indistinct. Of Aeschylus we possess (1) an isolated historical drama, *The Persians*, on the subject of the great victory at Salamis;[1] (2) three single plays out of trilogies: *The Suppliants*, the first of a group of three plays

[1] The astonishing distortion of historical truth in this play is well exposed and explained by Richmond Lattimore in *Classical Studies in honor of W. A. Oldfather* (Univ. of Illinois Press, 1943), pp. 82 ff.: according to Aeschylus, 'the battle of Psyttaleia was a major engagement [*Pers.* 435–7]; the battle of Plataea was an insignificant mopping-up operation' (op. cit., p. 91); in this and other respects the desire to glorify Athens suppresses or distorts the well-known facts.

concerning the misfortunes of the daughters of Danaus;
Prometheus Bound, one of three plays about the struggle of
man's benefactor, Prometheus, against man's enemy, Zeus;
and *The Seven against Thebes*, the last of three plays on the
legend of Oedipus; (3) *The Oresteia*, three consecutive plays
concerning the doom of the house of Agamemnon. That is
all, except a number of fragments. One trilogy, three fragments of trilogies, and one historical play which stands apart
from the main road of custom; and the only objective evidence in our possession assigns all these plays to the latter
part of the poet's lifetime, the years of his life between fifty
and sixty-five. At least seventy-three, and perhaps as many
as ninety, of his plays survived into the Christian era; and
we, who possess so small a proportion of his work, done in
so short a period of his life, can make no useful inference
about the development of his art and his thought. Indeed
the greatest caution is required in judging the few witnesses
who come before us. In *The Suppliants* the fifty daughters
of Danaus have fled to Argos, pursued by their fifty cousins
who claim the right to marry them. The women take refuge
in sanctuary; the high-minded king of Argos promises pro-
tection; the impatient cousins are taught a sharp lesson.
At the end of the play we are left with the comfortable feeling that right has prevailed over force, that the wicked are
baffled, the virtuous triumphant and secure. Now we do not
know much about the two plays which continued the theme,
but we do know that in the next one, *The Egyptians*, fortune
was reversed. Argos did not, after all, succeed in protecting
its suppliants; the wicked cousins did marry them, all fifty;
and all but one of the brides murdered each her own husband on the wedding-night. In the third play somebody
was put on trial, and Aphrodite spoke for the prosecution
or defence—whether of Danaus, because forty-nine
daughters had killed their husbands; or of the fiftieth,
because she had not. (See Robertson, *C.R.* xxxviii (1924)
51 ff.) What the moral of all this may have been, what the
rights of the rival parties—these are questions unanswerable

so long as we possess only one third of the story as Aeschylus told it.

Moreover our confidence (if we had any) has been shaken by the unexpected contents of two manuscripts, both of the second (or early third) century A.D., published in the last few years. One of these offers what appears to be part of a tragedy written by a contemporary of Aeschylus.[1] It is an historical drama of a kind hitherto unknown, at a stage of development hitherto unsuspected at so early an era—if indeed it is so early; on that point there is no general agreement, but the balance of argument so far seems to me to favour the Aeschylean date. Secondly, there was published in 1952 a piece of information about the play which we had been accustomed to regard as representing Greek drama in a relatively primitive form, *The Suppliants* of Aeschylus.[2] Our histories of Tragedy have generally been written on the assumption, which appeared an obviously safe one, that this is the earliest of the extant plays. And now we are informed that it was produced in a year in which Sophocles was competing for the prize; that must be, at the earliest, not more than some ten years before *The Oresteia*, towards the end of Aeschylus' life. There is no reasonable doubt that the fact is as stated, and that the evidence is reliable. It refers to a production by Aeschylus, not by somebody else after his death; and it is unlikely that anyone will for long take seriously the suggestion that the play was written in the poet's youth but withheld from the theatre until the later years of his life.

In the circumstances it seems imprudent to make general statements about the nature and development of Aeschylean tragedy: we may, however, observe, as an objective fact,

---

[1] E. Lobel, *Proceedings of the British Academy* xxxv (1950) 1 ff.; the case in favour of the early date is summarized in my *New Chapter in the History of Greek Tragedy* (Cambridge, 1951; in favour of a later date see especially A. Lesky, *Hermes* 81 (1953) 1 ff.).

[2] *The Oxyrhynchus Papyri* xx (1952), no. 2256, fr. 3; the best appreciation is that of A. Lesky in *Hermes* 82 (1954) 1 ff.

one feature common to all the plays which we possess—the simplicity of their design in plot and character. A single action prevails in all; in all there is a single main point at issue between two persons or parties—the Danaids against their cousins; Prometheus against Zeus; Eteocles against Polynices; Agamemnon against Clytemnestra and Aegisthus; Orestes and Electra against the same pair; Orestes and Apollo against the Furies. The line of development is straight, without turnings or byways or complexities. And, further, the conflict is always between the parties, never within the heart of one party. The principal Aeschylean characters have no doubts or self-questionings. Prometheus, Eteocles, the Danaids, Clytemnestra, the Furies, are haunted by no misgivings. Orestes may hesitate a moment before he kills his mother, but his hesitation could not be briefer or more easily turned to action; at no time is there any doubt in his mind about what his duty requires and his inclination approves.

The quest for a useful definition of Greek Tragedy is likely to be vain. How could there be one formula which applied equally to *The Persians*, *Philoctetes*, and *Helen*? It is nevertheless tenable that of many forms there is one, the highest, exemplified in a few plays; and that *The Oresteia*, *Oedipus Tyrannus*, *Hippolytus*, and *The Bacchae* most nearly represent the ideal. It was said by Goethe that the conflict on which a tragedy is founded must be one for which there is no possible reconciliation. Tragedy is concerned with problems which are insoluble; solve the problem, and there is no tragedy left. Now it is certain that many of the dramas which we call tragedies are of this inferior type, problems to which solutions are at least offered. But it may be observed that those Greek tragedies which universal opinion has deemed to be the best are of the higher type defined by Goethe. Consider, for example, *The Oresteia*. Agamemnon must pay with his life for a life which he destroyed; and his murderess must pay with her life for taking his; and her son must be brought to justice for killing her. That is the central theme: but are we then to infer that Aeschylus was primarily concerned to expound and solve the problem of the inherited blood-feud? Of course not. That problem had been solved by Attic law for at least a century and a half; and there was nobody now alive in Athens who supposed that he was permitted, let alone required, to take action against a homicide except through the machinery of the courts. The blood-feud had long been obsolete in Athens as in other civilized states. But though it was no longer a problem to be solved, it was still a framework for the highest type of Tragedy, in which men and women could be entangled in toils from which there was no escape. In *Agamemnon* and *The Choephoroe* the conflict is of such a kind that, in the circumstances given, no reconciliation, no comfortable justifying of the ways of god to man, is conceivable. It is not a struggle of Justice against Injustice, but something different in kind—the conflict of equal, or at least irreconcilable rights, of Justice against Justice; Ἄρης Ἄρει ξυμβαλεῖ, Δίκᾳ Δίκα.[1] It was right (θέμις[2]) that the army at Aulis should demand the death of Iphigeneia; it was right that Clytemnestra should avenge her daughter's death; and it was right that Orestes should kill her in turn. Even in the hour of utmost horror, after Agamemnon has fallen murdered, the Chorus, loathing and reviling Clytemnestra, can still confess that it is hard to see where the true judgement lies, δύσμαχα δ' ἐστὶ κρῖναι:[3] and that this too is the will of Zeus, διαὶ Διὸς παναιτίου πανεργέτα.[4] And in *The Seven against Thebes*, the last play of its trilogy, we observe that it is *Polynices* who wears the blazon 'Justice' on his shield:[5] it is not a simple story of the good brother defending the city from the bad brother; ξυμβαλεῖ Δίκᾳ Δίκα, it is the conflict of Right against Right.

There can be no solution, there can only be an end. And it is instructive to observe how the poets end these, their

---

[1] *Cho.* 461.   [2] *Agam.* 217.   [3] Ibid. 1561.

[4] Ibid. 1485 f.   [5] *ScT* 646.

greatest tragedies. In *Oedipus Tyrannus* and *The Bacchae*, for example, there is no attempt to solve problems or to alleviate disasters. Oedipus must go out into exile, blind and accursed; nothing remains for him but the threat of further disaster. In *The Bacchae* there is no hope, no comfort for Agave; and certainly none for Pentheus. In *The Oresteia* patriotic pride and the historical sense are appeased, if not satisfied, by the ending of the blood-feud in a court of law, and by the reconciliation of the Furies to the service of Athens: thus by artificial contrivance a particular purpose is fulfilled, and the play may come to an end.[1] But what of Agamemnon and Clytemnestra? From their perplexities no such escape was offered; their rights and wrongs were not to be reconciled; they must go their ways inevitably doomed. *Agamemnon* and *The Choephoroe* are, *The Eumenides* is not, the highest form of Tragedy, 'an image of ideal sorrow', in which men and women fulfil a destiny from which there is no resting or respite in this world; θανὼν δ' οὐκ ἄγαν ἐλεύθερος.

Moreover in Tragedy of this type the beginning is no less inevitable than the end. At the end there was no escape from the present or hope for the future; but neither at the beginning was there any means of prevention or evasion. The wrongs which Oedipus did he must do; there was no conceivable means by which he could have avoided doing them. He perfectly exemplifies the type described by Solon, 'The man who tries to deal justly, but because he cannot see what lies ahead falls into great and grievous ruin'.[2] And as

[1] It was evidently Aeschylus' purpose in *The Eumenides* to maintain his audience's interest by an almost continuous display of highly spectacular theatrical effects—the priestess running on all fours; the disgusting exhibition of the Furies; the ghost of Clytemnestra; the pursuit of Orestes to Athens; the arrival of Athena, air-borne; the representation of a law court, complete with jury; the torchlit procession at the end. The trial-scene itself is, and surely seemed to its audience, rather weak: but its faults might be excused as congenital to its purely antiquarian purpose, and overlooked in the brilliance of the spectacle which it provided.

[2] Solon fr. 1. 67 f. ὁ μὲν εὖ ἔρδειν πειρώμενος, οὐ προνοήσας, | εἰς μεγάλην ἄτην καὶ χαλεπὴν ἔπεσεν.

much must be said of Agamemnon and Eteocles, at least in the plays of Aeschylus. These are the extreme cases, in which the sinner is neither originally free to refrain from sin nor finally able to escape or atone for its consequences. It has long been observed, and marked as a great mystery, that Aeschylus imposes upon Agamemnon the necessity of killing his daughter, without assigning to him any fault which might be regarded as the cause of that effect; thereby ignoring the popular tradition, which alleged that Agamemnon insulted Artemis, who punished him for his offence in this way. Of course the doom of Agamemnon is ultimately justified as requital for a crime committed by his father: but this victim, in this play, has no choice but to do what he does, and no possible escape from the consequences. And that is the essence of Tragedy in its highest form, the Tragedy which is concerned with the darkest inexplicable, the unforgivable sin committed unwillingly or even unawares.

This statement, *that Agamemnon has no choice but to do what he does*, is contrary to the general opinion and may be thought to need some clarification.

The first point to notice is the extraordinary reason given by Aeschylus for Artemis' anger against the Atridae. The common story, in more than one form,[1] told of a deed of insolence or utterance of folly by Agamemnon, action or boast by which the goddess was offended. Here was a suitable background for Aeschylus' narrative: the mortal offends the goddess, and her anger involves him in further wrongdoing; the original wrong was his fault, and all that follows can be traced back to it. Alternatively (and better) the wrath of Artemis might have been more closely linked to the chain of destiny which binds the house of Atreus. As Aeschylus actually tells the story, Agamemnon is *compelled, for no fault of his own*, to sacrifice his daughter. Zeus has approved,[2] indeed he has dispatched,[3] the expedition to

---

[1] S. *El.* 563 ff., E. *IT* 20 ff.   [2] 114 ff., the favourable omen.
[3] 60 ff. Ἀτρέως παῖδας . . . ἐπ᾽ Ἀλεξάνδρῳ πέμπει . . . Ζεύς; 362 ff. Δία . . . τὸν τάδε πράξαντα; 367 Διὸς πλαγάν; 748 πομπᾷ Διός; 813 ff., al.

Troy: it is his will that Troy should fall; it is nowhere suggested that Agamemnon might have disbanded his army;[1] indeed it is said that the army will think it 'right and proper'[2] that Iphigeneia should be sacrificed. Iphigeneia is clearly doomed, whatever Agamemnon may do. His only way out is *to desert*, λιπόναυς γενέσθαι: that would be contrary to the will of Zeus, and it would not save his daughter. Desertion is not a *real* alternative: nobody except Agamemnon even mentions it as being even theoreticaliy possible; and he mentions it only to rule it out at once on the ground[3] that it would not save his daughter. The sacrifice of Iphigeneia, once demanded by Artemis, is an absolute *necessity*: and *necessity* is the word by which Aeschylus describes Agamemnon's submission to the will of Artemis;[4] what he bowed to was (it could not be more plainly stated) *compulsion, ἀνάγκη*.

Now this crime, the sacrifice of Iphigeneia, is given by Aeschylus the most extraordinary motive. Instead of tracing

[1] In Sophocles' *Electra*, Electra expressly says that there was no question of disbanding the army: οὐ γὰρ ἦν λύσις | ἄλλη στρατῷ πρὸς οἶκον: nor does Clytemnestra (ibid. 530 ff.) refer to any such possibility, sorely though she needed so strong an argument. The earlier dramatists ignore the point or dismiss it as wholly impracticable, taking it (naturally enough) for granted that the φιλόμαχοι βραβῆς would not go home simply because Agamemnon told them to: it is characteristic of Euripides that he should at last bring this matter into the open (*IA* 94 ff., 352 f., 495, 515).

[2] 217 θέμις.

[3] 214 γάρ.

[4] 218 ἀνάγκας: see note ad loc. The modern critics say that Agamemnon made a voluntary, however painful, decision; Aeschylus says that what he submitted to was *necessity*. I do not see how these statements can be reconciled. It cannot be argued that the poet *meant* (he certainly does not say it) that the matter only became a 'necessity' *after* he had made his choice: that would be an impossible abuse of the word ἀνάγκη, and a most arbitrary distortion of the surface meaning of the whole. Nor yet can ἀνάγκη be toned down to something like 'painful decision': the word means 'necessity', 'compulsion', always with a connotation of *inevitability*; the whole course of Aeschylus' exposition shows the clear intention of absolving Agamemnon from responsibility, ἀνάγκη in 218 merely adds the final and decisive touch.

it back to the mortal's offence against divinity, or otherwise linking it to the destiny of the house of Atreus, the poet tells us in plain language that Artemis was enraged *because eagles, sent by Zeus to be an encouraging portent, happened to devour a hare together with its unborn young; she therefore demanded a 'second sacrifice', the death of Iphigeneia, in return for the death of the hare and its young.* That is what is in the text; and, however crude and inadequate it may appear, in the text it remains, it cannot be removed. The sacrifice of Iphigeneia, with its terrible consequences to Agamemnon and others, is demanded by Artemis not because he has done or left undone anything, but because two eagles, sent by Zeus himself to encourage Agamemnon, have devoured a pregnant hare. This plain testimony of the text is so displeasing that attempts have been made, all in vain, to substitute explanations other than, and inconsistent with, that which the poet offers. Artemis is angry, it is said, because the killing of the hare symbolizes the future destruction of the young in Troy: so it does; but it is the will of Zeus that Troy shall fall. Agamemnon has done, and will do, nothing contrary to the will of Zeus; and no attempt is made to explain why Agamemnon must suffer for his obedience. Professor Fraenkel, admitting (as we all must) that Aeschylus has 'eliminated the act of Agamemnon which incensed the goddess' and that 'while suppressing the cause, he elaborated the details of the sign (portending) the disapproval of Artemis', calls this extraordinary procedure a 'bold stroke' and a 'solution'. It is hard to see what it solves: it leaves the wrath of Artemis without a motive in any act of Agamemnon; and Professor Fraenkel's statement, that 'all the evil that is to befall Agamemnon has its origin in his own voluntary decision', is contradicted by the text of Aeschylus, which calls his decision a 'necessity' (218), and which goes out of its way to suppress all evidence of any *guilt* on the part of Agamemnon at any stage of the proceedings, at least up to his final acceptance of the necessity of sacrificing Iphigeneia—and that was the will of Artemis, not of

Agamemnon. Zeus has approved and dispatched the expedition to Troy, as the poet repeatedly tells us. Artemis demands that Iphigeneia must be killed before they sail. Agamemnon's first thought is to consider whether this command can be disobeyed (206 τὸ μὴ πιθέσθαι). There is no question of abandoning the expedition; nor does Aeschylus ever suggest that he might have done so. The chieftains will think it 'right and proper' (217 θέμις) that Iphigeneia should be sacrificed according to Artemis' command: her doom is therefore certain; and the question remains, what course except obedience to Artemis is open to Agamemnon? The answer is plainly given: he might *desert*, run away from his allies; who will then sacrifice his daughter and proceed without him. But it is unthinkable that the King of kings should turn deserter, λιπόναυς, a common criminal; and if he did, it would certainly incur the wrath of Zeus, whose vice-gerent he is in this expedition against Troy; nor could he save his daughter—he could only save himself from presiding at her sacrifice. Well might he exclaim τί τῶνδ' ἄνευ κακῶν;—nowhere does Aeschylus suggest that he *ought* to have deserted: the possibility is dismissed as unpractical; and the poet is at pains to give his opinion that Agamemnon *could* not desert his divinely-appointed command, telling us that the harness which he put on was the harness of *necessity*. Of course the killing of Iphigeneia was 'impious, unsanctified, unholy' (219 f.) and 'of the uttermost audacity' (221); and Agamemnon, after he understood that he had no choice (218 ἀνάγκας), did make up his mind to do the deed (μετέγνω)—a mind that must first be *deranged*, the poet adds (παρακοπά). But the question is not whether the deed was abominable, but whether it was voluntary: let us ask of the poet certain questions:—(1) Who ordered the expedition against Troy?—*Zeus*. (2) Who demanded the sacrifice of Iphigeneia?—*Artemis*. (3) Is the imposition of this dreadful burden upon Agamemnon justified, in this play, as punishment for previous wrong-doing?—*Decidedly not: on the contrary, all versions of the story in which it was so justified are totally suppressed.* (4) What is Agamemnon's first reaction to the information that Artemis requires his daughter's death?—*He reflects on the possibility of disobedience, τὸ μὴ πιθέσθαι.* (5) What possibility is there? Might he disband his army?—*No: that question is never even raised. Agamemnon guesses that his commanders will think it right and proper to obey Artemis: they will obey her, whether he will or not.* (6) What other possibility is there?—*The one that is mentioned: he might desert, λιπόναυς γενέσθαι.* (7) Would not that be contrary to the will of Zeus, who has ordained the expedition to Troy?—*Yes.* (8) Would it save the life of Iphigeneia?—*Of course not: the commanders would sacrifice her and proceed to Troy.* (9) Is this possibility of desertion treated by you, or by any of your characters, as a real alternative?—*No: it is not even mentioned by anybody except Agamemnon, who rejects it at once on the ground that he would not thus save his daughter.* (10) Your critics have sometimes said that Artemis presented Agamemnon with alternative courses—either to kill his daughter and sail to Troy, or to stay at home and so spare his daughter: is this what you intended?—*It was neither said nor intended. The death of Iphigeneia is claimed in requital for a death (that of the hare and its offspring) which has already taken place: her sacrifice is related to a past fact, not to a future condition; nowhere is there the slightest indication that Artemis offered Agamemnon a choice between alternatives, and he himself very quickly sees that he has no choice.* (11) If it was your purpose to show that Agamemnon had no choice whatever in the matter, could you not have made this very important fact a little plainer? —*No: it is definitely stated that he put on the harness of Necessity: a man who acts under Necessity is not acting voluntarily. It is further stated in unambiguous terms that his mind was deranged (παρακοπά) before the trouble could be begun (πρωτοπήμων).* (12) How is this consistent with the statement that his spirit 'changed direction', and thereafter was 'impious' and 'unholy', and that he 'altered his mind' in favour of a course of 'uttermost daring'?—*The 'change of mind' simply represents the fact. When Agamemnon saw that he had no choice in the matter* (ἀνάγκας ἔδυ λέπαδνον), *he now made up his mind to obey, having first looked in vain for some means of disobeying. It was not until he recognized the burden as a compulsory one that he made up his mind to the act* (ἐπεὶ . . . τόθεν). *As for the moralizing adjectives: let us not confuse two very different things.—nobody denies that he made up his mind to the act, or that the act was abominable: the question remains, had he any choice? It is clearly stated that Artemis compelled Agamemnon to commit the crime, and that she did so for no fault on his part: it remains nevertheless an abominable crime, and he committed it, and he must pay for it. The plea of compulsion will not avail him, any more than the plea of total unawareness availed Oedipus.* (13) Would it not have been simpler to portray him as committing the crime as a result of his own decision, not under divine compulsion?— *Only if this had been a simple tale of Crime and Punishment; but it is not. It is a Tragedy, the Tragedy of Man's destiny; and that is most moving when the human victim is involved against his will (like Agamemnon) or unawares (like Oedipus) in criminal error for which the penalty must be paid. Agamemnon in this Chorus is depicted as a man who has no choice but to kill what is dearest to him—a much likelier and more interesting figure than the weak-willed butcher whom some would apparently prefer to see portrayed.*

Zeus in Aeschylus is a stern and terrible god. In *Agamemnon* he is the inflexible punisher of wrong-doing which arises inevitably out of an enterprise which he himself had approved and abetted. He moves in a mysterious way: in the words of Niobe, 'when the god desires utterly to destroy a family, *he creates a fault in man*'[1]—the sins of the father

---

[1] Aeschylus, *Niobe* (*Greek Literary Papyri*, Loeb 3rd ed. 1950, no. 1. 15 f.): θεὸς μὲν αἰτίαν φύει βροτοῖς | ὅταν κακῶσαι δῶμα παμπήδην θέλῃ. Schmid–Staehlin, *Gr. Lit.* i. 2, p. 270, needs correction. The statement that the lines are 'purely personal to Niobe,' and have nothing to do with Aeschylus' beliefs' is in its first half arbitrary and improbable and in its second half almost certainly false. There is no reason whatever to suppose that what Niobe here says is at variance with the facts of the

Atreus must be visited on the head of the son Agamemnon; so the gods 'create a fault' in Agamemnon, they compel him to commit a crime which only his own death can expiate. It is indeed remarkable what pains the poet will take to avoid imputing the primary blame to his victims. The crime of Paris, one might think, was a clear enough example of voluntary wrong-doing: did he not freely elope with Helen, the wife of his host? Not so, according to Aeschylus: Paris was *compelled* by the demon 'Persuasion', the *intolerable* daughter of another demon, 'Ruin' (or 'Infatuation'); the episode was *planned beforehand* by her, and there was *no remedy*.[1]

It does not follow that Aeschylus absolves mankind from all responsibility. When Zeus 'creates a fault in man', he is not moved by wilful malice. His wrath is visited upon those —or their unfortunate posterity—whose conduct offends against his rule of law among men. But the visitation of fathers' sins upon children's heads creates such ideal subjects of Tragedy as Agamemnon and Oedipus, where the primary wrong-doing lies in the antecedent legend, and the present sufferers are involved against their will and without defence.[2]

Ταῖς τε γὰρ ὄψεσι καὶ τοῖς μύθοις πρὸς ἔκπληξιν τερατώδη μᾶλλον ἢ πρὸς ἀπάτην κέχρηται.[3] Tragedy is to be seen as well

case; which would then provide an exact parallel to the treatment of Agamemnon in our play. The further statement, that the force of Niobe's words is broken by what follows in the next two lines, should be struck out: we do not know what was said in the next two lines; what remains of them can very easily be supplemented to make harmony with *θεὸς μὲν κτλ.* (see, for example, the version offered in the text quoted at the beginning of this note).

[1] See the Commentary on 386 ff.

[2] Aristotle in *The Poetics* 1453[a] comes close to this position. Although he says (1452[b] fin.) that 'a good man must not be seen passing from happiness to misery', he insists (1453[a] 14 ff.) that the cause of the hero's suffering 'must lie not in any depravity but in some great *ἁμαρτία* on his part': since he illustrates his theme with the example of *Oedipus* (among others), it is clear that he is thinking of *involuntary* *ἁμαρτία*.

[3] From the ancient *Life of Aeschylus* (printed at the end of *Aeschyli Tragoediae* in the Oxford Classical Texts series).

as heard; and it was long remembered of Aeschylus that he
was pleased to entertain, or even to appal, his audience with
the display of abnormal and sometimes astounding theatrical devices. Aristophanes has something to say about this in
The Frogs; and we need look no farther than the extant
plays for examples. *Prometheus* opens with the clang of
hammers upon chains; the principal character, whether real
or a dummy, is being riveted to a rock. There will be no
means of getting him off the scene except in an earthquake:
let him be engulfed in a general convulsion of nature at the
end of the play. So remote is the action, on the uttermost
verges of the earth, that the entry of other persons by foot
or in chariots would be ludicrous: let them arrive by air, in
wonderful contrivances visible to the spectator. The Chorus
appears in winged vehicles, their father displays his flying-
machine propelled by an ingenious fowl; 'with four legs', he
says, though four wings would have been more useful.
Consider *The Suppliants*, where the spectacular entertain-
ment is of a different type. It is a play of movements and
multitudes. The scene is filled, and vacated, by very large
throngs of persons, for the most part of dusky complexion
and unfamiliar costume. There is a moment when we stop
to ask, how many persons are in sight? On a mound or
platform are Danaus and his fifty daughters, each (unless
the poet misleads us) with an attendant girl; in the scene
below are a herald and his Egyptian escort, presumably
equal in number to the screaming women whom they would
carry away; to them enters the king of Argos with a bodyguard presumably equal in number to the Egyptians whom
they repulse. Can the total be less than 203?[1] The multitudes, the outlandish costumes, the black faces, the threats
of the one party and screams of the other, compose a scene
without parallel in the remains of Greek Tragedy.

Aeschylus' delight in theatrical effects was manifested
in the most various phenomena. Niobe sat veiled on her

[1] Perhaps it can be reduced to 51 (assuming a Chorus of 12, contrary
to the surface evidence): that is still a considerable crowd.

children's tomb without uttering a word until the play was more than half done. Eos, who must descend from the sky to fetch the body of her son, came flying through the air at the end of a rope suspended from a crane. Earth opens and emits uncomfortable ghosts: an ominous Darius, a vindictive Clytemnestra. Longest remembered, and repeated not without exaggeration, was the story of the sufferings of women and children in the audience at the beginning of *The Eumenides*, when Aeschylus suddenly disclosed the interior of the temple and revealed the figures of the Furies— black, hideous, with noses snorting and eyes oozing, creatures so disgusting that the priestess who first saw them could no longer stand upright; here she comes crawling or scampering on all fours[1] to tell the story.

These devices went out of fashion fairly soon. Such pantomime was put away in the age of enlightened decadence. Euripidean characters as a general rule enter the scene on foot at ground level. The earth does not gape, the heavens let down no ropes, the air is not black with birds.

Agamemnon begins. We look, and nobody is on the scene; there is a palace, but nobody comes out of it. The voice comes from the roof, of all places; and the speaker is not even standing up.

In a few words he tells us most of what we need to know. He is a watchman on the roof of Agamemnon's palace at Argos, watching for the beacon which is to announce the fall of Troy. His vigil has lasted a whole year, and he is heartily tired of it. He is frightened of being caught by Clytemnestra sleeping at his post; so he whistles or hums a tune and walks about to keep awake. He knows that things are not as they should be in the palace: already in the prologue Aeschylus begins to create that feeling of foreboding, of impending inevitable disaster, which grows in intensity up to the moment, late in the play, when a scream is heard from inside the palace, and all is over: King Agamemnon is

[1] *Eum.* 37.

dead. Suddenly a beacon is seen: the watchman shouts and capers; but rejoicing is soon damped by the cloud of fear. However, he thinks it better to say nothing: a great ox (that is his homely phrase) has stepped upon his tongue. He is a lively person, this watchman; an individual drawn with zest and sympathy. Aeschylus' principal characters are often larger than life; his minor characters are sometimes more naturally drawn.

It is now clear enough what will happen. Agamemnon is to return home, and we can guess the welcome that awaits him from his wife and her lover. But the story is not properly understood unless it is seen as the inevitable consequence of happenings in the past. There enters a Chorus, men of high rank in the state, whose memories reach far back. They tell the story of Agamemnon's doom: how the army, assembled to sail for Troy, was detained by adverse weather at Aulis; how Artemis was angry, and compelled Agamemnon to kill his daughter Iphigeneia as a sacrifice on behalf of the fleet. The Chorus knows that Clytemnestra has not forgiven the killing of her daughter; they have no doubt that Agamemnon will be in deadly danger when he comes.

The workings of destiny are clearly seen: there is no hope; and the news of the fall of Troy, which might have been so joyfully received, means that the doom of Agamemnon is near its end, can no longer be deferred. The Chorus tries hard to reject the evidence, to disbelieve the message of the beacons; better that the war should last for ever, than that Agamemnon should come home to be murdered by his wife.

All this time, ever since the entry of the Chorus, the sinister figure of Clytemnestra has been visible to the spectators, mutely significant in the background. Now she comes forward and describes the relay of beacons which have brought the news from Troy across four hundred miles of land and sea. She describes the scene in Troy at this hour as she imagines it; gloats over the sufferings of the conquered; darkly rejoices that the dangers of the conquerors are not yet past. She has been waiting ten years for this moment; and her plans are laid.

The Greek army arrives at Argos, half an hour after the beacons have announced the fall of Troy. That is warm work, if it were reckoned thus: certainly it was not so reckoned by the Athenian spectator, who expected to see Agamemnon at any moment now, the sooner the better. But the suspense is increased by the arrival of an unforeseen person, a herald, announcing the return of his master. This is another good minor character, carefully portrayed. He knows nothing of what is to happen; he is delighted to be home; alone of all characters in *The Oresteia* he has no forebodings. The tension is tautened by his futile cheerfulness; we wish he would go away, that we might know the worst at once. He has a habit, if the text may be trusted so far, of forgetting the beginnings of his sentences, starting afresh when they become too complicated. He paints a realistic picture of the hardships of the army at Troy. Descriptions of warfare in Greek Tragedy (and elsewhere) are as a rule rather conventional; this one is a notable exception. The worst of war is not its occasional dangers but its perpetual discomforts; so the herald tells us how disagreeable the sleeping quarters were, whether on ship with people stepping over you or on you, or on land where the dewfall drenches you and the clothes breed vermin. And now there is more good news for Clytemnestra: the herald reports that the fleet has been scattered by a storm; only Agamemnon's ship is so far safely home. His brother Menelaus is lost: he will come, then, not surrounded by his soldiers, supported by his brother, but alone, an easy victim.

The play is half finished before Agamemnon appears, and he is present for only one-tenth of its course. His first address does not endear him. He is ready with pious phrases; he greets success with gratitude but without surprise. He is mistrustful of man's friendship—only one comrade, he says, was true to him, Odysseus; though what fault he had to find with Nestor, Diomede, and others remains a great mystery.

He neither mentions his wife nor expresses pleasure at his home-coming. He looks forward to dealing with ten years' arrears of domestic crime: he assumes that there will be diseases to be cured; and we shall cure them, he says, by knife or burning, εὐφρόνως, with the best intentions.

A strange homily; but stranger still the address of Clytemnestra. Here are king and queen who have not met for ten years: what will she say to him? Nothing, at least for some time. She turns to the Chorus, and defends herself against the charge (if anyone should care to make it) of infidelity to her husband. Agamemnon, whom she calls 'this man here', listens patiently or impatiently. The Chorus knows, or at least suspects, the truth: she tries to ensure their silence by anticipating their accusation. She has a plan to be fulfilled this hour: not a whisper of suspicion, not a word of danger, must reach the king.

To him at last she speaks with gross adulation and rank hypocrisy. 'She winds about him coil after coil of her glittering rhetoric',[1] and prostrates herself like a grovelling oriental before the pompous King of kings. Agamemnon replies in words which become rougher as his speech progresses. He rejects all that she offers. His annoyance is natural: for here and now, at the climax of his triumphant return from Troy, his wife proposes to him a course which (if he is fool enough to follow it) will alienate the sympathy of men and incur the severest displeasure of the gods. She has spread purple vestments in his path, and she tempts him to walk indoors along them. He knows, and says, that these objects belong to the worship of the gods. It is not for man to trample on them; or, if he does, he need expect no mercy from heaven. And yet the temptation is great, too great: 'Lord, if this be sin, pardon this my sin.' Agamemnon is gone, trampling on purple and silver vestments; we know that he will not be seen alive again.

The conventions of Greek Tragedy require that his murder take place out of sight; and it may be expected that after

[1] Weir Smyth, op. cit., p. 168.

the event some person will come out to tell us what happened. That expectation is not fulfilled; Aeschylus makes an experiment unique in ancient drama.

When Agamemnon entered the scene he brought with him a silent companion, a young woman, Cassandra. Now Cassandra has the gift of second sight; past and future reveal themselves to her. Let her then dream a vision of Agamemnon's murder before it occurs; and let her describe it as if it were now occurring, in the open theatre for all to see. And so it is done. Cassandra has a vision of the doom of the house of Atreus, from the beginning to the end. She sees, and makes the audience imagine they see, each horror in order, as it has been and as it will be. Here, in her vision, is Clytemnestra planning the murder; here she approaches her victim, reaches out her arms towards him, flings a net over him, and while he is entangled, defenceless, she strikes; and he falls dead. There is no more imaginative and unorthodox scene in Greek Tragedy.[1]

Now we have actually seen the murder, or seemed to see it. Will somebody come from the palace to tell us that it was so? There is hardly time to wonder, when a scream is heard, and then another, and then no more; that is how Aeschylus announces the death of Agamemnon. The tension has been stretched to breaking-point; and now it breaks, with an appalling sound. We are shown, in a moment of silence, the interior scene: Clytemnestra standing triumphant, red-handed, above her victims. We have now to listen to her, boasting and self-justifying, as cold-hearted a murderess as ever man saw, untouched by pity or regret or even fear. She sees in this execution the will of Zeus, in her sword the agent of his justice; and even the chorus must confess that this is so.[2]

The play is nearly over; but first we must watch, with whatever emotions, the antics of Aegisthus. A disagreeable person, this shadowy figure who sat at home for ten years making love to Clytemnestra and helping to plan the murder

[1] See further, pp. 164 ff. below. [2] 1481–8 n.

of her husband. Justice, he can prove to you, is on his side; and so it is,[1] but we do not love him the more. He claims all the credit for what has happened, neither speaking to Clytemnestra nor even mentioning her name. The future is bright; and he and his bodyguard will make short work of the Chorus if they interfere. So the end comes, with Aegisthus and Clytemnestra triumphant. But yet there is a hint that their days too are numbered; that not all justice has yet been done; that soon they will lie where Agamemnon and Cassandra lie, their penalty paid.

THE TRANSMISSION OF THE TEXT[2]

The fame of Aeschylus was great in the latter part of his lifetime, and endured for some decades thereafter. It was permitted, as a mark of special honour, to reproduce his plays in the theatre after his death;[3] and although he appeared old-fashioned to the enlightened spirits of the era of the Sophists, *The Frogs* of Aristophanes suggests that he was still well known and highly esteemed at the end of the fifth century B.C. From that time onwards he yielded place in popular favour to Euripides, whose peculiar talents were in all respects more congenial to the spirit of Athens in the generations of her decline. There are few quotations from Aeschylus in authors of the fourth century B.C.; Aristotle in *The Poetics* has remarkably little to say about him; and our evidence indicates that his plays were no longer to be seen in the theatre. Yet more than seventy, perhaps as many as ninety,[4] of his plays survived into the era of Alexandrian scholarship, when a more or less standard text was made and

---

[1] 1607 n.

[2] See esp. Wilamowitz, *Einleitung in die gr. Tragödie*, ch. iii; *Aeschyli Tragoediae* (1914), *Praefatio*. The facts about Aeschylus are fully and lucidly marshalled in Schmid–Stählin, *Gr. Lit.* i. 2, pp. 302–7.

[3] *Vita Aeschyli* 12.

[4] The catalogue of his plays in codd. MV has 73 titles, to which 10 may be added from other sources; Suidas gives the total as 90.

multiplied. Adaptation of some of his plays by Ennius and Accius[1] may indicate a temporary revival of public interest at this time; and discoveries of papyrus-texts, especially at Oxyrhynchus in Egypt,[2] prove that numerous plays were still being copied and read up to the third century A.D.; though in the meantime only a few learned men, such as Plutarch and Seneca,[3] reveal much knowledge of him, and the general opinion is probably reflected in the harsh verdict of Quintilian.[4]

It is probable that a selection of plays, the seven which we possess, was made in the third century A.D. and furnished with commentaries (which are represented by the 'scholia' in our MSS) for use in schools; and that the gradual disappearance of the remainder began about that era as a natural consequence.[5] This selection was later reduced from seven to three, the so-called 'Byzantine Triad', *Prometheus Vinctus*, *Persians*, *Seven against Thebes*: upon these three the attention of Byzantine scholarship, culminating in the work of Thomas Magister and Demetrius Triclinius in the late 13th and early 14th centuries A.D., was concentrated. At some time (we do not know when) *Agamemnon* and *The Eumenides* were taken back into the fold: and the modern world would possess five, instead of seven, Aeschylean plays, derived solely from this tradition of Byzantine scholarship, if Giovanni Aurispa had not brought from Constantinople to Italy in or about the year A.D. 1423 a single, and much older, representative of a purer source. This, commonly called 'the Medicean', written

---

[1] Ennius: *Nemea, Eumenides*, prob. *Hectoris Lutra*; Accius: *Prometheus, Myrmidones*.

[2] See esp. *The Oxyrhynchus Papyri* xviii (1941), nos. 2159–64, 2178–9; xx (1952), nos. 2245–56; xxii (1954), nos. 2333–4.

[3] Seneca esp. in his *Agamemnon*. See also Dio Chrysostom, *orat.* 52, §§ 4 ff.

[4] *sublimis et gravis et grandiloquus saepe usque ad vitium, sed rudis in plerisque et incompositus* (*inst.* x. 1. 66).

[5] The copious writings of the well-read Julian, Themistius, and Libanius contribute altogether *only two* quotations from Aeschylus (Schmid–Stählin, op. cit., p. 304).

in minuscule letters *c.* A.D. 1000 (over 200 years earlier than any other extant manuscript of Aeschylus), is a solitary survivor of the Greco-Roman selection of seven plays, a descendant—not of the first generation—of a manuscript written in uncial letters not later than *c.* A.D. 800 and perhaps (or even probably) much earlier. It is our sole authority for *Supplices* and *The Choephoroe,* and our best witness to the text of the other five plays. Unfortunately the greater part of *Agamemnon* is missing: the Medicean has only vv. 1–310 and 1067–1159, and for the rest the text depends upon two degenerate sources.[1] Of these two sources the one, cod. **V**, fails after *Agam.* 348: the other is represented by two manuscripts written in the fourteenth century, codd. **F** and **Tr**, and by one written in the fifteenth century, cod. **G**. Cod. **Tr** is the autograph edition of *Agamemnon* by the Byzantine scholar Demetrius Triclinius: it offers a debased tradition further distorted by arbitrary conjectures, sometimes (but seldom) improved by clever ones. It is well that we possess cod. **F**, which represents the same tradition at an earlier stage—bad enough, but free from 'the violent critical manœuvres, . . . the particularly reckless, though often ingenious, conjectures of Triclinius'.[2]

The value of cod. **G**, which reads almost (but not quite) as if it were a mere copy of cod. **F**, could not be less than it is without entirely ceasing to exist. It is doubtful whether there is a single place in *Agamemnon* where its reading

---

[1] The present note on the manuscripts has been greatly abbreviated, since it is now possible to refer to two works in English which put the facts in a very clear light: Fraenkel, *Agam.* i, *Prolegomena* I; Turyn, *The Manuscript Tradition of the Tragedies of Aeschylus,* 1943, esp. pp. 100–16.

[2] Fraenkel, i, p. 33. There is still considerable doubt about the relation of **F** to **Tr**. R. Sealey (*CQ* n.s. V (1955) 119 ff.) offers what appears to be weighty evidence (derived from the relation between the metrical scholia in the two MSS.) that **F** is, as Turyn held, copied from a recension by Triclinius earlier than that which we call **Tr**. If this is so, the fact remains that the text of **F** is, as Fraenkel says, relatively free from the characteristic Triclinian maltreatment apparent in **Tr**.

assists either to clarify the tradition or to emend a corrupt place. It is practically ignored in the present edition.[1]

On these decayed and patched foundations the greater part of our text of *Agamemnon* must be built. A little assistance is offered by quotations, much more is given by the marginal annotations called *scholia*. In the Medicean, so far as it goes, these annotations include valuable relics of ancient learning, their pedigree reaching back to remote antiquity. In Triclinius' manuscript they are of two kinds: σχόλια παλαιά (called 'Schol. vet(era)' in this edition), often of great interest and value; and Triclinius' own annotations, distinguished by the word ἡμέτερον (or ἡμέτερα) and a cross, or by a cross alone. Cod. **V** has no scholia, cod. **F** nothing of much value except a few notes on the prologue and parodos.[2]

M (Mediceus) = Bibl. Laurenziana, cod. 32. 9, Florence: parchment, saec. x fin., with corrections by a contemporary *diorthotes* (= m). *Agam.* 1–310, 1067–1159, with scholia. Facsimile published with introduction by E. Rostagno, *L'Eschilo Laurenziano*, Florence 1896.

V (Venetus) = Bibl. Marciana, cod. gr. 468 (now 653), Venice: paper, saec. xiii. *Agam.* 1–348, without scholia.

Tr (Triclinius) = Bibl. Nazionale, cod. II F 31, Naples: paper, saec. xiv (first quarter), in the hand of Demetrius Triclinius. *Agam.* entire, with scholia.

F = Bibl. Laurenziana, cod. 31. 8, Florence: paper, between *c.* 1330 and 1374. *Agam.* entire, with scholia.

G = Bibl. Marciana, cod. gr. 616 (now 663), Venice: parchment, saec. xv. *Agam.* 1–45, 1095–end, with metrical scholia only.

P.Oxy. = *The Oxyrhynchus Papyri* xviii (1941), no. 2178, pp. 101 f.: small remnants of the beginnings of *Agam.* 7–30, from a copy of the play written on papyrus in the second century A.D.

For the relations of these manuscripts one to another see Fraenkel, i p. 32: the earliest minuscule manuscript of Aeschylus (9th century) left to posterity three descendants: (*a*) the Medicean, (*b*) the ancestor of cod. **V**, (*c*) the ancestor of the common source of codd. **F**, **Tr**, and **G**.

[1] On cod. **G** see Fraenkel, i, pp. 30 f.
[2] On the Scholia see especially Fraenkel, i, pp. 16 ff.

ΑΓΑΜΕΜΝΩΝ

ΑΓΑΜΕΜΝΩΝ

ἐδιδάχθη τὸ δρᾶμα ἐπὶ ἄρχοντος Φιλοκλέους ὀλυμπιάδι ὀγδοηκοστῇ ἔτει δευτέρῳ (*vere anni 458 a.C.*). πρῶτος Αἰσχύλος Ἀγαμέμνονι, Χοηφόροις, Εὐμενίσι, Πρωτεῖ σατυρικῷ. ἐχορήγει Ξενοκλῆς Ἀφιδναῖος.

ΤΑ ΤΟΥ ΔΡΑΜΑΤΟΣ ΠΡΟΣΩΠΑ

ΦΥΛΑΞ	*ΧΟΡΟΣ*	*[ΑΓΓΕΛΟΣ]*
ΚΛΥΤΑΙΜΗΣΤΡΑ		*[ΤΑΛΘΥΒΙΟΣ] ΚΗΡΥΞ*
ΑΓΑΜΕΜΝΩΝ		*ΚΑΣΣΑΝΔΡΑ*
	ΑΙΓΙΣΘΟΣ	

Ἄγγελος *et* Ταλθύβιος seclusit Stanley

ΑΓΑΜΕΜΝΩΝ

ΦΥΛΑΞ

θεοὺς μὲν αἰτῶ τῶνδ' ἀπαλλαγὴν πόνων,
φρουρᾶς ἐτείας μῆκος, ἣν κοιμώμενος
στέγαις Ἀτρειδῶν ἄγκαθεν, κυνὸς δίκην,
ἄστρων κάτοιδα νυκτέρων ὁμήγυριν,
καὶ τοὺς φέροντας χεῖμα καὶ θέρος βροτοῖς   5
λαμπροὺς δυνάστας, ἐμπρέποντας αἰθέρι
ἀστέρας, ὅταν φθίνωσιν ἀντολαῖς τε τῶν.
καὶ νῦν φυλάσσω λαμπάδος τὸ σύμβολον,
αὐγὴν πυρὸς φέρουσαν ἐκ Τροίας φάτιν
ἁλώσιμόν τε βάξιν· ὧδε γὰρ κρατεῖ   10
γυναικὸς ἀνδρόβουλον ἐλπίζον κέαρ.
εὖτ' ἂν δὲ νυκτίπλαγκτον ἔνδροσόν τ' ἔχω
εὐνὴν ὀνείροις οὐκ ἐπισκοπουμένην
ἐμήν· φόβος γὰρ ἀνθ' ὕπνου παραστατεῖ
τὸ μὴ βεβαίως βλέφαρα συμβαλεῖν ὕπνῳ·   15
ὅταν δ' ἀείδειν ἢ μινύρεσθαι δοκῶ,
ὕπνου τόδ' ἀντίμολπον ἐντέμνων ἄκος,
κλαίω τότ' οἴκου τοῦδε συμφορὰν στένων
οὐχ ὡς τὰ πρόσθ' ἄριστα διαπονουμένου.
νῦν δ' εὐτυχὴς γένοιτ' ἀπαλλαγὴ πόνων,   20
εὐαγγέλου φανέντος ὀρφναίου πυρός.
ὦ χαῖρε λαμπτὴρ νυκτὸς ἡμερήσιον
φάος πιφαύσκων καὶ χορῶν κατάστασιν
πολλῶν ἐν Ἄργει τῆσδε συμφορᾶς χάριν.

MVFTr   2 δ' ἦν MV   4–6 cit. Achill. in Arat. p. 28 Maass
5 βροτοῖς θέρος FTr   6 αἰθέρι MFTr : ἐν θέρει V   7–30
initia exstant in P. Oxy. 2178   7 Margoliouth : ἀντολάς codd.
11 cit. Io. Siceliota, schol. ad Hermog. π. ἰδ. vi. 225 Walz   ἐλπί-
ζῶν MV, -ζων Io. Sicel.   12 sup. δὲ scr. γε F   17 ἐκτέμνων
(sscr. ἐν) F, ἐκτ- etiam G   23 φάος MV et procul dubio P. Oxy. :
νῦν φῶς FTr

ἰοὺ ἰού·　　　　　　　　　　　　　　　　　　25
Ἀγαμέμνονος γυναικὶ σημαίνω τορῶς
εὐνῆς ἐπαντείλασαν ὡς τάχος δόμοις
ὀλολυγμὸν εὐφημοῦντα τῇδε λαμπάδι
ἐπορθιάζειν, εἴπερ Ἰλίου πόλις
ἑάλωκεν, ὡς ὁ φρυκτὸς ἀγγέλλων πρέπει·　　30
αὐτός τ' ἔγωγε φροίμιον χορεύσομαι·
τὰ δεσποτῶν γὰρ εὖ πεσόντα θήσομαι,
τρὶς ἓξ βαλούσης τῆσδέ μοι φρυκτωρίας.
γένοιτο δ' οὖν μολόντος εὐφιλῆ χέρα
ἄνακτος οἴκων τῇδε βαστάσαι χερί·　　　35
τὰ δ' ἄλλα σιγῶ· βοῦς ἐπὶ γλώσσῃ μέγας
βέβηκεν· οἶκος δ' αὐτός, εἰ φθογγὴν λάβοι,
σαφέστατ' ἂν λέξειεν· ὡς ἑκὼν ἐγώ
μαθοῦσιν αὐδῶ κοὐ μαθοῦσι λήθομαι.

ΧΟΡΟΣ
δέκατον μὲν ἔτος τόδ' ἐπεὶ Πριάμου　　　40
μέγας ἀντίδικος,
Μενέλαος ἄναξ ἠδ' Ἀγαμέμνων,
διθρόνου Διόθεν καὶ δισκήπτρου
τιμῆς ὀχυρὸν ζεῦγος Ἀτρειδᾶν,
στόλον Ἀργείων χιλιοναύτην　　　　　　45
τῆσδ' ἀπὸ χώρας
ἦραν, στρατιῶτιν ἀρωγήν,
μεγάλ' ἐκ θυμοῦ κλάζοντες Ἄρη,
τρόπον αἰγυπιῶν οἵτ' ἐκπατίοις
ἄλγεσι παίδων ὕπατοι λεχέων　　　　　50
στροφοδινοῦνται
πτερύγων ἐρετμοῖσιν ἐρεσσόμενοι,

MVFTr　　26 M: σημανῶ rell.　29 -ορθρι- MV　30 fort.
πέ[π]τωκεν, certe non ἑάλωκεν, P. Oxy.　Tr: ἀγγέλων MVF　38
λέξει F　39 αὐδῶν οὐ V　40 πριάμω MV　45 -ναύταν
codd., sup. αν scr. η MTr; γρ. ἴλιον αὔταν m F　47 ἀρωγὰν codd.,
η sscr. MTr　48 scripsimus: μέγαν codd.　κλάγξαντες FTr

δεμνιοτήρη
πόνον ὀρταλίχων ὀλέσαντες·
ὕπατος δ' αἴων ἤ τις Ἀπόλλων 55
ἢ Πὰν ἢ Ζεὺς οἰωνόθροον
γόον ὀξυβόαν τῶνδε μετοίκων
ὑστερόποινον
πέμπει παραβᾶσιν Ἐρινύν·
οὕτω δ' Ἀτρέως παῖδας ὁ κρείσσων 60
ἐπ' Ἀλεξάνδρῳ πέμπει ξένιος
Ζεύς, πολυάνορος ἀμφὶ γυναικὸς
πολλὰ παλαίσματα καὶ γυιοβαρῆ,
γόνατος κονίαισιν ἐρειδομένου
διακναιομένης τ' ἐν προτελείοις 65
κάμακος, θήσων Δαναοῖσιν
Τρωσί θ' ὁμοίως. ἔστι δ' ὅπῃ νῦν
ἔστι· τελεῖται δ' ἐς τὸ πεπρωμένον·
οὔθ' ὑποκαίων οὔτ' ἀπολείβων
ἀπύρων ἱερῶν 70
ὀργὰς ἀτενεῖς παραθέλξει.
ἡμεῖς δ' ἀτίται σαρκὶ παλαιᾷ
τῆς τότ' ἀρωγῆς ὑπολειφθέντες
μίμνομεν ἰσχὺν
ἰσόπαιδα νέμοντες ἐπὶ σκήπτροις· 75
ὅ τε γὰρ νεαρὸς μυελὸς στέρνων
ἐντὸς ἀνάσσων
ἰσόπρεσβυς, Ἄρης δ' οὐκ ἐνὶ χώρᾳ·
τό θ' ὑπέργηρων φυλλάδος ἤδη
κατακαρφομένης τρίποδας μὲν ὁδοὺς 80
στείχει, παιδὸς δ' οὐδὲν ἀρείων

MVFTr   64 ἐρειπο- FTr, 80 sscr. F   69 Casaubon : ὑπο-
κλαίων codd., unde glossema οὔτε δακρύων post -λείβων omnes, del.
Bamberger   Beattie : οὔθ' ὑπολείβων codd.   72 ἀτίται ex ἀτίτα✱
M, ἀτίται F : ἀτίταια V, ἀτιταὶ Tr   77 Hermann : ἀνάσσων codd.
78 ἐνὶ V : ἐνι M, ἐνί FTr   79 Tr : τίθιπεργήρως M, τόθιπεργήρως
VF   80 τρίποδος FTr   81 δ' om. V

ὄναρ ἡμερόφαντον ἀλαίνει.

<u>σὺ δέ, Τυνδάρεω</u>
θύγατερ, βασίλεια Κλυταιμήστρα,
τί χρέος; τί νέον; τί δ' ἐπαισθομένη,   85
τίνος ἀγγελίας
πειθοῖ περίπεμπτα θυοσκεῖς;
πάντων δὲ θεῶν τῶν ἀστυνόμων,
ὑπάτων, χθονίων, τῶν τε θυραίων
τῶν τ' ἀγοραίων,   90
βωμοὶ δώροισι φλέγονται·
ἄλλη δ' ἄλλοθεν οὐρανομήκης
λαμπὰς ἀνίσχει,
φαρμασσομένη χρίματος ἁγνοῦ
μαλακαῖς ἀδόλοισι παρηγορίαις,   95
πελανῷ μυχόθεν βασιλείῳ.
τούτων λέξασ' ὅ τι καὶ δυνατὸν
καὶ θέμις, αἴνει παιών τε γενοῦ
τῆσδε μερίμνης,
ἢ νῦν τοτὲ μὲν κακόφρων τελέθει,   100
τοτὲ δ' ἐκ θυσιῶν ἃς ἀναφαίνεις
ἐλπὶς ἀμύνει φροντίδ' ἄπληστον
†τὴν θυμοφθόρον λύπης φρένα.†

κύριός εἰμι θροεῖν ὅδιον κράτος αἴσιον ἀνδρῶν   Str.
ἐκτελέων· ἔτι γὰρ θεόθεν καταπνείει   105
Πειθώ, μολπᾷ δ' ἀλκᾶν σύμφυτος αἰών·

MVFTr   82 -φατον MV   83 τυνδάρεῶ M   87 πυθοῖ F Turnebus: θυοσκοεῖς v.l. in schol. vet. Tr, θυοσκινεῖς MTr, θυόσκινεῖς
(deleto accentu priore F) VF   89 τῶν τε θυραίων Enger: τῶν τ'
οὐρανίων codd.   91 Tr: δώροις rell.   94 χρήμ- V, χρίσμ- F Tr
98 Wieseler: αἰνεῖν MV, εἰπεῖν FTr   101 Ahrens: ἀγανὰ φαίνεις
M, ἀγανὰ φαίνει V, ἀγανὰ φαίνουσ' FTr   102 ἄπλειστον M   103
ita MV: θυμοβόρον FTr, tum λυποφρένα Tr   104 cit. Ar. Ran. 1276,
ubi ὃς δῖον R, ὅσιον rell.   105 ed. Aldina: -πνεύει VFTr et ut
vid. M   106 scripsimus: μολπὰν (ex ὰν factum in M) ἀλκὰν codd.

ὅπως Ἀχαιῶν δίθρονον κράτος, Ἑλλάδος ἥβας
    ξύμφρονα ταγάν,   110
πέμπει ξὺν δορὶ καὶ χερὶ πράκτορι
    θούριος ὄρνις Τευκρίδ᾽ ἐπ᾽ αἶαν,
οἰωνῶν βασιλεὺς βασιλεῦσι νε-
    ῶν, ὁ κελαινὸς ὅ τ᾽ ἐξόπιν ἀργᾶς,   115
φανέντες ἵκταρ μελάθρων χερὸς ἐκ δοριπάλτου
παμπρέπτοις ἐν ἕδραισιν,
βοσκομένω λαγίναν ἐρικύμονα φέρματι γένναν,
βλάψαντε λοισθίων δρόμων.   120
αἴλινον αἴλινον εἰπέ, τὸ δ᾽ εὖ νικάτω.

κεδνὸς δὲ στρατόμαντις ἰδὼν δύο λήμασι δισσοὺς   Ant.
Ἀτρεΐδας μαχίμους ἐδάη λαγοδαίτας,
πομποὺς ἀρχᾶς· οὕτω δ᾽ εἶπε τεράζων·   125
‘ χρόνῳ μὲν ἀγρεῖ Πριάμου πόλιν ἅδε κέλευθος,
    πάντα δὲ πύργων
κτήνη πρόσθετα δημιοπληθῆ
    μοῖρα λαπάξει πρὸς τὸ βίαιον·   130
οἷον μή τις ἄγα θεόθεν κνεφά-
    σῃ προτυπὲν στόμιον μέγα Τροίας
στρατωθέν· οἴκτῳ γὰρ ἐπίφθονος Ἄρτεμις ἁγνὰ
πτανοῖσιν κυσὶ πατρὸς   135
αὐτότοκον πρὸ λόχου μογερὰν πτάκα θυομένοισιν·

MVFTr   108 ὅπως–109 ἥβας cit. Ar. Ran. 1285: ἥβαν (ex -ᾶν M)
codd.   110 συμ- VFTr   τᾶν γᾶν m   111 cit. Ar. Ran. 1289:
ξὺν (σὺν m) δορὶ δίκας πράκτορι codd.   115 Blomfield: ἀργίας
codd.   116 οἱ φανέντες F   Turnebus: δορυπ- codd.   117
παμπρέποισιν ἔδραις F, παμπρέπτεσιν ἔδραις Tr   118 scripsimus:
βοσκόμενοι MVF, -ην Tr   119 ἐρικύματα M   φέρβοντο FTr
120 scripsimus: βλαβέντα codd.   122 λήμμασι FTr   123 λογο-
MV   124 Rauchenstein: τ᾽ (del. Thiersch) ἀρχὰς MV, τ᾽ ἀρχοὺς
FTr   125 δ᾽ οὖν εἶπε F   129 προσθετὰ M, πρόσθε τὰ VFTr
130 Elmsley: μοῖρ᾽ ἀλ- codd.   131 Hermann: ἄτα codd.   134
Scaliger: οἴκῳ codd.   137 πτάωνκα V, πτῶκα FTr

στυγεῖ δὲ δεῖπνον αἰετῶν.'
αἴλινον αἴλινον εἰπέ, τὸ δ' εὖ νικάτω.

' τόσον περ εὔφρων ἀ καλὰ   Epod.
δρόσοις ἀέπτοις μαλερῶν λεόντων   141
πάντων τ' ἀγρονόμων φιλομάστοις
θηρῶν ὀβρικάλοισι τερπνά,
τούτων αἰτεῖ ξύμβολα κρᾶναι.
δεξιὰ μὲν κατάμομφα δὲ φάσματα ⟨κρίνω·⟩   145
ἰήιον δὲ καλέω Παιᾶνα,
μή τινας ἀντιπνόους Δαναοῖς χρονί-
    as ἐχενῇδας ἀπλοίας
τεύξῃ, σπευδομένα θυσίαν ἑτέραν ἄνομόν τιν' ἄδαιτον,
νεικέων τέκτονα σύμφυτον, οὐ δει-   151
    σήνορα· μίμνει γὰρ φοβερὰ παλίνορτος
οἰκονόμος δολία, μνάμων Μῆνις τεκνόποινος.'   155
τοιάδε Κάλχας ξὺν μεγάλοις ἀγαθοῖς ἀπέκλαγξεν
μόρσιμ' ἀπ' ὀρνίθων ὁδίων οἴκοις βασιλείοις·
τοῖς δ' ὁμόφωνον
αἴλινον αἴλινον εἰπέ, τὸ δ' εὖ νικάτω.   159

Ζεὺς ὅστις πότ' ἐστίν, εἰ τόδ' αὐ-   Str.
    τῷ φίλον κεκλημένῳ,
τοῦτό νιν προσεννέπω·
οὐκ ἔχω προσεικάσαι
    πάντ' ἐπισταθμώμενος

MVFTr   140 τόσσων M   ἀ FTr: om. MV   141 δρόσοις Tr:
-οισιν rell.   ἀέπτοις VF: -οισι Tr, ἀέλπτοις M (sed ἀέπτοις explicat
schol. ibidem)   λεόντων ex Et. Mag. (Et. Gen.) 377. 37: ὄντων MV,
om. FTr   143 -κάλοις FTr   144 κράναι MV   145 post
φάσματα, στρουθῶν MV, τῶν στρ. FTr; glossema del. Porson, versum
ex. grat. supplevimus (κρίνων iam Schwerdt)   150 ἀπλοίδας FTr
151 σύμφυτον MFTr: συμμενεῖ φυτόν V   154 γὰρ om. FTr   163
προσεικάσαι ex προσηκᾶσαι corr. M

πλὴν Διός, εἰ τὸ μάταν ἀπὸ φροντίδος ἄχθος   165
χρὴ βαλεῖν ἐτητύμως·

οὐδ' ὅστις πάροιθεν ἦν μέγας,   Ant.
  παμμάχῳ θράσει βρύων,
οὐδὲ λέξεται πρὶν ὤν·   170
ὃς δ' ἔπειτ' ἔφυ, τρια-
  κτῆρος οἴχεται τυχών·
Ζῆνα δέ τις προφρόνως ἐπινίκια κλάζων
τεύξεται φρενῶν τὸ πᾶν·   175

τὸν φρονεῖν βροτοὺς ὁδώ-   Str.
  σαντα, τὸν πάθει μάθος
θέντα κυρίως ἔχειν·
στάζει δ' ἀνθ' ὕπνου πρὸ καρδίας
μνησιπήμων πόνος· καὶ παρ' ἄ-   180
  κοντας ἦλθε σωφρονεῖν·
δαιμόνων δέ που χάρις βίαιος
σέλμα σεμνὸν ἡμένων.

καὶ τόθ' ἡγεμὼν ὁ πρέ-   Ant.
  σβυς νεῶν Ἀχαιϊκῶν,   185
μάντιν οὔτινα ψέγων,
ἐμπαίοις τύχαισι συμπνέων,
εὖτ' ἀπλοίᾳ κεναγγεῖ βαρύνοντ' Ἀχαιϊκὸς λεώς,
Χαλκίδος πέραν ἔχων παλιρρό-   190
  χθοις ἐν Αὐλίδος τόποις·

πνοαὶ δ' ἀπὸ Στρυμόνος μολοῦσαι   Str.
κακόσχολοι, νήστιδες, δύσορμοι,

MVFTr   165 Pauw: εἰ τόδε MVF, εἴ γε Tr   170 Ahrens:
οὐδὲν λέξαι MVF, οὐδέν τι λέξαι Tr   177 Schütz: τῶι πάθει codd.
179 Emperius: ἔν (ἔν M) θ' ὕπνωι codd.   182 Turnebus: βιαίως
codd.   190 Ahrens: παλιρρόθοις codd.

βροτῶν ἄλαι,
ναῶν ⟨τε⟩ καὶ πεισμάτων ἀφειδεῖς,   195
παλιμμήκη χρόνον τιθεῖσαι
τρίβῳ κατέξαινον ἄνθος Ἀργεί-
    ων· ἐπεὶ δὲ καὶ πικροῦ
χείματος ἄλλο μῆχαρ
βριθύτερον πρόμοισιν   200
μάντις ἔκλαγξεν προφέρων
Ἄρτεμιν, ὥστε χθόνα βά-
    κτροις ἐπικρούσαντας Ἀτρεί-
δας δάκρυ μὴ κατασχεῖν·

ἄναξ δ' ὁ πρέσβυς τόδ' εἶπε φωνῶν·   Ant.
' βαρεῖα μὲν κὴρ τὸ μὴ πιθέσθαι,   206
βαρεῖα δ', εἰ
τέκνον δαΐξω, δόμων ἄγαλμα,
μιαίνων παρθενοσφάγοισιν
ῥείθροις πατρῴους χέρας πέλας βω-   210
    μοῦ· τί τῶνδ' ἄνευ κακῶν;
πῶς λιπόναυς γένωμαι
ξυμμαχίας ἁμαρτών;
παυσανέμου γὰρ θυσίας
παρθενίου θ' αἵματος ὀρ-   215
    γᾷ περιοργῷ σ⟨φ'⟩ ἐπιθυ-
μεῖν θέμις· εὖ γὰρ εἴη.'

ἐπεὶ δ' ἀνάγκας ἔδυ λέπαδνον   Str.
φρενὸς πνέων δυσσεβῆ τροπαίαν
ἄναγνον, ἀνίερον, τόθεν   220
τὸ παντότολμον φρονεῖν μετέγνω·

MVFTr   195 τε suppl. Porson   196 πολυμήκη (sscr. παλιμμ
F) VF   206 Turnebus: πειθέσθαι MV, πείθ- FTr   210 Tr:
ῥεέθροις rell.   Blomfield: βωμοῦ πέλας codd.   212 Tr: τί πῶς
λιπόναυς τε rell.   215 ὀργᾶι MVF: γρ. αὐδᾶ in marg. M, αὐδᾷ
Tr; tum περιόργως codd., corr. Bamberger

βροτοὺς θρασύνει γὰρ αἰσχρόμητις
τάλαινα παρακοπὰ πρωτοπήμων·   *deranged*
ἔτλα δ' οὖν θυτὴρ γενέ-
  σθαι θυγατρός, γυναικοποί-   225
  νων πολέμων ἀρωγὰν
καὶ προτέλεια ναῶν.

λιτὰς δὲ καὶ κληδόνας πατρῴους   Ant.
παρ' οὐδὲν αἰῶνα παρθένειον ⟨τ'⟩
valued ἔθεντο φιλόμαχοι βραβῆς·   230
φράσεν δ' ἀόζοις πατὴρ μετ' εὐχὰν
δίκαν χιμαίρας ὕπερθε βωμοῦ
πέπλοισι περιπετῆ παντὶ θυμῷ   *see notes*
προνωπῆ λαβεῖν ἀέρ-
  δην στόματός τε καλλιπρώ-   235
  ρου φυλακᾷ κατασχεῖν
φθόγγον ἀραῖον οἴκοις,

βίᾳ χαλινῶν τ' ἀναύδῳ μένει·   Str.
κρόκου βαφὰς δ' ἐς πέδον χέουσα
ἔβαλλ' ἕκαστον θυτή-
  ρων ἀπ' ὄμματος βέλει φιλοίκτῳ,   240
πρέπουσά θ' ὡς ἐν γραφαῖς, προσεννέπειν
θέλουσ', ἐπεὶ πολλάκις
πατρὸς κατ' ἀνδρῶνας εὐτραπέζους
ἔμελψεν, ἁγνᾷ δ' ἀταύρωτος αὐδᾷ πατρὸς   245
φίλου τριτόσπονδον εὔποτμον παι-
  ῶνα φίλως ἐτίμα.

τὰ δ' ἔνθεν οὔτ' εἶδον οὔτ' ἐννέπω·   Ant.

MVFTr   222 Spanheim : βροτοῖς. θρασύνει codd.   229 τ'
suppl. Elmsley   230 βραβεῖς VFTr   236 Blomfield : φυλακὰν
codd.   238 τ' MVF : δ' Tr   239 δ' om. Tr   χέουσ' F
245 Tr : ἁγνὰ MVF   FTr : αὐδὰ MV   246 εὔποτμον ex εὐπόταμον M : εὐπόταμον VF, εὔποτον Tr   246–7 Hartung : αἰῶνα codd.

τέχναι δὲ Κάλχαντος οὐκ ἄκραντοι·
Δίκα δὲ τοῖς μὲν παθοῦ-
σιν μαθεῖν ἐπιρρέπει· τὸ μέλλον ⟨δ'⟩   250
ἐπεὶ γένοιτ' ἂν κλύοις· πρὸ χαιρέτω·
ἴσον δὲ τῷ προστένειν·
τορὸν γὰρ ἥξει σύνορθρον αὐγαῖς·
πέλοιτο δ' οὖν τἀπὶ τούτοισιν εὖ πρᾶξις, ὡς   255
θέλει τόδ' ἄγχιστον Ἀπίας γαί-
ας μονόφρουρον ἕρκος.

ἥκω σεβίζων σὸν Κλυταιμήστρα κράτος·
δίκη γάρ ἐστι φωτὸς ἀρχηγοῦ τίειν
γυναῖκ' ἐρημωθέντος ἄρσενος θρόνου·   260
σὺ δ' εἴ τι κεδνὸν εἴτε μὴ πεπυσμένη
εὐαγγέλοισιν ἐλπίσιν θυηπολεῖς
κλύοιμ' ἂν εὔφρων· οὐδὲ σιγώσῃ φθόνος.

ΚΛΥΤΑΙΜΗΣΤΡΑ

εὐάγγελος μέν, ὥσπερ ἡ παροιμία,
ἕως γένοιτο μητρὸς εὐφρόνης πάρα·   265
πεύσῃ δὲ χάρμα μεῖζον ἐλπίδος κλύειν·
Πριάμου γὰρ ἡρήκασιν Ἀργεῖοι πόλιν.

Χο. πῶς φῇς; πέφευγε τοὔπος ἐξ ἀπιστίας.

Κλ. Τροίαν Ἀχαιῶν οὖσαν· ἢ τορῶς λέγω;

Χο. χαρά μ' ὑφέρπει δάκρυον ἐκκαλουμένη.   270

Κλ. εὖ γὰρ φρονοῦντος ὄμμα σοῦ κατηγορεῖ.

Χο. τί γὰρ τὸ πιστόν; ἔστι τῶνδέ σοι τέκμαρ;

MVFTr   251 δ' suppl. Elmsley   post μέλλον habent τὸ δὲ προ-
κλύειν m VF   252 Ahrens: προχαιρέτω codd.   254 Wellauer:
συνορθὸν M, σὺν ὀρθον V, σύναρθρον FTr   Hermann: αὐταῖς codd.
255 Lobeck: εὔπραξις codd.   258 sqq. personarum notas resti-
tuit Casaubon   261 Auratus: εἰ τὸ M, εἴτε m VFTr   262
ἐλπίσειν M   263 σιγῶντι FTr (apud quos loquitur Clyt.)
264 sq. cit. Eust. 22. 32   270 cit. schol. Hom. Od. 19. 471, cf.
Eust. 1872. 65   271 φρονούσης FTr (apud quos loquitur ἄγγελος)

Κλ. ἔστιν· τί δ' οὐχί; μὴ δολώσαντος θεοῦ.

Χο. πότερα δ' ὀνείρων φάσματ' εὐπειθῆ σέβεις;

Κλ. οὐ δόξαν ἂν λάβοιμι βριζούσης φρενός.　　275

Χο. ἀλλ' ἦ σ' ἐπίανέν τις ἄπτερος φάτις;　feed on

Κλ. παιδὸς νέας ὡς κάρτ' ἐμωμήσω φρένας.

Χο. ποίου χρόνου δὲ καὶ πεπόρθηται πόλις;

Κλ. τῆς νῦν τεκούσης φῶς τόδ' εὐφρόνης λέγω.

Χο. καὶ τίς τόδ' ἐξίκοιτ' ἂν ἀγγέλων τάχος;　　280

Κλ. Ἥφαιστος, Ἴδης λαμπρὸν ἐκπέμπων σέλας·
　　φρυκτὸς δὲ φρυκτὸν δεῦρ' ἀπ' ἀγγάρου πυρός
　　ἔπεμπεν· Ἴδη μὲν πρὸς Ἑρμαῖον λέπας
　　Λήμνου· μέγαν δὲ πανὸν ἐκ νήσου τρίτον
　　Ἀθῷον αἶπος Ζηνὸς ἐξεδέξατο·　　285
　　ὑπερτελής τε πόντον ὥστε νωτίσαι
　　ἰσχὺς πορευτοῦ λαμπάδος †πρὸς ἡδονήν†

.　　.　　.　　.　　.　　.　　.　　.

　　πεύκη τὸ χρυσοφεγγὲς ὥς τις ἥλιος
　　σέλας παραγγείλασα Μακίστου σκοπαῖς·　water-towers
　　ὁ δ' οὔτι μέλλων οὐδ' ἀφρασμόνως ὕπνῳ　　290
　　νικώμενος παρῆκεν ἀγγέλου μέρος,
　　ἑκὰς δὲ φρυκτοῦ φῶς ἐπ' Εὐρίπου ῥοάς
　　Μεσσαπίου φύλαξι σημαίνει μολόν·
　　οἱ δ' ἀντέλαμψαν καὶ παρήγγειλαν πρόσω　blaze in turn
　　γραίας ἐρείκης θωμὸν ἅψαντες πυρί·　　295
　　σθένουσα λαμπὰς δ' οὐδέ πω μαυρουμένη,
　　ὑπερθοροῦσα πεδίον Ἀσωποῦ, δίκην
　　φαιδρᾶς σελήνης, πρὸς Κιθαιρῶνος λέπας
　　ἤγειρεν ἄλλην ἐκδοχὴν πομποῦ πυρός·

M V F Tr　282 ἀγγάρου Et. Mag., Phot., Suid., Eust.: ἀγγέλου codd.
284 πανὸν Athen. xv. 700 e, Phot.: φανὸν codd.　　286 M V: ὑπεὶρ
ἔλης F Tr et schol. vet. Tr　　287–8 lacunam indic. Paley　　289
Turnebus: σκοπὰς codd.　　294 οἵ τ' F　　297 F Tr: παιδίον
ὠποῦ M V

φάος δὲ τηλέπομπον οὐκ ἠναίνετο   300
φρουρά, πλέον καίουσα τῶν εἰρημένων·
λίμνην δ' ὑπὲρ Γοργῶπιν ἔσκηψεν φάος,
ὅρος τ' ἐπ' αἰγίπλαγκτον ἐξικνούμενον
ὤτρυνε θεσμὸν μὴ †χαρίζεσθαι† πυρός·
πέμπουσι δ' ἀνδαίοντες ἀφθόνῳ μένει   305
φλογὸς μέγαν πώγωνα †καὶ Σαρωνικοῦ
πορθμοῦ κάτοπτον πρῶν' ὑπερβάλλειν πρόσω
φλέγουσαν·† εἶτ' ἔσκηψεν, εἶτ' ἀφίκετο
Ἀραχναῖον αἶπος, ἀστυγείτονας σκοπάς·
κἄπειτ' Ἀτρειδῶν ἐς τόδε σκήπτει στέγος   310
φάος τόδ' οὐκ ἄπαππον Ἰδαίου πυρός.
τοιοίδε τοί μοι λαμπαδηφόρων νόμοι,
ἄλλος παρ' ἄλλου διαδοχαῖς πληρούμενοι·
νικᾷ δ' ὁ πρῶτος καὶ τελευταῖος δραμών.
τέκμαρ τοιοῦτον σύμβολόν τέ σοι λέγω   315
ἀνδρὸς παραγγείλαντος ἐκ Τροίας ἐμοί.

Χο. θεοῖς μὲν αὖθις, ὦ γύναι, προσεύξομαι·
λόγους δ' ἀκοῦσαι τούσδε κἀποθαυμάσαι
διηνεκῶς θέλοιμ' ἄν, ὡς λέγοις πάλιν.

Κλ. Τροίαν Ἀχαιοὶ τῇδ' ἔχουσ' ἐν ἡμέρᾳ·   320
οἶμαι βοὴν ἄμεικτον ἐν πόλει πρέπειν·
ὄξος τ' ἄλειφά τ' ἐγχέας ταὐτῷ κύτει
διχοστατοῦντ' ἂν οὐ φίλω προσεννέποις·
καὶ τῶν ἁλόντων καὶ κρατησάντων δίχα
φθογγὰς ἀκούειν ἔστι συμφορᾶς διπλῆς·   325
οἱ μὲν γὰρ ἀμφὶ σώμασιν πεπτωκότες
ἀνδρῶν κασιγνήτων τε καὶ †φυταλμίων

MVFTr   304 δὴ χαρίζεσθαι Tr   306–8 corrupti, nisi post 307
versus excidit   307 Canter: κάτοπτρον codd.   310 FTr:
τόγε σκήπτει Μ, τόδ' ἐνσκήπτει V   311–1066 desunt cod. Μ
312 Schütz: τοιοίδ' ἕτοιμοι (ἔτυμοι F) codd.   319 λέγεις V   321
ἄμικτον codd.   322 Canter: ἐκχέας codd.   323 Stanley:
φίλως codd.

παῖδες γερόντων† οὐκέτ᾽ ἐξ ἐλευθέρου
δέρης ἀποιμώζουσι φιλτάτων μόρον·
τοὺς δ᾽ αὖτε νυκτίπλαγκτος ἐκ μάχης πόνος   330
νήστεις πρὸς ἀρίστοισιν ὧν ἔχει πόλις
τάσσει, πρὸς οὐδὲν ἐν μέρει τεκμήριον,
ἀλλ᾽ ὡς ἕκαστος ἔσπασεν τύχης πάλον.
ἐν ⟨δ᾽⟩ αἰχμαλώτοις Τρωϊκοῖς οἰκήμασιν
ναίουσιν ἤδη, τῶν ὑπαιθρίων πάγων   335
δρόσων τ᾽ ἀπαλλαχθέντες, ὡς δ᾽ εὐδαίμονες
ἀφύλακτον εὐδήσουσι πᾶσαν εὐφρόνην.
εἰ δ᾽ εὐσεβοῦσι τοὺς πολισσούχους θεούς
τοὺς τῆς ἁλούσης γῆς θεῶν θ᾽ ἱδρύματα,
οὔ τἂν ἑλόντες αὖθις ἀνθαλοῖεν ἄν·   340
ἔρως δὲ μή τις πρότερον ἐμπίπτῃ στρατῷ
πορθεῖν ἃ μὴ χρὴ κέρδεσιν νικωμένους·
δεῖ γὰρ πρὸς οἴκους νοστίμου σωτηρίας,
κάμψαι διαύλου θάτερον κῶλον πάλιν·
θεοῖς δ᾽ ἀναμπλάκητος εἰ μόλοι στρατός,   345
ἐγρηγορὸς τὸ πῆμα τῶν ὀλωλότων
γένοιτ᾽ ἄν, εἰ πρόσπαια μὴ τύχοι κακά.   *unexpected*
τοιαῦτά τοι γυναικὸς ἐξ ἐμοῦ κλύεις·
τὸ δ᾽ εὖ κρατοίη μὴ διχορρόπως ἰδεῖν·
πολλῶν γὰρ ἐσθλῶν τὴν ὄνησιν εἱλόμην.   350

Χο. γύναι, κατ᾽ ἄνδρα σώφρον᾽ εὐφρόνως λέγεις·
ἐγὼ δ᾽ ἀκούσας πιστά σου τεκμήρια
θεοὺς προσειπεῖν εὖ παρασκευάζομαι·
χάρις γὰρ οὐκ ἄτιμος εἴργασται πόνων.

ὦ Ζεῦ βασιλεῦ καὶ Νὺξ φιλία   355

VFTr   331 Tr: νῆστις F, νήστισι V   334 suppl. Pauw   336
ἀπαλλαγέντες F Tr   Casaubon : ὡς δυσδαίμονες codd. et schol. vet.
Tr   340 Hermann : οὐκ ἀνελόντες V, οὐκ ἄν γ᾽ ἑλόντες F Tr   Auratus : ἂν θάνοιεν V, αὖ θάνοιεν F Tr   341 πρῶτον V   ἐμπίπτῃ (sup. η
scr. οι) F : -πτει V, -ποι Tr   342 τὰ μὴ V   346 Porson : ἐγρήγορον
codd.   347 τύχη Tr   348 κλύοις F Tr   Post h.v. deficit V

μεγάλων κόσμων κτεάτειρα,
ἥτ' ἐπὶ Τροίας πύργοις ἔβαλες
στεγανὸν δίκτυον ὡς μήτε μέγαν
μήτ' οὖν νεαρῶν τιν' ὑπερτελέσαι
μέγα δουλείας   360
γάγγαμον ἄτης παναλώτου·
Δία τοι ξένιον μέγαν αἰδοῦμαι
τὸν τάδε πράξαντ', ἐπ' Ἀλεξάνδρῳ
τείνοντα πάλαι τόξον, ὅπως ἂν
μήτε πρὸ καιροῦ μήθ' ὑπὲρ ἄστρων   365
βέλος ἡλίθιον σκήψειεν.

Διὸς πλαγὰν ἔχουσιν εἰπεῖν,   Str.
πάρεστιν τοῦτό γ' ἐξιχνεῦσαι·
ἔπραξεν ὡς ἔκρανεν. οὐκ ἔφα τις
θεοὺς βροτῶν ἀξιοῦσθαι μέλειν   370
ὅσοις ἀθίκτων χάρις
πατοῖθ'· ὁ δ' οὐκ εὐσεβής·
πέφανται δ' ἐγγόνοις
†ἀτολμήτων ἄρη†   375
πνεόντων μεῖζον ἢ δικαίως,
φλεόντων δωμάτων ὑπέρφευ,
ὑπὲρ τὸ βέλτιστον· ἔστω δ' ἀπήμαντον, ὥστ' ἀπαρκεῖν
εὖ πραπίδων λαχόντι.   380
οὐ γὰρ ἔστιν ἔπαλξις
πλούτου πρὸς Κόρον ἀνδρὶ
λακτίσαντι μέγαν Δίκας
βωμὸν εἰς ἀφάνειαν.

FTr   356 τῶν μεγ. Tr   367 ἔχουσαν in ἔχουσ' mut. F   368
πάρεστι FTr, ν add. Hartung τοῦτ' F   369 Hermann: ὡς ἔπραξεν
ὡς FTr   374 Casaubon: ἐγγόνους (sup. prius γ scr. κ Tr) FTr
379 ὥστε κἀπαρκεῖν Tr   380 Auratus: λαχόντα FTr   383
ἐκλακτ- Tr   Canter: μεγάλα FTr

βιᾶται δ' ἁ τάλαινα Πειθώ,　　　　　Ant.

προβούλου παῖς ἄφερτος Ἄτας·　　　386

ἄκος δὲ πᾶν μάταιον· οὐκ ἐκρύφθη,

πρέπει δέ, φῶς αἰνολαμπές, σίνος·

κακοῦ δὲ χαλκοῦ τρόπον　　　　　　390

τρίβῳ τε καὶ προσβολαῖς

μελαμπαγὴς πέλει

δικαιωθείς, ἐπεὶ

διώκει παῖς ποτανὸν ὄρνιν,

πόλει πρόστριμμα θεὶς ἄφερτον·　　　395

λιτᾶν δ' ἀκούει μὲν οὔτις θεῶν,

　　τὸν δ' ἐπίστροφον τῶν

φῶτ' ἄδικον καθαιρεῖ.

　　οἷος καὶ Πάρις ἐλθὼν

　　ἐς δόμον τὸν Ἀτρειδᾶν　　　　　400

　　ᾔσχυνε ξενίαν τράπε-

　　　ζαν κλοπαῖσι γυναικός.

λιποῦσα δ' ἀστοῖσιν ἀσπίστορας　　　Str.

κλόνους λοχισμούς τε καὶ

　　ναυβάτας ὁπλισμούς,　　　　　　405

ἄγουσά τ' ἀντίφερνον Ἰλίῳ φθοράν,

βεβάκει ῥίμφα διὰ

　　πυλᾶν ἄτλητα τλᾶσα· πολλὰ δ' ἔστενον

τόδ' ἐννέποντες δόμων προφῆται·

' ἰὼ ἰὼ δῶμα δῶμα καὶ πρόμοι,　　　410

ἰὼ λέχος καὶ στίβοι φιλάνορες·

FTr　　386 Hartung: προβουλόπαις FTr　　387 ὡς ἄκος Tr　Musgrave: παμμάταιον FTr　　389 σέλας schol. vet. Tr, et sup. σίνος scr. Tr　　391 τε om. F　　Casaubon: προβ- FTr　　394 Schütz: πτανὸν F, πτανόν τιν' Tr　　395 Wilamowitz: πρόστριμμ' ἄφερτον θεὶς F, π. ἄ. ἐνθεὶς Tr　　397 Klausen: ἐπίστροφον τῶνδε FTr　400 ἐς δόμον τῶν F, εἰς οἶκον τὸν Tr　　401 τὴν ξενίαν Tr　　402 κλοπαῖς F　　404 Heyse: λογχίμους FTr　　407 Keck: βέβακε F, -κεν Tr　　408 πολὺ δ' ἀνέστενον F　　410 ἰώ et δῶμα semel F

πάρεστι †σιγᾶς ἄτιμος ἀλοίδορος
ἄδιστος ἀφεμένων† ἰδεῖν·
πόθῳ δ' ὑπερποντίας
φάσμα δόξει δόμων ἀνάσσειν·　　　　　　　415
εὐμόρφων δὲ κολοσσῶν
ἔχθεται χάρις ἀνδρί·
ὀμμάτων δ' ἐν ἀχηνίαις
ἔρρει πᾶσ' Ἀφροδίτα·

ὀνειρόφαντοι δὲ πενθήμονες　　　　　　Ant.
πάρεισι δόξαι φέρου-　　　　　　　　　421
σαι χάριν ματαίαν·
μάταν γάρ, εὖτ' ἂν ἐσθλά τις δοκοῦνθ' ὁρᾷ,
παραλλάξασα διὰ
χερῶν βέβακεν ὄψις, οὐ μεθύστερον　　　425
πτεροῖς ὀπαδοῦσ' ὕπνου κελεύθοις.'
τὰ μὲν κατ' οἴκους ἐφ' ἑστίας ἄχη
τάδ' ἐστί, καὶ τῶνδ' ὑπερβατώτερα·
τὸ πᾶν δ' ἀφ' Ἕλλανος αἴας συνορμένοισι πένθεια τλησικάρδιος　　　　　　　　　　430
δόμῳ 'ν ἑκάστου πρέπει·
πολλὰ γοῦν θιγγάνει πρὸς ἧπαρ·
οὓς μὲν γάρ ⟨τις⟩ ἔπεμψεν
οἶδεν, ἀντὶ δὲ φωτῶν
τεύχη καὶ σποδὸς εἰς ἑκά-　　　　　　435
στου δόμους ἀφικνεῖται.

ὁ χρυσαμοιβὸς δ' Ἄρης σωμάτων　　　　Str.
καὶ ταλαντοῦχος ἐν μάχῃ δορὸς

FTr　　　412 πάρεστιν F　　　416 δὲ F : γὰρ Tr　　　417 τἀνδρί
Tr　　419 Ἀφροδίτη F　　　423 Salzmann : δοκῶν ὁρᾶν FTr
425 χειρῶν F　　　426 Dobree : ὀπαδοῖς FTr　　　429 Bamberger :
ἑλλάδος FTr　　　συνορμένοις FTr, -ι add. Schwerdt　　　431 Dobree :
δόμων FTr　　　433 suppl. Porson　　　πέμψεν Tr　　　434 ἀντὶ δὲ
βροτῶν Tr　　　435 sq. πρὸς ἑκάστου τοὺς δόμους εἰσαφ- Tr

πυρωθὲν ἐξ Ἰλίου   440
φίλοισι πέμπει βαρὺ
ψῆγμα δυσδάκρυτον ἀν-
 τήνορος σποδοῦ γεμί-
 ζων λέβητας εὐθέτου.
στένουσι δ' εὖ λέγοντες ἄν-   445
 δρα τὸν μὲν ὡς μάχης ἴδρις,
τὸν δ' ἐν φοναῖς καλῶς πεσόντ'
 ἀλλοτρίας διαὶ γυναι-
 κός. τάδε σῖγά τις βαΰ-
ζει· φθονερὸν δ' ὑπ' ἄλγος ἕρ-   450
πει προδίκοις Ἀτρείδαις.
οἱ δ' αὐτοῦ περὶ τεῖχος
 θήκας Ἰλιάδος γᾶς
 εὔμορφοι κατέχουσιν· ἐχ-
 θρὰ δ' ἔχοντας ἔκρυψεν.   455

βαρεῖα δ' ἀστῶν φάτις σὺν κότῳ·   Ant.
δημοκράντου δ' ἀρᾶς τίνει χρέος· ǀ
μένει δ' ἀκοῦσαί τί μου
μέριμνα νυκτηρεφές·   460
τῶν πολυκτόνων γὰρ οὐκ
 ἄσκοποι θεοί· κελαι-
 ναὶ δ' Ἐρινύες χρόνῳ
τυχηρὸν ὄντ' ἄνευ δίκας
 παλιντυχεῖ τριβᾷ βίου   465
τιθεῖσ' ἀμαυρόν, ἐν δ' ἀΐ-
 στοις τελέθοντος οὔτις ἀλ-
 κά· τὸ δ' ὑπερκόπως κλύειν

FTr   444 τοὺς λέβ. Tr   448 διαὶ An. Ox. Cramer i. 119.
10 sqq.: διὰ F, γε διὰ Tr   449 σιγᾷ F   451 -κοισιν F   452
οἶδ' FTr, distinxit Victorius   454-5 ἐχθρῶς Tr   457 Porson:
-κράτου FTr   462 ἀπόσκοποι F   463 δ' οὖν Tr   465 Scaliger:
-τυχῇ F, -τυχῇ Tr   468 Casaubon: -κότως FTr

εὖ βαρύ· βάλλεται γὰρ †ὅσ-
σοις† Διόθεν κεραυνός.   470
κρίνω δ' ἄφθονον ὄλβον·
μήτ' εἴην πτολιπόρθης,
μήτ' οὖν αὐτὸς ἁλοὺς ὑπ' ἄλλῳ βίον κατίδοιμι.

— πυρὸς δ' ὑπ' εὐαγγέλου   475
πόλιν διήκει θοὰ
βάξις· εἰ δ' ἐτήτυμος,
τίς οἶδεν; ἤ τι θεῖόν ἐστιν ἢ ψύθος.
— τίς ὧδε παιδνὸς ἢ φρενῶν κεκομμένος,
φλογὸς παραγγέλμασιν   480
νέοις πυρωθέντα καρδίαν ἔπειτ'
ἀλλαγᾷ λόγου καμεῖν;
— γυναικὸς αἰχμᾷ πρέπει
πρὸ τοῦ φανέντος χάριν ξυναινέσαι·
πιθανὸς ἄγαν ὁ θῆλυς ὅρος ἐπινέμεται   485
ταχύπορος· ἀλλὰ ταχύμορον
γυναικογήρυτον ὄλλυται κλέος.

ΚΛ. τάχ' εἰσόμεσθα λαμπάδων φαεσφόρων
φρυκτωριῶν τε καὶ πυρὸς παραλλαγάς,   490
εἴτ' οὖν ἀληθεῖς εἴτ' ὀνειράτων δίκην
τερπνὸν τόδ' ἐλθὸν φῶς ἐφήλωσεν φρένας·
κήρυκ' ἀπ' ἀκτῆς τόνδ' ὁρῶ κατάσκιον
κλάδοις ἐλαίας· μαρτυρεῖ δέ μοι κάσις
πηλοῦ ξύνουρος διψία κόνις τάδε,   495
ὡς οὔτ' ἄναυδος οὔτε σοι δαίων φλόγα
ὕλης ὀρείας σημανεῖ καπνῷ πυρός·

FTr   472 μὴ δ' F   -πόρθις F   473 Karsten : ἄλλων FTr
476 τὴν πόλιν Tr   477 Auratus : ἐτητύμως FTr   478 ἤ (sscr.
ει) τοι F, ἤ τοι Tr, ἐστὶ (-τὶν F) μὴ FTr, corr. Hermann (τι), Lobel
(ἐστιν ἢ)   481-2 καρδίαν ἔπει | ἔπειτ' ἀλλαγᾷ F   482 λόγους F
483 Scaliger : ἐν γυναικὸς FTr   492 -ωσεν schol. vet. Tr, -ωσε FTr

ἀλλ' ἢ τὸ χαίρειν μᾶλλον ἐκβάξει λέγων,
τὸν ἀντίον δὲ τοῖσδ' ἀποστέργω λόγον·
εὖ γὰρ πρὸς εὖ φανεῖσι προσθήκη πέλοι.   500

Χο. ὅστις τάδ' ἄλλως τῇδ' ἐπεύχεται πόλει,
αὐτὸς φρενῶν καρποῖτο τὴν ἁμαρτίαν.

ΚΗΡΥΞ

ἰὼ πατρῷον οὖδας Ἀργείας χθονός,
δεκάτου σε φέγγει τῷδ' ἀφικόμην ἔτους,
πολλῶν ῥαγεισῶν ἐλπίδων μιᾶς τυχών·   505
οὐ γάρ ποτ' ηὔχουν τῇδ' ἐν Ἀργείᾳ χθονί
θανὼν μεθέξειν φιλτάτου τάφου μέρος.
νῦν χαῖρε μὲν χθών, χαῖρε δ' ἡλίου φάος,
ὕπατός τε χώρας Ζεύς, ὁ Πύθιός τ' ἄναξ,
τόξοις ἰάπτων μηκέτ' εἰς ἡμᾶς βέλη·   510
ἅλις παρὰ Σκάμανδρον ἦσθ' ἀνάρσιος·
νῦν δ' αὖτε σωτὴρ ἴσθι καὶ παιώνιος,
ἄναξ Ἄπολλον· τούς τ' ἀγωνίους θεούς
πάντας προσαυδῶ, τόν τ' ἐμὸν τιμάορον
Ἑρμῆν, φίλον κήρυκα, κηρύκων σέβας,   515
ἥρως τε τοὺς πέμψαντας, εὐμενεῖς πάλιν
στρατὸν δέχεσθαι τὸν λελειμμένον δορός.
ἰὼ μέλαθρα βασιλέων, φίλαι στέγαι,
σεμνοί τε θᾶκοι, δαίμονές τ' ἀντήλιοι,
εἴ που πάλαι, φαιδροῖσι τοισίδ' ὄμμασιν   520
δέξασθε κόσμῳ βασιλέα πολλῷ χρόνῳ·
ἥκει γὰρ ὑμῖν φῶς ἐν εὐφρόνῃ φέρων
καὶ τοῖσδ' ἅπασι κοινὸν Ἀγαμέμνων ἄναξ.
ἀλλ' εὖ νιν ἀσπάσασθε, καὶ γὰρ οὖν πρέπει,
Τροίαν κατασκάψαντα τοῦ δικηφόρου   525

FTr   504 Jacob: δεκάτῳ codd.   511 Needham: ἦλθ' (sscr. ες)
F, ἦλθες Tr   512 Dobree: καὶ παγώνιος F, κἀπαγώνιος Tr   520
Auratus: ἦ που FTr   τοῖσιν Tr   521 δέξαισθε Tr   522
ἡμῖν F

Διὸς μακέλλῃ, τῇ κατείργασται πέδον·
βωμοὶ δ' ἄιστοι καὶ θεῶν ἱδρύματα,
καὶ σπέρμα πάσης ἐξαπόλλυται χθονός.
τοιόνδε Τροίᾳ περιβαλὼν ζευκτήριον
ἄναξ Ἀτρείδης πρέσβυς εὐδαίμων ἀνήρ   530
ἥκει, τίεσθαι δ' ἀξιώτατος βροτῶν
τῶν νῦν· Πάρις γὰρ οὔτε συντελὴς πόλις   *accomplice*
ἐξεύχεται τὸ δρᾶμα τοῦ πάθους πλέον·
ὀφλὼν γὰρ ἁρπαγῆς τε καὶ κλοπῆς δίκην
τοῦ ῥυσίου θ' ἥμαρτε καὶ πανώλεθρον   535
αὐτόχθονον πατρῷον ἔθρισεν δόμον·
διπλᾶ δ' ἔτεισαν Πριαμίδαι θἀμάρτια.

Χο. κῆρυξ Ἀχαιῶν χαῖρε τῶν ἀπὸ στρατοῦ.

Κη. χαίρω, ⟨τὸ⟩ τεθνάναι δ' οὐκέτ' ἀντερῶ θεοῖς.

Χο. ἔρως πατρῴας τῆσδε γῆς σ' ἐγύμνασεν;   540

Κη. ὥστ' ἐνδακρύειν γ' ὄμμασιν χαρᾶς ὕπο.

Χο. τερπνῆς ἄρ' ἦστε τῆσδ' ἐπήβολοι νόσου.

Κη. πῶς δή; διδαχθεὶς τοῦδε δεσπόσω λόγου.

Χο. τῶν ἀντερώντων ἱμέρῳ πεπληγμένοι.

Κη. ποθεῖν ποθοῦντα τήνδε γῆν στρατὸν λέγεις;   545

Χο. ὡς πόλλ' ἀμαυρᾶς ἐκ φρενός ⟨μ'⟩ ἀναστένειν.

Κη. πόθεν τὸ δύσφρον τοῦτ' ἐπῆν στύγος στρατοῦ;

Χο. πάλαι τὸ σιγᾶν φάρμακον βλάβης ἔχω.

Κη. καὶ πῶς; ἀπόντων κοιράνων ἔτρεις τινάς;

Χο. ὡς νῦν, τὸ σὸν δή, καὶ θανεῖν πολλὴ χάρις.   550

Κη. εὖ γὰρ πέπρακται· ταῦτα δ' ἐν πολλῷ χρόνῳ

FTr   537 ἔτισαν FTr   539 Schneidewin : τεθνᾶναι FTr   οὐκ F
541 ἐκδακρ- Tr   542 Ahrens : ἴστε F, ἦτε Tr   544 Tyrwhitt :
-μένος FTr   546 suppl. Scaliger   547 Auratus : στρατῶι FTr
549 κοιράνων Tr : τυράννων F   550 ὡς Scaliger, Auratus : ὧν
FTr   551 Haupt : ταῦτα FTr

τὰ μέν τις ἂν λέξειεν εὐπετῶς ἔχειν,
τὰ δ' αὖτε κἀπίμομφα· τίς δὲ πλὴν θεῶν
ἅπαντ' ἀπήμων τὸν δι' αἰῶνος χρόνον;
μόχθους γὰρ εἰ λέγοιμι καὶ δυσαυλίας,   555
σπαρνὰς παρήξεις καὶ κακοστρώτους, τί δ' οὐ
στένοντες, οὐ λαχόντες ἤματος μέρος;
τὰ δ' αὖτε χέρσῳ καὶ προσῆν πλέον στύγος·
εὐναὶ γὰρ ἦσαν δαΐων πρὸς τείχεσιν,
ἐξ οὐρανοῦ δὲ κἀπὸ γῆς λειμώνιαι   560
δρόσοι κατεψάκαζον, ἔμπεδον σίνος,
ἐσθημάτων τιθέντες ἔνθηρον τρίχα.
χειμῶνα δ' εἰ λέγοι τις οἰωνοκτόνον,
οἷον παρεῖχ' ἄφερτον Ἰδαία χιών,
ἢ θάλπος, εὖτε πόντος ἐν μεσημβριναῖς   565
κοίταις ἀκύμων νηνέμοις εὕδοι πεσών·
τί ταῦτα πενθεῖν δεῖ; παροίχεται πόνος·
παροίχεται δέ, τοῖσι μὲν τεθνηκόσιν
τὸ μήποτ' αὖθις μηδ' ἀναστῆναι μέλειν·   569
ἡμῖν δὲ τοῖς λοιποῖσιν Ἀργείων στρατοῦ   573
νικᾷ τὸ κέρδος, πῆμα δ' οὐκ ἀντιρρέπει·   574
τί τοὺς ἀναλωθέντας ἐν ψήφῳ λέγειν,   570
τὸν ζῶντα δ' ἀλγεῖν χρὴ τύχης παλιγκότου;
καὶ πολλὰ χαίρειν συμφοραῖς καταξιῶ,   572
ὡς κομπάσαι τῷδ' εἰκὸς ἡλίου φάει   575
ὑπὲρ θαλάσσης καὶ χθονὸς ποτωμένοις·
' Τροίαν ἑλόντες δή ποτ' Ἀργείων στόλος
θεοῖς λάφυρα ταῦτα τοῖς καθ' Ἑλλάδα
δόμοις ἐπασσάλευσαν ἀρχαῖον γάνος.'   ?
τοιαῦτα χρὴ κλύοντας εὐλογεῖν πόλιν   580

FTr   552 ἂν Auratus : εὖ FTr   553 τάδ' FTr, distinxit
Heath   556 κακοτρ- F   558 τάδ' FTr, distinxit Victorius
559 Dindorf: δηίων FTr   560 δὲ Pearson : γὰρ FTr   -ωνίαι FTr
561 -ψεκ- FTr, corr. Dindorf   563 λέγει Tr   573–4 transposuit Elberling   577 Τροίην F, fort. recte

καὶ τοὺς στρατηγούς· καὶ χάρις τιμήσεται
Διὸς τάδ᾽ ἐκπράξασα. πάντ᾽ ἔχεις λόγον.

Χο. νικώμενος λόγοισιν οὐκ ἀναίνομαι·
ἀεὶ γὰρ ἡβᾷ τοῖς γέρουσιν εὐμαθεῖν·
δόμοις δὲ ταῦτα καὶ Κλυταιμήστρᾳ μέλειν   585
εἰκὸς μάλιστα, σὺν δὲ πλουτίζειν ἐμέ.

Κλ. ἀνωλόλυξα μὲν πάλαι χαρᾶς ὕπο,
ὅτ᾽ ἦλθ᾽ ὁ πρῶτος νύχιος ἄγγελος πυρός,
φράζων ἅλωσιν Ἰλίου τ᾽ ἀνάστασιν·
καί τίς μ᾽ ἐνίπτων εἶπε· ʽ φρυκτωρῶν διά   590
πεισθεῖσα Τροίαν νῦν πεπορθῆσθαι δοκεῖς;
ἦ κάρτα πρὸς γυναικὸς αἴρεσθαι κέαρ.ʼ
λόγοις τοιούτοις πλαγκτὸς οὖσ᾽ ἐφαινόμην·
ὅμως δ᾽ ἔθυον, καὶ γυναικείῳ νόμῳ
ὀλολυγμὸν ἄλλος ἄλλοθεν κατὰ πτόλιν   ˎ   595
ἔλασκον εὐφημοῦντες, ἐν θεῶν ἕδραις
θυηφάγον κοιμῶντες εὐώδη φλόγα.
καὶ νῦν τὰ μάσσω μὲν τί δεῖ σ᾽ ἐμοὶ λέγειν;
ἄνακτος αὐτοῦ πάντα πεύσομαι λόγον·
ὅπως δ᾽ ἄριστα τὸν ἐμὸν αἰδοῖον πόσιν   600
σπεύσω πάλιν μολόντα δέξασθαι· τί γάρ
γυναικὶ τούτου φέγγος ἥδιον δρακεῖν,
ἀπὸ στρατείας ἄνδρα σώσαντος θεοῦ
πύλας ἀνοῖξαι; ταῦτ᾽ ἀπάγγειλον πόσει·
ἥκειν ὅπως τάχιστ᾽ ἐράσμιον πόλει·   605
γυναῖκα πιστὴν δ᾽ ἐν δόμοις εὕροι μολών
οἵανπερ οὖν ἔλειπε, δωμάτων κύνα
ἐσθλὴν ἐκείνῳ, πολεμίαν τοῖς δύσφροσιν,
καὶ τἄλλ᾽ ὁμοίαν πάντα, σημαντήριον
οὐδὲν διαφθείρασαν ἐν μήκει χρόνου·   610
οὐδ᾽ οἶδα τέρψιν οὐδ᾽ ἐπίψογον φάτιν

FTr   584 Headlam: εὖ μαθεῖν FTr   587 ἀνωλολύξαμεν FTr,
distinxit H. Stephanus   590 ἐνίπτων F   593 πλακτὸς Tr
596 ἐνθέων F

ἄλλου πρὸς ἀνδρὸς μᾶλλον ἢ χαλκοῦ βαφάς·
τοιόσδ᾽ ὁ κόμπος, τῆς ἀληθείας γέμων,
οὐκ αἰσχρὸς ὡς γυναικὶ γενναίᾳ λακεῖν.

Χο. αὕτη μὲν οὕτως εἶπε μανθάνοντί σοι,   615
τοροῖσιν ἑρμηνεῦσιν εὐπρεπῶς λόγον·
σὺ δ᾽ εἰπέ, κῆρυξ, Μενέλεων δὲ πεύθομαι,
εἰ νόστιμός τε καὶ σεσωμένος πάλιν
ἥκει σὺν ὑμῖν, τῆσδε γῆς φίλον κράτος.

Κη. οὐκ ἔσθ᾽ ὅπως λέξαιμι τὰ ψευδῆ καλά   620
ἐς τὸν πολὺν φίλοισι καρποῦσθαι χρόνον.

Χο. πῶς δῆτ᾽ ἂν εἰπὼν κεδνὰ τἀληθῆ τύχοις;
σχισθέντα δ᾽ οὐκ εὔκρυπτα γίγνεται τάδε.

Κη. ἀνὴρ ἄφαντος ἐξ Ἀχαϊκοῦ στρατοῦ,
αὐτός τε καὶ τὸ πλοῖον· οὐ ψευδῆ λέγω.   625

Χο. πότερον ἀναχθεὶς ἐμφανῶς ἐξ Ἰλίου,
ἢ χεῖμα, κοινὸν ἄχθος, ἥρπασε στρατοῦ;

Κη. ἔκυρσας ὥστε τοξότης ἄκρος σκοποῦ·
μακρὸν δὲ πῆμα συντόμως ἐφημίσω.

Χο. πότερα γὰρ αὐτοῦ ζῶντος ἢ τεθνηκότος   630
φάτις πρὸς ἄλλων ναυτίλων ἐκλῄζετο;

Κη. οὐκ οἶδεν οὐδεὶς ὥστ᾽ ἀπαγγεῖλαι τορῶς,
πλὴν τοῦ τρέφοντος Ἡλίου χθονὸς φύσιν.

Χο. πῶς γὰρ λέγεις χειμῶνα ναυτικῷ στρατῷ
ἐλθεῖν τελευτῆσαί τε δαιμόνων κότῳ;   635

Κη. εὔφημον ἦμαρ οὐ πρέπει κακαγγέλῳ
γλώσσῃ μιαίνειν· χωρὶς ἡ τιμὴ θεῶν·
ὅταν δ᾽ ἀπευκτὰ πήματ᾽ ἄγγελος πόλει
στυγνῷ προσώπῳ πτωσίμου στρατοῦ φέρῃ,

FTr   618 τε Hermann : γε FTr   σεσωσμ- FTr   619
Karsten : ἥξει FTr   622 Porson : τύχης FTr   624 ἀνὴρ
FTr, corr. Hermann   639 σμοιῷ pro στυγνῷ ex Hesych. (σμοιῷ
προσώπῳ) M. Schmidt

πόλει μὲν ἕλκος ἓν τὸ δήμιον τυχεῖν,　　　　640
'πολλοὺς δὲ πολλῶν ἐξαγισθέντας δόμων
ἄνδρας διπλῇ μάστιγι, τὴν Ἄρης φιλεῖ,
δίλογχον ἄτην, φοινίαν ξυνωρίδα·
τοιῶνδε μέντοι πημάτων σεσαγμένον
πρέπει λέγειν παιᾶνα τόνδ' Ἐρινύων·　　　　645
σωτηρίων δὲ πραγμάτων εὐάγγελον
ἥκοντα πρὸς χαίρουσαν εὐεστοῖ πόλιν,
πῶς κεδνὰ τοῖς κακοῖσι συμμείξω, λέγων
χειμῶν' †Ἀχαιῶν οὐκ ἀμήνιτον θεοῖς†;
ξυνώμοσαν γάρ, ὄντες ἔχθιστοι τὸ πρίν,　　　650
πῦρ καὶ θάλασσα, καὶ τὰ πίστ' ἐδειξάτην
φθείροντε τὸν δύστηνον Ἀργείων στρατόν.
ἐν νυκτὶ δυσκύμαντα δ' ὠρώρει κακά·
ναῦς γὰρ πρὸς ἀλλήλησι Θρήκιαι πνοαί
ἤρεικον· αἱ δὲ κεροτυπούμεναι βίᾳ　　　　655
χειμῶνι τυφῶ σὺν ζάλῃ τ' ὀμβροκτύπῳ,
ᾤχοντ' ἄφαντοι, ποιμένος κακοῦ στρόβῳ.
ἐπεὶ δ' ἀνῆλθε λαμπρὸν ἡλίου φάος,
ὁρῶμεν ἀνθοῦν πέλαγος Αἰγαῖον νεκροῖς
ἀνδρῶν Ἀχαιῶν ναυτικοῖς τ' ἐρειπίοις·　　　660
ἡμᾶς γε μὲν δὴ ναῦν τ' ἀκήρατον σκάφος
ἤτοι τις ἐξέκλεψεν ἢ 'ξῃτήσατο,
θεός τις, οὐκ ἄνθρωπος, οἴακος θιγών·
Τύχη δὲ σωτὴρ ναῦν θέλουσ' ἐφέζετο,
ὡς μήτ' ἐν ὅρμῳ κύματος ζάλην ἔχειν　　　665
μήτ' ἐξοκεῖλαι πρὸς κραταίλεως χθόνα.
ἔπειτα δ' ᾅδην πόντιον πεφευγότες,
λευκὸν κατ' ἦμαρ, οὐ πεποιθότες τύχῃ,
ἐβουκολοῦμεν φροντίσιν νέον πάθος,
στρατοῦ καμόντος καὶ κακῶς σποδουμένου.　　670

FTr　　644 Schütz : σεσαγμένων FTr　　648 -μίξω FTr　　654
-λαισι Tr　　655 ἤρειπον Tr　　κερω- FTr　　660 Auratus :
ναυτικῶν τ' ἐριπίων FTr

καὶ νῦν ἐκείνων εἴ τις ἐστὶν ἐμπνέων,
λέγουσιν ἡμᾶς ὡς ὀλωλότας, τί μήν;
ἡμεῖς τ᾽ ἐκείνους ταῦτ᾽ ἔχειν δοξάζομεν.
γένοιτο δ᾽ ὡς ἄριστα· Μενέλεων γὰρ οὖν
πρῶτόν τε καὶ μάλιστα προσδόκα μολεῖν·   675
εἰ δ᾽ οὖν τις ἀκτὶς ἡλίου νιν ἱστορεῖ
καὶ ζῶντα καὶ βλέποντα, μηχαναῖς Διός
οὔπω θέλοντος ἐξαναλῶσαι γένος,
ἐλπίς τις αὐτὸν πρὸς δόμους ἥξειν πάλιν.
τοσαῦτ᾽ ἀκούσας ἴσθι τἀληθῆ κλυών.   680

Χο. τίς ποτ᾽ ὠνόμαζεν ὧδ᾽   Str.
    ἐς τὸ πᾶν ἐτητύμως·
    μή τις ὄντιν᾽ οὐχ ὁρῶμεν προνοί-
    αισι τοῦ πεπρωμένου
    γλῶσσαν ἐν τύχᾳ νέμων;   685
    τὰν δορίγαμβρον ἀμφινει-
        κῆ θ᾽ Ἑλέναν; ἐπεὶ πρεπόντως
    ἑλένας, ἕλανδρος, ἑλέ-
        πτολις, ἐκ τῶν ἁβροπήνων   690
    προκαλυμμάτων ἔπλευσεν
    ζεφύρου γίγαντος αὔρᾳ,
    πολύανδροί τε φεράσπιδες κυναγοὶ
        κατ᾽ ἴχνος πλατᾶν ἄφαντον   695
    κέλσαν, τὰς Σιμόεντος ἀ-
        κτὰς ἐπ᾽ ἀεξιφύλλους
    δι᾽ Ἔριν αἱματόεσσαν.

    Ἰλίῳ δὲ κῆδος ὀρ-   Ant.
        θώνυμον τελεσσίφρων   700

FTr   672 Linwood : τί μή FTr   673 Casaubon : ταῦτ᾽ FTr
677 χλωρόν τε καὶ βλέποντα· ἀντὶ τοῦ ζῶντα Hesych., unde χλωρόν τε
hic Toup   680 κλύειν Tr, -ων (sscr. -ειν) F   681 ὠνόμαξεν F
683 Pauw : προνοίαις FTr   690 Salmasius : ἁβροτίμων FTr   695
Heath : πλάταν FTr   696 Auratus (ἔκελσαν τὰς) : κελσάντων FTr
696-7 ἀκτᾶς F   697 ἐπ᾽ ἀξι- F, εἰς ἀεξι- Tr

Μῆνις ἤλασεν, τραπέζας ἀτί-
μωσιν ὑστέρῳ χρόνῳ
καὶ ξυνεστίου Διὸς
πρασσομένα τὸ νυμφότι-   705
μον μέλος ἐκφάτως τίοντας,
ὑμέναιον ὃς τότ' ἐπέρ-
ρεπε γαμβροῖσιν ἀείδειν·
μεταμανθάνουσα δ' ὕμνον
Πριάμου πόλις γεραιὰ   710
πολύθρηνον μέγα που στένει, κικλήσκου-
σα Πάριν τὸν αἰνόλεκτρον,
†παμπρόσθη πολύθρηνον
αἰῶν' ἀμφὶ πολίταν†   715
μέλεον αἷμ' ἀνατλᾶσα.

ἔθρεψεν δὲ λέοντος ἴ-   Str.
νιν δόμοις ἀγάλακτον οὕ-
τως ἀνὴρ φιλόμαστον,
ἐν βιότου προτελείοις   720
ἄμερον, εὐφιλόπαιδα
καὶ γεραροῖς ἐπίχαρτον·
πολέα δ' ἔσχ' ἐν ἀγκάλαις,
νεοτρόφου τέκνου δίκαν,
φαιδρωπὸς ποτὶ χεῖρα σαί-   725
νων τε γαστρὸς ἀνάγκαις.

χρονισθεὶς δ' ἀπέδειξεν ἦ-   Ant.
θος τὸ πρὸς τοκέων· χάριν
γὰρ τροφεῦσιν ἀμείβων

FTr   701 ἤλασε FTr, ν add. Porson   701-2 Canter : ἀτίμως
ἵν' F, ἀτίμως Tr   707-8 ἐπέρρεπεν F, ν del. Porson ; ἐπέπρεπεν
Tr   717-18 Conington : λέοντα σίνιν FTr   718-19 οὗτος
(sscr. ως) F   727-8 Conington : ἔθος FTr   728 τοκήων F
729 τροφᾶς F

μηλοφόνοισι ⟨σὺ⟩ν ἄταις   730
δαῖτ' ἀκέλευστος ἔτευξεν·
αἵματι δ' οἶκος ἐφύρθη,
ἄμαχον ἄλγος οἰκέταις,
μέγα σίνος πολύκτονον·
ἐκ θεοῦ δ' ἱερεύς τις Ἄ-   735
τας δόμοις προσεθρέφθη.

πάραυτα δ' ἐλθεῖν ἐς Ἰλίου πόλιν   Str.
λέγοιμ' ἂν φρόνημα μὲν
    νηνέμου γαλάνας,   740
ἀκασκαῖον ⟨δ'⟩ ἄγαλμα πλούτου,
μαλθακὸν ὀμμάτων βέλος,
δηξίθυμον ἔρωτος ἄνθος.
παρακλίνασ' ἐπέκρανεν
    δὲ γάμου πικρὰς τελευτάς,   745
δύσεδρος καὶ δυσόμιλος
συμένα Πριαμίδαισιν,
πομπᾷ Διὸς ξενίου,
νυμφόκλαυτος Ἐρινύς.   749

παλαίφατος δ' ἐν βροτοῖς γέρων λόγος   Ant.
τέτυκται, μέγαν τελε-
    σθέντα φωτὸς ὄλβον
τεκνοῦσθαι μηδ' ἄπαιδα θνῄσκειν.
ἐκ δ' ἀγαθᾶς τύχας γένει   755
βλαστάνειν ἀκόρεστον οἰζύν·
δίχα δ' ἄλλων μονόφρων εἰ-
    μί· τὸ δυσσεβὲς γὰρ ἔργον
μετὰ μὲν πλείονα τίκτει,

σφετέρᾳ δ' εἰκότα γέννα·   760
οἴκων γὰρ εὐθυδίκων
καλλίπαις πότμος αἰεί.

φιλεῖ δὲ τίκτειν ὕβρις   Str.
  μὲν παλαιὰ νεά-
  ζουσαν ἐν κακοῖς βροτῶν   765
ὕβριν τότ' ἢ τόθ', ὅτε τὸ κύ-
  ριον μόλῃ φάος τόκου,
δαίμονά τε τὰν ἄμαχον ἀπόλε-
  μον, ἀνίερον θράσος μελαί-
νας μελάθροισιν ἄτας,   770
εἰδομένας τοκεῦσιν.

Δίκα δὲ λάμπει μὲν ἐν   Ant.
  δυσκάπνοις δώμασιν,
  τὸν δ' ἐναίσιμον τίει [βίον]·   775
τὰ χρυσόπαστα δ' ἔδεθλα σὺν
  πίνῳ χερῶν παλιντρόποις
ὄμμασι λιποῦσ' ὅσια †προσέβα
  τοῦ†, δύναμιν οὐ σέβουσα πλού-
του παράσημον αἴνῳ·   780
πᾶν δ' ἐπὶ τέρμα νωμᾷ.

ἄγε δή, βασιλεῦ, Τροίας πτολίπορθ',
Ἀτρέως γένεθλον,
πῶς σε προσείπω; πῶς σε σεβίξω,   785
μήθ' ὑπεράρας μήθ' ὑποκάμψας
καιρὸν χάριτος;

FTr   766 ὅτε Klausen: ὅταν FTr   767 Ahrens: μόλῃ νεαρὰ
φάους κότον FTr   768 Hermann: τε τὸν FTr   ἄμαχον om. Tr
770 μελάθροις F   771 Casaubon: -μέναν FTr   775 βίον del.
Ahrens   776 Auratus: -παστα δ' ἐσθλὰ F, -παστ' ἐσθλὰ Tr   777
παλίντροπ' Tr   783 Blomfield: πολί- FTr   785 -ίζω in -ίξω
mut. F, -ίζω Tr

πολλοὶ δὲ βροτῶν τὸ δοκεῖν εἶναι
προτίουσι δίκην παραβάντες·
τῷ δυσπραγοῦντι δ' ἐπιστενάχειν   790
πᾶς τις ἕτοιμος· δῆγμα δὲ λύπης
οὐδὲν ἐφ' ἧπαρ προσικνεῖται·
καὶ ξυγχαίρουσιν ὁμοιοπρεπεῖς
ἀγέλαστα πρόσωπα βιαζόμενοι

.   .   .   .   .   .

ὅστις δ' ἀγαθὸς προβατογνώμων,   795
οὐκ ἔστι λαθεῖν ὄμματα φωτὸς
τὰ δοκοῦντ' εὔφρονος ἐκ διανοίας
ὑδαρεῖ σαίνειν φιλότητι.
σὺ δέ μοι τότε μὲν στέλλων στρατιὰν
'Ελένης ἕνεκ', οὐκ ἐπικεύσω,   800
κάρτ' ἀπομούσως ἦσθα γεγραμμένος
οὐδ' εὖ πραπίδων οἴακα νέμων,
θράσος ἐκ θυσιῶν
ἀνδράσι θνήσκουσι κομίζων·
νῦν δ' οὐκ ἀπ' ἄκρας φρενὸς οὐδ' ἀφίλως   805
εὔφρων πόνον εὖ τελέσασιν ⟨ἐγώ⟩·
γνώσῃ δὲ χρόνῳ διαπευθόμενος
τόν τε δικαίως καὶ τὸν ἀκαίρως
πόλιν οἰκουροῦντα πολιτῶν.

ΑΓΑΜΕΜΝΩΝ

πρῶτον μὲν Ἄργος καὶ θεοὺς ἐγχωρίους   810
δίκῃ προσειπεῖν, τοὺς ἐμοὶ μεταιτίους
νόστου δικαίων θ' ὧν ἐπραξάμην πόλιν
Πριάμου· δίκας γὰρ οὐκ ἀπὸ γλώσσης θεοί

FTr   789 -βαίνοντες Tr   790–4 cit. Stob. *Flor.* 112. 12   791
δεῖγμα F   792 προσεφικν- Tr   793 καὶ νυκτὶ δὲ Stob.   794–
5 lacunam indic. Hermann   800 οὐκ Hermann : οὐ γὰρ F Tr
803 Ahrens : θράσος ἑκούσιον F, θάρσος ἐκ. Tr   804 ἀνδράσιν εὖ
θν. Tr   806 εὔφρων τις Tr   Auratus : πόνος FTr   ἐγώ suppl.
Wilamowitz

κλυόντες ἀνδροθνῆτας Ἰλιοφθόρους
ἐς αἱματηρὸν τεῦχος οὐ διχορρόπως   815
ψήφους ἔθεντο· τῷ δ' ἐναντίῳ κύτει
ἐλπὶς προσῄει χειρὸς οὐ πληρουμένῳ.
καπνῷ δ' ἁλοῦσα νῦν ἔτ' εὔσημος πόλις·
ἄτης θύελλαι ζῶσι, δυσθνῄσκουσα δέ
σποδὸς προπέμπει πίονας πλούτου πνοάς.   820
τούτων θεοῖσι χρὴ πολύμνηστον χάριν
τίνειν, ἐπείπερ χάρπαγας ὑπερκόπους
ἐπραξάμεσθα, καὶ γυναικὸς οὕνεκα
πόλιν διημάθυνεν Ἀργεῖον δάκος,
ἵππου νεοσσός, ἀσπιδηφόρος λεώς,   825
<u>πήδημ' ὀρούσας ἀμφὶ Πλειάδων δύσιν·</u>
ὑπερθορὼν δὲ πύργον ὠμηστὴς λέων
ᾅδην ἔλειξεν αἵματος τυραννικοῦ.
θεοῖς μὲν ἐξέτεινα φροίμιον τόδε·
τὰ δ' ἐς τὸ σὸν φρόνημα, μέμνημαι κλυών   830
καὶ φημὶ ταὐτὰ καὶ συνήγορόν μ' ἔχεις·
παύροις γὰρ ἀνδρῶν ἐστι συγγενὲς τόδε,
φίλον τὸν εὐτυχοῦντ' ἄνευ φθόνων σέβειν·
δύσφρων γὰρ ἰὸς καρδίαν προσήμενος
ἄχθος διπλοίζει τῷ πεπαμένῳ νόσον·   835
τοῖς τ' αὐτὸς αὐτοῦ πήμασιν βαρύνεται
καὶ τὸν θυραῖον ὄλβον εἰσορῶν στένει·
<u>εἰδὼς λέγοιμ' ἄν, εὖ γὰρ ἐξεπίσταμαι</u>
ὁμιλίας κάτοπτρον, εἴδωλον σκιᾶς,
δοκοῦντας εἶναι κάρτα πρευμενεῖς ἐμοί·   840
μόνος δ' Ὀδυσσεύς, ὅσπερ οὐχ ἑκὼν ἔπλει,
ζευχθεὶς ἑτοῖμος ἦν ἐμοὶ σειραφόρος·

FTr   814 κλύ- FTr   Karsten: ἰλίου φθορᾶς FTr   819 Enger:
συνθνήσκουσα FTr   822 Tyrwhitt: καὶ παγᾶς FTr   Heath:
-κότους FTr   825 Blomfield: -ηστρόφος F, -οστρόφος Tr   828
ᾅδδην Tr   830 κλύ- FTr   831 Auratus: ταῦτα FTr
833 φθόνου Tr, ψόγου Stob. *Flor.* 38. 28   835 Porson: πεπαμμ-
FTr

εἴτ' οὖν θανόντος εἴτε καὶ ζῶντος πέρι
λέγω. τὰ δ' ἄλλα πρὸς πόλιν τε καὶ θεούς
κοινοὺς ἀγῶνας θέντες ἐν πανηγύρει   845
βουλευσόμεσθα· καὶ τὸ μὲν καλῶς ἔχον
ὅπως χρονίζον εὖ μενεῖ βουλευτέον·
ὅτῳ δὲ καὶ δεῖ φαρμάκων παιωνίων,
ἤτοι κέαντες ἢ τεμόντες εὐφρόνως
πειρασόμεσθα πῆμ' ἀποστρέψαι νόσου.   850
νῦν δ' ἐς μέλαθρα καὶ δόμους ἐφεστίους
ἐλθὼν θεοῖσι πρῶτα δεξιώσομαι,
οἵπερ πρόσω πέμψαντες ἤγαγον πάλιν·
νίκη δ', ἐπείπερ ἕσπετ', ἐμπέδως μένοι.

Κλ. ἄνδρες πολῖται, πρέσβος Ἀργείων τόδε,   855
οὐκ αἰσχυνοῦμαι τοὺς φιλάνορας τρόπους
λέξαι πρὸς ὑμᾶς· ἐν χρόνῳ δ' ἀποφθίνει
τὸ τάρβος ἀνθρώποισιν· οὐκ ἄλλων πάρα
μαθοῦσ', ἐμαυτῆς δύσφορον λέξω βίον
τοσόνδ' ὅσονπερ οὗτος ἦν ὑπ' Ἰλίῳ.   860
τὸ μὲν γυναῖκα πρῶτον ἄρσενος δίχα
ἧσθαι δόμοις ἔρημον ἔκπαγλον κακόν,
πολλὰς κλύουσαν κληδόνας παλιγκότους,
καὶ τὸν μὲν ἥκειν, τὸν δ' ἐπεισφέρειν κακοῦ
κάκιον ἄλλο πῆμα, λάσκοντας δόμοις·   865
καὶ τραυμάτων μὲν εἰ τόσων ἐτύγχανεν
ἀνὴρ ὅδ' ὡς πρὸς οἶκον ὠχετεύετο
φάτις, τέτρηται δικτύου πλέω λέγειν·
εἰ δ' ἦν τεθνηκὼς ὡς ἐπλήθυον λόγοι,
τρισώματός τἂν Γηρυὼν ὁ δεύτερος   870
πολλὴν ἄνωθεν, τὴν κάτω γὰρ οὐ λέγω,
χθονὸς τρίμοιρον χλαῖναν ἐξηύχει λαβών,

FTr   850 Porson: πήματος τρέψαι νόσον FTr   860 ἐπ' ἰλίωι Tr
863 Auratus: ἠδονὰς FTr   867 ἀνὴρ et ὠχ- FTr   868 Ahrens:
τέτρωται FTr   869 Porson: ἐπλήθυνον FTr   870 Wellauer:
τ' ἂν FTr

ἅπαξ ἑκάστῳ κατθανὼν μορφώματι.
τοιῶνδ' ἔκατι κληδόνων παλιγκότων
πολλὰς ἄνωθεν ἀρτάνας ἐμῆς δέρης   875
ἔλυσαν ἄλλοι πρὸς βίαν λελημμένης.
ἐκ τῶνδέ τοι παῖς ἐνθάδ' οὐ παραστατεῖ,
ἐμῶν τε καὶ σῶν κύριος πιστωμάτων,
ὡς χρῆν, Ὀρέστης· μηδὲ θαυμάσῃς τόδε·
τρέφει γὰρ αὐτὸν εὐμενὴς δορύξενος,   880
Στροφίος ὁ Φωκεύς, ἀμφίλεκτα πήματα
ἐμοὶ προφωνῶν, τόν θ' ὑπ' Ἰλίῳ σέθεν
κίνδυνον, εἴ τε δημόθρους ἀναρχία
βουλὴν καταρρίψειεν, ὥς τι σύγγονον
βροτοῖσι τὸν πεσόντα λακτίσαι πλέον·   885
τοιάδε μέντοι σκῆψις οὐ δόλον φέρει.
ἔμοιγε μὲν δὴ κλαυμάτων ἐπίσσυτοι
πηγαὶ κατεσβήκασιν, οὐδ' ἔνι σταγών·
ἐν ὀψικοίτοις δ' ὄμμασιν βλάβας ἔχω
τὰς ἀμφί σοι κλαίουσα λαμπτηρουχίας   890
ἀτημελήτους αἰέν· ἐν δ' ὀνείρασιν
λεπταῖς ὑπαὶ κώνωπος ἐξηγειρόμην
ῥιπαῖσι θωύσσοντος, ἀμφί σοι πάθη
ὁρῶσα πλείω τοῦ ξυνεύδοντος χρόνου.
νῦν, ταῦτα πάντα τλᾶσ', ἀπενθήτῳ φρενί   895
λέγοιμ' ἂν ἄνδρα τόνδε τῶν σταθμῶν κύνα,
σωτῆρα ναὸς πρότονον, ὑψηλῆς στέγης
στῦλον ποδήρη, μονογενὲς τέκνον πατρί,
καὶ γῆν φανεῖσαν ναυτίλοις παρ' ἐλπίδα,
κάλλιστον ἦμαρ εἰσιδεῖν ἐκ χείματος,   900
ὁδοιπόρῳ διψῶντι πηγαῖον ῥέος·

FTr   878 Spanheim: πιστευμάτων FTr   881 στρόφ- FTr   882
τ' ὑπ' Tr   884 Hartung: ὥστε FTr   888 κατεσβ. in καθεστή-
κασιν mut. F   889 κλάβας F   890 ἀμφὶ σοὶ FTr, idem 893
898 στῦλον Tr, στόλον F   898 sqq. vera falsis secernere nequi-
mus: fort. aut 901 post 898 transponendus (Bothe), aut γαῖαν (Blomfield) pro καὶ γῆν 899 legendum et 900, 902 expellendi

τερπνὸν δὲ τἀναγκαῖον ἐκφυγεῖν ἅπαν·
τοιοῖσδέ τοί νιν ἀξιῶ προσφθέγμασιν·
φθόνος δ' ἀπέστω· πολλὰ γὰρ τὰ πρὶν κακά
ἠνειχόμεσθα. νῦν δέ μοι, φίλον κάρα,   905
ἔκβαιν' ἀπήνης τῆσδε, μὴ χαμαὶ τιθείς
τὸν σὸν πόδ', ὦναξ, Ἰλίου πορθήτορα.
δμωαί, τί μέλλεθ', αἷς ἐπέσταλται τέλος
πέδον κελεύθου στορνύναι πετάσμασιν;
εὐθὺς γενέσθω πορφυρόστρωτος πόρος,   910
ἐς δῶμ' ἄελπτον ὡς ἂν ἡγῆται Δίκη.
τὰ δ' ἄλλα φροντὶς οὐχ ὕπνῳ νικωμένη
θήσει δικαίως σὺν θεοῖς θειμαρμένα.

Αγ. Λήδας γένεθλον, δωμάτων ἐμῶν φύλαξ,
ἀπουσίᾳ μὲν εἶπας εἰκότως ἐμῇ,   915
μακρὰν γὰρ ἐξέτεινας· ἀλλ' ἐναισίμως
αἰνεῖν, παρ' ἄλλων χρὴ τόδ' ἔρχεσθαι γέρας.
καὶ τἄλλα μὴ γυναικὸς ἐν τρόποις ἐμέ
ἅβρυνε, μηδὲ βαρβάρου φωτὸς δίκην
χαμαιπετὲς βόαμα προσχάνῃς ἐμοί,   920
μηδ' εἵμασι στρώσασ' ἐπίφθονον πόρον
τίθει· θεούς τοι τοῖσδε τιμαλφεῖν χρεών·
ἐν ποικίλοις δὲ θνητὸν ὄντα κάλλεσιν
βαίνειν ἐμοὶ μὲν οὐδαμῶς ἄνευ φόβου·
λέγω κατ' ἄνδρα, μὴ θεόν, σέβειν ἐμέ·   925
χωρὶς ποδοψήστρων τε καὶ τῶν ποικίλων
κληδὼν ἀυτεῖ· καὶ τὸ μὴ κακῶς φρονεῖν
θεοῦ μέγιστον δῶρον· ὀλβίσαι δὲ χρή
βίον τελευτήσαντ' ἐν εὐεστοῖ φίλῃ.
εἰ πάντα δ' ὡς πράσσοιμ' ἄν, εὐθαρσὴς ἐγώ.   930

Κλ. καὶ μὴν τόδ' εἰπὲ μὴ παρὰ γνώμην ἐμοί.

FTr   903 Schütz: τοίνυν FTr   905 Bothe: δ' ἐμοὶ FTr   907
ἄναξ F   908 τέλος F: τάδε Tr   909 Elmsley: στρωννύναι FTr
913 scripsimus: εἱμαρμένα codd.   920 βόημα Tr, et (η sup. α(μ)
scr.) F

Αγ. γνώμην μὲν ἴσθι μὴ διαφθεροῦντ' ἐμέ.

Κλ. ηὔξω θεοῖς δείσας ἂν ὧδ' ἔρδειν τάδε;

Αγ. εἴπερ τις εἰδώς γ' εὖ τόδ' ἐξεῖπεν τέλος.

Κλ. τί δ' ἂν δοκεῖ σοι Πρίαμος, εἰ τάδ' ἤνυσεν; 935

Αγ. ἐν ποικίλοις ἂν κάρτα μοι βῆναι δοκεῖ.

Κλ. μή νυν τὸν ἀνθρώπειον αἰδεσθῇς ψόγον.

Αγ. φήμη γε μέντοι δημόθρους μέγα σθένει.

Κλ. ὁ δ' ἀφθόνητός γ' οὐκ ἐπίζηλος πέλει.

Αγ. οὔτοι γυναικός ἐστιν ἱμείρειν μάχης. 940

Κλ. τοῖς δ' ὀλβίοις γε καὶ τὸ νικᾶσθαι πρέπει.

Αγ. ἦ καὶ σὺ νίκην τήνδε δήριος τίεις;

Κλ. πιθοῦ, †κράτος μέντοι πάρες γ'† ἑκὼν ἐμοί.

Αγ. ἀλλ', εἰ δοκεῖ σοι ταῦθ', ὑπαί τις ἀρβύλας
λύοι τάχος, πρόδουλον ἔμβασιν ποδός· 945
καὶ τοῖσδέ μ' ἐμβαίνονθ' ἁλουργέσιν θεῶν
μή τις πρόσωθεν ὄμματος βάλοι φθόνος·
πολλὴ γὰρ αἰδὼς δωματοφθορεῖν ποσίν
φθείροντα πλοῦτον ἀργυρωνήτους θ' ὑφάς.
τούτων μὲν οὕτω· τὴν ξένην δὲ πρευμενῶς 950
τήνδ' ἐσκόμιζε· τὸν κρατοῦντα μαλθακῶς
θεὸς πρόσωθεν εὐμενῶς προσδέρκεται·
ἑκὼν γὰρ οὐδεὶς δουλίῳ χρῆται ζυγῷ,
αὕτη δὲ πολλῶν χρημάτων ἐξαίρετον
ἄνθος, στρατοῦ δώρημ', ἐμοὶ ξυνέσπετο. 955
ἐπεὶ δ' ἀκούειν σοῦ κατέστραμμαι τάδε,
εἶμ' ἐς δόμων μέλαθρα πορφύρας πατῶν.

FTr 933 ἔρδ- F 934 Auratus: -εἶπον FTr 935 Stanley: δοκῇ FTr 936 δοκεῖ in δοκῇ mut. F, δοκεῖ sscr. η Tr 937 νῦν F αἰδεσθεὶς F 946 καὶ F: σὺν Tr -νοντ' ἀλ- FTr 948 Schütz: σωματοφθ. FTr ποσὶν Scaliger: πόσιν FTr 954 Auratus: αὐτὴ FTr 956 κατέσταμαι Tr (schol. εὕρηται καὶ κατέστραμμαι)

Κλ. ἔστιν θάλασσα· τίς δέ νιν κατασβέσει;
τρέφουσα πολλῆς πορφύρας ἰσάργυρον
κηκῖδα παγκαίνιστον, εἱμάτων βαφάς·   960
οἶκος δ' ὑπάρχει τῶνδε σὺν θεοῖς, ἄναξ,
ἔχειν· πένεσθαι δ' οὐκ ἐπίσταται δόμος.
πολλῶν πατησμὸν δ' εἱμάτων ἂν ηὐξάμην,
δόμοισι προυνεχθέντος ἐν χρηστηρίοις
ψυχῆς κόμιστρα τῆσδε μηχανωμένῃ·   965
ῥίζης γὰρ οὔσης φυλλὰς ἵκετ' ἐς δόμους,
σκιὰν ὑπερτείνασα σειρίου κυνός·
καὶ σοῦ μολόντος δωματῖτιν ἑστίαν,
θάλπος μὲν ἐν χειμῶνι σημαίνει μολόν,
ὅταν δὲ τεύχῃ Ζεὺς ἀπ' ὄμφακος πικρᾶς   970
οἶνον, τότ' ἤδη ψῦχος ἐν δόμοις πέλει,
ἀνδρὸς τελείου δῶμ' ἐπιστρωφωμένου.
Ζεῦ Ζεῦ τέλειε, τὰς ἐμὰς εὐχὰς τέλει·
μέλοι δέ τοί σοι τῶνπερ ἂν μέλλῃς τελεῖν.

Χο. τίπτε μοι τόδ' ἐμπέδως   Str.
δεῖμα προστατήριον   976
καρδίας τερασκόπου ποτᾶται;
μαντιπολεῖ δ' ἀκέλευστος ἄμισθος ἀοιδά,
οὐδ' ἀποπτύσαι δίκαν   980
δυσκρίτων ὀνειράτων
θάρσος εὐπειθὲς ἵ-
ζει φρενὸς φίλον θρόνον.
χρόνος δ', †ἐπεὶ πρυμνησίων ξυνεμβόλοις

FTr   959 Salmasius : εἰς ἄργυρον FTr   963 δειμ- FTr, distinxit
Canter   εὐξ- FTr .   965 κομίστρα F   Abresch : -μένης FTr
967 -τίνασα F   969 σημαίνει Karsten, μολόν H. Voss : σημαίνεις
μολών FTr   970 τ' ἀπ' FTr, τ' del. Auratus   972 Victorius :
-στρεφ- F, -στροφ- Tr   974 τοι σοι Tr : σοι F (et μέλη in -οι corr.)
976 δεῖγμα F   978–9 ποτᾶτ' ἄμισθος ἀοιδά. μαντιπολεῖ δ' ἀκέλευστος Tr   980 -πτύσας F   982 Jacob : εὐπιθὲς FTr   982–3
Scaliger : ἵξει F, ἵζει Tr   984 ἐπὶ Tr

ψαμμίας ἀκάτα† παρή-   985
βησεν, εὖθ' ὑπ' Ἴλιον
ὦρτο ναυβάτας στρατός·

πεύθομαι δ' ἀπ' ὀμμάτων   Ant.
νόστον, αὐτόμαρτυς ὤν·
τὸν δ' ἄνευ λύρας ὅμως ὑμνῳδεῖ   990
θρῆνον Ἐρινύος αὐτοδίδακτος ἔσωθεν
θυμός, οὐ τὸ πᾶν ἔχων
ἐλπίδος φίλον θράσος.

σπλάγχνα δ' οὔτοι ματᾴ-   995
ζει πρὸς ἐνδίκοις φρεσὶν
τελεσφόροις δίναις κυκλούμενον κέαρ·
εὔχομαι δ' ἐξ ἐμᾶς
ἐλπίδος ψύθη πεσεῖν
ἐς τὸ μὴ τελεσφόρον.   1000

†μάλα γάρ τοι τᾶς πολλᾶς ὑγιείας†   Str.
ἀκόρεστον τέρμα· νόσος γὰρ
γείτων ὁμότοιχος ἐρείδει.
καὶ πότμος εὐθυπορῶν   1005

.   .   .   .   .   .

ἀνδρὸς ἔπαισεν ἄφαντον ἕρμα·
καὶ τὸ μὲν πρὸ χρημάτων
κτησίων ὄκνος βαλὼν
σφενδόνας ἀπ' εὐμέτρου,   1010
οὐκ ἔδυ πρόπας δόμος
πλησμονᾶς γέμων ἄγαν,

FTr   985 ἀκάτας Tr   985–6 παρήβησ' Tr   990 Auratus :
ὅπως FTr   991 Porson : ἐρινὺς FTr   995–6 ματάζει FTr
998 ἀπ' ἐμᾶς τοι Tr   999 H. Stephanus : ψύδη FTr   1001
μάλα γέ (sscr. γὰρ) τοι δὴ Tr   lacunam post 1005 indic. Heath
(post 1004 Klausen)   1007 ἕρμα FTr   1012 Schütz : πημονὰς
FTr

οὐδ' ἐπόντισε σκάφος·
πολλά τοι δόσις ἐκ Διὸς ἀμφιλα-　1015
φής τε καὶ ἐξ ἀλόκων ἐπετειᾶν
νῆστιν ὤλεσεν νόσον·

τὸ δ' ἐπὶ γᾶν πεσὸν ἅπαξ θανάσιμον　　Ant.
πρόπαρ ἀνδρὸς μέλαν αἷμα τίς ἂν　1020
πάλιν ἀγκαλέσαιτ' ἐπαείδων;
οὐδὲ τὸν ὀρθοδαῆ
τῶν φθιμένων ἀνάγειν
Ζεὺς ἀπέπαυσεν ἐπ' ἀβλαβείᾳ.
εἰ δὲ μὴ τεταγμένα　1025
μοῖρα μοῖραν ἐκ θεῶν
εἶργε μὴ πλέον φέρειν,
προφθάσασα καρδία
γλῶσσαν ἂν τάδ' ἐξέχει·
νῦν δ' ὑπὸ σκότῳ βρέμει　1030
θυμαλγής τε καὶ οὐδὲν ἐπελπομέ-
να ποτὲ καίριον ἐκτολυπεύσειν
ζωπυρουμένας φρενός.

Κλ. εἴσω κομίζου καὶ σύ, Κασσάνδραν λέγω·　1035
ἐπεί σ' ἔθηκε Ζεὺς ἀμηνίτως δόμοις
κοινωνὸν εἶναι χερνίβων, πολλῶν μέτα
δούλων σταθεῖσαν κτησίου βωμοῦ πέλας,
ἔκβαιν' ἀπήνης τῆσδε μηδ' ὑπερφρόνει·
καὶ παῖδα γάρ τοί φασιν Ἀλκμήνης ποτέ　1040
πραθέντα τλῆναι †δουλίας μάζης βία.†
εἰ δ' οὖν ἀνάγκη τῆσδ' ἐπιρρέποι τύχης,

FTr　　1015 ἐκ om. Tr　　1016 κἀξ F　　1018 Auratus :
πεσόνθ' FTr　　1019 προπάροιθ' Tr　　1020–1 τίς τ' ἀγκαλ- Tr
1024 Hartung : αὔτ' ἔπαυσ' FTr　　ἀβλαβείᾳ γε Tr, αὐλαβεία F　　1030
βλέπ- in βρέμ- mut. F　　1031 θυμαλγής τε καὶ οὐδὲν ἐπ om. Tr
1035 Κασσ- Hermann : κασ- FTr　　1041 δουλείας μάζης βία F, καὶ
ζυγῶν θίγειν βία Tr　　1042 -ρέπει Tr

ἀρχαιοπλούτων δεσποτῶν πολλὴ χάρις·
οἳ δ᾽ οὔποτ᾽ ἐλπίσαντες ἤμησαν καλῶς,
ὠμοί τε δούλοις πάντα, καὶ παρὰ στάθμην   1045

. . . .

ἔχεις παρ᾽ ἡμῶν οἷάπερ νομίζεται.

Χο. σοί τοι λέγουσα παύεται σαφῆ λόγον·
ἐντὸς δ᾽ ἁλοῦσα μορσίμων ἀγρευμάτων
πείθοι᾽ ἄν, εἰ πείθοι᾽· ἀπειθοίης δ᾽ ἴσως.

Κλ. ἀλλ᾽ εἴπερ ἐστὶ μὴ χελιδόνος δίκην   1050
ἀγνῶτα φωνὴν βάρβαρον κεκτημένη,
ἔσω φρενῶν λέγουσα πείθω νιν λόγῳ.

Χο. ἕπου· τὰ λῷστα τῶν παρεστώτων λέγει·
πειθοῦ λιποῦσα τόνδ᾽ ἁμαξήρη θρόνον.

Κλ. οὔτοι θυραίᾳ τῇδ᾽ ἐμοὶ σχολὴ πάρα   1055
τρίβειν· τὰ μὲν γὰρ ἑστίας μεσομφάλου
ἕστηκεν ἤδη μῆλα †πρὸς σφαγὰς πυρός,†
ὡς οὔποτ᾽ ἐλπίσασι τήνδ᾽ ἕξειν χάριν.
σὺ δ᾽ εἴ τι δράσεις τῶνδε, μὴ σχολὴν τίθει·
εἰ δ᾽ ἀξυνήμων οὖσα μὴ δέχῃ λόγον,   1060
σὺ δ᾽ ἀντὶ φωνῆς φράζε καρβάνῳ χερί.

Χο. ἑρμηνέως ἔοικεν ἡ ξένη τοροῦ
δεῖσθαι· τρόπος δὲ θηρὸς ὡς νεαιρέτου.

Κλ. ἦ μαίνεταί γε καὶ κακῶν κλύει φρενῶν,
ἥτις λιποῦσα μὲν πόλιν νεαίρετον   1065
ἥκει, χαλινὸν δ᾽ οὐκ ἐπίσταται φέρειν,
πρὶν αἱματηρὸν ἐξαφρίζεσθαι μένος·
οὐ μὴν πλέω ῥίψασ᾽ ἀτιμασθήσομαι.

(M)FTr   1044 οἶδ᾽ FTr   1045 παραστάθμων F   1045–6
lacunam indic. Hartung   1048 C. G. Haupt: ἂν οὖσα FTr
1055 Casaubon: θυραίαν FTr   Musgrave: τήνδ᾽ FTr   1064 ἦ
F   φρενῶν κλύει F, ordinem corr. ipse   1067 iterum incipit
cod. M   1068 μὴ M, corr. m

Χο. ἐγὼ δ', ἐποικτίρω γάρ, οὐ θυμώσομαι·
ἴθ', ὦ τάλαινα, τόνδ' ἐρημώσασ' ὄχον·　　　1070
εἴκουσ' ἀνάγκῃ τῇδε καίνισον ζυγόν.

ΚΑΣΣΑΝΔΡΑ

ὀτοτοτοῖ πόποι δᾶ·　　　　　　　Str. 1
ὦπολλον, ὦπολλον.

Χο. τί ταῦτ' ἀνωτότυξας ἀμφὶ Λοξίου;
οὐ γὰρ τοιοῦτος ὥστε θρηνητοῦ τυχεῖν.　　　1075

Κα. ὀτοτοτοῖ πόποι δᾶ·　　　　　　　Ant. 1
ὦπολλον, ὦπολλον.

Χο. ἥδ' αὖτε δυσφημοῦσα τὸν θεὸν καλεῖ
οὐδὲν προσήκοντ' ἐν γόοις παραστατεῖν.

Κα. ὦπολλον, ὦπολλον,　　　　　　　Str. 2
ἀγυιᾶτ', ἀπόλλων ἐμός·　　　　　　　1081
ἀπώλεσας γὰρ οὐ μόλις τὸ δεύτερον.

Χο. χρήσειν ἔοικεν ἀμφὶ τῶν αὑτῆς κακῶν·
μένει τὸ θεῖον δουλίᾳ περ ἐν φρενί.

Κα. ὦπολλον, ὦπολλον,　　　　　　　Ant. 2
ἀγυιᾶτ', ἀπόλλων ἐμός·　　　　　　　1086
ἆ ποῖ ποτ' ἤγαγές με; πρὸς ποίαν στέγην;

Χο. πρὸς τὴν Ἀτρειδῶν· εἰ σὺ μὴ τόδ' ἐννοεῖς,
ἐγὼ λέγω σοι· καὶ τάδ' οὐκ ἐρεῖς ψύθη.

MFTr　1069 -οικτείρ- codd.　1071 Robortello : ἑκοῦσ' codd.
1072 et 1076 ὀτοτοτοτοῖ M　1073 et 1077 ἄπολλον ἄπολλον FTr
1074-5 cit. schol. E. *Ph.* 1028, ubi ἀνωλόλυξας　1078 ἡ δ' M
1080 et 1085 ἄπολλον ἄπολλον codd.　1083 αὑτῆς codd.　1084
Schütz : παρ' ἐν M, παρὲν F, παρὸν Tr　1088 εἰ σὺ· τὸ, μὴ δ'
ἐννοεῖς F, εἰ. τό περ μὴ δ' ἐννοεῖς Tr　1089 κᾆτα δ' FTr　ψύθη
Tr

Κα. ἆ ἆ·   Str. 3

  μισόθεον μὲν οὖν, πολλὰ συνίστορα   1090

\| αὐτοφόνα κακὰ †καρτάναι†

  ἀνδροσφαγεῖον καὶ πέδον ῥαντήριον.

Χο. ἔοικεν εὔρις ἡ ξένη κυνὸς δίκην

  εἶναι, ματεύει δ' ὧν ἀνευρήσει φόνον.

Κα. μαρτυρίοισι γὰρ τοῖσδ' ἐπιπείθομαι   Ant. 3

  κλαιόμενα τάδε βρέφη σφαγὰς   1096

  ὀπτάς τε σάρκας πρὸς πατρὸς βεβρωμένας.

Χο. ἦ μὴν κλέος σου μαντικὸν πεπυσμένοι

  ἦμεν· προφήτας δ' οὔτινας ματεύομεν.

Κα. ἰὼ πόποι, τί ποτε μήδεται;   Str. 4

  τί τόδε νέον ἄχος; μέγα   1101

  μέγ' ἐν δόμοισι τοῖσδε μήδεται κακὸν

  ἄφερτον φίλοισιν, δυσίατον, ἀλκὰ δ'

    ἑκὰς ἀποστατεῖ.

Χο. τούτων ἄιδρίς εἰμι τῶν μαντευμάτων,   1105

  ἐκεῖνα δ' ἔγνων· πᾶσα γὰρ πόλις βοᾷ.

Κα. ἰὼ τάλαινα, τόδε γὰρ τελεῖς;   Ant. 4

  τὸν ὁμοδέμνιον πόσιν

  λουτροῖσι φαιδρύνασα, πῶς φράσω τέλος;

  τάχος γὰρ τόδ' ἔσται· προτείνει δὲ χεῖρ' ἐκ   1110

  χερὸς ὀρεγομένα.

MFTr   1090 ἆ ἆ om. FTr   ξυνίστ- M   1091 αὐτόφονα M,
corr. m   καρτάναι M, κἀρτάναι F, κἀρτάνας Tr   1092 Casaubon,
Dobree : ἀνδρὸς σφάγιον codd.   πεδόρραντ- M, corr. m   1093 εὔρις
M, εὔ- FTr   1094 μαντεύει M   Porson : ἂν εὑρήσῃ M, ἐφευρήσει FTr
1095 Pauw : μαρτυρίοις codd.   μὲν γὰρ FTr   Abresch : τοῖσδε πε-
πείθομαι codd.   1096 τάδε M : τὰ FTr   1098 ἦμην (sscr. ἦμεν)
M, ἦμεν FTr   1099 ἦμεν M   Schütz : μαστ- codd.   1101
ἄχθος, sscr. ἄχος, M   1103 -οισι MF   ἀλκὰν F   1106 βοᾷ
πόλις FTr   1110 χεὶρ FTr et M ante correctionem   1111
χειρὸς M   ὀρεγμένα FTr (-όμενα ante correctionem M)

Χο. οὔπω ξυνῆκα· νῦν γὰρ ἐξ αἰνιγμάτων
ἐπαργέμοισι θεσφάτοις ἀμηχανῶ.

Κα. ἒ ἔ, παπαῖ παπαῖ, τί τόδε φαίνεται;   Str. 5
ἦ δίκτυόν τί γ' Ἅιδου;   1115
ἀλλ' ἄρκυς ἡ ξύνευνος, ἡ ξυναιτία
φόνου· στάσις δ' ἀκόρετος γένει
κατολολυξάτω θύματος λευσίμου.

Χο. ποίαν Ἐρινὺν τήνδε δώμασιν κέλη
ἐπορθιάζειν; οὔ με φαιδρύνει λόγος.   1120
ἐπὶ δὲ καρδίαν ἔδραμε κροκοβαφὴς
σταγών, ἅτε †καὶ δορία πτώσιμος†
ξυνανύτει βίου δύντος αὐγαῖς·
ταχεῖα δ' ἄτα πέλει.

Κα. ἃ ἃ ἰδοὺ ἰδού, ἄπεχε τῆς βοὸς   Ant. 5
τὸν ταῦρον· ἐν πέπλοισιν   1126
μελαγκέρῳ λαβοῦσα μηχανήματι
τύπτει· πίτνει δ' ⟨ἐν⟩ ἐνύδρῳ τεύχει·
δολοφόνου λέβητος τύχαν σοι λέγω.

Χο. οὐ κομπάσαιμ' ἂν θεσφάτων γνώμων ἄκρος   1130
εἶναι, κακῷ δέ τῳ προσεικάζω τάδε.
ἀπὸ δὲ θεσφάτων τίς ἀγαθὰ φάτις
βροτοῖς στέλλεται; κακῶν γὰρ διαὶ
πολυεπεῖς τέχναι θεσπιῳδῶν
φόβον φέρουσιν μαθεῖν.   1135

Κα. ἰὼ ἰὼ ταλαίνας κακόποτμοι τύχαι·   Str. 6

MFTr   1113 ἐπ' ἀργ- FTr   1115 ἦ FTr   ἀίδου codd.
1117 Bothe : ἀκόρεστος codd.   1122 καὶ δορία M, καὶ δωρία F,
δωρία Tr   1125 ἃ ἅ FTr   βοῆς Tr   1127 μελάγκέρωι M, ι ex
ν factum, sscr. ·ν· : μελαγκέρων F, μελάγκερων Tr   λαθοῦσα schol. M
1128 suppl. Schütz   1132 τις M   1133 -οῖσι F   Hermann : δὴ
αἱ FTr, διὰ M   1134 Casaubon : θεσπιωιδὸν codd.   1135 -ουσι
MF

τὸ γὰρ ἐμὸν θροῶ πάθος †ἐπεγχέασα†.
ποῖ δή με δεῦρο τὴν τάλαιναν ἤγαγες,
οὐδέν ποτ' εἰ μὴ ξυνθανουμένην; τί γάρ;

Χο. φρενομανής τις εἶ θεοφόρητος, ἀμ-   1140
 φὶ δ' αὐτᾶς θροεῖς
 νόμον ἄνομον, οἷά τις ξουθὰ
 ἀκόρετος βοᾶς, φεῦ, ταλαίναις φρεσὶν
 "Ιτυν "Ιτυν στένουσ' ἀμφιθαλῆ κακοῖς
 ἀηδὼν μόρον.   1145

Κα. ἰὼ ἰὼ λιγείας βίος ἀηδόνος·   Ant. 6
 περέβαλον γάρ οἱ πτεροφόρον δέμας
 θεοὶ γλυκύν τ' αἰῶνα κλαυμάτων ἄτερ·
 ἐμοὶ δὲ μίμνει σχισμὸς ἀμφήκει δορί.

Χο. πόθεν ἐπισσύτους θεοφόρους τ' ἔχεις   1150
 ματαίους δύας,
 τὰ δ' ἐπίφοβα δυσφάτῳ κλαγγᾷ
 μελοτυπεῖς ὁμοῦ τ' ὀρθίοις ἐν νόμοις;
 πόθεν ὅρους ἔχεις θεσπεσίας ὁδοῦ
 κακορρήμονας;   1155

Κα. ἰὼ γάμοι γάμοι Πάριδος ὀλέθριοι φίλων· Str. 7
 ἰὼ Σκαμάνδρου πάτριον ποτόν·
 τότε μὲν ἀμφὶ σὰς ἀιόνας τάλαιν'
  ἠνυτόμαν τροφαῖς·
 νῦν δ' ἀμφὶ Κωκυτόν τε κἀχερουσίους   1160

MFTr 1137 ita M: ἐπαγχ- FTr 1139 οὐδέποτ' F, οὐ δή
ποτ' Tr 1141 αὐτᾶς M 1142 ἄνομόν γ' Tr 1143 editio
Aldina: -εστος codd. βοᾶις M, βορᾶς Tr φεῦ om. FTr φιλοίκτοις ταλαίναις F, φιλοίκτοισι (om. ταλ.) Tr 1145-6 scripsimus:
ἀηδὼν βίον et λιγείας ἀηδόνος μόρον codd. 1147 Hermann
(περίβ-): περεβάλοντο M, περιβαλόντες FTr 1148 ἀγῶνα MFTr,
sed γρ. αἰῶνα in marg. m 1151 δοιάς M in δύας corr. m 1152
ἐπὶ φόβῳ m F²Tr² post 1159 deficit M

ὄχθους ἔοικα θεσπιῳδήσειν τάχα.

Χο. τί τόδε τορὸν ἄγαν ἔπος ἐφημίσω;
νεογνὸς ἂν ἀΐων μάθοι·
πέπληγμαι δ' ὑπαὶ δήγματι φοινίῳ
δυσαλγεῖ τύχᾳ μινυρὰ [κακὰ] θρεομένας,   1165
θραύματ' ἐμοὶ κλύειν.

Κα. ἰὼ πόνοι πόνοι πόλεος ὀλομένας τὸ πᾶν·   Ant. 7
ἰὼ πρόπυργοι θυσίαι πατρὸς
✗ πολυκανεῖς βοτῶν ποιονόμων· ἄκος δ'
οὐδὲν ἐπήρκεσαν   1170
τὸ μὴ πόλιν μὲν ὥσπερ οὖν ἐχρῆν παθεῖν·
ἐγὼ δὲ †θερμόνους τάχ' ἐμπέδῳ βαλῶ.†

Χο. ἑπόμενα προτέροισι τάδ' ἐφημίσω.
καί τίς σε κακοφρονῶν τίθη-
σι δαίμων ὑπερβαρὴς ἐμπίτνων   1175
μελίζειν πάθη γοερὰ θανατοφόρα·
τέρμα δ' ἀμηχανῶ.

Κα. καὶ μὴν ὁ χρησμὸς οὐκέτ' ἐκ καλυμμάτων
ἔσται δεδορκὼς νεογάμου νύμφης δίκην·
λαμπρὸς δ' ἔοικεν ἡλίου πρὸς ἀντολάς   1180
πνέων ἐφήξειν, ὥστε κύματος δίκην
κλύζειν πρὸς αὐγὰς τοῦδε πήματος πολύ
μεῖζον· φρενώσω δ' οὐκέτ' ἐξ αἰνιγμάτων·   ) I will instruct
καὶ μαρτυρεῖτε συνδρόμως ἴχνος κακῶν
ῥινηλατούσῃ τῶν πάλαι πεπραγμένων·   1185

FTr   1163 Karsten: ἀνθρώπων FTr   1164 -ημαι Tr   ὑπὸ F
1165 Canter: δυσαγγεῖ FTr   κακὰ del. Schütz   1166 θαύμ-
Tr   1167 πόλεως F   Casaubon: ὀλωμ- F, ὀλουμ- Tr   1171
Maas: ἔχειν παθεῖν F, ἔχει παθεῖν Tr   1173 Pauw: -οις FTr
1174 καὶ τίς σε F, τίς σε καὶ Tr   Schütz: -φρονεῖν FTr   κακο-
φρονεῖν δαίμων ποιεῖ ὑπερβαρὺς Tr   1176 θανατηφόρα Tr   1179
νύμφας F   1181 scripsimus: ἐς ἥξειν FTr   1182 Auratus:
κλύειν FTr

τὴν γὰρ στέγην τήνδ' οὔποτ' ἐκλείπει χορός
ξύμφθογγος οὐκ εὔφωνος· οὐ γὰρ εὖ λέγει·
καὶ μὴν πεπωκώς γ', ὡς θρασύνεσθαι πλέον,
βρότειον αἷμα κῶμος ἐν δόμοις μένει,
δύσπεμπτος ἔξω, συγγόνων Ἐρινύων·   1190
ὑμνοῦσι δ' ὕμνον δώμασιν προσήμεναι
πρώταρχον ἄτην, ἐν μέρει δ' ἀπέπτυσαν
εὐνὰς ἀδελφοῦ τῷ πατοῦντι δυσμενεῖς.
ἥμαρτον, ἢ †τηρῶ† τι τοξότης τις ὥς;
ἢ ψευδόμαντίς εἰμι θυροκόπος φλέδων;   1195
ἐκμαρτύρησον προυμόσας τό μ' εἰδέναι
λόγῳ παλαιὰς τῶνδ' ἁμαρτίας δόμων.

Χο. καὶ πῶς ἂν ὅρκου πῆγμα γενναίως παγέν
παιώνιον γένοιτο; θαυμάζω δέ σου,
πόντου πέραν τραφεῖσαν ἀλλόθρουν πόλιν   1200
κυρεῖν λέγουσαν ὥσπερ εἰ παρεστάτεις.

Κα. μάντις μ' Ἀπόλλων τῷδ' ἐπέστησεν τέλει.

Χο. μῶν καὶ θεός περ ἱμέρῳ πεπληγμένος;   1204

Κα. πρὸ τοῦ μὲν αἰδὼς ἦν ἐμοὶ λέγειν τάδε.   1203

Χο. ἁβρύνεται γὰρ πᾶς τις εὖ πράσσων πλέον.   1205

Κα. ἀλλ' ἦν παλαιστὴς κάρτ' ἐμοὶ πνέων χάριν.

Χο. ἦ καὶ τέκνων εἰς ἔργον ἠλθέτην ὁμοῦ;

Κα. ξυναινέσασα Λοξίαν ἐψευσάμην.

Χο. ἤδη τέχναισιν ἐνθέοις ᾑρημένη;

Κα. ἤδη πολίταις πάντ' ἐθέσπιζον πάθη.   1210

Χο. πῶς δῆτ' ἄνατος ἦσθα Λοξίου κότῳ;

FTr   1187 σύμφογγος F   1191 δώμασι FTr, ν add.
Porson   1192 -αρχος F   1196 καὶ μαρτ. Tr   1198 Auratus :
ὅρκος πῆμα FTr   1204 traiecit Hermann   1203 προτοῦ
FTr, sed cf. M in Eum. 462   1205 βαρύνεται Tr   1207
Elmsley : ἤλθετον FTr   Butler : νόμῳ FTr   1211 Canter :
ἄνακτος FTr

Κα. ἔπειθον οὐδέν᾽ οὐδέν, ὡς τάδ᾽ ἤμπλακον.

Χο. ἡμῖν γε μὲν δὴ πιστὰ θεσπίζειν δοκεῖς.

Κα. ἰοὺ ἰού, ὦ ὦ κακά·
 ὑπ᾽ αὖ με δεινὸς ὀρθομαντείας πόνος   1215
 στροβεῖ ταράσσων φροιμίοις ⟨δυσφροιμίοις⟩.
 ὁρᾶτε τούσδε τοὺς δόμοις ἐφημένους
 νέους, ὀνείρων προσφερεῖς μορφώμασιν;
 παῖδες θανόντες ὡσπερεὶ πρὸς τῶν φίλων,
 χεῖρας κρεῶν πλήθοντες, οἰκείας βορᾶς,   1220
 σὺν ἐντέροις τε σπλάγχν᾽, ἐποίκτιστον γέμος,
 πρέπουσ᾽ ἔχοντες, ὧν πατὴρ ἐγεύσατο.
 ἐκ τῶνδε ποινάς φημι βουλεύειν τινά
 λέοντ᾽ ἄναλκιν ἐν λέχει στρωφώμενον
 οἰκουρὸν ὠμὸν τῷ μολόντι δεσπότῃ   1225
 ἐμῷ· φέρειν γὰρ χρὴ τὸ δούλιον ζυγόν·
 νεῶν δ᾽ ἄπαρχος Ἰλίου τ᾽ ἀναστάτης
 οὐκ οἶδεν οἷα γλῶσσα μισητῆς κυνός,
 λέξασα κἀκτείνασα φαιδρόνους δίκην,
 ἄτης λαθραίου τεύξεται κακῇ τύχῃ.   1230
 τοιαῦτα τολμᾷ· θῆλυς ἄρσενος φονεύς
 ἐστίν· τί νιν καλοῦσα δυσφιλὲς δάκος
 τύχοιμ᾽ ἄν; ἀμφίσβαιναν, ἢ Σκύλλαν τινά
 οἰκοῦσαν ἐν πέτραισι, ναυτίλων βλάβην,
 θύουσαν Ἅιδου μητέρ᾽ ἄσπονδόν τ᾽ Ἄρη   1235
 φίλοις πνέουσαν; ὡς δ᾽ ἐπωλολύξατο
 ἡ παντότολμος, ὥσπερ ἐν μάχης τροπῇ·
 δοκεῖ δὲ χαίρειν νοστίμῳ σωτηρίᾳ.
 καὶ τῶνδ᾽ ὁμοῖον εἴ τι μὴ πείθω· τί γάρ;

FTr 1212 Canter: οὐδὲν οὐδὲν FTr 1216 suppl. Hermann: φροιμίοις ἐφημένους (-οις sscr. Tr) FTr 1225 scripsimus: οἰκουρὸν οἴμοι FTr 1226 δούλειον Tr ζυγὸν ex -ω corr. F versum del. A. Ludwig, fort. recte 1227 G. Vossius: νεῶν τ᾽ FTr 1228 εὖ οἶδεν Tr οἷα FTr 1229 Canter: καὶ κτείνᾱσα FTr 1231 τοιάδε F 1232 -φιλεὺς F 1235 Franz (Ἄρην iam anonymus): ἀρὰν FTr

τὸ μέλλον ἥξει· καὶ σύ μ᾽ ἐν τάχει παρών   1240
ἄγαν γ᾽ ἀληθόμαντιν οἰκτίρας ἐρεῖς.

Χο. τὴν μὲν Θυέστου δαῖτα παιδείων κρεῶν
ξυνῆκα καὶ πέφρικα καὶ φόβος μ᾽ ἔχει
κλυόντ᾽ ἀληθῶς οὐδὲν ἐξηκασμένα·
τὰ δ᾽ ἄλλ᾽ ἀκούσας ἐκ δρόμου πεσὼν τρέχω.   1245

Κα. Ἀγαμέμνονός σέ φημ᾽ ἐπόψεσθαι μόρον.

Χο. εὔφημον, ὦ τάλαινα, κοίμησον στόμα.

Κα. ἀλλ᾽ οὔτι παιὼν τῷδ᾽ ἐπιστατεῖ λόγῳ.

Χο. οὔκ, εἴπερ ἔσται γ᾽· ἀλλὰ μὴ γένοιτό πως.

Κα. σὺ μὲν κατεύχῃ, τοῖς δ᾽ ἀποκτείνειν μέλει.   1250

Χο. τίνος πρὸς ἀνδρὸς τοῦτ᾽ ἄχος πορσύνεται;

Κα. ἦ κάρτα λίαν παρεκόπης χρησμῶν ἐμῶν.

Χο. τοῦ γὰρ τελοῦντος οὐ ξυνῆκα μηχανήν.

Κα. καὶ μὴν ἄγαν γ᾽ Ἕλλην᾽ ἐπίσταμαι φάτιν.

Χο. καὶ γὰρ τὰ πυθόκραντα· δυσμαθῆ δ᾽ ὅμως.   1255

Κα. παπαῖ· οἷον τὸ πῦρ· ἐπέρχεται δέ μοι·
ὀτοτοῖ, Λύκει᾽ Ἄπολλον, οἳ ἐγὼ ἐγώ.
αὕτη δίπους λέαινα συγκοιμωμένη
λύκῳ, λέοντος εὐγενοῦς ἀπουσίᾳ,
κτενεῖ με τὴν τάλαιναν· ὡς δὲ φάρμακον   1260
τεύχουσα κἀμοῦ μισθὸν ἐνθήσει κότῳ·
ἐπεύχεται, θήγουσα φωτὶ φάσγανον,
ἐμῆς ἀγωγῆς ἀντιτείσεσθαι φόνον.
τί δῆτ᾽ ἐμαυτῆς καταγέλωτ᾽ ἔχω τάδε
καὶ σκῆπτρα καὶ μαντεῖα περὶ δέρῃ στέφη;   1265

FTr   1240 Auratus : μὴν FTr   1241 οἰκτεί- FTr   1242
παιδίων FTr   1244 κλύ- FTr   ἐξεικ- Tr   1247 κοίμισον
Tr   1249 Schütz : εἰ παρέσται FTr   1252 Mazon : κάρτ᾽ ἄρ᾽
ἂν FTr   Hartung : παρεσκόπεις (sup. ει scr. η) F, -πης Tr   1255
δυσπαθῆ F   1258 Victorius : δίπλους FTr   1261 μνείαν
sup. μισθὸν scr F.   ἐνθήσειν Tr²   1263 Blomfield : -σασθαι FTr

σὲ μὲν πρὸ μοίρας τῆς ἐμῆς διαφθερῶ·
ἴτ' ἐς φθόρον· πεσόντα γ' ὧδ' ἀμείβομαι·
ἄλλην τιν' ἄτης ἀντ' ἐμοῦ πλουτίζετε.
ἰδοὺ δ', Ἀπόλλων αὐτὸς ἐκδύων ἐμέ
χρηστηρίαν ἐσθῆτ', ἐποπτεύσας δέ με   1270
κἂν τοῖσδε κόσμοις καταγελωμένην μέγα
φίλων ὑπ' ἐχθρῶν οὐ διχορρόπως †μάτην· †
καλουμένη δὲ φοιτὰς ὡς ἀγύρτρια
πτωχὸς τάλαινα λιμοθνὴς ἠνεσχόμην·
καὶ νῦν ὁ μάντις μάντιν ἐκπράξας ἐμέ   1275
ἀπήγαγ' ἐς τοιάσδε θανασίμους τύχας·
βωμοῦ πατρῴου δ' ἀντ' ἐπίξηνον μένει,
θερμῷ κοπείσης φοίνιον προσφάγματι.
οὐ μὴν ἄτιμοί γ' ἐκ θεῶν τεθνήξομεν·
ἥξει γὰρ ἡμῶν ἄλλος αὖ τιμάορος,   1280
μητροκτόνον φίτυμα, ποινάτωρ πατρός·
φυγὰς δ' ἀλήτης τῆσδε γῆς ἀπόξενος
κάτεισιν, ἄτας τάσδε θριγκώσων φίλοις·
ὀμώμοται γὰρ ὅρκος ἐκ θεῶν μέγας,   1290
ἄξειν νιν ὑπτίασμα κειμένου πατρός.
τί δῆτ' ἐγὼ κάτοικτος ὧδ' ἀναστένω;   1285
ἐπεὶ τὸ πρῶτον εἶδον Ἰλίου πόλιν
πράξασαν ὡς ἔπραξεν, οἳ δ' εἶλον πόλιν
οὕτως ἀπαλλάσσουσιν ἐν θεῶν κρίσει,
ἰοῦσ' ἀπάρξω, τλήσομαι τὸ κατθανεῖν·   1289
Ἅιδου πύλας δὲ τάσδ' ἐγὼ προσεννέπω·   1291
ἐπεύχομαι δὲ καιρίας πληγῆς τυχεῖν,

FTr   1267 Jacob: πεσόντ' ἀγαθὼ δ' FTr   ἀμείψ- Tr et post
correctionem F   1268 Stanley: ἄτην FTr   1270 ἐπώπτ- Tr
1271 Hermann: μέτα FTr   1277 ἀντεπίξηνον FTr, distinxit
Auratus   1278 C. G. Haupt: φοινίῳ FTr   1279 ἄτιμοί F²Tr:
-μόν F   1290 huc transtulit Hermann   1284 ἄξει Tr   1285
Scaliger: κάτοικος FTr   1287 οἶδ' FTr   Musgrave: εἶχον FTr
1288 ἐκ F   1289 scripsimus: ἰοῦσα πράξω FTr   1291
Auratus: τὰς λέγω FTr

ὡς ἀσφάδαστος, αἱμάτων εὐθνησίμων
ἀπορρυέντων, ὄμμα συμβάλω τόδε.

Χο. ὦ πολλὰ μὲν τάλαινα, πολλὰ δ' αὖ σοφή   1295
γύναι, μακρὰν ἔτεινας· εἰ δ' ἐτητύμως
μόρον τὸν αὑτῆς οἶσθα, πῶς θεηλάτου
βοὸς δίκην πρὸς βωμὸν εὐτόλμως πατεῖς;

Κα. οὐκ ἔστ' ἄλυξις, οὔ, ξένοι, χρόνον πλέω.

Χο. ὁ δ' ὕστατός γε τοῦ χρόνου πρεσβεύεται.   1300

Κα. ἥκει τόδ' ἦμαρ· σμικρὰ κερδανῶ φυγῇ.

Χο. ἀλλ' ἴσθι τλήμων οὖσ' ἀπ' εὐτόλμου φρενός.

Κα. οὐδεὶς ἀκούει ταῦτα τῶν εὐδαιμόνων.

Χο. ἀλλ' εὐκλεῶς τοι κατθανεῖν χάρις βροτῷ.

Κα. ἰὼ πάτερ σοῦ σῶν τε γενναίων τέκνων.   1305

Χο. τί δ' ἐστὶ χρῆμα; τίς σ' ἀποστρέφει φόβος;

Κα. φεῦ φεῦ.

Χο. τί τοῦτ' ἔφευξας; εἴ τι μὴ φρενῶν στύγος.

Κα. φόνον δόμοι πνέουσιν αἱματοσταγῆ.

Χο. καὶ πῶς; τόδ' ὄζει θυμάτων ἐφεστίων.   1310

Κα. ὁμοῖος ἀτμὸς ὥσπερ ἐκ τάφου πρέπει.

Χο. οὐ Σύριον ἀγλάϊσμα δώμασιν λέγεις.

Κα. ἀλλ' εἶμι κἂν δόμοισι κωκύσουσ' ἐμήν
Ἀγαμέμνονός τε μοῖραν· ἀρκείτω βίος. ✦
ἰὼ ξένοι·   1315
οὔτοι δυσοίζω θάμνον ὡς ὄρνις φόβῳ,
ἀλλ' ὡς θανούσῃ μαρτυρῆτέ μοι τόδε,
ὅταν γυνὴ γυναικὸς ἀντ' ἐμοῦ θάνῃ
ἀνήρ τε δυσδάμαρτος ἀντ' ἀνδρὸς πέσῃ·

FTr   1295 δὲ σοφὴ F   1297 αὑτῆς F   1299 Hermann :
χρόνῳ πλέω (-ῳ Tr) FTr   1305 Auratus : τῶν τε FTr   1309
φόβον FTr, ν sup. β scr. Tr   1317 Orelli : -ρεῖτε FTr

ἐπιξενοῦμαι ταῦτα δ' ὡς θανουμένη.   1320

Χο. ὦ τλῆμον, οἰκτίρω σε θεσφάτου μόρου.

Κα. ἅπαξ ἔτ' εἰπεῖν ῥῆσιν ἢ θρῆνον θέλω
ἐμὸν τὸν αὐτῆς· ἡλίῳ δ' ἐπεύχομαι
πρὸς ὕστατον φῶς †τοῖς ἐμοῖς τιμαόροις
ἐχθροῖς φονεῦσι τοῖς ἐμοῖς τίνειν ὁμοῦ†   1325
δούλης θανούσης, εὐμαροῦς χειρώματος.
ἰὼ βρότεια πράγματ'· εὐτυχοῦντα μέν
σκιᾷ τις ἂν πρέψειεν· εἰ δὲ δυστυχῇ,
βολαῖς ὑγρώσσων σπόγγος ὤλεσεν γραφήν·
καὶ ταῦτ' ἐκείνων μᾶλλον οἰκτίρω πολύ.   1330

Χο. τὸ μὲν εὖ πράσσειν ἀκόρεστον ἔφυ
πᾶσι βροτοῖσιν· δακτυλοδείκτων δ'
οὔτις ἀπειπὼν εἴργει μελάθρων,
μηκέτ' ἐσέλθῃς τάδε φωνῶν.
καὶ τῷδε πόλιν μὲν ἑλεῖν ἔδοσαν   1335
μάκαρες Πριάμου,
θεοτίμητος δ' οἴκαδ' ἱκάνει·
νῦν δ' εἰ προτέρων αἷμ' ἀποτείσῃ
καὶ τοῖσι θανοῦσι θανὼν ἄλλων
ποινὰς θανάτων ἐπικράνῃ,   1340
τίς κἂν εὔξαιτο βροτῶν ἀσινεῖ
δαίμονι φῦναι τάδ' ἀκούων;

Αγ. ὤμοι, πέπληγμαι καιρίαν πληγὴν ἔσω.

Χο. σῖγα· τίς πληγὴν ἀυτεῖ καιρίως οὐτασμένος;

Αγ. ὤμοι μάλ' αὖθις δευτέραν πεπληγμένος.   1345

FTr   1321 οἰκτεῖ· FTr   1324 τους in τοῖς corr. F   1328
Wieseler, Boissonade: σκιά τις ἀντρέψειεν FTr   -τυχῇ FTr   1329
ὤλεσε FTr, ν add. Porson   1330 οἰκτεῖ· FTr   1331 Porson:
πράττειν FTr   1332 Pauw: -οῖς FTr   -δεικτῶν FTr et schol.
vet.   1334 Hermann: μηκέτι δ' εἰσέλθῃς FTr   1338 Sidgwick:
-τίσει FTr   1340 Sidgwick: ἐπικρανεῖ F, ἄγαν ἐπικρανεῖ Tr   1341
Lobel: τίς ἂν FTr

Χο. τοὖργον εἰργάσθαι δοκεῖ μοι βασιλέως οἰμώγμασιν·
ἀλλὰ κοινωσώμεθ᾽ ἤν πως ἀσφαλῆ βουλεύματ᾽ ⟨ᾖ⟩.

— ἐγὼ μὲν ὑμῖν τὴν ἐμὴν γνώμην λέγω,
πρὸς δῶμα δεῦρ᾽ ἀστοῖσι κηρύσσειν βοήν.

— ἐμοὶ δ᾽ ὅπως τάχιστά γ᾽ ἐμπεσεῖν δοκεῖ   1350
καὶ πρᾶγμ᾽ ἐλέγχειν σὺν νεορρύτῳ ξίφει.

— κἀγὼ τοιούτου γνώματος κοινωνὸς ὤν
ψηφίζομαι τὸ δρᾶν τι· μὴ μέλλειν δ᾽ ἀκμή.

— ὁρᾶν πάρεστι· φροιμιάζονται γὰρ ὡς
τυραννίδος σημεῖα πράσσοντες πόλει.   1355

— χρονίζομεν γάρ· οἱ δὲ τῆς μελλοῦς κλέος
πέδον πατοῦντες οὐ καθεύδουσιν χερί.

— οὐκ οἶδα βουλῆς ἧστινος τυχὼν λέγω·
τοῦ δρῶντός ἐστι καὶ τὸ βουλεῦσαι †πέρι†.

— κἀγὼ τοιοῦτός εἰμ᾽, ἐπεὶ δυσμηχανῶ   1360
λόγοισι τὸν θανόντ᾽ ἀνιστάναι πάλιν.

— ἦ καὶ βίον τείνοντες ὧδ᾽ ὑπείξομεν
δόμων καταισχυντῆρσι τοῖσδ᾽ ἡγουμένοις;

— ἀλλ᾽ οὐκ ἀνεκτόν, ἀλλὰ κατθανεῖν κρατεῖ·
πεπαιτέρα γὰρ μοῖρα τῆς τυραννίδος.   1365

— ἦ γὰρ τεκμηρίοισιν ἐξ οἰμωγμάτων
μαντευσόμεσθα τἀνδρὸς ὡς ὀλωλότος;

— σάφ᾽ εἰδότας χρὴ τῶνδε μυθεῖσθαι πέρι·
τὸ γὰρ τοπάζειν τοῦ σάφ᾽ εἰδέναι δίχα.

— ταύτην ἐπαινεῖν πάντοθεν πληθύνομαι,   1370
τρανῶς Ἀτρείδην εἰδέναι κυροῦνθ᾽ ὅπως.

FTr   1346 -ᾶσθαι FTr   1347 Paley : ἄν πως FTr   ᾖ suppl.
Enger   1353 Musgrave : τι δρᾶν· τὸ FTr   1356 Blomfield
ex Tryphone περὶ τρόπων, Rhet. Graec. viii. 741. 9 Walz ὧδε τῆς
μελλοῦς χάριν : τῆς (om. Tr) μελλούσης κλέος FTr   1357
καθεύδουσι F   1362 Canter : κτείνοντες FTr   1364 Casaubon :
κράτει FTr   1367 -σόμεθα F   1368 J. G. Schneider : θυμοῦ-
σθαι FTr

Κλ. πολλῶν πάροιθεν καιρίως εἰρημένων
τἀναντί' εἰπεῖν οὐκ ἐπαισχυνθήσομαι·
πῶς γάρ τις ἐχθροῖς ἐχθρὰ πορσύνων, φίλοις
δοκοῦσιν εἶναι, πημονῆς ἀρκύστατ' ἂν   1375
φάρξειεν ὕψος κρεῖσσον ἐκπηδήματος;
ἐμοὶ δ' ἀγὼν ὅδ' οὐκ ἀφρόντιστος πάλαι
νείκης παλαιᾶς ἦλθε, σὺν χρόνῳ γε μήν·
ἕστηκα δ' ἔνθ' ἔπαισ' ἐπ' ἐξειργασμένοις.
οὕτω δ' ἔπραξα, καὶ τάδ' οὐκ ἀρνήσομαι,   1380
ὡς μήτε φεύγειν μήτ' ἀμύνεσθαι μόρον·
ἄπειρον ἀμφίβληστρον, ὥσπερ ἰχθύων,
περιστιχίζω, πλοῦτον εἵματος κακόν·
παίω δέ νιν δίς, κἀν δυοῖν οἰμώγμασιν
μεθῆκεν αὐτοῦ κῶλα, καὶ πεπτωκότι   1385
τρίτην ἐπενδίδωμι, τοῦ κατὰ χθονὸς
Διὸς νεκρῶν σωτῆρος εὐκταίαν χάριν.
οὕτω τὸν αὑτοῦ θυμὸν †ὁρμαίνει† πεσών,
κἀκφυσιῶν ὀξεῖαν αἵματος σφαγὴν
βάλλει μ' ἐρεμνῇ ψακάδι φοινίας δρόσου,   1390
χαίρουσαν οὐδὲν ἧσσον ἢ διοσδότῳ
γάνει σπορητὸς κάλυκος ἐν λοχεύμασιν.
ὡς ὧδ' ἐχόντων, πρέσβος Ἀργείων τόδε,
χαίροιτ' ἄν, εἰ χαίροιτ', ἐγὼ δ' ἐπεύχομαι·
εἰ δ' ἦν πρεπόντως ὥστ' ἐπισπένδειν νεκρῷ,   1395
τάδ' ἂν δικαίως ἦν, ὑπερδίκως μὲν οὖν·
τοσῶνδε κρατῆρ' ἐν δόμοις κακῶν ὅδε
πλήσας ἀραίων αὐτὸς ἐκπίνει μολών.

Χο. θαυμάζομέν σου γλῶσσαν, ὡς θρασύστομος,
ἥτις τοιόνδ' ἐπ' ἀνδρὶ κομπάζεις λόγον.   1400

FTr   1375 Auratus: πημονὴν FTr   Elmsley: ἀρκύστατον FTr
1378 Heath: νείκης FTr   1379 ἔπεσ' F   1381 Victorius:
ἀμύνασθαι FTr   1383 -στοιχίζων F   1387 Διὸς Enger: ᾄδου
FTr   1388 αὑτοῦ FTr   1391-2 Porson, nisi Διὸς νότῳ |
γαθεῖ (Lloyd-Jones) praeferendum: διὸς νότῳ | γᾶν εἰ FTr   1392
σπόρητος FTr   1395 Is. Vossius: πρεπόντων FTr

Κλ. πειρᾶσθέ μου γυναικὸς ὡς ἀφράσμονος·
   ἐγὼ δ᾽ ἀτρέστῳ καρδίᾳ πρὸς εἰδότας
   λέγω· σὺ δ᾽ αἰνεῖν εἴτε με ψέγειν θέλεις,
   ὁμοῖον· οὗτός ἐστιν Ἀγαμέμνων, ἐμός
   πόσις, νεκρὸς δέ, τῆσδε δεξιᾶς χερός   1405
   ἔργον, δικαίας τέκτονος. τάδ᾽ ὧδ᾽ ἔχει.

Χο. τί κακόν, ὦ γύναι,   Str.
   χθονοτρεφὲς ἐδανὸν ἢ ποτὸν
   πασαμένα ῥυτᾶς ἐξ ἁλὸς ὀρόμενον
   τόδ᾽ ἐπέθου θύος, δημοθρόους τ᾽ ἀρὰς
   ἀπέδικες ἀπέταμες· ἀπόπολις δ᾽ ἔσῃ,   1410
   μῖσος ὄβριμον ἀστοῖς.

Κλ. νῦν μὲν δικάζεις ἐκ πόλεως φυγὴν ἐμοί
   καὶ μῖσος ἀστῶν δημόθρους τ᾽ ἔχειν ἀράς,
   οὐδὲν τότ᾽ ἀνδρὶ τῷδ᾽ ἐναντίον φέρων,
   ὃς οὐ προτιμῶν, ὡσπερεὶ βοτοῦ μόρον,   1415
   μήλων φλεόντων εὐπόκοις νομεύμασιν,
   ἔθυσεν αὑτοῦ παῖδα, φιλτάτην ἐμοί
   ὠδῖν᾽, ἐπῳδὸν Θρῃκίων ἀημάτων·
   οὐ τοῦτον ἐκ γῆς τῆσδε χρῆν σ᾽ ἀνδρηλατεῖν
   μιασμάτων ἄποιν᾽; ἐπήκοος δ᾽ ἐμῶν   1420
   ἔργων δικαστὴς τραχὺς εἶ. λέγω δέ σοι
   τοιαῦτ᾽ ἀπειλεῖν, ὡς παρεσκευασμένης
   ἐκ τῶν ὁμοίων, χειρὶ νικήσαντ᾽ ἐμοῦ
   ἄρχειν· ἐὰν δὲ τοὔμπαλιν κραίνῃ θεός,
   γνώσῃ διδαχθεὶς ὀψὲ γοῦν τὸ σωφρονεῖν.   1425

Χο. μεγαλόμητις εἶ,   Ant.
   περίφρονα δ᾽ ἔλακες· ὥσπερ οὖν

FTr   1406 δικαίως Tr   1408 Stanley : ῥύσας F, ῥυσᾶς
Tr   Canter : ὀρώμενον F, ὀρώμ- Tr   1409 ἐπεύθου Tr   1410 ε
sup. -ταμ- scr. F, a sup. -τεμ- Tr   Casaubon : ἄπολις FTr   1411
Porson : ὄμβρ- FTr   1414 τότ᾽ Is. Vossius : τόδ᾽ FTr   1417 αὐτοῦ
FTr   1418 Canter : τὲ (τε Tr) λημμάτων FTr   1419 Porson :
χρή FTr

φονολιβεῖ τύχᾳ φρὴν ἐπιμαίνεται,
λίβος ἐπ' ὀμμάτων αἵματος ἐμπρέπει.
ἄντιτον ἔτι σε χρὴ στερομέναν φίλων
τύμμα τύμμα⟨τι⟩ τεῖσαι.   1430

Κλ. καὶ τήνδ' ἀκούεις ὁρκίων ἐμῶν θέμιν·
μὰ τὴν τέλειον τῆς ἐμῆς παιδὸς Δίκην,
Ἄτην Ἐρινύν θ', αἷσι τόνδ' ἔσφαξ' ἐγώ,
οὔ μοι φόβου μέλαθρον ἐλπὶς ἐμπατεῖ,
ἕως ἂν αἴθῃ πῦρ ἐφ' ἑστίας ἐμῆς   1435
Αἴγισθος, ὡς τὸ πρόσθεν εὖ φρονῶν ἐμοί·
οὗτος γὰρ ἡμῖν ἀσπὶς οὐ σμικρὰ θράσους.
κεῖται γυναικὸς τῆσδ' ὁ λυμαντήριος,
Χρυσηΐδων μείλιγμα τῶν ὑπ' Ἰλίῳ,
ἥ τ' αἰχμάλωτος ἥδε καὶ τερασκόπος   1440
καὶ κοινόλεκτρος τοῦδε, θεσφατηλόγος
πιστὴ ξύνευνος, ναυτίλων δὲ σελμάτων
†ἱστοτρίβης†. ἄτιμα δ' οὐκ ἐπραξάτην·
ὁ μὲν γὰρ οὕτως, ἡ δέ τοι κύκνου δίκην
τὸν ὕστατον μέλψασα θανάσιμον γόον   1445
κεῖται φιλήτωρ τοῦδ', ἐμοὶ δ' ἐπήγαγεν
†εὐνῆς παροψώνημα τῆς ἐμῆς χλιδῆς†.

Χο. φεῦ, τίς ἂν ἐν τάχει μὴ περιώδυνος   Str.
    μηδὲ δεμνιοτήρης
μόλοι τὸν ἀεὶ φέρουσ' ἐν ἡμῖν   1450
μοῖρ' ἀτέλευτον ὕπνον, δαμέντος
φύλακος εὐμενεστάτου [καὶ]
πολλὰ τλάντος γυναικὸς διαί;
πρὸς γυναικὸς δ' ἀπέφθισεν βίον.

FTr   1428 Casaubon : λῖπος FTr   Auratus : εὖ πρέπει FTr
1428–9 Weil : πρέπειαν τίετον F, πρέπει ἀτίετον Tr   1430 suppl.
Casaubon τίσαι FTr   1435 Porson : ἐμὰς FTr   1437 μικρὰ
FTr   1438 Kayser : τῆσδε λυμ. FTr   1446 φιλήτως F   1447
παροψόνημα FTr   1452 καὶ del. Franz   1453 διὰ Tr

ἰώ· παράνους Ἑλένα, 1455
μία τὰς πολλάς, τὰς πάνυ πολλὰς
ψυχὰς ὀλέσασ᾽ ὑπὸ Τροίᾳ,
νῦν †δὲ τελείαν† πολύμναστον ἐπηνθίσω
δι᾽ αἷμ᾽ ἄνιπτον· ἦ τις ἦν τότ᾽ ἐν δόμοις 1460
Ἔρις ἐρίδματος ἀνδρὸς οἰζύς.

Κλ. μηδὲν θανάτου μοῖραν ἐπεύχου
τοῖσδε βαρυνθείς·
μηδ᾽ εἰς Ἑλένην κότον ἐκτρέψῃς,
ὡς ἀνδρολέτειρ᾽, ὡς μία πολλῶν 1465
ἀνδρῶν ψυχὰς Δαναῶν ὀλέσασ᾽
ἀξύστατον ἄλγος ἔπραξεν.

Χο. δαῖμον, ὃς ἐμπίτνεις δώμασι καὶ διφυί- Ant.
οισι Τανταλίδαισιν,
κράτος ⟨τ᾽⟩ ἰσόψυχον ἐκ γυναικῶν 1470
καρδιόδηκτον ἐμοὶ κρατύνεις·
ἐπὶ δὲ σώματος δίκαν [μοι]
κόρακος ἐχθροῦ σταθεῖσ᾽ ἐκνόμως
ὕμνον ὑμνεῖν ἐπεύχεται ⟨ ◡ – ⟩.

Κλ. νῦν δ᾽ ὤρθωσας στόματος γνώμην, 1475
τὸν τριπάχυντον
δαίμονα γέννης τῆσδε κικλήσκων·
ἐκ τοῦ γὰρ ἔρως αἱματολοιχὸς
νείρᾳ τρέφεται· πρὶν καταλῆξαι
τὸ παλαιὸν ἄχος, νέος ἰχώρ. 1480

Χο. ἦ μέγαν †οἴκοις τοῖσδε† Str.
δαίμονα καὶ βαρύμηνιν αἰνεῖς,

FTr   1455 Hermann: παρανόμους FTr   1460 Schütz: ἤτις
FTr   1464 ἐκτρέχης F   1466 ὀλέσαν F   1468 Canter:
ἐμπίπτεις FTr   1468–9 Hermann: διφυεῖσι FTr   1469
-ίδεσιν F   1470 suppl. Hermann   1471 Abresch: καρδίᾳ
δηκτὸν FTr   1472 μοι del. Dindorf   1473 Stanley: σταθεὶς
FTr   ἐκνόμως schol. vet. in Tr et post correctionem Tr: ἐνν-
F   1476 Bamberger: -πάχυιον FTr   1477 γέννας Tr et
sscr. F   1479 Casaubon (νείρῃ): νείρει FTr

φεῦ φεῦ, κακὸν αἶνον ἀτη-
ρᾶς τύχας ἀκορέστου·
ἰὼ ἰή, διαὶ Διὸς   1485
παναιτίου πανεργέτα·
τί γὰρ βροτοῖς ἄνευ Διὸς τελεῖται;
τί τῶνδ' οὐ θεόκραντόν ἐστιν;

ἰὼ ἰὼ βασιλεῦ βασιλεῦ,
πῶς σε δακρύσω;   1490
φρενὸς ἐκ φιλίας τί ποτ' εἴπω;
κεῖσαι δ' ἀράχνης ἐν ὑφάσματι τῷδ'
ἀσεβεῖ θανάτῳ βίον ἐκπνέων.
ὤμοι μοι, κοίταν τάνδ' ἀνελεύθερον
δολίῳ μόρῳ δαμεὶς   1495
ἐκ χερὸς ἀμφιτόμῳ βελέμνῳ.

Κλ. αὐχεῖς εἶναι τόδε τοὔργον ἐμὸν
†μηδ' ἐπιλεχθῇς†
Ἀγαμεμνονίαν εἶναί μ' ἄλοχον·
φανταζόμενος δὲ γυναικὶ νεκροῦ   1500
τοῦδ' ὁ παλαιὸς δριμὺς ἀλάστωρ
Ἀτρέως χαλεποῦ θοινατῆρος
τόνδ' ἀπέτεισεν
τέλεον νεαροῖς ἐπιθύσας.

Χο. ὡς μὲν ἀναίτιος εἶ   Ant.
τοῦδε φόνου τίς ὁ μαρτυρήσων;   1506
πῶ πῶ; πατρόθεν δὲ συλλή-
πτωρ γένοιτ' ἂν ἀλάστωρ·
βιάζεται δ' ὁμοσπόροις
ἐπιρροαῖσιν αἱμάτων   1510
μέλας Ἄρης, ὅποι δίκαν προβαίνων

FTr   1486 -γέταν (ex -γάταν corr.) F   1489 ἰὼ semel F
1491 ποτ' ἄρ' εἴπω Tr   1493 ἐκπνείων Tr   1494 τᾶνδ' F
ἀνελεύθερα Tr   1497 τοὔργον ἐμὸν τόδε; Tr   1498 μὴ δ' FTr
1503 -τισεν FTr   1504 νεκροῖς Tr   1507 δὲ om. Tr   1511
Butler: δὲ καὶ FTr   Canter: προσβ- FTr

πάχνᾳ κουροβόρῳ παρέξει.

ἰὼ ἰὼ βασιλεῦ βασιλεῦ,
πῶς σε δακρύσω;
φρενὸς ἐκ φιλίας τί ποτ᾽ εἴπω;　　　　　　　1515
κεῖσαι δ᾽ ἀράχνης ἐν ὑφάσματι τῷδ᾽
ἀσεβεῖ θανάτῳ βίον ἐκπνέων.
ὤμοι μοι, κοίταν τάνδ᾽ ἀνελεύθερον
δολίῳ μόρῳ δαμεὶς
ἐκ χερὸς ἀμφιτόμῳ βελέμνῳ.　　　　　　　1520

Κλ. οὔτ᾽ ἀνελεύθερον οἶμαι θάνατον
τῷδε γενέσθαι· ⟨　　　　　　　⟩
⟨　　　　　　　　　　　　⟩
οὐδὲ γὰρ οὗτος δολίαν ἄτην
οἴκοισιν ἔθηκ᾽;
ἀλλ᾽ ἐμὸν ἐκ τοῦδ᾽ ἔρνος ἀερθὲν　　　　　1525
τὴν πολυκλαύτην
Ἰφιγένειαν ἀνάξια δράσας
ἄξια πάσχων μηδὲν ἐν Ἅιδου
μεγαλαυχείτω, ξιφοδηλήτῳ
θανάτῳ τείσας ἅπερ ἦρξεν.

Χο. ἀμηχανῶ φροντίδος στερηθεὶς　　　　Str.
εὐπάλαμον μέριμναν　　　　　　　　　1531
ὅπᾳ τράπωμαι, πίτνοντος οἴκου·
δέδοικα δ᾽ ὄμβρου κτύπον δομοσφαλῆ
τὸν αἱματηρόν· ψακὰς δὲ λήγει.
Δίκα δ᾽ ἐπ᾽ ἄλλο πρᾶγμα θήγεται βλάβης　1535
πρὸς ἄλλαις θηγάναισι Μοίρας.

FTr　　1512 πάχνα κουροβόρω (-ῳ Tr) FTr　　1513 ἰὼ semel F
1515 ποτ᾽ ἀρ᾽ εἴπω Tr　　1517 εὐσεβεῖ F　ἐκπνείων Tr　　1518
ἀνελεύθερα Tr　　1522–3 lacunam indic. Wilamowitz　　1526 Porson: -κλαυτόν τ᾽ FTr　　1529 τίσας FTr　　1530 φροντίδων Tr
1531 Porson: εὐπάλαμνον FTr　　1532 ὅπα (sscr. η Tr) FTr　　1534
ψεκ- FTr　　1535 δίκη F: δίκᾳ, sscr. η, Tr　Emperius: θήγει
FTr 1536 Pauw: θηγάναις FTr　Emperius: μοῖρα FTr

ἰὼ γᾶ γᾶ, εἴθ' ἔμ' ἐδέξω,
πρὶν τόνδ' ἐπιδεῖν ἀργυροτοίχου
δροίτης κατέχοντα χάμευναν.   1540
τίς ὁ θάψων νιν; τίς ὁ θρηνήσων;
ἢ σὺ τόδ' ἔρξαι τλήσῃ, κτείνασ'
ἄνδρα τὸν αὑτῆς ἀποκωκῦσαι
ψυχῇ τ' ἄχαριν χάριν ἀντ' ἔργων   1545
μεγάλων ἀδίκως ἐπικρᾶναι;
τίς δ' ἐπιτύμβιον αἶνον ἐπ' ἀνδρὶ θείῳ
σὺν δακρύοις ἰάπτων
ἀληθείᾳ φρενῶν πονήσει;   1550

Κλ. οὐ σὲ προσήκει τὸ μέλημ' ἀλέγειν
τοῦτο· πρὸς ἡμῶν
κάππεσε κάτθανε καὶ καταθάψομεν,
οὐχ ὑπὸ κλαυθμῶν τῶν ἐξ οἴκων,
ἀλλ' Ἰφιγένειά νιν ἀσπασίως   1555
θυγάτηρ, ὡς χρή,
πατέρ' ἀντιάσασα πρὸς ὠκύπορον
πόρθμευμ' ἀχέων
περὶ χεῖρα βαλοῦσα φιλήσει.

Χο. ὄνειδος ἥκει τόδ' ἀντ' ὀνείδους,   Ant.
δύσμαχα δ' ἐστὶ κρῖναι·   1561
φέρει φέροντ', ἐκτίνει δ' ὁ καίνων·
μίμνει δὲ μίμνοντος ἐν θρόνῳ Διὸς
παθεῖν τὸν ἔρξαντα· θέσμιον γάρ.
τίς ἂν γονὰν ἀραῖον ἐκβάλοι δόμων;   1565
κεκόλληται γένος πρὸς ἄτᾳ.

FTr   1537 εἴθε μ' Tr   1540 δροίτας FTr   νῦν κατέχ. Tr
χαμεύναν FTr   1542 ἔρξαι F   1545 E. A. J. Ahrens: ψυχὴν
ἄχαριν FTr   1547 Casaubon: ἐπιτύμβιος αἶνος FTr   1551 οὔ σε
F, οὔτε Tr   Karsten: μέλημα λέγειν FTr   1553 κάπτεσε κάτ-
θανεν Tr   1555 Auratus: -νειαν· ἵν' FTr   1559 Stanley:
φιλήσῃ FTr   1563 Schütz: χρόνῳ (-ῳ Tr) FTr   1565 Hermann: ῥᾶον F, ῥᾷον Tr   1566 Blomfield: προσάψαι FTr

Κλ. ἐς τόνδ᾽ ἐνέβης ξὺν ἀληθείᾳ
χρησμόν· ἐγὼ δ᾽ οὖν
ἐθέλω δαίμονι τῷ Πλεισθενιδᾶν
ὅρκους θεμένη τάδε μὲν στέργειν   1570
δύστλητά περ ὄνθ᾽, ὃ δὲ λοιπόν, ἰόντ᾽
ἐκ τῶνδε δόμων ἄλλην γενεὰν
τρίβειν θανάτοις αὐθένταισιν·
κτεάνων δὲ μέρος βαιὸν ἐχούσῃ
πᾶν ἀπόχρη μοι μανίας μελάθρων   1575
ἀλληλοφόνους ἀφελούσῃ.

ΑΙΓΙΣΘΟΣ

ὦ φέγγος εὖφρον ἡμέρας δικηφόρου·
φαίην ἂν ἤδη νῦν βροτῶν τιμαόρους
θεοὺς ἄνωθεν γῆς ἐποπτεύειν ἄχη,
ἰδὼν ὑφαντοῖς ἐν πέπλοις Ἐρινύων   1580
τὸν ἄνδρα τόνδε κείμενον φίλως ἐμοί
χερὸς πατρῴας ἐκτίνοντα μηχανάς.
Ἀτρεὺς γὰρ ἄρχων τῆσδε γῆς, τούτου πατήρ,
πατέρα Θυέστην τὸν ἐμόν, ὡς τορῶς φράσαι,
αὐτοῦ δ᾽ ἀδελφόν, ἀμφίλεκτος ὢν κράτει,   1585
ἠνδρηλάτησεν ἐκ πόλεώς τε καὶ δόμων·
καὶ προστρόπαιος ἑστίας μολὼν πάλιν
τλήμων Θυέστης μοῖραν ηὗρετ᾽ ἀσφαλῆ,
τὸ μὴ θανὼν πατρῷον αἱμάξαι πέδον
αὐτοῦ· ξένια δὲ τοῦδε δύσθεος πατήρ   1590
Ἀτρεύς, προθύμως μᾶλλον ἢ φίλως, πατρί
τὠμῷ, κρεουργὸν ἦμαρ εὐθύμως ἄγειν
δοκῶν, παρέσχε δαῖτα παιδείων κρεῶν.

FTr   1567 Canter: ἐνέβη FTr   1569 -ιδῶν sscr. Tr
1570 θεμένα (sscr. η) Tr   1571 δύσπλητά F   1573 om. Tr   1574
δὲ Auratus: τε FTr   1575–6 πᾶν, ἀπόχρη μοι δ᾽ ἀλληλ. μαν. μελ.
ἀφελούσῃ (-ῃ Tr) FTr, transposuit Erfurdt, δ᾽ del. Canter   1582
χειρὸς Tr   1585 Elmsley: αὐτοῦ τ᾽ FTr   1588 εὗρετ᾽ FTr
1590 ξενίᾳ Tr

τὰ μὲν ποδήρη καὶ χερῶν ἄκρους κτένας
†ἔθρυπτ᾽ ἄνωθεν ἀνδρακὰς καθήμενος†   1595
ἄσημα δ᾽ αὐτῶν αὐτίκ᾽ ἀγνοίᾳ λαβών
ἔσθει, βορὰν ἄσωτον, ὡς ὁρᾷς, γένει·
κἄπειτ᾽ ἐπιγνοὺς ἔργον οὐ καταίσιον
ᾤμωξεν, ἀμπίπτει δ᾽ ἀπὸ σφαγὴν ἐρῶν,
μόρον δ᾽ ἄφερτον Πελοπίδαις ἐπεύχεται,   1600
λάκτισμα δείπνου ξυνδίκως τιθεὶς ἀρᾷ·
οὕτως ὀλέσθαι πᾶν τὸ Πλεισθένους γένος.
ἐκ τῶνδέ σοι πεσόντα τόνδ᾽ ἰδεῖν πάρα·
κἀγὼ δίκαιος τοῦδε τοῦ φόνου ῥαφεύς·
τρίτον γὰρ ὄντα μ᾽ †ἐπὶ δέκ᾽† ἀθλίῳ πατρί   1605
συνεξελαύνει τυτθὸν ὄντ᾽ ἐν σπαργάνοις·
τραφέντα δ᾽ αὖθις ἡ Δίκη κατήγαγεν
καὶ τοῦδε τἀνδρὸς ἡψάμην θυραῖος ὤν,
πᾶσαν συνάψας μηχανὴν δυσβουλίας.
οὕτω καλὸν δὴ καὶ τὸ κατθανεῖν ἐμοί,   1610
ἰδόντα τοῦτον τῆς Δίκης ἐν ἔρκεσιν.

Χο. Αἴγισθ᾽, ὑβρίζοντ᾽ ἐν κακοῖσιν οὐ σέβω·
σὺ δ᾽ ἄνδρα τόνδε φὴς ἑκὼν κατακτανεῖν,
μόνος δ᾽ ἔποικτον τόνδε βουλεῦσαι φόνον·
οὔ φημ᾽ ἀλύξειν ἐν δίκῃ τὸ σὸν κάρα   1615
δημορριφεῖς, σάφ᾽ ἴσθι, λευσίμους ἀράς.

Αι. σὺ ταῦτα φωνεῖς, νερτέρᾳ προσήμενος
κώπῃ, κρατούντων τῶν ἐπὶ ζυγῷ δορός;
γνώσῃ γέρων ὢν ὡς διδάσκεσθαι βαρύ
τῷ τηλικούτῳ, σωφρονεῖν εἰρημένον·   1620
δεσμὸς δὲ καὶ τὸ γῆρας αἵ τε νήστιδες
δύαι διδάσκειν ἐξοχώταται φρενῶν

FTr   1594 χερῶν Tr : χρεῶν F   1599 Canter : ἄν· πίπτει
FTr   Auratus : σφαγῆς FTr   1602 Tzetzes (An. Ox. Cramer
iii. 378. 10) : ὀλέσθη FTr   1609 ξυν- Tr   1611 ἰδόντι Tr
1612 Heyse : ὑβρίζειν FTr   1613 Pauw : τόνδ᾽ ἔφης FTr   1617
νετέρᾳ F   1621 δεσμὸν F, fort. recte

ἰατρομάντεις. οὐχ ὁρᾷς ὁρῶν τάδε;
πρὸς κέντρα μὴ λάκτιζε, μὴ παίσας μογῇς.

Χο. γύναι, σὺ τοὺς ἥκοντας ἐκ μάχης μένων   1625
οἰκουρὸς εὐνὴν ἀνδρὸς αἰσχύνων ἅμα
ἀνδρὶ στρατηγῷ τόνδ᾽ ἐβούλευσας μόρον;

Αι. καὶ ταῦτα τἄπη κλαυμάτων ἀρχηγενῆ·
'Ορφεῖ δὲ γλῶσσαν τὴν ἐναντίαν ἔχεις·
ὁ μὲν γὰρ ἦγε πάντ᾽ ἀπὸ φθογγῆς χαρᾷ,   1630
σὺ δ᾽ ἐξορίνας νηπίοις ὑλάγμασιν
ἄξῃ· κρατηθεὶς δ᾽ ἡμερώτερος φανῇ.

Χο. ὡς δὴ σύ μοι τύραννος Ἀργείων ἔσῃ,
ὃς οὐκ, ἐπειδὴ τῷδ᾽ ἐβούλευσας μόρον,
δρᾶσαι τόδ᾽ ἔργον οὐκ ἔτλης αὐτοκτόνως.   1635

Αι. τὸ γὰρ δολῶσαι πρὸς γυναικὸς ἦν σαφῶς·
ἐγὼ δ᾽ ὕποπτος εχθρὸς ἦ παλαιγενής.
ἐκ τῶν δὲ τοῦδε χρημάτων πειράσομαι
ἄρχειν πολιτῶν· τὸν δὲ μὴ πειθάνορα
ζεύξω βαρείαις, οὔτι μὴ σειραφόρον   1640
κριθῶντα πῶλον, ἀλλ᾽ ὁ δυσφιλὴς σκότῳ
λιμὸς ξύνοικος μαλθακόν σφ᾽ ἐπόψεται.

Χο. τί δὴ τὸν ἄνδρα τόνδ᾽ ἀπὸ ψυχῆς κακῆς
οὐκ αὐτὸς ἠνάριζες, ἀλλὰ σὺν γυνή,
χώρας μίασμα καὶ θεῶν ἐγχωρίων,   1645
ἔκτειν᾽; 'Ορέστης ἀρά που βλέπει φάος,
ὅπως κατελθὼν δεῦρο πρευμενεῖ τύχῃ
ἀμφοῖν γένηται τοῖνδε παγκρατὴς φονεύς.

Αι. ἀλλ᾽ ἐπεὶ δοκεῖς τάδ᾽ ἔρδειν καὶ λέγειν, γνώσῃ τάχα.

FTr   1624 schol. Pind. Pyth. ii. 173: πήσας FTr   1625
μένων Wieseler: νέον FTr   1626 Keck: αἰσχύνουσ᾽ FTr   1631
Jacob: ἠπίοις FTr   1634 τῷδε βουλεύσας F   1637 ἢ Porson:
ἢ FTr   1638 Casaubon: τῶνδε FTr   1641 Auratus: κότω
FTr   1646 ἆρα ποῦ Tr

Χο. εἶα δή, φίλοι λοχῖται, τοὔργον οὐχ ἑκὰς τόδε.   1650

Αι. εἶα δή, ξίφος πρόκωπον πᾶς τις εὐτρεπιζέτω.

Χο. ἀλλὰ κἀγὼ μὴν πρόκωπος, οὐδ᾽ ἀναίνομαι θανεῖν.

Αι. δεχομένοις λέγεις θανεῖν γε· τὴν τύχην δ᾽ αἱρούμεθα.

Κλ. μηδαμῶς, ὦ φίλτατ᾽ ἀνδρῶν, ἄλλα δράσωμεν κακά·
    ἀλλὰ καὶ τάδ᾽ ἐξαμῆσαι πολλά, δύστηνον θέρος·   1655
    πημονῆς δ᾽ ἅλις γ᾽ ὑπάρχει· μηδὲν αἱματώμεθα.
    †στείχετε δ᾽ οἵ† γέροντες πρὸς δόμους [πεπρωμένους
    τούσδε]
    πρὶν παθεῖν ἔρξαντα· κυροῦν χρὴ τάδ᾽ ὡς ἐπράξαμεν·
    εἰ δέ τοι μόχθων γένοιτο τῶνδ᾽ †ἅλις†, δεχοίμεθ᾽ ἄν,
    δαίμονος χηλῇ βαρείᾳ δυστυχῶς πεπληγμένοι.   1660
    ὧδ᾽ ἔχει λόγος γυναικός, εἴ τις ἀξιοῖ μαθεῖν.

Αι. ἀλλὰ τούσδ᾽ ἐμοὶ ματαίαν γλῶσσαν ὧδ᾽ †ἀπανθίσαι†
    κἀκβαλεῖν ἔπη τοιαῦτα δαίμονος πειρωμένους,
    σώφρονος γνώμης δ᾽ ἁμαρτεῖν τὸν κρατοῦντά ⟨θ᾽ ὑβρίσαι⟩.

Χο. οὐκ ἂν Ἀργείων τόδ᾽ εἴη, φῶτα προσσαίνειν κακόν.   1665

Αι. ἀλλ᾽ ἐγώ σ᾽ ἐν ὑστέραισιν ἡμέραις μέτειμ᾽ ἔτι.

Χο. οὔκ, ἐὰν δαίμων Ὀρέστην δεῦρ᾽ ἀπευθύνῃ μολεῖν.

Αι. οἶδ᾽ ἐγὼ φεύγοντας ἄνδρας ἐλπίδας σιτουμένους.

Χο. πρᾶσσε, πιαίνου, μιαίνων τὴν δίκην, ἐπεὶ πάρα.

FTr   1651 αἴγ(ισθος) primitus, mox χορὸς praefixit F: nota
nulla Tr   1652 choro, 1653 Aegistho dedit Stanley: contrarie FTr
1652 πρόκωπος post correctionem G: -κοπος F, -κοπτος Tr   οὐδ᾽
Lobel, nisi κοὐκ (Fraenkel) praeferendum: οὐκ FTr   1653
γε Lobel: σε FTr   Auratus: ἐρούμ- FTr   1654 Victorius:
δράσομεν FTr   1655 θέρος Schütz: ὁ ἔρως FTr   1656
Scaliger: ὕπαρχε FTr   Jacob: ἡματ- FTr   1658 ἔρξαντες
F   scripsimus: καιρὸν χρὴν (χρὴ Hartung) FTr   Victorius: ἐπραξάμην FTr   1659 Hermann: γ᾽ ἐχοίμεθ᾽ FTr   1662 Is. Vossius:
τούσδε μοι FTr   1663 Casaubon: δαίμονας FTr   1664
Casaubon: δ᾽ ἁμαρτῆτον FTr   finem suppl. Blomfield   1665
προσαίνειν F

64   ΑΓΑΜΕΜΝΩΝ

Αι. ἴσθι μοι δώσων ἄποινα τῆσδε μωρίας χάριν.   1670

Χο. κόμπασον θαρσῶν, ἀλέκτωρ ὥστε θηλείας πέλας.

Κλ. μὴ προτιμήσῃς ματαίων τῶνδ᾽ ὑλαγμάτων· ⟨ἐγώ⟩
     καὶ σὺ θήσομεν κρατοῦντε τῶνδε δωμάτων ⟨καλῶς⟩.

FTr   1671 θαρρῶν FTr   Canter: ὥσπερ FTr   1672–3
suppl. Auratus, Canter, ex schol. vet. Tr; sed τῶνδε suspectum

COMMENTARY

1 ff. The Watchman is lying on the roof of the Atridae's palace, looking out into the night. The principal theme of the play is indirectly revealed in the first few lines: the audience at once recognizes the man whom Aegisthus posted to give warning of the arrival of Agamemnon (*Od.* 4. 524 ff.); though here he is soon observed to be a loyal servant of Agamemnon, not as in the *Odyssey* a hired spy.

This simple man's feelings, his fear of his mistress and affection for his master, are delicately portrayed in a brief space; and the note of foreboding, which gathers volume steadily as the play proceeds, is already sounded here (19, 36–39). In the whole of extant Greek Tragedy there are few characters of such brief appearance so memorably drawn.

1. For the use of μέν at the start of a work, with or without a subsequent δέ or equivalent, see *Gk. Particles*, pp. 382 f. Here as in *Suppl.* 1 the initial μέν is solitary; neither καὶ νῦν in 8 nor νῦν δέ in 20 provides a formal answer to it.

2. φρουρᾶς: in apposition to πόνων, explaining it; 'release from toils— the yearlong vigil . . .'. μῆκος is adverbial, 'of a year *in length*', the normal idiom in definitions of measure. It may have been specially intended to clarify ἐτείας here: unlike ἐνιαύσιος, which may mean either 'yearlong' or 'annual', ἔτειος elsewhere is restricted to the meaning 'annual', and would naturally convey that meaning here if μῆκος did not assist it. In general cf. *Od.* 4. 526, of the watchman appointed by Aegisthus: φύλασσε δ' ὅγ' εἰς ἐνιαυτόν. ἣν κοιμώμενος: φρουρὰν κοιμῶμαι may stand for φρουρὰν κοιμώμενος φρουρῶ, 'vigil which I keep while lying abed', whether we call this an extension of the cognate accus. (φρουρὰν κοιμώμενος for φρουρὰν φρουρῶν) or simply a condensed expression (brachylogy) of a type common in Aeschylus; cf. 10 below, where ὧδε κελεύει κρατοῦσα is abbreviated to ὧδε κρατεῖ. κοιμώμενος: though the Watchman speaks of his bed (13) and describes himself as dozing (15) he does not mean here that he *goes to sleep* during his watch (though that is what κοιμᾶσθαι usually implies). He means 'lying abed' without sleeping; cf. *Od.* 20. 4, where Odysseus goes to bed and Eurynome ἐπὶ χλαῖναν βάλε κοιμηθέντι, 'when he was in bed' (not 'asleep', as v. 6 shows, κεῖτ' ἐγρηγορόων).

3. 'At the house of the Atreidae, up aloft, like a dog.' στέγαις (locative) gives the general situation; ἄγκαθεν (equivalent to ἄνωθεν) adds the detail 'up above', i.e. on the roof; κυνὸς δίκην illustrates ἄγκαθεν, since the roof is the place where you might expect to find the house-dog sleeping at night (see Fraenkel for evidence on this point). ἄγκαθεν was correctly explained by Schneidewin in *Philol.* iii (1848) 116 ff.: it is a contraction of ἀνάκαθεν, which corresponds to ἀνακάς, 'above', as ἔκαθεν to ἑκάς; cf. Hesych. ἀνακάς· . . . ἄνωθεν, ἐν ὕψει, ἄνω, and Pind. *Ol.* 2. 22 where ἀνακάς has been corrupted to ἀναβᾶσ' in some MSS. and in others to ἀνεκάς (which is the regular spelling of this word elsewhere: ἀνεκάς, ἀνέκαθεν, probably under the mistaken impression that it is related to ἑκάς, ἔκαθεν). The form ἄγκαθεν, '(from) above', recurs at *Eum.* 373 ἄγκαθεν (commonly altered by edd. to ἀνέκαθεν) βαρυπεσῆ καταφέρω ποδὸς ἀκμάν. Although in *Eum.* 80, ἄγκαθεν λαβὼν βρέτας, the meaning is undoubtedly 'in your arms' (ἄγκαθεν for ἀγκάς), as 259 shows, yet it remains certain that ἄγκαθεν could not mean 'in (or on) my arms' in *Agam.* 3: ἄγκαθεν κοιμώμενος might possibly (with ἄγκαθεν for ἀγκάς) be said of *A* reclining in *B*'s arms: it could not possibly describe a man resting on *his own* arms (or elbows); moreover a man in such an attitude would not noticeably resemble a dog (κυνὸς δίκην); nor would it be possible to adopt a more uncomfortable posture for observing the stars.

For στέγαις, perhaps στέγης (Schneidewin), governed by ἄγκαθεν, 'on top of the roof'.

4 ff. The 'bright potentates conspicuous in the sky' (6, the more important stars and constellations) are contrasted with the commonalty (ὁμήγυριν), and the word δυνάστας glances at the fact that they control some of man's most important affairs, especially the seasons in farming and navigation.

7. There are difficulties here which are most commonly solved by removing the line from the text. That seems a desperate remedy, since nobody can give a plausible reason why such a line should have been added; indeed the theory of interpolation is practically ruled out by the language—an interpolator, wishing to say 'whensoever they set or rise', would probably have written δύνωσιν for φθίνωσιν and ἀν(α)τέλλωσί τε for the rest; he would certainly not have ended his phrase with the definite article τῶν used as a demonstrative pronoun (= αὐτῶν, 'of them'). Against these considerations we have to set certain objections to the word ἀστέρας: (1) It seems weak and repetitive, especially after the powerful λαμπροὺς δυνάστας; the force of this objection, in itself not very great, is further reduced by the numerous parallel examples of this trick of style adduced by Headlam–Thomson from Aeschylus. (2) It is contrary to Aeschylus' practice to begin an iambic trimeter with a word of dactylic scansion (ἀστέρᾰς|): an abnormality of this type may be thought to weigh lightly in the scales; *Cho.* 986 begins with ἠλῐŏς, and it seems very special pleading to urge that ἥλιος there is a proper name, and that proper names might have special treatment; moreover, as Maas points out, *Cho.*

216 καὶ τίνα at the beginning of an iamb. trim. is equally unparalleled in Aeschylus. (The beginning of a line in this position, compatible with ἀ]στέ[ρας, is now attested by a papyrus-text of the second century A.D. (P. Oxy. 2178): this means that the line already existed in the Alexandrian edition of Aeschylus; and though there remains a possibility that an interpolation of the kind in question here *might* have established itself securely in the standard texts before the era of Alexandrian scholarship, our first duty must be to inquire what meaning the great scholars of the third and second centuries B.C. attached to the texts which they published.)

If the text is substantially correct, its interpretation must start from the following points: (1) as Fraenkel puts it, 'ὅταν φθίνωσιν . . . cannot stand in an indirect question [see further A. G. Laird in *CR* xvi (1922) 37 ff., replying to A. C. Pearson in *AJP* 33. 426 ff.], but can only mean "whensoever they disappear"'; (2) the sentence provides only one possible antecedent to ὅταν φθίνωσιν, viz. τοὺς φέροντας χεῖμα καὶ θέρος, 'the stars which bring winter and summer . . . whensoever they set or rise'; these are especially the Pleiads, but other stars (e.g. Arcturus, Sirius) may be and probably are included here. To this it has been fairly objected that the separation of the governing clause (τοὺς . . . βροτοῖς, or τοὺς . . . δυνάστας) from the governed (ὅταν φθίνωσιν) by the additional descriptive phrase (ἐμπρέπ. . . . ἀστέρας, or λαμπροὺς . . . ἀστέρας) is abnormal and displeasing: it is indeed so, but it is what our MSS. offer, and we have no alternative but either to tolerate it or to find a better solution than the removal of a line from the text. It is by no means certain that anything is fatally amiss until we come to the words ἀντολάς τε τῶν: here we must face the fact that, since ὅταν φθίνωσιν and what follows must depend on τοὺς φέροντας χεῖμα καὶ θέρος, the accusative ἀντολάς is unintelligible. 'Whensoever they fade or rise' might be expressed in the form ὅταν φθίνωσιν ἀντολαῖς τε τῶν, 'whensoever they fade and by their risings'; but an accus. case, ἀντολάς τε, would be utterly inexplicable. Why the poet wrote ἀντολαῖς τε τῶν instead of ἀντολαῖσί τε, it is impossible to guess and may be vain to inquire; we can only be certain that an interpolator would not have written so.

Tr. 'I know the assembly of the stars at night, and those which bring winter and summer to mortals—bright potentates, stars conspicuous in the sky—whensoever they set and by their risings.'

8. 'And so now, I am keeping watch for the prearranged sign (τὸ σύμβολον) of the torch (= the beacon, cf. 28, 287, 296, 312).' **φυλάσσω** as in *Il.* 2. 251, LSJ s.v. B 2.

9–10. For the use of τε, joining ἀλ. βάξιν to that which it defines (φάτιν), see *Gk. Particles*, p. 502. 'Tidings of capture'; cf. *ScT* 635 ἁλώσιμον παιᾶνα, 'paean celebrating capture'.

10. **κρατεῖ**: 'exercises power' (*dominatur*, not *iubet*; Fraenkel ad loc.).

11. Lit. 'a woman's manly-purposed heart expectant': Clytemnestra, full of guilty fear (because of her dealings with Aegisthus) and eagerness (to avenge the death of Iphigeneia) seems constantly to *expect* the signal for Agamemnon's return in this tenth year.

12–16. εὖτ' ἂν δέ is resumed by ὅταν δέ below, after the interruption caused by the parenthetic γάρ-clause, which takes the thought a stage farther; the fresh start at ὅταν, instead of repeating the content of εὖτ' ἂν κτλ., proceeds from the point attained at the end of the parenthesis.

12. νυκτίπλαγκτον: the Watchman gets up at intervals and walks about to keep himself awake. He lies down now in one place, now in another; it is not only he, but also the place where he lies (εὐνή), that changes position. νυκτίπλαγκτος εὐνή exactly describes the fact.

13 ff. Robertson, *CR* lviii (1944) 34 f., makes the attractive suggestion that the medical metaphor in 17 is to be recognized already in ἐπισκοπουμένην and παραστατεῖ: ἐπισκοπεῖσθαι = 'watch over the sick-bed', cf. [Demo.] *in Neaeram* 56 τὰ πρόσφορα τῇ νόσῳ φέρουσαι καὶ ἐπισκοπούμεναι; the Dreams, like Fear and Sleep in the next line, are more or less personified. With παραστατεῖ Robertson compares S. *Phil.* 674 f., τὸ γὰρ | νοσοῦν ποθεῖ σε ξυμπαραστάτην λαβεῖν, and Hierocles, p. 54 von Arnim, οἷα δὲ δὴ ἐν νόσοις παραστάτις.

14. It is possible, but not certain, that some emphasis was intended to fall on ἐμήν: if so, the emphasis comes not from its position in the line (see Headlam, *On Editing Aeschylus*, pp. 5 ff.) but from its position in the sentence, divided as it is from its noun by the participial clause. The suggested meaning would then be: '*other people* may go to sleep and dream, but not *I*'.

15. For τὸ μή with infin., of *prevention*, cf. 1589 below, Goodwin, *MT*, § 811 ff.

16. τοῦτο κατὰ τὴν παροιμίαν φησὶ τὴν λέγουσαν ' φρουρᾶς ᾄδει ', Schol. vet. Cf. Ar. *Nub.* 721 φρουρᾶς ᾄδων, 'singing on sentry-go'.　δοκῶ: 'have a fancy to . . .', LSJ s.v. I. 3 b.

17. 'Incising a cure' is a typically condensed expression for 'curing by means of incision', τομῇ; a common metaphor (cf. 849 below, *Cho.* 539 ἄκος τομαῖον) in fifth-century literature. The object of ἐν- in ἐντέμνων is 'the patient' (here 'myself'; -όμενος would have been apt, but is not specially called for).　ἀντίμολπον: the phraseology in E. *Med.* 1176 f. is (no doubt fortuitously) very similar, ἀντίμολπον ὀλολυγῆς κωκυτόν. Lit. 'Incising this remedy, a song-antidote to sleep', i.e. singing as a cure for, and antidote to, sleep.

19. διαπονουμένου: apparently 'being managed', 'being taken care of'; the verb here lacks the emphasis on 'hard work' which is expected and always found elsewhere.

21. ὀρφναίου: 'in the darkness'; elsewhere always 'dark'.

21–22. δεῖ διαστήματος ὀλίγου, εἶτα ἀνακραγεῖν ὡς θεασάμενον τὸν πυρσόν (Schol. vet.): the Watchman leaps up in joy and amazement at the sight of the beacon; there is no need to suppose a pause or interval of any noticeable duration.

22. νυκτός: better with λαμπτήρ, 'lamp of night' (def. gen.) than adverbially with ἡμερήσιον φάος, 'showing light of day by night'; the verbal contrast, νυκτὸς ἡμερήσιον, is obvious in either case.

23. πιφαύσκων: with φάος, 'making manifest' (cf. *Pers.* 662); with χορῶν κατάστασιν, 'giving the signal for' (cf. *Eum.* 620, where βουλῇ πιφαύσκω δ' ὕμμ' ἐπισπέσθαι πατρός = 'I give you the signal to, i.e. order you to, conform to my father's will.'). **χορῶν κατάστασιν**: a common way of celebrating success, cf. E. *Alc.* 1154 f., *H.* 763 f., and S. *El.* 278 ff., where Clytemnestra is said to set up dances, χοροὺς ἵστησι, to mark the anniversary of Agamemnon's murder.

26. σημαίνω, not σημανῶ: he refers to his cry ἰοὺ ἰού; 'by this shrill cry I am announcing to the queen that she should rise etc.', Paley.

27. ἐπαντείλασαν: rising from her bed. ὡς ἐπὶ ἄστρου ἢ σελήνης, Schol.: but it is a disagreeable conceit, that Clytemnestra should be asked to 'rise' like the stars or moon. The verb ἐπανατέλλω has no such implication in (e.g.) *Cho.* 282, E. *H.* 1053, *Ph.* 105.

27 ff. λαμπάδι is best taken with ἐπ-ορθιάζειν, **δόμοις** with the content of the whole, 'for the benefit of the house'; i.e. 'raise, for the household, a loud cry of good omen over this beacon'. ὀλολυγμός is a loud cheerful cry, especially uttered by women; cf. 594 ff. below, γυναικείῳ νόμῳ | ὀλολυγμὸν ... | ἔλασκον εὐφημοῦντες; E. *Med.* 1173 n.

29. εἴπερ: as usual, confident in tone, almost 'since ...', whereas εἰ δή is usually sceptical; *Gk. Particles*, p. 223, n. 1.

30. The Oxyrhynchus Papyrus no. 2178, a text of the second century A.D., preserves traces of the first two letters of this line: ἑάλωκεν was certainly not its reading, πέ[πτωκεν may have been. **ἀγγέλλων πρέπει**: lit. 'is conspicuous announcing'.

31. The idea that the Watchman dances a *pas seul* at this point is not supported by the text, which refers the activity to the future, χορεύσομαι not χορεύομαι.

32–33. The metaphor is taken from a game played with pieces moved on a board according to the fall of dice. Treble six, τρὶς ἕξ, won the game outright; θέσθαι was the regular term for moving the pieces in accordance with the fall of the dice. (LSJ s.v. A vii. 2. θέσθαι in this sense should govern the piece, ψῆφον, not the dice-throw as apparently here: τὰ εὖ πεσόντα θήσομαι is probably a condensed expression of Aeschylean type, 'I shall move the throw' standing for 'I shall move the pieces according to the throw.' Quite different are Sophocles fr. 947 P., στέργειν δὲ τἀκπεσόντα καὶ θέσθαι χρεών, where ψῆφον, if anything, is to be understood with θέσθαι, 'put up with the fall of the dice, and make your move'; and Socrates in Stobaeus iv. 56. 39, where the phrase τίθεσθαι τὸ συμβαῖνον is at once clarified by ὥσπερ ψῆφόν τινα.)

The literal meaning may then be: 'Since this beacon-watching has thrown me a treble-six' (i.e. a win outright, victory; he may now expect the reward of his services, and share in the general rejoicings), '*I shall move my master's lucky throw.*' What this means is shown by γάρ in 32, which attaches these lines closely to 31, 'I myself shall dance the prelude': the connexion of thought is, 'My masters having had a winning throw, I shall move their pieces accordingly', i.e. I shall do what the victor does to declare his success—in the game, the moving of the pieces into the winning positions, in this context the starting of a dance of celebration: 'I myself shall dance a prelude; what I mean is (γάρ), I shall make the move consequent upon my masters' successful throw.'

34 ff. The Watchman's jubilation is brief. Agamemnon has a long way to come; and when he does reach home, what a home it is! He moderates his tone: 'Well, the great thing is (**δ' οὖν**), may he get safely home.' **βαστάσαι** suggests a warm, prolonged handclasp: but Agamemnon, when he appears, does not impress us as a man accustomed to greeting his servants warmly.

36. βοῦς ἐπὶ γλώσσῃ: this homely phrase is found also in Theognis 815, Strattis (*Comic. Attic. Fragmenta* i, p. 731 Kock) fr. 67; παροιμία ἐπὶ τῶν μὴ δυναμένων παρρησιάζεσθαι, Hesychius. Elsewhere we find the less undignified image of a key, a seal, or a door.

37 f. As Thomson says, 'possibly the phraseology is designed to indicate the nature of the secret: E. *Hipp.* 415 ff. (of adulterers), πῶς ποτ' ... | βλέπουσιν ἐς πρόσωπα τῶν ξυνευνετῶν, | οὐδὲ σκότον φρίσσουσι τὸν ξυνεργάτην, | τέραμνά τ' οἴκων, μή ποτε φθογγὴν ἀφῇ;'

38–39. ἑκών: to be taken with both parts of what follows; the meaning is 'I am careful so to express myself that the initiated will understand, while to anyone who is not in the secret I can say "I have no recollection of hinting at anything at all".'

40–103. The Chorus tell of the setting forth of the Greek army years ago (40–71); they explain that they were too old to join the expedition (72–82), and give the reason for their presence now on the scene (80–103: they have come to find out the cause 'of this post-haste and romage in the land'). The emotions described in the opening are those which the Chorus felt when the army sailed for Troy; though they later claim to have had misgivings even then (799–804). But at 62 a shadow falls over the picture of righteous heaven-sent vengeance: after all, the cause of this great enterprise was πολυάνωρ γυνή, a promiscuous woman; and Greeks, no less than Trojans, will lose their lives. Present and future alike are ominous: the gods, it is clearly hinted, are angry and will prove implacable (71). At 99–103 the

Chorus's misgivings are plainly expressed: they proceed (104-257) to tell in full the story which explains their anxiety.

40. μέν implies the apodosis '(it is ten years since the fleet sailed), *and now* . . .': but the μέν-clause is greatly protracted, and the nearest thing to an answering δέ-clause is 67 f. ἔστι δ' ὅπῃ νῦν ἔστι.   ἐπεί: 'from the time when . . .'.

41. ἀντίδικος: adversary at law. This metaphor recurs often in *The Oresteia*: Priam is the defendant, Menelaus the plaintiff; Zeus gives judgement against Paris, and sends the Atridae to reclaim the stolen property and to exact the penalty awarded by the court.

43 f. διθρόνου τιμῆς ζεῦγος: the phrase naturally describes two persons joined together in the honour of kingship; the genitive is descriptive, defining that of which the ζεῦγος consists. And now a further defining genitive is added to ζεῦγος: the 'yoke' or 'pair' consists of 'the Atridae'; the whole is heavy but clear, 'the steadfast Atridae-partnership of two-throned and two-sceptred privilege from Zeus'.

45 ff. στόλον . . . ἦραν: 'put their fleet to sea', not '*raised* a fleet'.

47. ἀρωγήν is in apposition to the content of the preceding clause, a common idiom. The word here probably has a legal colour; see Fraenkel.

48. κλάζοντες Ἄρη: 'shouting warlike cries', cf. A. *PV* 355 συρίζων φόβον, *ScT* 386 κλάζουσι . . . φόβον. μέγαν (codd.) is awkward, and the small and easy change to **μεγάλ'** is supported by *Il.* 16. 428 f. ὥστ' αἰγυπιοὶ . . . μεγάλα κλάζοντε, evidently in Aeschylus' memory at this moment. (μεγάλα, adverbial, not elsewhere in Aesch. (but Eur. *Andr.* 189, *Tro.* 1277, al.; A. *Eum.* 791 leg. μεγάλατοι) here directly taken from the Epic model.)

49 ff. The vultures' nest has been robbed: the gods send the Erinyes to punish the robber. In the other term of the comparison the Atridae represent *both* the robbed vultures *and* the avenging Erinyes—it is they whom Zeus sends to punish the robber (60 f.). The detail is difficult at two points: (1) **ἐκπατίοις ἄλγεσι:** the adjective would naturally mean 'off the beaten track (πάτος)'; and so it does, according to Schol. here (ἔξω τῆς ὁδοῦ), Hesychius (ἐκπάτιον· τὸ ἔξω πάτου) and Erotian on Hippocrates (41. 16 Nachm. ἐκπατίως· ἐκτρόπως—a unique and ambiguous word—καὶ [. . .] ὁδοῦ ἀγνοοῦντες). There is no other evidence about the word, and no indication that it might mean anything else, except that the analogy of ἔκτοπος suggests the possibility of its meaning 'extraordinary', 'out-of-the-way' in the sense 'excessive', 'extreme', or the like. (If this meaning is adopted, it will be preferable, if not necessary, to interpret παίδων as objective genitive, 'in extreme grief *for* their children'; E. *Hec.* 1256, K.-G. i. 335.)

But if, as the evidence indicates, ἐκπατίοις would be understood to mean 'off the beaten track', this was surely not intended to be merely a mode of describing the region where vultures are normally at home: 'eagles and vultures were notoriously remote and solitary', as Headlam says; from the vultures' point of view (and also from the poet's) 'off the beaten track' is their proper place, and we must not introduce a note of false pathos by imagining that the poet thought that the 'sufferings' of the nestlings were any the worse for being 'off the beaten track' in this sense, as if some special hardship were involved therein. The truth is surely quite different. The whole point of the word lies in the fact that the nestlings are *not* in their natural home; they are *missing*; the 'children' ($\pi\alpha\acute{\iota}\delta\omega\nu$) are not to be found in their 'beds' ($\lambda\epsilon\chi\acute{\epsilon}\omega\nu$); that is why the parent-vultures are so distressed, and, in such a context, there is no other conceivable reference for $\acute{\epsilon}\kappa\pi\alpha$-$\tau\acute{\iota}o\iota s$—the nestlings are suffering in some (*to them and their parents*) unknown and unfriendly region, they are $\acute{\epsilon}\kappa\pi\acute{\alpha}\tau\iota o\iota$, 'missing from their familiar ground'. The attachment of the adjective to the sufferings instead of the sufferers is unusually bold, comparable with $\chi\lambda o\epsilon\rho\alpha\hat{\iota}s$ $\lambda\epsilon\acute{\iota}\mu\alpha\kappa os$ $\mathring{\eta}\delta o\nu\alpha\hat{\iota}s$ in E. *Ba.* 866 f.

With the causal dative **ἄλγεσι** compare $\phi\acute{o}\beta o\iota\sigma\iota$ in S. *Ajax* 531 (Fraenkel). **παίδων** here, like $\emph{ἶνιν}$ in 717 below, is abnormal (usually only of *human* offspring).

(2) **ὕπατοι λεχέων**: see especially Housman *J.Phil.* xvi (1888) 247, Headlam ad loc. $\emph{ὕπατος}$, a superlative form, does not (it is alleged) elsewhere govern a genitive with the sense 'high above something'; hence the attractive conjecture $\emph{ὑπατηλεχέων}$ (Headlam). Yet it is not by any means certain that $\emph{ὕπατοι λεχέων}$ cannot stand here in the sense required: for what exactly is the difference between this phrase and $\emph{ὕπατος χώρας}$ in 509 below? Most edd. seem to think that the meaning in 509 is 'highest *of* the land', i.e. the highest possessed by, belonging to, the land. That may be a possible, but it is certainly not a natural, way of describing the supreme authority of Zeus: much more probably $\emph{ὕπατος χώρας Ζεύς}$ in 509 means (as LSJ say) 'supreme *over* the land'; and, if so, it is no longer reasonable to object to $\emph{ὕπατοι λεχέων}$ in the sense 'very high above the nest', since in each place the genitive denotes that above which the subject is elevated ($\emph{ὕπατος}$)—in 509 metaphorically, in this place literally; and what is permitted in the metaph. usage must be permissible in the literal one.

For $\lambda\acute{\epsilon}\chi os$ of a bird's nest, Fraenkel compares *ScT* 293, S. *Ant.* 423 ff.

52. A ship is often said to 'fly' (though its 'wings' are usually sails, not oars): here and in a few other places the reverse metaphor occurs, and a bird is said to 'row'; E. *IT* 289 $\pi\tau\epsilon\rho o\hat{\iota}s$ $\acute{\epsilon}\rho\acute{\epsilon}\sigma\sigma\epsilon\iota$, *Ion* 161 $\acute{\epsilon}\rho\acute{\epsilon}\sigma\sigma\epsilon\iota$ $\kappa\acute{\upsilon}\kappa\nu os$, Virgil's *remigio alarum.*

53. **δεμνιοτήρη**: their labour involves 'watching over the bed' of their offspring; *cubiliprema* (better *cubiliserva*) *cura pullorum,* Hermann.

54. πόνον ὀρταλίχων: 'toil over their brood'; E. *Suppl.* 1135 πόνος . . . τέκνων, *Med.* 1261 μόχθος . . . τέκνων, 'labour *for* children'. ὀλέσαντες: it was a labour which they were unwilling to give up; they may be said to have *lost* it.

55. In the Epic, ὕπατος is used only of Zeus, and is always metaphorical ('supreme in power'). Here it evidently covers Apollo and Pan as well as Zeus, and the meaning must therefore be literal ('on the heights').

It is natural to say of Zeus and Pan that they dwell 'high up', and that they avenge the wrong done to birds; one would not have expected to find Apollo in this company. See Fraenkel's discussion.

56–57. Lit. 'shrill-cried lamentation uttered by the birds'. γόον: 'lament *for the dead*', as usual; the vultures know that they will not see their brood again.

57. τῶνδε μετοίκων: this use of the demonstrative pronoun ὅδε, to denote something of which mention was made a moment ago, is rare; there is a clear example in Hesiod, *op.* 80 f. ὀνόμηνε δὲ τήνδε γυναῖκα | Πανδώρην, where τήνδε means (like τῶνδε here) 'the one of whom I was just speaking'. There is a still more remarkable use in this play, at 645 below, παιᾶνα τόνδ' Ἐρινύων, where '*this* paean' means 'the one I *implied* a moment ago' (viz. in 636 κακαγγέλῳ γλώσσῃ). μετοίκων: 'Those lofty regions belong really to the gods; they alone have full rights of citizenship therein. The birds that are permitted to live there too are μέτοικοι in the heavenly πόλις; they stand accordingly under the protection of heaven', Fraenkel.

58. ὑστερόποινον: 'late-avenging', LSJ. That would suit the punishment of Paris, delayed ten years, but not the matter to which it is applied—requital for the vultures. Probably 'avenging after the act', as in *Cho.* 383, cf. ὑστεροφθόροι . . . Ἐρινύες in S. *Ant.* 1074 f., without any idea of lateness. The Erinyes execute the will of Zeus as well in the animal as in the human world: *Il.* 19. 418 Ἐρινύες ἔσχεθον αὐδήν, of the horse Xanthus.

60. ὁ κρείσσων is odd and unusual, perhaps corrupt.

61. ξένιος: Paris was a guest under Menelaus' roof at the time when he eloped with Helen; the point is often made (e.g. 399 ff. below) that it was especially this breach of the laws of hospitality which incurred the displeasure of Zeus. That Zeus *sent* the avenging army to Troy, and that it was his will that Troy should fall, is repeatedly stated: cf. also 362 f. Δία . . . τὸν τάδε πράξαντα, 367 Διὸς πλαγάν, 526 Διὸς μακέλλῃ, 701 ff., 748 πομπᾷ Διός, 813 ff. See the Introduction, p. xxiii n. 3.

62. πολυάνορος: Helen had several 'husbands' (Theseus, Menelaus, Paris, and yet others according to some authorities).

63. παλαίσματα is separated from the verb (θήσων) which governs it by the two genitive absolute phrases.

65. προτελείοις: the meaning here is unknown. προτέλεια, without further qualification, means 'rites preliminary *to marriage*' (κυρίως ταῖς πρὸ γάμου θυσίαις, Schol.); and since Paris and Helen are mentioned at the beginning of this sentence it is the more natural to suppose that ἐν προτελείοις here alludes to their wedding. Indeed it is hard to see what else could possibly fit both the phrase and the context: but we must then suppose that Aeschylus for the moment forgets that the wedding of Paris and Helen *preceded* the fighting at Troy (699 ff. below).

(No other explanation takes proper account of the marriage-association of the word προτέλεια; nor is any plausible answer given to the question '*to what* are these preliminaries (if they have nothing to do with a wedding-ceremony) *preliminary*?'—'To the ultimate fall of Troy', according to the Scholiast: the context is strongly against it. 'Spears shattered *preliminary to the use of swords*', Schütz: this may securely be left out of the discussion. Simply 'in the prelude of the battle', Sidgwick: but what could be the point of confining the πολλὰ παλαίσματα to the *prelude* of the battle?)

67 f. 'Things are wherever now they are; and are being fulfilled to their fated end.' The Chorus (who do not know 'how things now are') mean simply that there is no way of altering the course of events. The idiom is to be distinguished from examples of the type of E. *Med.* 889 ἐσμὲν οἷόν ἐσμεν, S. *OC* 273 ἱκόμην ἵν' ἱκόμην, which are euphemistic, the answers to the implied questions being perfectly well known to the speakers.

69–71. See Farnell, *CR* xi (1897) 293 ff. (1) οὔτε δακρύων is probably a gloss on the impossible οὔθ' ὑποκλαίων, corrected by Casaubon to οὔθ' ὑποκαίων: 'In a Christian narrative the repentant sinner might naturally be said to . . . weep bitterly; but with Greek methods of atonement for sin weeping and tears have nothing to do' (l.c., p. 296). (2) ὑπο- in ὑπολείβων is meaningless and therefore presumably corrupt; although, as Prof. Dover observes, there is a tendency in Greek to use the same prefix with co-ordinate verbs when the prefix is appropriate to only one of the two, as in Antiphon, 3 β 8 οὐ συνηδομένων [μὲν] οὐδὲ συνεθελόντων, συναλγούντων δὲ καὶ συλλυπουμένων, where συν- makes sense with the second pair but not with the first. ἐπιλείβων is good, ἀπολείβων better (cf. Hesiod, *theog.* 793). (3) Greek sacrifices may be broadly distinguished as either ἔμπυρα (esp. animals, killed and burnt) or ἄπυρα (esp. fruits and wine, not burnt). The antithesis here is plain: 'neither with burnt sacrifice (ὑποκαίων, sc. ἔμπυρα) nor with pouring from unburnt offerings (ἀπύρων ἱερῶν partitive gen. with ἀπολείβων).' (Fraenkel states as a 'decisive objection' that 'ἐπιλείβων . . . clearly means the pouring of a libation over burnt sacrifice': it is hard to see the force of this, for whatever the libation is poured *over*, it is poured *from* 'unburnt' sacrifices (e.g. wine); and

the common distinction between burnt and unburnt could not be
more clearly marked.)

71. With ὀργὰς ἀτενεῖς we must supply 'of the gods', and with **παραθέλξει** the subject 'anybody'. The former supplement is not very
easy in the context, the latter usage is highly abnormal in Tragedy
(though, as Prof. Dover observes, the nom. participles ὑποκαίων,
ἀπολείβων do much to help). Perhaps something like ⟨βροτὸς ἀθανά-
των⟩ has dropped out before ὀργὰς κτλ.

72. ἀτίται: 'unhonoured' seems the only possible sense here, though
the passive use of an agent-noun is illogical and abnormal, and the
word itself would be expected to mean 'not paying', from τίνω, not
τίω, as in *Eum.* 257. (The suggestion that 'not paying' here could
stand for 'unable to pay the debt of military service to the state', i.e.
simply 'unfit for military service', is not supported by the usage of
τίνω and its cognates, and is surely ruled out by its obscurity.)

75 f. For the use of νέμειν see LSJ s.v. A III. 2.

76 f. Since the point is the *weakness* of the youthful body the lordly
word ἀνάσσων seems out of place. ἀνᾴσσων, 'leaping up', 'rushing up',
is no great improvement in this respect, and is an unnatural term to
describe the movement of the marrow in the bones: but, as Prof. Dover
suggests, Aeschylus may have believed that marrow was pumped
through the bones like sap, and that this process accompanied
growth; thus here he may be referring to the time of life when one is
still growing. (There seems to be no useful parallel: Aristotle, *hist.
anim.* 521ᵇ8, implies only that the marrow is *fluid* in young bodies,
fatty or lardy in adults.)

78. 'And Ares is not at his station', i.e. warlike spirit has not yet occupied its proper place in the body. (Fraenkel objects that 'ἐνί equivalent to ἐν does not occur in drama': but ἐνί here is not 'equivalent to
ἐν', since ἐστί must obviously be supplied with it. When the verb
εἶναι is omitted, the longer form of a preposition is normally used
(Wackernagel, *Synt.* ii. 166): thus ἔνι for ἔνεστι in *Pers.* 738, *PV* 294,
and ἐνι (however accented) for ἐστὶν ἐν here; note that οὐκ ἐστιν ἐν
χώρᾳ, 'is not at his station', differs in sense from οὐκ ἔνεστι χώρᾳ, 'is not
in the district'.)

79 ff. 'And extreme old age, its leafage already withering, goes its ways
on three feet' (i.e. with a staff to support its two feet).

81. ἀρείων: masculine πρὸς τὸ σημαινόμενον, as Triclinius says, 'in view
of the sense', though the neuter τὸ ὑπέργηρων is formally the subject
of the sentence. It remains, however, very doubtful whether the true
reading has been recovered at the beginning of 79.

83 ff. The form and content of this address to Clytemnestra strongly
and immediately suggest that she is present on the scene. There is
nothing (either here or at any later point) to show at what moment
she entered: but we are evidently meant to understand that she is

now, and remains throughout the choral song down to 258, present and engaged in sacrificial ritual (87 θυοσκεῖς, of which we are reminded in 262 θυηπολεῖς). That one who may fairly be called the principal person in the play should enter thus unannounced and remain silent, not even replying to questions directly addressed to her, throughout the Parodos (about one-eighth of the play), is a procedure so extraordinary—however dramatically effective—that many have denied its possibility, preferring an opinion equally anomalous, viz. that questions of this nature might be addressed to a person who is *not* on the scene. (E. *Hipp.* 141 ff. is fundamentally different: in *Agam.*, the Chorus know what the Queen is doing and ask her—several times, as if expecting an answer—why she is doing it; in *Hipp.* the Chorus do not know what the Queen is doing, and make suggestions, put in the form of questions to which, in the context, it is obvious that no answer is expected. S. *Ajax* 134 ff. is so different in kind that it may be left out of the discussion.) It is to be noticed that at 255 ff. neither Clytemnestra nor the Chorus refers to an *entrance*: on the contrary the Chorus refer to an activity in which the Queen is at that moment engaged, offering sacrifice (262 θυηπολεῖς). (It is perfectly natural that the Chorus should not formally draw attention to the fact of their arrival until the Parodos is finished; 258, ἥκω—a word, incidentally, as a rule spoken by *the later* of two arrivals.)

87. περίπεμπτα: the Queen sends heralds (cf. *Od.* 20. 276 f.) round the city ordering sacrifices, which are therefore poetically called περίπεμπτα, an accusative cognate to the verb θυοσκεῖς. Lit. 'By persuasion of what message do you supervise sacrifices sent round about?'

88. ἀστυνόμων: 'administering the city', having the city under their management. As a rule 'city' in the political sense is πόλις, not ἄστυ, and the gods are more often called πολιοῦχοι, πολισσοῦχοι; but cf. *Suppl.* 1018 ff. ἀστυάνακτας μάκαρας θεοὺς γανάοντες πολιούχους.

89. τ' οὐρανίων codd.: but the θεοὶ ἀστυνόμοι have just been divided into two main categories, those 'above' and those 'below', i.e. Olympians and Chthonic deities (cf. *Suppl.* 24 f. ὕπατοι . . . καὶ βαρύτιμοι χθόνιοι); it seems clumsy now to append to this a subdivision of the former category, τῶν ὑπάτων, distinguishing them as either οὐράνιοι (which means the same thing as ὕπατοι in this context) and ἀγοραῖοι. For θεοὶ θυραῖοι see Tertullian, *de Idol.* 15, *de cor. mil.* 13 (Maas).

94 ff. Lit. 'Medicined by the soft guileless comfort of holy unguent, an oil belonging to the royal house, from the inner chambers.' Flames are springing up everywhere, not only from altars but also from torches fed by oil. **χρίματος**: χρῖμα means an *unguent*, and oil might be so called because used for that purpose; it seems odd to call it an 'unguent' in a context in which it is being used as *fuel*. **ἀδόλοισι**: genuine, i.e. unadulterated.   **παρηγορίαις**: παρηγορεῖν implies 'soothing, giving *comforting* advice'. On πελανῷ see Fraenkel and LSJ s.v. I.

97 ff. In 98 codd. M V have αἰνεῖν, F Tr εἰπεῖν: but τε in παιῶν τε γενοῦ must originally have coupled γενοῦ to another imperative. αἶνει ('consent', imperative) was mistakenly altered to αἰνεῖν under the impression that it was governed by θέμις. 'Tell us what you can and may, and consent and be healer . . . .' (It is not possible to treat λέξασα αἶνει as if it were equivalent to αἰνέσασα λέξον, in the general sense of *placeat tibi dixisse*.)

101. ἃς ἀναφαίνεις: ἀγανὴ (sc. ἐλπίς) φαίνουσ' is more imaginative and would do very well here; but it would then be hard to explain why cod. M has ἀγανά and φαίνεις.

103. The metre is so thoroughly dislocated, and the MSS.' variants so widely divergent (probably including glosses mixed with text), that nothing but merest guesswork is possible here.

104–257. The Chorus describe a portent, sent to the Atridae at Aulis, and Calchas' interpretation thereof. Two eagles devoured a pregnant hare: Calchas infers that the eagles represent the two Atridae, the hare the city of Troy; he concludes that the Atridae will capture Troy.

Calchas is a reader of signs (125 τεράζων), not an inspired visionary (like Cassandra, for example): but the poet's purpose requires that he should take a step beyond his brief, and draw a further conclusion only indirectly suggested by the visible portent. He therefore suggests that Artemis is likely to be offended by the death of the mother hare, and that she will not leave it unrequited: the portent has a bad side as well as a good, and trouble may be expected for the army at Aulis and for the house of Atreus hereafter.

Aeschylus' treatment of this portent, and in particular of Artemis' anger against Agamemnon, is in some respects obscure and in others plainly unsatisfactory; some indication of the difficulties is given in the Introduction, pp. xxiii ff.

104. κύριός εἰμι: 'I have full authority'; they were eyewitnesses of the events.   **ὅδιον κράτος αἴσιον:** Aeschylus uses language with remarkable freedom: κράτος, 'command', here can signify nothing but 'the commanders', the Atridae; yet both ὅδιον and αἴσιον are adjectives applicable to portents, not to those who receive portents. (For ὅδιος cf. 157 ὀρνίθων ὁδίων, the only other occurrence of the word except by conjecture in E. *El.* 162, *Hypsipyle* I. iv. 30; Hesychius (= Trag. Adesp. 242) gives it as an epithet of Hermes, cf. *Il.* 24. 375 f. ὁδοιπόρον . . . αἴσιον, of Hermes.) 'The auspicious command on the road' means 'the commanders who met with auspicious omens on the road'.

104–5. ἀνδρῶν ἐκτελέων. '(command) of young men in their prime'.

ἐκτελής = 'full-grown', as in E. *Ion* 780 ἐκτελῆ νεανίαν; cf. *Pers.* 218, Hes. *op.* 466. ἀνδρῶν is objective genitive; κράτος ἀνδρῶν here means the same thing as Ἀχαιῶν κράτος and Ἑλλάδος ἥβας ταγάν in the immediate sequel.

105–7. The subject of καταπνείει is πειθώ (for its action here, cf. *Eum.* 885 f., 970 f.); it cannot be αἰών, for a man's 'age' (time of life) could not be said to '*breathe down*' upon him, especially '*from the gods*'. This part of the sentence is clear and certain: 'For still from heaven Persuasion breathes down (upon me)'; καταπνείει as in Plato Comicus fr. 173. 14 K. μή σοι νέμεσις θεόθεν καταπνεύσῃ.

The following jumble of words, μολπὰν ἀλκὰν σύμφυτος αἰών, defies interpretation. Adequate sense is given by the text offered here, **μολπᾷ δ' ἀλκᾶν κτλ.**, 'and my time of life (αἰών) is naturally adapted to (σύμφυτος) a song of valorous deeds' (ἀλκαί, as in Pind. *Nem.* 7. 12, Bacchylides 11. 126, E. *Rhes.* 933). **σύμφυτος**: 'congenital' passes easily into the sense 'congenial', 'naturally adapted to', cf. Plato, *Laws* 844ᵇ ἀνδρία . . . τισὶ τόποις σύμφυτος; Aristotle, *de anim.* 420ᵃ4 ἀκοῇ συμφυὴς ἀήρ.

110. ταγάν: on the prosody see Fraenkel; elsewhere τᾱγα, but τᾱγος, hence ξύμφρονε ταγώ conj. Dindorf.

111. δορὶ δίκας πράκτορι codd.: a gloss δίκης, explaining πράκτορι, has invaded the text, ousting καὶ χερί, restored from the quotation of this passage by Aristophanes, *Ran.* 1289.

114 f. 'The King of birds—the dark one, and the one white from behind —appearing to the King of ships'; the balance οἰωνῶν βασιλεύς— βασιλεῦσι νεῶν is highly artificial.   **ὁ κελαινός**: the Golden Eagle (Aristotle's μελανάετος, the Homeric μέλας or μορφνὸς θηρητήρ). **ὁ ἐξόπιν ἀργᾶς**: the White-tailed Eagle, or Erne, vulgarly called πύγαργος.   **ἀργᾶς**: a contraction of ἀργάεις (codd. ἀργίας is an unintelligible form), exactly like τιμῆς for τιμήεις in *Il.* 9. 605. Heath's conjecture ἀργής has the advantage of being a word found elsewhere in Tragedy, but is perhaps not so likely to have been corrupted.

116. χερὸς ἐκ δοριπάλτου: 'on the spear-brandishing hand', i.e. on the right, therefore well-omened, hand.

117. ἕδραισιν: places where they sit or settle (not 'quarters of the sky').

118 f. Text and interpretation are uncertain. βοσκ. λαγίναν γένναν has been said to mean *vescentes leporino genere*, where 'family of hares' stands for 'hare' simply: but this is intolerable in a context which is dealing with 'the hare's family' in a very different sense ('offspring'). Presumably γέννα here means not 'birth' but 'bearer', an anomaly parallel to that in *PV* 850, where γέννημα, elsewhere always 'thing begotten', means 'begetting'; and to that in Alcaeus fr. 129. 7, where Hera is called πάντων γενέθλαν, '*mother* of all'. The expression λαγίνα γέννα = 'hare-mother', is suitable to the oracular style, though in this context the ambiguity is displeasing.   ἐρικύμονα

φέρματι (the best that can be made of the corrupt tradition) = 'pregnant with that-which-is-born', 'with offspring'.

120. βλαβέντα codd., but γένναν βλαβέντα (for βλαβεῖσαν) is intolerable. From Fraenkel's discussion on 562 below it appears that the only other clearly attested examples of masc. participle with fem. substantive in classical Greek are Pind. *Ol.* 6. 15 πυρᾶν νεκρῶν τελεσθέντων (certainly corrupt: see Robertson, *Proceedings of the Cambridge Philological Society*, 1924, 35) and *Agam.* 561-2 δρόσοι . . . τιθέντες, where, however, the noun is widely separated from the participle, and the incoherence may have been intentional. Metathesis converts βλάψαντε to βλάψεντα, and the change to βλαβέντα was then easy enough. It is not certain that the consequential change of βοσκόμενοι to -ομένω need be adopted, for fluctuation between dual and plural is not uncommon (K.–G. i. 73). Lit. 'Having hindered (the hare-mother) from its last runnings', i.e. having prevented it from achieving what is in fact its last course. For the phrase and construction cf. *Od.* I. 195 ἀλλά νυ τόν γε θεοὶ βλάπτουσι κελεύθου; Oppian, *Hal.* ii. 441 καί μιν ὁδοῦ βλάπτουσι.

122 ff. Of several ways in which these words might be construed, the context suggests as preferable the following: (1) **ἰδών** governs 'the portent': cf. Rose, *JHS* lxxii (1952) 131; there is no point in saying that at this moment he *saw* the Atridae, who had been present throughout. (2) **δύο . . . Ἀτρεῖδας** is the predicate, **λαγοδαίτας (πομπούς ἀρχᾶς)** the direct object of **ἐδάη**; **μαχίμους** is perhaps better taken with the Atridae than with the eagles: 'he understood the devourers of the hare to be the two warlike Atridae twain in temper'. The eagles are **πομπούς ἀρχᾶς**: that this is a likely interpretation of the ambiguous MS. tradition is shown by 110 above, ταγὰν πέμπει . . . θούριος ὄρνις; the eagles are said to give a send-off to the commanders —'command' here for 'commanders', cf. 104 κράτος. **λήμασι δισσούς** is an obscure expression. **δισσούς** must mean 'double' in the sense 'divided' (see Jebb on S. *El.* 645): but since δισσ. Ἀτρείδ. is a common expression for 'the two Atridae', the word here is something of an abuse. As for **λήμασι**: though λῆμα often connotes *courage*, the distinction here is not between the courage of Agamemnon and the cowardice of Menelaus. Though the latter is once called μαλθακὸς αἰχμητής in the *Iliad* (17. 587 f.) by an enemy who has a motive for decrying his valour (see Schol. and Leaf ad loc.); and though a similar taunt is found in E. *Or.* 754, 1201 f., and a few other places; yet in general his reputation is that of a good fighter, ἀρηίφιλος, βοὴν ἀγαθός, δουρὶ κλειτός, and nowhere in this play is his courage called in question—least of all in the present passage, where μαχίμους applies to both Kings equally, even if it be taken in agreement with λαγοδαίτας. The difference in temperament between Agamemnon, the supreme commander, choleric, vain, and selfish, and Menelaus, the inferior chieftain, uxorious, unpretentious, is clearly marked in the Epic tradition: and it is hard to see what except this general difference is intended by λήμασι δισσούς here. Menelaus is in general a less dominating character than Agamemnon, just as the White-tailed Eagle was in general thought to be inferior to the Golden Eagle. In neither term of the comparison is the *cowardice* of the inferior party implied—indeed it is ruled out for both by the adjective μαχίμους. Whatever Sophocles may have said about the cowardice of the White-tailed Eagle (fr. 1085 P., πύγαργος . . . ἐπὶ τοῦ δειλοῦ), no such allusion is possible here.

126. ἀγρεῖ: a characteristic use of present for future tense in prophecy.

127 ff. πύργων κτήνη προσθετὰ cod. M. If κτήνη here means, as usual, 'herds' (the sense 'possessions', offered by Schol. here and Hesychius, is not found elsewhere, though some have assumed it in Hesiod fr. 94. 49), we must divide πρόσθε from τά and render lit. 'all the herds, the numerous public ones, in front of the towers . . .'. This has some very unwelcome features: (1) in the portent, the eagles devour the hare with the (unborn) young *inside* it; how could this portend the destruction of cattle *outside* Troy? And what is the point of referring to the destruction of *cattle outside Troy*, when the destruction of *humans inside Troy* is a much more serious matter? Who can believe that Aeschylus wrote anything so disappointing as this, 'Troy will fall—*and all the cattle outside its walls will be destroyed*'? (2) The article τά with the adj. δημιοπληθῆ is not wanted, indeed hardly intelligible. (3) The interruption of πύργων πρόσθε by the object of the sentence, κτήνη, is very harsh (Pind. *Ol.* 3. 12, γλεφάρων Αἰτωλὸς ἀνὴρ ὕψοθεν, quoted by Fraenkel, is almost if not quite as harsh; *Il.* 4. 54, 12. 445 f., where the intervening words are of a fundamentally different nature, are not comparable).

The reading of cod. M is not much more satisfactory, for (1) πύργων, denoting the fortress as a whole without reference to its fortifications, is abnormal; (2) κτήνη will have to mean 'possessions'; these two objections are perhaps not unanswerable, but (3) πρόσθετα is very difficult: the sense 'additional' is out of place, and the only other possibility is 'given up', 'made over' (by debtor to creditor), a sense attested in an inscription of the mid-fourth century from Mylasa (*SIG* 167. 12 = Schwyzer 746 A 12), (κτήματα) πρόσθετα ποιήσαντες Μανσσώλλῳ; LSJ s.v. II.

δημιοπληθῆ (-θέα O. Müller, to restore exact metrical correspondence): consisting of many δήμια, public properties. Cf. *Pers.* 122 γυναικοπληθὴς ὅμιλος, a crowd of many women, *Suppl.* 29 f. ἀρσενοπληθῆ ἐσμόν, a swarm of many males.

130. μοῖρα: 'doom' in the sense 'death' (not 'division', 'apportionment').

131 ff. 'Only let no malice from the gods darken the great curb of

Troy, struck beforehand, marshalled as an army.' προτυπέν: struck before they even start for Troy, clarified by στρατωθέν: 'formed as an army' (i.e. assembled to form an army *at Aulis*). The mixture of metaphors is reckless: 'overcloud' does not suit 'curb', and προτυπέν, στρατωθέν proceed without regard for the meaning of στόμιον.

134. οἴκῳ codd., which would have to be taken with ἐπίφθονος, leaving the dative κυσὶ πατρός (= the eagles) without any possible means of attachment to the sentence.

136. αὐτότοκον = σὺν αὐτῷ τῷ τόκῳ, Schol. πρὸ λόχου: before birth-giving; λόχος here and *Suppl.* 677 only in this sense.

140–5. Text and interpretation are extremely doubtful.

περ: see *Gk. Particles*, pp. 481 ff., whence it appears that περ in τόσον περ is likely to be intensive, not concessive; and indeed the intensive force is the more natural here—'Artemis is angry with the eagles for killing the hare; *being, as she is, so well-disposed* to all young animals, she demands fulfilment of what this act portends. But perhaps Apollo will intervene and prevent her from going so far as to demand a death in return for the hare's death.' That seems to be the general sense of this corrupt and in other respects difficult passage. Calchas has said that divine wrath threatens the army because the eagles have offended Artemis by killing and eating a mother-hare: here he continues: 'The Fair Goddess, being so well-disposed to the cubs of fierce lions, and pleasing to the suckling young of all beasts that roam the fields, begs to fulfil what these things portend' (i.e. what the killing of the hare betokens, viz. the retributive death of Iphigeneia). But there are difficulties, some of them apparently insuperable, in the detail: (1) It is uncertain whether the Attic τόσον should be preferred to τόσσ- (cod. M), which recurs in *Pers.* 864, S. *Ajax* 184. (2) ἁ καλά (the indispensable definite article is wanting in cod. M) is an extraordinary appellation for Artemis; but the difficulty here is the less since καλλίστη was a common culttitle for her, and since there is at least no doubt here who is meant. (3) The tradition offers δρόσοις ἀέπτοις: see Etym. Mag. 377. 37 (Aristonicus on *Od.* 9. 222), Αἰσχύλος ἐν Ἀγαμέμνονι τοὺς σκύμνους τῶν λεόντων δρόσους κέκληκε. This unparalleled usage of δρόσος was presumably related to, or inspired by, the Epic ἔρσαι in the sense 'lambs' (as if from ἔρσα, 'dew', though in fact ἔρσαι probably means 'males', and has nothing to do with 'dew'; Giles, *CR* iii (1889) 3. Sophocles fr. 793 P., ψακαλοῦχοι μητέρες, affords no help, since there is no proof that ψακαλός is related to ψακάς or that it has anything to do with 'dew'). (4) What the ancients made of ἀέπτοις here is given by the Schol., τοῖς ἕπεσθαι τοῖς γονεῦσι ⟨μὴ⟩ δυναμένοις: it is natural to say that the cubs cannot *walk* (Aristotle, *hist. anim.* 579ᵇ17), but it seems less natural to express this by saying that they cannot *follow* (cf.

however Aelian, *VH* i 6). Perhaps ἀέπτοις here = Epic ἀάπτοις, 'not to be touched' (see Bechtel, *Lexilogus* s.v.): the lions are fierce (μαλερῶν), and even their cubs are dangerous, not to be handled; the goddess delights in the young of all animals, even the most dangerous. (The conjecture λεπτοῖς is unacceptable, since this adjective is not applicable to such a subject as the young of men or animals.) (5) **μαλερῶν**: presumably 'violent', 'fierce', or the like. In the Epic always of *fire*; of an emotion, *Pers.* 62 (πόθος); of a person or animal, only here and S. *OT* 190 (Ἄρεα τὸν μαλερόν). (6) **ὀβρικάλοισι**: another extraordinary word for 'the young of animals'. (7) **τερπνά**: the context clearly suggests 'taking pleasure in . . .' (cf. *Od.* 6. 104), but 'pleasing to . . .', however unsuitable here, is the only known usage. (8) **τούτων αἰτεῖ ξύμβολα κρᾶναι**: there is no difficulty in αἰτεῖ κρᾶναι, 'she begs to fulfil . . .'; aor. infin. after αἰτεῖ signifies the action for which permission is sought, as in E. *Hec.* 40 f. αἰτεῖ δ' ἀδελφὴν . . . λαβεῖν; the implied object of αἰτεῖ is τὸν Δία—it is a commonplace from the Epic onwards that the lesser gods appeal for authority to Zeus, especially in a matter in which, as here, Zeus himself is closely concerned. τούτων ξύμβολα is much more condensed and cryptic: χειμῶνος σύμβολον, for example, would normally mean 'that which portends a storm', not 'that which a storm portends'; here, however, the genitive must be of the latter type, 'things portended by these events' (viz. by the killing of the mother-hare, the subject under consideration since 131; to Artemis it is a *token* or *portent* of a 'second sacrifice', the death of Iphigeneia). (9) How the next line, **δεξιὰ κτλ.**, fitted on, it is impossible to say, for the explanatory gloss (τῶν) στρουθῶν ('of the birds', explaining what the φάσματα were) has ousted a word, and that word may have given the key to the meaning of the whole. In the text offered here, **δεξιὰ . . . κρίνω** sums up the whole of what precedes and makes an easy transition to the sequel, 'There is a bad side as well as a good one to the visions which I am interpreting: but I entreat Apollo to intervene in our favour . . . .'

150. θυσίαν ἑτέραν: the death of Iphigeneia is called a 'second sacrifice' because 'sacrifice' was the term used of the death of the mother-hare, 137 θυομένοισι.   **ἄνομον**: 'unaccompanied by the flute'; see Lloyd-Jones, *CQ* n.s. iii (1953) 96.

151. σύμφυτον: the sacrifice of Iphigeneia is called an 'innate' feud-maker; it is an integral, ingrained, element in the fabric of destiny. (Auratus' συμφύτων injures the metre, giving an isolated glyconic among the dactyls.)

152 f. The sacrifice of Iphigeneia has been called an 'innate maker of strife', and its character and the nature of the 'strife' are now further indicated by **οὐ δεισήνορα**, 'it has no fear of *any man* (Agamemnon)'; this is further clarified by what follows, lit. 'for there waits a terrible treacherous *housekeeper* (οἰκονόμος is substantive, not adj.),

rising up again, unforgetting child-avenging Wrath', i.e. Clytemnestra will nurse her anger at home until her husband's return, and
will then exact a terrible and treacherous revenge for her daughter's
death. **παλίνορτος**: rising up *in future*; cf. the usage of πάλιν
in *Cho.* 258, *Eum.* 720.

156. ἀπέκλαγξε: ἀπό as in ἀπόφημι (*Il.* 7. 362), 'speak out', 'declare
plainly'; Fraenkel compares further *Hymn. Merc.* 280 μάκρ' ἀποσυ-
ρίζων, S. *Ant.* 1021.

157. μόρσιμα: see Fraenkel; often in a neutral sense, 'destined', sometimes sinister, 'of evil destiny', and so here contrasted with μεγάλοις
ἀγαθοῖς. **ἀπ' ὀρνίθων**: ἀπό of the source from which the forecast comes. **οἴκοις**: dative of that to which speech is addressed.

160 ff. The Chorus has in mind (153 ff.) the danger which impends
over Agamemnon on his return. This heavy burden of anxiety (165)
compels them to turn toward Zeus, to whom alone they can pray for
relief (163–6), for with him alone rests the power (167–75). The transition here to Zeus appears at first sight a little abrupt, but only so
long as we fail to remember that it was he who was responsible for
the gathering at Aulis (60 ff.), he whose action led to the wrath of
Artemis against Agamemnon (114 ff.).

It is vain to search for profound philosophy in 160–83: these simple
lines neither say nor imply more than the man in the street might
have said—that Zeus alone can give relief from the heaviest burdens,
Zeus is all-powerful, Zeus teaches man a hard lesson of 'learning
through suffering' (see on 184 ff. below); and that if you want proof
of his power, consider how he overthrew his own father (cf. *Eum.*
641), just as that father had overthrown his. 176 ff. link this prayer
to Zeus with what follows: Zeus brings understanding to men; the
lesson is compulsory, and a hard one; its pains are not easily forgotten (179–80). His favour is done by force (182–3), as you may see in
the example of Agamemnon (184 ff.).

160. Ζεύς: the nominative is 'pendent', the structure of the sentence
taking a different turn after the long interruption ὅστις . . . προσεν-
νέπω. **τόδ' . . . τοῦτο**: the use of ὅδε and οὗτος as synonyms,
closely together, is found even in the most elegant writing, S. *Ant.*
296 f. τοῦτο καὶ πόλεις | πορθεῖ, τόδ' ἄνδρας κτλ., E. *Med.* 1046, S. *El.* 981.

163 ff. προσεικάσαι means 'liken', 'compare', not 'guess'. Since neither
the accus. of the object nor the dative of that to which the object is
compared is here expressed, it follows that we must recognize an
anacoluthon, an incoherence in the structure of the sentence. The
natural sequel to οὐκ ἔχω προσεικάσαι would be οὐδὲν Διί, 'I cannot compare anything to Zeus', but the coherence is broken
by the participial clause, in which πάντα πλὴν Διός does all that
οὐδὲν Διί could have done, and makes it impossible to revert to the

construction promised by οὐκ ἔχω προσεικάσαι. 'I cannot compare'—
he was going to say 'anything to Zeus'—'weighing in the balance
everything other than Zeus . . .' (οὐκ ἔχω in 163 can only mean
'I cannot': Fraenkel's English, 'I *have nothing whereto* to liken *him*',
is not in the Greek).

165 f. 'If need arises truly to cast away (ἀπό with βαλεῖν) the vain
burden of anxiety.' **μάταν**: *futile*, because being anxious does
nothing to help matters, no good or profit will come of it; 1151
ματαίους δύας is similar. **ἐτητύμως**: as opposed to the unreal,
apparent relief which might be sought or found in other quarters.
The general sense is: in a case where one feels the need to shift from
one's shoulders the burden of care, there is nothing to compare with
Zeus as a source of relief.

168 ff. The references are to Uranus (168–70) and Cronus (171–2). The
poet here illustrates the power of Zeus by alluding to the savage
tales of early Greek theogony: Uranus was once supreme, but overthrown by Cronus; Cronus in turn was dethroned by Zeus.

170. οὐδὲ λέξεται: this seems to be the best that can be done with the
inscrutable οὐδὲν λέξαι of codd.   **πρὶν ὤν**: '(shall not even be
spoken of) as existing formerly'; construction as in E. *IT* 1047
λέξεται . . . ἔχων, 'shall be spoken of as having . . .'.

171 f. τριακτῆρος: 'overthrower', properly of the wrestler who throws
his opponent thrice.

174. ἐπινίκια κλάζων closely together, governing Ζῆνα, 'shouting a
victory-song to Zeus'.

175. τεύξεται φρενῶν τὸ πᾶν: ὁλοσχερῶς φρόνιμος ἔσται, Schol. An odd
expression, apparently 'shall attain good sense in all respects', as
opposed to φρενῶν ἁμαρτάνειν (E. *Alc.* 327), 'to fall short of good
sense'. *Od.* 8. 547, ὀλίγον περ ἐπιψαύῃ πραπίδεσσιν, is similar.

176 f. 'He who set men on the path to understanding, who laid down
the law, "learning through suffering", to hold good' (κυρίως ἔχειν as
in Isaeus 7. 26). The meaningless dative article τῷ (codd.) before
πάθει must be altered to **τόν**: corruption through assimilation of
case-endings, as very commonly.

179 f. Lit. 'Instead of sleep there drips before the heart the pain that
reminds of suffering': this seems to mean that the memory of past
'sufferings' inflicted in the cause of 'understanding' may keep a man
awake at night. The connexions with what follows and what precedes
are abrupt, but the general sense is clear enough: 176–8, Zeus teaches
man a hard lesson; 179–80, not even sleep brings him freedom to
forget it; 180–1, whether he welcomes it or not, he is subject to this
stern discipline.

σωφρονεῖν: see Fraenkel on 584 below, replying to Housman, *CR*
ii (1888) 244, who held that the infinitive without the article cannot
stand as the subject of a verb (except in a well-defined class with the

verbs ἐστί, γίγνεται, ξυμβαίνει). The only examples among those adduced by Fraenkel which appear plainly contrary to Housman's rule are the present passage and 584 below: the latter might be emended or otherwise explained, and here perhaps πόνος is subject of ἦλθε, with σωφρονεῖν = ὥστε σωφρονεῖν. Cf. however the aberration in Lucretius, 4. 765, where the infin. *meminisse* is subject of *iacet*.

182. 'The favour of the gods is forceful': the 'favour' is the privilege of being educated in this manner (πάθει μάθος) by Zeus; **βίαιος** repeats the sense of παρ' ἄκοντας—the lesson is enforced even against the will. Codd. have βιαίως, which would have to be taken with ἡμένων; but the perfect participle, 'being seated', could not possibly be qualified by such an adverb as βιαίως, 'violently'—a man may *sit down* forcibly, he cannot *be seated* forcibly, i.e. *be in a state of sitting down* by force. Nor is βιαίως ἧσθαι conceivable Greek for 'sit, using force' (Fraenkel). Nor yet can it be argued that since σέλμα σεμνὸν ἡμένων means in effect 'being in supreme authority', the adverb βιαίως may qualify the way in which the authority is exercised: 'exercising authority violently' is normal language, 'being seated on the throne of authority violently' is impossible.

183. σέλμα: metaph. from the bench of the steersman in a ship.

184 ff. The antistrophe applies the doctrine of the strophe to the particular case of Agamemnon: he is a victim of the χάρις βίαιος of Zeus.

What exactly is meant by this doctrine, πάθει μάθος? Is it not merely that popular piece of worldly wisdom, *experientia docet*? That is what παθήματα μαθήματα means in Herodotus: is it otherwise here?—Aeschylus tells us that Justice is not man-made: it is a rule for life on earth imposed by Zeus. If you break his law, he will teach you to mend your ways by inflicting punishment; you will learn perforce not to ignore the divine origin and sanction of the rules of conduct which govern civilized society. In effect, πάθει μάθος and δράσαντι παθεῖν are hardly distinguishable maxims: both imply that crime will be followed by punishment, the stern discipline of Zeus will teach you to mend your ways. Does Aeschylus mean no more than this, a doctrine familiar to an Athenian audience since the time of Solon if not earlier? Or is it possible that he may imply something more elevated—for example, that sufferings on earth are divinely imposed in order to refine and purify human character? That life is a path through tribulation toward perfection; that moral and spiritual enlightenment is forged in a furnace of suffering? That punishment is inflicted by Zeus not in exercise of vengeance or abstract justice, but for the instruction and improvement of the sinner? It would be difficult to find in his plays any clear evidence of any such doctrine, and quite impossible to apply it to the case of Agamemnon.

Agamemnon's *sufferings* are indeed clear enough. Zeus has commanded him to go to Troy, Artemis has demanded the death of his daughter beforehand: the deed which he must perform is one of the utmost horror; and he is doomed to be slain by his wife. His μάθος, on the other hand, what he *learns* from all this, is hard to see. Nobody supposes that he was morally improved by the divinely thrust-on killing of his daughter; or that, even if he had emerged from that experience a wiser and better man, his ultimate doom would have been different. And it is obvious that his final suffering, his own death, taught him no lesson at all. Of course others may learn from the example of his fate: this is how Zeus puts mankind in general on the road to understanding, φρονεῖν βροτοὺς ὁδώσαντα; only the sinner himself is excluded from the company of learners. Yet this explanation—that Aeschylus meant that the rest of the world should mark the sinner's doom and accordingly mend its ways—is plainly unsatisfactory, for 179 ff. strongly suggest that it is the sinner himself who is to 'learn through suffering': in Agamemnon's case, at least, it is beyond doubt that πάθει μάθος means no more than δράσαντι παθεῖν; he shall learn that man cannot escape the punishment imposed by Zeus on crime; what he does, he must pay for.

184. πρέσβυς = πρεσβύτερος, as in 205, 530 below; an abnormal usage. This nominative has no verb: the thread is broken at the subordinate clause εὖτε κτλ. 188, and is never resumed.

186. μάντιν οὔτινα ψέγων: 'not blaming any prophet'; the meaning is clear, the idiomatic use of οὔτις is abnormal, but cf. 1099 below.

ἐμπαίοις τύχαισι συμπνέων: lit. 'blowing in the same direction as the events which struck against him', i.e. not resisting the impact of disaster. He neither charged Calchas with untruth (187) nor offered any resistance to the misfortune (of detention at Aulis: the matter of Iphigeneia's sacrifice has not yet been made clear to him) which was forecast by Calchas and which now followed at once. A similar metaphor occurs in 219 below, q.v.

188. κεναγγεῖ: the long delay 'empties the jars' of provisions. (The doctors and comedians use κεν(ε)αγγία and its cognates of *evacuation of the body*: so crude an expression need not, and should not, be detected here.)

188–9. βαρύνοντ' = ἐβαρύνοντο.

190. πέραν accus. of πέρα, 'land opposite'; 'holding' (or simply 'being on') the shore opposite to Chalcis', i.e. at Aulis.

193. '(winds) of harmful idleness, of hunger, of ill-anchorage': the army has more leisure than it wants, it is starved, and its anchorage is turned into a bad one (cf. 195).

194. βροτῶν ἄλαι: the men 'wander' in search of provisions; cf. *Od*. 12. 329 f. ἀλλ' ὅτε δὴ νηὸς ἐξέφθιτο ἤια πάντα, | καὶ δὴ ἄγρην ἐφέπεσκον ἀλητεύοντες ἀνάγκῃ (Prof. Dover compares Thuc. vii. 4. 6, 13. 2). It may be thought that a non-physical sense of ἄλαι, 'distractions (madness)', loosely in apposition to 'the winds', would run smoothly in this context.

196. παλιμμήκη (the word here only): perhaps '(making the time) as long again'; their stay at Aulis is twice as long as it should have been.

197. τρίβῳ: 'by wearing out' (not 'by delay', τριβῇ).

199-200. ἄλλο μῆχαρ βριθύτερον: not 'a further heavier remedy' but 'a remedy additional to the disease and worse than it'; something else worse than the disease, viz. its cure.

201. προφέρων: 'bringing forward' as warrant or authority; cf. 964 προυνεχθέντος.

202 f. For this gesture, denoting distress, cf. *Od.* 2. 80 ὡς φάτο χωόμενος ποτὶ δὲ σκῆπτρον βάλε γαίῃ.

205. For δέ in apodosis see *Gk. Particles*, pp. 177 ff. τότ' (Stanley) is a likely conjecture for τόδ'.

206 ff. δαίξω, ῥείθροις are harsh terms, deliberately chosen.   **λιπόναυς** (212) is, as Fraenkel says, an 'ugly word', signifying a 'criminal act'. It should be obvious that the question in 212 is purely rhetorical: it has only to be stated in this harsh manner for the impossibility of such action to be apparent. Neither Aeschylus nor his audience supposes that the criminal act in question is, for Agamemnon, a real alternative; see the Introduction, pp. xxiv ff.

213. ξυμμαχίας ἁμαρτών: the meaning is uncertain. 'Erring in respect of alliance' in the sense 'failing in duty to allies' involves a use of ἁμαρτάνω c. gen. for which no parallel is forthcoming except possibly *Il.* 24. 68 οὔ τι φίλων ἡμάρτανε δώρων. 'Losing my league' may be preferred (the tense of ἁμαρτών is proper for the act considered in isolation), but is less suitable to the context.

214 ff. θέμις: it is said to be not merely reasonable but actually *right and proper* that the confederate chiefs should demand the sacrifice of Iphigeneia. Agamemnon's position is hopeless from this point of view too: the world at large thinks it his *duty* to do what Artemis commands; and it is certain that Agamemnon's *desertion* (212) would not save the life of Iphigeneia.

σφ(ε): the allies, understood from ξυμμαχίας, or from the context at large. (The MSS. ὀργᾷ—cod. M has the inexplicable marginal variant αὐδᾷ—περιόργως, 'with (?) anger very angrily' is, as one would expect, unparalleled in Greek. The phrases quoted by Fraenkel, *PV* 944 τὸν πικρῶς ὑπέρπικρον, *Il.* 16. 776 μέγας μεγαλωστί, E. *Or.* 811 πάλαι παλαιᾶς ἀπὸ συμφορᾶς δόμων, have no relevance here; they only illustrate adjectives juxtaposed to cognate adverbs; the Latin examples are not more helpful. The Homeric αἴνοθεν αἰνῶς, however it is to be explained, does not noticeably resemble an alleged ὀργῇ περιόργως. What is needed for a parallel is not πικρῶς ὑπέρπικρος or *impudenter impudens* but πικρότητι ὑπέρπικρος or *impudentiā impudens*.)

218. **λέπαδνον**: not the yoke, but the strap which fastens the neck to the yoke. ἀνάγκη here must mean what it says: it is absolutely inconsistent with the idea that Agamemnon had any freedom of choice; what he put on was the harness of *necessity, compulsion*. Aeschylus does not say, what some of the modern critics say, that the necessity was 'self-imposed', 'developed only as a result of his decision to kill his daughter'—ἀνάγκη is the last word a Greek would have chosen to describe or refer to a voluntary decision. (In case anybody should wish to import into this context from LSJ s.v. I. 4 a toned-down meaning, 'bodily pain', 'anguish', it may be worth mentioning that ἀνάγκη in that sense is—as one would expect—used only of *inevitable* pains, *involuntarily* undergone. It hardly needs adding that nobody can seriously believe that the reference in ἀνάγκη here is not to the action which he now undertakes but to *the inevitable consequences of that action*.)

219. 'Breathing his spirit's changing-wind, an impious one'; i.e. as the wind veers from one quarter to another, so his mind changed direction in the instant when he resolved that the command of Artemis must be obeyed. There is no special connexion, apart from similarity of metaphor, between this passage and 187 above. Cf. *ScT* 706 λήματος . . . τροπαίᾳ.

220. **τόθεν**: correlative to ἐπεί, 'from that moment . . .'.

221. **φρονεῖν** is directly governed by μετέγνω (not explanatory infin.), 'decided instead to entertain thoughts of uttermost audacity'. The phraseology is in several respects abnormal, as Professor A. Y. Campbell observes; in particular, μεταγνῶναι regularly means 'to *reverse* a decision, *from bad to good*', and the use with an infinitive (φρονεῖν) is very uncommon (Thuc. i. 44. 1).

222 f. **παρακοπά** is not 'infatuation' or the like, but 'being out of one's wits', 'deranged' ('delirium' in the Greek doctors; cf. *Eum.* 329 f. παρακοπά, παραφορὰ φρενοδαλής). In face of the necessity of performing this appalling act, Agamemnon's state of mind becomes altogether abnormal (219–21): and this is the reason why (γάρ 222) he can bring himself to perform it—because, when a man is out of his proper mind (παρακοπά), his madness suggests evil means to him (αἰσχρόμητις) and emboldens him (θρασύνει) to perform the end; in his right mind he could not perform or even contemplate it. **πρωτοπήμων**: it is this temporary insanity which is the first cause, so far as the human agent is concerned, of the disasters which are to follow; the deed argues an abnormal state of mind, and not until that derangement is present will the thought be translated into action and so the trouble begun.

224. ἔτλα δ' οὖν 'And so (being as he was, mentally deranged,) he had the heart to . . .'; *Gk. Particles*, p. 463.

225. γυναικοποίνων: cf. 62, 447, 779 f. It is all very well to blame Agamemnon for going to war for a woman's sake; but Aeschylus has made it very plain that Zeus thought it was the right thing to do (61 f. *πέμπει Ζεὺς πολυάνορος ἀμφὶ γυναικός*), and (especially) that the nature of the cause of the war had nothing whatever to do with Artemis' demand for the death of Iphigeneia.

226. ἀρωγάν: accus. in apposition to the content of the whole of the preceding clause.

227. προτέλεια ναῶν: 'preliminary sacrifice on behalf of the ships'. Though *προτέλεια* properly means 'rites preliminary to marriage' (see 65 n.), it is very unlikely that there is any allusion here to Iphigeneia's deceptive betrothal to Achilles, a matter ignored by Aeschylus in this play.

228. κληδόνας πατρῴους: an extraordinary expression for 'her cries of "Father"'.

229 f. παρ' οὐδὲν . . . ἔθεντο: 'set at naught', LSJ s.v. *τίθημι* B II. 3. Between these words, perhaps rather *αἰῶ* (= *αἰῶνα*, *Cho.* 350) ⟨τε⟩ *παρθένειον* (conj. O. Müller). For the alleged displacement of *τε* (following noun+adj.) cf. *Suppl.* 282 Κύπριος χαρακτήρ τ'.

230. βραβῆς: normally 'judge' or the like; here and *Pers.* 302 the context requires 'chieftains', an idea easily derived (judge—umpire or overseer—man in charge).

231. μετ' εὐχάν: 'after the prayer'; so in E. *Hec.* 534 the prayer precedes the killing.

232. δίκαν χιμαίρας: this is specially apt, for it was customary to sacrifice a *χίμαιρα* to Artemis Agrotera; see Wecklein and Fraenkel. **ὕπερθε βωμοῦ**: the victim must be firmly held with its throat immediately above the altar, to ensure that the blood fell thereon; see Pearson on E. *Hel.* 1561.

233 f. πέπλοισι περιπετῆ: see especially Lloyd-Jones, *CR* n.s. ii (1952) 132 ff. (1) If *περιπετής* is related to *περιπίπτω*, both normal usage and the fact that *πίπτω* has no passive require that it should be active in meaning; but 'falling around her robes' is mere verbiage; a person cannot *fall around* his clothes, though his clothes may fall around him. If *περιπετής* were, exceptionally, passive (as it appears to be in S. *Ai.* 906 f.: but *περιπετοῦς*, active, may be the true reading there), the meaning would be 'fallen around by her robes', an unnatural expression in itself, absolutely excluded here since Iphigeneia's robes are certainly not falling off her. (2) If *περιπετής* were related to *περιπετάννυμι*, the meaning would be 'spread around by her robes', again an unnatural expression, presumably signifying that her clothes were wrapped round her, or simply that she was covered by her clothes; the sense is unsatisfactory, and *-πετής* from πετάννυμι is not found earlier than medical writers of the following century.

Lloyd-Jones suggests an entirely different approach: πέπλοισι περιπετῆ means '(Iphigeneia) *falling around his* (Agamemnon's) *robes*', as a suppliant; cf. S. *Ant.* 1223 ἀμφὶ μέσσῃ περιπετῆ, E. *Suppl.* 279 ἀμφιπίτνουσα, *Hec.* 787 ἀμφὶ . . . πίπτω, and other passages, of suppliants. This interpretation has great advantages: the thought and the language are now both of a normal type, and—this is a most important point—it becomes possible for the first time to make sense of the following words **παντὶ θυμῷ**, which qualify the idea of supplication implicit in πέπλοισι περιπετῆ, 'fallen about his robes (as a suppliant) with all her heart', cf. Pind. *Nem.* 5. 31 παντὶ θυμῷ . . . λιτάνευεν. On any other view παντὶ θυμῷ has to be taken with λαβεῖν ἀέρδην, and it is really intolerable that Agamemnon should make a point of telling the attendants 'not to be half-hearted' about their task, to act 'with all their heart'; 'with all their strength', if the words could mean that, would be even more grotesque.

It may be objected that the *order* of the phrases is displeasing (πέπλοισι περιπετῆ breaking the coherence of ὕπερθε βωμοῦ—λαβεῖν ἀέρδην): judgement in such a case is specially hazardous and uncertain. If an author had written ἐκέλευσεν ὑπὲρ βωμοῦ τὴν παντὶ θυμῷ ἱκετεύουσαν αἴρειν, nobody would have found much fault with the order of the words; the expression in our text is only a poetical variation of that, and the word-order is at least not so clumsy as in other places, e.g. 1621 f. below.

προνωπῆ: this difficult word of uncertain derivation is taken to mean 'facing downwards', i.e. her throat is above and facing the surface of the altar, so that her blood may fall thereon.

234 ff. 'and with a guard of (= bridle on, cf. χαλινῶν below) her lovely mouth, to restrain a sound which would act as a curse against the house'. Any appeal or cry of pain would be of ill omen, like a curse, at this stage of the ritual; the sacrifice must appear to be voluntary.

καλλιπρῴρου: an extreme example of its type, the compound adjective of which the latter element is meaningless; *ScT* 533 βλάστημα καλλίπρωρον, ἀνδρόπαις ἀνήρ.

239. See Lloyd-Jones, l.c., pp. 134 f. Disrobing by Iphigeneia, whether accidental or deliberate, is out of the question: she has no freedom of movement, being firmly held aloft by the attendants; nor is there the least likelihood that she would do anything so ἀπρεπές ('an unnecessary piece of exhibitionism', as Lloyd-Jones calls it) even if she were able; nor could the action, in this context, have been described by the *present* participle. The phrase means 'pouring her saffron-dyed garment toward the ground': the picture is of a girl held more or less horizontally (see the illustration in Maas's article, *CQ* xliv (1951) 94), wearing a peplos; the lower fulness of her robe, and the upper over-fall, then naturally flow downwards, in the direction of the ground. **χέουσα** (for the interlinear hiatus, see pp. 239 f. below): she is said to be 'pouring them', because they are flowing down from her; thus a charioteer 'pours' the reins to the ground when he lets them fall (*Il.* 17. 619), a woman 'pours' her head-dress when she lets it fall (*Il.* 22. 468 χέε : v.l. βάλε Aristarchus and a few MSS.). The phrase is purely descriptive, and is naturally joined by τε to the other descriptive phrase πρέπουσα κτλ.   **ἐς πέδον** = 'toward the ground' (not '*to* the ground'); cf. S. *Ant.* 269 f. ἐς πέδον κάρα | νεῦσαι, 441 νεύουσαν ἐς πέδον κάρα (quoted by Lloyd-Jones).

(The suggestion that κρόκου βαφάς might signify *blood* (cf. 1121 κροκοβαφὴς σταγών) is ruled out by the context : if Iphigeneia's throat has already been cut, she is in no condition to cast piteous glances at her sacrificers—*each in turn*, 240—and the idea of προσεννέπειν θέλουσα becomes positively macabre.)

241. φιλοίκτῳ: the context demands 'pitiable', which is not what the formation suggests; see LSJ s.v. φιλοικτίρμων and cognates.

242. ἐν γραφαῖς: 'in pictures'. This is not entirely clarified until προσ-εννέπειν θέλουσα is reached : she is the central figure (πρέπουσα) in a painting, but like the figure in the painting she cannot *speak*, though she looks as though she were trying to (θέλουσα).

242 ff. See Fraenkel : it is unheard of in Attic society that the daughter of the house should join the company of men at table in the ἀνδρών, even for the purpose of singing the customary 'paean' at the end of the meal, before the drinking began. It has been suggested that Aeschylus supposed this to be a practice of the Heroic age; but it would be hard to find anything similar in the Homeric poems.

244 f. ἀταύρωτος: elsewhere only Ar. *Lys.* 217, whence it appears that this extraordinary and apparently brutal word means in effect 'chaste'.

246. τριτόσπονδον: 'accompanying the third libation'; the singing of the paean at the end of the meal was accompanied (or preceded) by the pouring of a triple libation.   **φίλου ... φίλως**: see 362 n.   **ἐτίμα**: i.e. sang reverently.

247. τὰ δ' ἔνθεν οὔτ' εἶδον: the implication is that they did see what happened up to this point; if then τὰ ἔνθεν refers to the actual killing of Iphigeneia, it is a fair question to ask how they could have failed to see that too. It appears reasonably certain that τὰ ἔνθεν refers to all that happened *after* the death of Iphigeneia. The Chorus did not accompany the fleet which then sailed from Aulis : they did not see, and do not know, anything further. Here they confine themselves to the safe general statement that Calchas does not make mistakes : he said that Troy would fall (126 ff.), and the Chorus is confident that the Trojans are now getting their deserts.

249 ff. Δίκα κτλ.: lit. 'Justice is coming down (like the scale of a balance) to the disadvantage of the one party (τοῖς μέν), so that they learn through suffering.' ἐπιρρέπει intransitive, cf. *Il.* 14. 99 ὄλεθρος ἐπιρρέπῃ. μαθεῖν is explanatory infin., = ὥστε παθόντας μαθεῖν; ὥστε being omitted, παθόντας must take the case of τοῖς, hence παθοῦσιν.

What persons are meant by τοῖς μέν? And what is the relation of the μέν-clause to what follows? Whether ⟨δ'⟩ is supplied after τὸ μέλλον or not, the contrast between the present (τοῖς μὲν . . . ἐπιρρέπει) and the future (τὸ μέλλον) is strongly marked. The context suggests that τοῖς μέν refers to *the Trojans*: Paris did wrong, and Troy must suffer; the Chorus, confident in Calchas' powers, assume that Troy is getting its deserts—that for them, the Trojans, the scale of Justice is inclining, and they are learning their hard lesson that wrong-doing does not go unpunished. So much for the Trojans, τοῖς μέν: and what about the Greeks? The Chorus are reluctant to express their forebodings: Calchas prophesied victory over Troy, and the Chorus assume that that prophecy is being fulfilled. But Calchas prophesied something else thereafter—a spirit of wrath waiting at home to avenge a daughter's death (154 f.). The Chorus might have continued: τοὺς δὲ (sc. the Greeks) μῆνις μένει τεκνόποινος. But they are, naturally, not so outspoken: they say in effect 'For the present, Justice is paying out the Trojans; as for the future, and our own people, the outlook is dark, but let us not cry before we are hurt.'

251 f. τὸ μέλλον κτλ.: 'As for the future, you will hear about it when it happens; beforehand (πρό), dismiss it from your thought (χαιρέτω, let it go, away with it, LSJ s.v. III. 2 b). It (sc. anticipating the future) is like crying before you are hurt. Clear will it (sc. the future) come together with the rays of early morning.' Such is the surface-meaning: the sense is clear and apt, though it is quite easy to find fault with the detail of the expression. (Some have diagnosed corruption, others have interpreted differently: the rendering by Fraenkel, προχαιρέτω, ἴσον δὲ τῷ προστένειν = 'let it be greeted in advance—but that is equal to being lamented in advance', offers a difficult sequence of thought, in which the relation between ἐπεὶ γένοιτ' ἂν κλύοις, '*you will hear about it when it happens*', and προχαιρέτω, '*greet it in advance*', is particularly obscure.)

254. σύνορθρον αὐγαῖς: if the text is correct, the use of αὐγαί, without specifying whose or what rays they are, is abnormal; Pind. *Isthm.* 4 (3), 65, ἐν δυθμαῖσιν αὐγᾶν, is similar, and here -ορθρον perhaps gives sufficient indication (ὄρθρος is not 'dawn' but the morning twilight preceding sunrise).

255 f. Lit. 'As regards the immediate future (τὰ ἐπὶ τούτοισιν), may execution (accomplishment, or the like; πρᾶξις) turn out well (εὖ with πέλοιτο).' So Miss Lorimer, *CR* xlv (1933) 211.

255 ff. Lit. 'As this ever-present sole-guardian bulwark of the land of

Apia (= Argos, cf. *Suppl.* 260 ff.) desires.' The Chorus are hostile to Clytemnestra. They know, or at least suspect, her intrigue with Aegisthus, and are aware that Agamemnon is in danger of death at her hands on his return (154 f.). And now, according to most of the modern editors, they conclude by expressing the wish 'that all may turn out *as Clytemnestra desires*': the contradiction could hardly be grosser.

The ancients understood it correctly: ἐπεὶ μόνοι γέροντες ἐφύλασσον τὴν Ἑλλάδα, Schol.; i.e. the Chorus here refer *to themselves*, 'may all turn out well as *we* desire', the only thing possible in the context. They call themselves the only solid defence of the state (knowing what they do about Clytemnestra, they are not likely to call *her* the country's 'one and only guardian and protector'). They claim that Agamemnon will find that, so far as his realm has been properly preserved, that preservation is their work; πρέσβος Ἀργείων is their dignified title in 855, 1393 below.   ἄγχιστον: as in Pind. *Pyth.* 9. 64, 'a very present help', as Myers translated it; so also Paley, and similarly Verrall.

259-60. In spite of the deferential manner this is not altogether tactful: in saying that they pay homage to her not for her own sake but because she is a substitute for her absent husband, they betray something of their hostility and contempt toward the woman in power; it is not thus that the Senators address Atossa in *The Persians.*

260. ἄρσενος: governed by ἐρημωθέντος (not an adj. with θρόνου), 'when the throne has been bereft of, left empty by, the male'.

262. εὐαγγέλοισιν ἐλπίσιν: 'hopes of good news'; cf. E. *Med.* 1010 δόξης . . . εὐαγγέλου.

264 f. The 'proverb' is not found elsewhere. 'May dawn, (coming) from its mother Night, bring glad tidings.'

266. μεῖζον ἐλπίδος combines the meanings 'greater than (mere) hope' and 'beyond all hope'.

269. οὖσαν: for the participle after the (implied) verb of speaking, a rare construction, see Jebb on S. *OT* 463 εἶπε . . . τελέσαντα.

271. Elsewhere in Tragedy κατηγορεῖν connotes *accusation* (S. *Ajax* 907, E. fr. 690 are not exceptions): here simply 'declare', as often in Attic and Ionic prose.

272. 'What is it that convinces you? Have you some proof of these things?'

273. ἔστιν· τί δ' οὐχί: 'of course there is'; Fraenkel on 557 below.

275. λάβοιμι: equivalent to δεξαίμην, 'receive', as in *Od.* 7. 255; Fraenkel quotes similar examples from Comedy.

276. ἐπίανεν: 'fattened' (from πιαίνω; not ἐπ-ιαίνω, a non-existent and unlikely compound); the metaph. sense 'cheered', required here, does not recur in Greek until a much later era. The word may be deliberately offensive.   ἄπτερος : in *Eum.* 51, 250 = 'without wings (or feathers)'. Here metaph., as in the formula in the *Odyssey* (four times; not in *Il.*), τῇ δ' ἄπτερος ἔπλετο μῦθος—there, in each place, *A* tells *B* to do something, τῇ δ' ἄπτερος ἔπλετο μῦθος, and without further speech *B* does what she is told: the contexts would be satisfied by either (1) 'And for her his words had no wings', i.e. they did not fly away, but abode in her mind, and she did what she was told; or (2) 'And *her* speech was wingless', i.e. instead of becoming ἔπεα πτερόεντα her words did not issue from her, she made no reply.

In the present passage the meaning is uncertain: simplest is Hermann's interpretation, 'without wings', 'unfledged', in the sense 'immature', 'new-born'; Clytemnestra's reply shows that the Chorus had used uncomplimentary language. (For other views see Headlam–Thomson and Fraenkel.)

277. Cf. *PV* 986 ἐκερτόμησας δῆθεν ὡς παῖδ' ὄντα με.

278. ποίου χρόνου : Verrall's suggestion that this use of ποῖος for πόσος signifies contempt, impatience, or the like, is in accord with E. *IA* 815 ποῖον χρόνον κτλ., Ar. *Av.* 920 ἀπὸ ποίου χρόνου; contrast E. *Hel.* 111 πόσον χρόνον γὰρ διαπεπόρθηται πόλις;   **καί** : giving emphasis, 'and since *when* has the city been sacked?' (*Gk. Particles*, p. 312).

The genitive signifying *duration* of time, or time *within which*, is common: not so the present usage implying '*since what time* . . .'. Similar are Eupolis fr. 181. 1, πόσου χρόνου γὰρ συγγεγένησαι Νικίᾳ; and Ar. *Ach.* 83, πόσου δὲ τὸν πρωκτὸν χρόνου ξυνήγαγεν;

280. τίς with **ἀγγέλων, τόδε** with **τάχος** (adverbial accusative), 'what messenger could arrive with this speed?'

281 ff. The Beacons. Aeschylus' narrative is obscure to us in numerous details. Discussion of the problems, some of which are unsolved, is beyond our present scope. It must suffice to state the leading points briefly, referring the reader to A. C. Merriam, *Papers of the Archaeol. Inst. of America* (Classical Series III), 1890; Verrall, *Introduction*; Calder, *CR* xxxvi (1922) 155 ff.; and especially Fraenkel on 289, 302 f., 306–8, A. J. Beattie in *CR* n.s. iv (1954) 77 ff.

The following beacon-stages are mentioned : (1) From Mt. Ida in the Troad to the Rock of Hermes in Lemnos; over 90 miles as the crow flies. (2) From Lemnos to Mt. Athos; about 50 miles. (3) From Athos to Makistos (location unknown; if in Euboea, the length of the stage would be about 100 miles). (4) From Makistos to Mt. Messapium, overlooking the sea close to the strait of Euripus (if Makistos is in Euboea, the stage is very short, perhaps 15 miles). (5) From Messapium across the plain of Asopos to Mt. Cithaeron; about 26 miles. (6) From Cithaeron over the Lake Gorgopis to the Sheep-roamed mountain: neither of these two localities is certainly identified. (7)

Over the promontory that looks down on the Saronic strait to Mt. Arachnaeum (north of the road from Argos to Epidaurus; Frazer's *Pausanias*, vol. iii, pp. 233 f.).

The principal difficulties are as follows. Several places are unidentified: (i) Makistos: The Scholia's ὄρος Εὐβοίας may be a mere inference from ἐπ' Εὐρίπου ῥοάς. If so, it was not a necessary inference, for 292 f. may mean 'it signals from afar, to the watchers of Messapium, its coming to the streams of Euripus'—Εὐρίπου ῥοάς denoting its destination, since Mt. Messapium is very close thereto. If Makistos is (as is commonly supposed) in central Euboea, the stage preceding it seems unduly long (from Athos), and the stage following it unduly short (to Messapium). It remains very doubtful whether the suggested location is correct, and the difficulty is increased by the fact that there is probably a gap in our text between the mentions of Athos and Makistos. (ii) The 'Lake Gorgopis' and the 'Sheeproamed mountain' are mysterious. The prevailing assumption (it is nothing more) that the mountain is *Geraneia* is to be rejected. No lake (or none of sufficient size or fame to be worth mentioning) exists on the route from Cithaeron to Geraneia: thus the suggested identification has the unhappy result of making the word λίμνη as obscure as its adjective γοργῶπις. Beattie makes the attractive suggestion that αἰγί-πλαγκτον is intended to remind the listener of the island Αἴγι-να: the λίμνη is then satisfactorily identified as the western half of what we call the 'Saronic gulf', land-locked on three sides; while the adjective 'gorgon-eyed' remains as inscrutable as before. The Σαρωνικὸς πορθμός in 306 f. then denotes the crossing from Aegina to the Peloponnesian coast—a most welcome consequence, since the 'Saronic' waters took their name from a river and district on the coast of the Peloponnese more or less opposite the south aspect of Aegina: Σ. πορθμός here and Σ. πόντος in E. *Hipp.* 1200 will then both refer to the same area, the waters between the coast of Epidaurus and Aegina. (Aeschylus is apparently the first to use 'Saronic' of these waters: the use of the term to denote the whole bay from Sunium to the Isthmus is not found until much later, and there is no reason to suppose that Aeschylus could, or did, use it in that sense; in Euripides the limitation is clear enough.)

282. ἀπ': of the source from which the beacon came, viz. 'from the courier-fire'. **ἀγγάρου** (for the prosody see Harrison, *CR* lii (1938) 165; LSJ needs correction): the term used by Herodotus and others for the mounted courier of the Persian 'postal'-system.

285. Cf. Hesychius s.v. Ἀθῷος· ὁ ἐπὶ τοῦ Ἄθω τοῦ ὄρους ἱδρυμένος ἀνδριάς, ὁ Ζεύς; Sophocles fr. 237 P. Θρῇσσαν σκοπιὰν Ζηνὸς Ἀθῴου.

286. ὑπερτελής: 'rising above, aloft', as in E. *Ion* 1549 (not 'beyond the τέλος ', i.e. beyond a prescribed limit).

νωτίσαι: ὑπερβῆναι, Schol., 'to go over the back (of the sea)', over the εὐρέα νῶτα θαλάσσης. The usage is unique; but it is a characteristic of verbs in -ίζω that they adapt themselves to their contexts in a remarkable manner; cf. E. *Ph.* 654, *H.* 362, where νωτίζω, ἐπινωτίζω are used with as great a freedom; many examples in Rutherford, *New Phrynichus*, pp. 178 ff.

287. With ἰσχὺς . . . λαμπάδος compare 296 σθένουσα λαμπάς. πορευτός (the word here only in poetry) = 'travelling'.

The sentence offers insoluble problems. There are two nominative subjects (ἰσχὺς λαμπάδος, πεύκη) but no main verb. Moreover though πρὸς ἡδονήν might theoretically mean 'joyfully' (Fraenkel on 381–4 below), that is not its normal sense (LSJ s.v.: those versions which are compelled to take λαμπάδος πρὸς ἡδονήν together, 'at pleasure of the beacon', = 'delighting in the beacon', may be ruled out; πρὸς ἡδονήν c. gen., if there were such a phrase, would mean 'to the beacon's pleasure' (cf. S. *OC* 890), an absurdity in this context). A lacuna must be marked: Calder, *CR* xxxvi (1922) 155 ff., suggests that, since the beacon-stage from Athos to Euboea (if indeed Makistos is in Euboea) is abnormally long, an intermediate stage (e.g. the island Icus) may have been mentioned in the missing part.

(Ahrens's fanciful conjecture, ἰχθῦς for ἰσχύς in 287, has had a remarkable vogue, inspiring the further change of the innocent πορευτοῦ into πυρευτοῦ, χορευτούς, χορευτάς: see Thomson ad loc., Cornford in *CR* liii (1939) 162.)

289. Μακίστου: we might have expected Μηκ-, cf. μῆκος in 2, παλιμμήκη in 196; the question is fully discussed by G. Björck, *Das Alpha Impurum* (1950), pp. 59, 135 (criticized on this point by A. C. Moorhouse, *JHS* lxxiii (1953) 167).

σκοπαῖς: σκοπάς codd., which might be retained if the missing verb were of motion, e.g. ἀφίκετο; 'look-out places', 'watch-towers', or the like.

291. παρῆκεν: '(did not) neglect'; the negatives in 290 apply to the whole sentence.   **ἀγγέλου μέρος**: 'a messenger's share', i.e. 'his share in the messenger's duty' (Fraenkel).

292 f. φῶς is subject of σημαίνει; σημαίνει μολόν go together, cf. S. *Ant.* 20 δηλοῖς . . . καλχαίνουσα; ἐπ' Εὐρίπου ῥοάς is governed by μολόν: 'From afar the beacon's light signals to the watchmen of M. its coming to (or over) the streams of Euripus.'

296. οὐδέ πω: 'not *yet*' seems pointless here; perhaps 'not at all', as in Homer (Leaf on *Il.* 3. 306, Ebeling's Homeric Lexicon s.v. πω).

299. Lit. 'aroused another taking-up of the messenger-fire'.

301.: 'burning more than those aforementioned'. This, the obvious meaning of the words, rings dull and prosaic, and an alternative, 'more than what was ordered', has been suggested: but though εἴρητο, εἰρημένον can mean 'ordered', the phrase πλέον τῶν εἰρημέν ν in the sense 'beyond one's orders' seems unlikely and does not in fact occur.

302 f. See note on *The Beacons* above.

304: 'commanded them not to . . . the ordinance of the fire': what is the missing verb? χαρίζεσθαι is nonsense; χρονίζεσθαι, χατίζεσθαι are shown by Fraenkel to be very improbable conjectures. The truth is still to be found: there is not even a plausible suggestion to record.

306–8. The text is unsatisfactory: (i) φλέγουσαν has no noun in agreement (to understand φλόγα from φλογὸς πώγωνα is a far-fetched expedient, for which no parallel is forthcoming); (ii) though ὑπερβάλλειν could be an infin. of purpose after πέμπουσι (Goodwin, *MT*, §§ 770 ff.), the καί is unintelligible—'*even* to cross the coastal promontory' is out of place, this being one of the less remarkable feats described. (Fraenkel further objects to εἶτα . . . εἶτα in 308, mainly on the ground that 'no time can elapse between the moment of ἔσκηψεν and that of ἀφίκετο, so that the anaphoric εἶτα-phrases would not describe a progressive action but only a single event happening at one and the same moment'. Beattie, *CR* n.s. iv (1954) 79, justifiably replies that this objection would only hold if ἔσκηψεν meant 'come *to earth*', 'hit the ground': in fact ἔσκηψεν means no more than 'swooped downwards', unless πέδοι (or the like) is expressed; two successive stages are marked here by ἔσκηψεν and ἀφίκετο, exactly as by ἔσκηψεν and ἐξικνούμενον in 302 f.) Simple changes would give φλόγ' ἐς μέγαν πώγων', ἑκὰς Σαρωνικοῦ κτλ., '(kindled) the flame to a great beard, so as to pass above the promontory far away, flaming onwards, etc.': but Aeschylus does not elsewhere begin his verse with an elided disyllable, and we may prefer to favour the suggestion of Blomfield, that the trouble has been caused by the accidental omission of a line between 307 and 308, providing a verb to govern καὶ . . . ὑπερβάλλειν and a noun to agree with φλέγουσαν.

For κάτοπτον (-οπτρον codd.) see Fraenkel.

312. The division τοιοίδε τοί μοι is not entirely satisfactory, for μοι is not wanted and not easily interpreted. It would perhaps be easier with νομοί (Beattie: "arrangements") instead of νόμοι.

313. The nom. ἄλλος . . . πληρούμενοι is apposed to the preceding clause, giving the detail explaining the broader statement, exactly as in *PV* 200 ff., S. *Ant.* 259 f., E. *Ph.* 1462 ff. (all quoted by Fraenkel): 'supplied in succession, one from another'.

314. 'The victory is won by the first runner and the last.' Clytemnestra thinks of the passage of the beacons in terms of a relay-race, especially the well-known λαμπαδηφορία at Athens; and all she means is that just as much service is done by the man who ran the first lap (ὁ πρῶτος δραμών, as in Hdt. 8. 98. 2) as by the man who had the glory of running the last lap. (For the omission of the article in καὶ τελευταῖος cf. 324 below, τῶν ἁλόντων καὶ (sc. τῶν) κρατησάντων; *Il.* 2,

281 οἱ πρῶτοί τε καί (sc. οἱ) ὕστατοι.) The safe arrival of the beacon at its destination is naturally described as a 'victory'.

(It is unreasonable to object that since no *competitive* team is concerned in the beacon-race—as it was in the λαμπαδηφορία—the question 'who won?' (νικᾷ) is inappropriate; and that there is not much point in saying here (or rather implying) that all members of the beacon-team did equal service toward 'victory'. Clytemnestra says in effect: 'This was a kind of λαμπαδηφορία in which one received the torch from another in relays—a race in which all contribute equally toward ultimate success, as much service being done by the first runner as by the last.' Image and reality are not perfectly blent, as so often in Aeschylus.)

318. τούσδε can only refer to what Clytemnestra has been saying. The meaning must therefore be: 'I wish to hear from start to finish (διηνεκῶς here only in Tragedy; Attic would have been διᾱν-) what you have just said.' Clytemnestra does not comply with this remarkable request to repeat the story of the beacons, but gives instead an imaginative picture of the scene in the captured city of Troy.

319. ὡς λέγεις, 'I should like to hear this story again *as you tell it*' is not very satisfactory either in phrasing (Fraenkel compares *Od.* 23. 62, which is similar, *Il.* 7. 406 f., which seems quite different) or in sense; moreover it is surely preferable not to separate ὡς λέγ. from πάλιν. οὓς λέγεις sounds dull, especially so late in the sentence. **ὡς λέγοις πάλιν**, 'according as you would tell it again', may be correct (Sidgwick; λέγοις optative assimilated to θέλοιμι).

322 ff. Lit. 'Having poured vinegar and oil in the same vessel, quarreling as they do you would call them anything but friends' (οὐ φίλω = ἐχθρώ; οὐ φίλως codd., but φίλω is indispensable to the sense—οὐ φίλως would have to qualify διχοστατοῦντ', and the resulting phrase 'you would address them, quarrelling as they do in enmity', is obviously impossible here, for there is no point in saying 'you would *speak to* them', and the sense 'you would *address them by the name of* quarrelsome things' could not be represented in Greek by προσεννέποις ἄν with the participle). The fact that this usage of προσεννέπειν, 'call a thing so-and-so', does not recur elsewhere is of no importance, since the verb itself is rare, and its synonyms προσαγορεύειν, προσειπεῖν are used in just this way: Plato, *Tht.* 182ᵈ ἆρά ποτε οἷόν τέ τι προσειπεῖν χρῶμα, ὥστε καὶ ὀρθῶς προσαγορεύειν; 'is it possible to call a thing "colour", so as to call it by its proper name?' In A. *Cho.* 997 τί νιν προσείπω = 'what am I to call her?' in the sense 'how shall I describe her?' (not 'in what terms shall I *address* her?').

324. τῶν goes with both participles (cf. 314 n.).

324–5. δίχα with ἀκούειν ἔστι: 'one can hear *in two ways* the cries of vanquished and victors', i.e. one can hear a noise distinguishable into two different sounds.

325. συμφορᾶς διπλῆς: virtually genitive absolute, 'their fortunes being twofold'; strictly perhaps gen. of definition, with φθογγάς.

One expects a contrast between triumph and misery to follow: but the state of the victors turns out to be only relatively happy, and clouded with fears for the future.

326–8. 'The one party fallen about the bodies of husbands and brothers, and children (fallen about the bodies) of old men their procreators, are bewailing the death etc.'. The expression is awkward and the sense unsatisfactory: it is unexpected that the 'children' should be said to bewail the 'old men' in a context in which (naturally) the old men are usually said to bewail the young (see the examples in Headlam–Thomson). No doubt old men were killed at the fall of Troy: but the death of the young and lamentations of the old are much the more natural topics here as elsewhere. Hence φυτάλμιοι παίδων γέροντες Weil, 'old men, their fathers, (fallen about the bodies) of their children'. The change would be less and the sentence smoother with φυταλμίων παίδων γέροντες, 'old men (fallen about the bodies) of children whom they had begotten'; φυτάλμιος passive, as perhaps in S. *OC* 151 (despite Hermann and Jebb).

328. ἐλευθέρου: masc. for fem. as in E. *El.* 868.

330. ἐκ μάχης: 'after the battle'. Battle is succeeded not by well-earned luxury but by weary wandering about the city in search of food. When day breaks, the conquerors sit down to eat what they have collected; the phrase ὧν ἔχει πόλις is probably intended to suggest that this was not much—that Troy is badly off for provisions.

331 f. πρὸς ἀρίστοισιν ... τάσσει: 'places them at breakfast'. **πρὸς οὐδὲν ἐν μέρει τεκμήριον:** lit. 'according to no token in turn', with nothing to fix an order of precedence; clarified by the next line, 'but just as each drew the lot of chance'.

336. ὡς δ' εὐδαίμονες: '*like* happy men'. Their life is still most uncomfortable (330 ff.); they only resemble 'happy men' in sleeping without interruption till dawn.

337. ἀφύλακτον (adverbial): 'without having to stand sentry' or 'without being protected'.

338. On εὐσεβεῖν, εὖ σέβειν, see Fraenkel. 'If they are (at this moment) observing reverence': how they are in fact behaving is described at 524 ff.; they are, as Clytemnestra hopes, offending the gods gravely.

341. For μή c. subj. expressing *fear*, in independent clauses, see Fraenkel.

343. For δεῖ c. gen., followed by accus.+infin., cf. *Suppl.* 407 ff. The running-track was hairpin-shaped, consisting of two equal limbs, κῶλα, with a turning-point at the far end; hence δίαυλος, 'of two channels'. To carry oneself round the bend could be described as 'bending the track', κάμπτειν δρόμον, or more simply 'bending', κάμπτοντος ἵππου. The phrase here is of the condensed type, 'turn ⟨round the bend and traverse⟩ the second limb of the course'.

345–7. The war is over, but the army is not yet out of danger. Something may be done to offend the gods; or the dead may claim payment; or something unforeseen may occur. This sequence of thought is expressed thus: 'If the army should come safely home without offence against the *gods*, the sufferings of the *dead* may be aroused, if no *unexpected* calamity occurs', i.e. if they escape the first danger they still have to reckon with the second, not to mention *unexpected* calamities which may (and in fact do) await them. The necessary emphasis is given to θεοῖς and πρόσπαια by position in their clauses, to ὀλωλότων by antithesis with θεοῖς. By πῆμα τῶν ὀλωλότων Clytemnestra refers to Iphigeneia; the Chorus understands her to mean the dead at Troy, a theme which they take up at 456 ff.

εἰ in 347 must not be taken to stand for καὶ εἰ, '*even* if . . .': it is the position of πρόσπαια within its clause which justifies the emphasis, 'if no *new* obstacle arises'—Clytemnestra knows that in fact a 'new obstacle' *will* arise.   πρόσπαια: anciently said to mean 'recent', 'novel'. The extension of meaning to 'unexpected' makes better sense in S. *Ichneutae* 119 P., Lycophron 211, and much better sense in Nicander, *Ther.* 690. 'Sudden' does as well as (but not better than) 'new' in Aristotle, *Eth. Nic.* 1166ᵇ35, 1167ᵃ2, and Polybius vi. 43. 3. There seems to be no other example of the word.

349. 'Let the good prevail, in no doubtful fashion, (for men) to see.'

350. A cryptic sentence, capable of various interpretations. Best perhaps simply 'many are the blessings whose enjoyment I have chosen', i.e. '(I hope the army will get safely home, and all turn out well): in that case there will be many good things for me to enjoy' (she refers especially to vengeance for her daughter's death). Among possible alternatives: '*This* enjoyment (viz. enjoyment of the successful outcome implicit in τὸ εὖ κρατοίη) I have chosen in preference to a wealth of blessings', i.e. I would rather have this than anything else; for εἰλόμην τί τινος in this sense see Fraenkel, and Gow on Theocr. 11. 49. (This interpretation absolutely requires τήνδ' for τήν.)

351. κατ' ἄνδρα: the Chorus take notice of her ironical or indignant γυναικὸς ἐξ ἐμοῦ (348).

352. πιστὰ . . . τεκμήρια: this is not to be taken seriously; nothing that Clytemnestra has said affords evidence, let alone 'convincing proof', that the beacons betoken the fall of Troy. See further 475 ff. below.

353. See Headlam. If εὖ is correct, it must qualify προσειπεῖν: but εὖ προσειπεῖν is an expression not found elsewhere. αὖ (Paley) is no improvement, for there is no point in saying 'I will address the gods *again*' (as if they had already done so since they heard the news). Probably, as Fraenkel says, εὖ has no specially close relation to the verb, but qualifies it as any adverb might do, 'I will prepare to address the gods in a proper manner'.

354. Lit. 'A highly-prized return for troubles has been achieved.
χάρις = favourable return for service (LSJ s.v. III. 1 a). οὐκ
ἄτιμος = μεγαλότιμος.

356. κτεάτειρα (here only) ought to mean 'one who acquires (or has acquired) possession': but what then are the μεγάλοι κόσμοι, of which the Night is the 'possessor'? The rich booty from Troy, or the glory of victory over Troy, or both, according to some: but the plural κόσμοι seems abnormal and unnatural in that sense. Others interpret 'the stars, planets, moon': and this seems a much more natural way of understanding the simple phrase 'O friendly Night, possessor of great ornaments'. (Fraenkel calls it a 'vague lyricism': if so, it keeps good company in Aeschylus, cf. PV 24 where Night is called ποικιλείμων, 'of variegated robes', without any special relevance to the context.)

357. ἦτε: as often in Tragedy, similar to *quippe quae* (*Gk. Particles*, pp. 522 f.). Night is their friend, because Troy was taken under cover of her darkness.

358. στεγανόν: 'covering', as a roof covers; Night lays a net of darkness, like a roof or lid, on top of the city.

359. μήτ' οὖν: 'nor yet . . .'; one might have hoped that at least the young would be spared.

ὑπερτελέσαι: 'rise above' the net which lies on top of the city, covering it (στεγανόν). Since the meaning is 'surmount', it is hard to see why ὑπερτεῖλαι, aorist of the relevant verb ὑπερτέλλω, was not written here; ὑπερτελέσαι, from ὑπερτελέω (not found elsewhere in literature) is unexplained (cf. however ὑπερτελής in 286 above).

361. γάγγαμον: properly a fishing-net; the imagery recalls *Il.* 5. 487 ff.
παναλώτου: active, 'all-catching'. δουλείας depends on γάγγαμον, and the combination depends on ἄτης, 'Ruin's all-catching slavery-net'.

362. μέγαν: 356 μεγάλων, 357 μέγαν, 360 μέγα; this sort of repetition (without special significance) is common in Aeschylus as in many other Greek writers; see Pearson on E. *Hel.* 674; *Agam.* 246, 395, 433 ff., 948-9, 966 ff., 1065, 1592, 1608-9, 1626-7, nn.

364 ff. Zeus, in Olympus, is aiming at Alexander, in Troy. His shot is to be aimed neither too low nor too high. If it is aimed too low, it will fall short of the mark, πρὸ καιροῦ; if it is aimed too high, it will go soaring above the target. To say that it will soar so high as to rise 'above the stars' (or 'beyond the stars': a rare usage of ὑπέρ) seems unduly exaggerated; but it is picturesque, and by no means obscures the meaning, which is simply 'too high'—the arrow, aimed from

Olympus, will pass above Troy and finish up above, or beyond, the stars.

For ὅπως ἄν c. opt. see Goodwin, *MT*, §§ 349 ff.

367 ff. The strophe starts with *the Trojans*: the end of the antistrophe shows that *Paris* exemplifies what has been said. There is no suggestion that any other personal subject intervenes, and we must suppose that the Trojans and Paris are the theme throughout 367–402. It is not at first sight clear what the condemnation of excessive wealth, the compulsion exercised by Persuasion, and the plot concocted beforehand by Ruin, have to do with Troy and Paris; but see the notes on 374 f., 386 ff. below.

367. ἔχουσιν: the Trojans. 'They can tell of a blow from *Zeus*' (emphatic by position); 'that at least one can track out: he did as he decreed.' ἔπραξαν, 'they fared', would do as well, but no change is needed; cf. 363 τὸν τάδ- πράξαντα.

369. 'Some people deny . . .': τις = 'somebody, I don't know who . . .', as often.

370. ἀξιοῦσθαι: deign, think appropriate to their dignity.

371. ἀθίκτων χάρις: there is *grace*, almost *charm* or *beauty*, in the sanctities on which the sinner tramples; E. *Med.* 439 ὅρκων χάρις may be similar.

374 f. Whatever the truth may be about ἀτολμήτων ἄρη, it is likely that ἐγγόνοις (for -ους, codd.) is correct: the next stanza (see 385 n.) makes it plain that Paris is driven to his crime by supernatural powers against his better judgement; he is paying for the corruption of the society from which he comes, he is an example of the visitation of fathers' sins upon children's heads. Observe too that the preceding sentiment, 'that the gods are indifferent to human wrongdoing' (369–71), an opinion derived from observation of the fact that the ungodly often flourish, was traditionally answered in just this way: 'Not so; for if the father escapes, the son will suffer'; ἀναίτιοι ἔργα τίνουσιν | ἢ παῖδες παίδων ἢ γένος ἐξοπίσω (Solon fr. 1. 31 f.), παλαιγενῆ γὰρ λέγω παρβασίαν ὠκύποινον, αἰῶνα δ' ἐς τρίτον μένειν (*ScT* 742 ff.). In such a context ἔγγονος expresses exactly the idea we should be expecting.

If ἀτολμήτων ἀρή could mean 'penalty for wicked sin' (Headlam), no further change would be needed: 'penalty for wicked sin is made manifest to children's children'; exactly the sense required. ἀρή, cf. ἀρήμενος, in the Epic means something like 'harm': elsewhere it occurs only in Aeschylus *Suppl.* 84, where Schol. glosses it βλάβη (βλάβη ἡ ἐν τῷ Ἄρει, Hesychius). The idea that ἀτολμήτων ἀρή here could mean something like 'punishment for things which should not have been dared', is most hazardous but not quite out of the question.

376. πνεόντων: the antecedent clause being so obscure, there is no means of telling whether this is gen. absol., 'in a case where men are proud beyond what is right', or an ordinary gen. dependent on or agreeing with something that went before.

377. φλέοντων ... ὑπέρφευ: both words are very rare, probably old-fashioned; the latter word is clarified at once, in Aeschylean manner, by the simple ὑπὲρ τὸ βέλτιστον.

379. ἀπήμαντον: predicate; the subject is presumably τὸ πλουτεῖν. (Fraenkel takes ἀπήμαντον itself as subject of ἔστω: such a substantival use of the adjective without article or other qualification is contrary to normal Attic and Tragic style, but cf. *Suppl.* 79; Heracleitus frr. 88, 108, 126; Verdenius in *Mnemos.* 1955, on Ar. *Plut.* 578.)

379. ἀπαρκεῖν ... λαχόντι: 'so as to satisfy a man of good sense'.

381 ff. Cf. Hdt. 8. 77 δῖα Δίκη σβέσσει κρατερὸν Κόρον, Ὕβριος υἱόν: pride and wealth are very well so long as Justice is in the house; Κόρος, excess, is controlled only by Δίκη, Justice—expel Justice (383-4), and your wealth no longer has any safeguard against excess: 'For there is no safeguard in wealth against excess, once a man has spurned the great altar of Justice out of sight.' See further 756-62 n. below.

ἔπαλξις πλούτου: defence consisting in, or afforded by, wealth; πλούτου might, but less stylishly, be taken with πρὸς Κόρον, 'against excess of wealth'. For the metaphor in ἔπαλξις πρὸς Κόρον cf. Demo. 21. 138, 'rich men take their wealth as a τεῖχος πρὸς τὸ μηδὲν παθεῖν.'

384. εἰς ἀφάνειαν: *Eum.* 539 ff. is milder and more normal: βωμὸν αἴδεσαι Δίκας, μηδέ νιν κέρδος ἰδὼν ἀθέῳ ποδὶ λὰξ ἀτίσῃς—it is one thing to spurn the Great Altar of Justice and dishonour it, much more remarkable to 'Kick it *into invisibility*', if that is what the words here mean (into disappearance or destruction, LSJ); the altar of Justice abides for ever, and is not to be kicked εἰς ἀφάνειαν by the foot of a mortal engaged in a particular misdemeanour. Perhaps more vaguely, 'into obscurity', out of sight'; Prof. Dover compares Thuc. vii. 69. 2 τὰς πατρικὰς ἀρετὰς ... μὴ ἀφανίζειν.

385. Persuasion *compels* him: he talks himself, or is talked by others, into action against his better judgement. It is hard to see what this has to do with Paris' crime; and it is unusual to speak of Peitho in these terms (for her 'violence' cf. Pind. *Pyth.* 4. 219 μάστιγι Πειθοῦς). τάλαινα: 'persistent', almost 'relentless'; E. *El.* 1171 n.

386 ff. 'Persuasion' is said to be daughter of 'Infatuation' (or 'Spirit of Destruction'), who 'deliberates *beforehand*': i.e. Atê decides *in advance* what the man's doom shall be, and her daughter puts the plan into effect against his will (βιᾶται); he has no hope of resisting her (ἄφερτος); she causes in him a malady for which there is no cure (ἄκος κτλ.) and no concealment (οὐκ ἐκρύφθη).

It is particularly to be observed how strongly, with what emphatic words, the poet insists upon the helplessness of the human victim, and the premeditation and violence of the supernatural powers which drive him to sin. Once the wrath of heaven has been aroused by human wrong-doing, certain wretched victims, who are no more responsible than anyone else—perhaps not responsible at all—for the original sin, are driven against their will and judgement, by express plan of the powers above, to commit further crimes, for which they must then pay in full. This picture of Paris, *compelled* to commit his crime in accordance with a supernaturally preconceived plan, is an exact parallel to that of Agamemnon, *ordered* by Artemis to kill his daughter in requital of a deed in which he had no part; in both examples the victim's compulsory crime is the inevitable sequel of the earlier sins of a family or society. The relevance of ἐγγόνοις (374) is now plain: Paris, it is said here (399 οἷος καὶ Πάρις ...), was compelled by Peitho, in accordance with a preconceived plan of Atê; there is no cure, and no concealment; he is a helpless victim of circumstances—*what* circumstances? Troy has grown too wealthy and too proud (376–80); Justice has been kicked out of sight (381–4), and so the Trojans have destroyed their only bulwark against Excess and all its evil consequences. The flower of this plant will soon blossom: the son of this house will overstep all bounds, will show no respect for what is right toward god or man (400–2). It is perfectly clear that Aeschylus takes the sin of Paris to be not a cause but an effect: it is not, strictly speaking, 'his fault', it is the fault of the society which produced him. He is not the black sheep of an honest flock: what is happening is that the sins of his fathers are being visited on his head, he is the symbol and scapegoat of their corruption, the finished model of their craftsmanship.

390 f. κακοῦ δὲ χαλκοῦ τρόπον κτλ.: the meaning is that the baseness of the bad man is revealed by the wear and tear of social and political life, just as the baser metal of counterfeit bronze in a vessel or implement is revealed by rubbing or wear (τρίβῳ) and by incidental knocks (προσβολαῖς).

(There is no question here of *bronze coins* being *tested by touchstones*: Athens had no bronze coinage in, or for some time after, the time of Aeschylus; and though gold was tested on touchstones, bronze was not. See further Fraenkel, pp. 204 f.: 'bad bronze' means bronze adulterated with lead; lead on the surface spreads through rubbing and turns the surface black, μελαμπαγὴς πέλει.) **μελαμπαγής:** another very condensed expression; 'he is black-fixed' means 'blackness is fixed in him', i.e. indelibly ingrained in him. Much easier is the use in *ScT* 737, where the adjective is used of blood which is 'black' and 'fixed', i.e. thick or congealed.

393 ff. δικαιωθείς: the following clause, ἐπεὶ ... ὄρνιν, means in effect 'since he seeks the unattainable', and this is connected with the participial clause πόλει πρόστριμμα (ἐν)θείς, 'having brought pollution upon his city'. It is hard to see what 'seeks the unattainable' could mean in such a context, except 'hopes to escape punishment' or the like; but that would be much too obscurely allusive unless δικαιωθείς had already introduced the idea of 'punishment', or 'getting his deserts'. Can we then render 'having been punished, or sentenced'? Clearly not: for if δικαιωθείς must cohere with what follows, it must cohere no less with what precedes; and the expression 'he has a black stain fixed in him, *after he has been punished, or sentenced*', makes no sense. If the metaphor is legal, the 'black stain', the baseness of his metal, may be the cause of his arrest, or something which becomes apparent during examination: it cannot possibly be something which makes no appearance until *after* sentence has been passed or executed. Moreover the phrase to which δικαιωθείς is attached is not simply μελαμπαγὴς πέλει but τρίβῳ τε καὶ προσβολαῖς μ. π.: 'through rubbing and battering he is indelibly black'—now add '*after sentence has been passed on him*', and the incoherence is at once manifest.

There seems to be only one way of making δικαιωθείς suit the context in both directions: to take it as resuming the sense of (and perhaps directly connected with) τρίβῳ τε καὶ προσβολαῖς μ. π.; thus either (1) 'Through rubbing and battering his metal is black, *through the justice thereby done to him*', or (2) 'his metal is black, when by rubbing and battering justice has been done to him'. δικαιοῦν = 'provide someone with τὰ δίκαια', δικαιοῦσθαι 'to be provided with τὰ δίκαια', to get one's deserts.

395. πρόστριμμα: 'affliction'; LSJ s.v. προστρίβω III 1. Whether ἄφερτον θείς (cod. F) represents ἄφερτον ἐνθείς (Triclinius) or θεὶς ἄφερτον (Wilamowitz) we do not know.

397. τὸν δ᾽ ἐπίστροφον τῶν: τῶν (if that is the true text) stands for τούτων, 'those (blameworthy) things'. ἐπίστροφον perhaps means something like 'having dealings with', or 'familiar with'; *Od*. i. 177, Odysseus ἐπίστροφος ἦν ἀνθρώπων.

398. καθαιρεῖ: sc. θεῶν τις, understood from οὔτις θεῶν above; Sidgwick compares Horace, *Sat*. i. 1. 1 ff. qui fit, Maecenas, ut nemo . . . contentus uiuat, laudet diuersa sequentis, where the subject of laudet, 'a person', is understood from nemo; cf. also S. *Ajax* 482 (Fraenkel). But Blomfield's conjecture φῶτα Δίκα is attractive.

400. As if the Atridae lived together at home in the same palace: an innovation, but essential to the plan of this choral song.

404. λοχισμούς: formations into λόχοι, military companies. See Beattie, *CR* n.s. ii (1952) 71; Maas, *Stud. U. E. Paoli* (1955) 505 f.

407. βέβακε codd., but see Fraenkel: a 'resultative' perfect tense should not have an adverb attached to it qualifying the nature of the action which led to that result (ῥίμφα).

408. ἄτλατα Dindorf, but the evidence is decidedly against consistency in this respect. πολὺ δ᾽ ἀνέστενον cod. F: responsion of two short to one long syllable (πŏλŭ = ōŭ 425) is very rare in the lyrical iambics of

Aeschylus (Fraenkel, p. 351; cf. 1451–3 n. below); moreover πολλά, not πολύ, is Aeschylus' usual adverbial neuter (except with comparatives and superlatives). The text of Triclinius, πολλὰ δ' ἔστενον, looks like mere emendation, and cannot be preferred here with any confidence.

409. ἐννέποντες: where does their speech end? At 426, according to most editors, probably rightly; the tense of δόξει strongly suggests that the speech extends to 415, and the coherence of the subject-matter indicates that all is of a piece down to 426.

δόμων προφῆται: Menelaus is silent (412), but the matter cannot pass without comment; somebody must 'speak on behalf of the house'. The standing and identity of these speakers, quaintly called 'spokes-men on behalf of the house' (not 'belonging to the house'), is left vague: Elders of the royal Household, we may suppose—there is no evidence that kings or others included domestic seers or 'prophets' in their personal retinue, nor is anything of the kind suggested here. The circumstances are exceptional: Menelaus will say not a word, so somebody else must come forward and speak on his behalf.

410. πρόμοι: Agamemnon and Menelaus, who live under the same roof (400) and are alike offended by Paris' offence against the laws of hospitality.

411. στίβοι φιλάνορες: lit. 'husband-loving tracks', a typically Aeschy-lean condensation of 'places where one who loved her husband used to walk'. στίβος means (a) a treading, or footprint, (b) a trodden path; there is no special connexion between στίβοι and λέχος here.

412. πάρεστι σιγὰς ἀτίμους is a probable restoration; then ἀλοιδόρους, or better -ως (since ἀτίμους ἀλοιδόρους do not make a good pair); and ἀφημένων, 'sitting apart', is picturesque and apt enough. The main difficulty lies in ΑΔΙϹΤΟϹ: corruption in the antistrophe is an impediment, but the scansion ∪ – – is highly probable here; we need an adjective or adverb beginning with alpha privative, ending -ους or -ως, and with a stem which will account for ΔΙϹΤ. No convincing word has been found. (ἀλίστως suggests itself: he sits in silence, neither cursing (her departure) nor praying (her return), ἀλοιδόρως ἀλίστως. But it is not certain that such adverbs could qualify such a verb as 'sitting', or that ἀλίστως (an invented word) could mean 'not praying'. ἀπίστους, accepted by Fraenkel, is surely impossible: there is no question of Menelaus *not believing* that Helen has left him; σιγαὶ ἄπιστοι would be a most unnatural expression; and the trio ἀτίμους ἀλοιδόρους ἀπίστους are most uncomfortable yoke-fellows.

414–15. There are two possibilities, neither free from difficulty: (a) 'He (Menelaus) will think that an apparition rules in his palace, by reason of his longing for her who is overseas'; but *Helen's ghost* cannot well be said to *rule the house*; (b) 'because of his longing for her who etc., a mere ghost (φάσμα, of Menelaus) will seem to rule the house': but this sense of the isolated φάσμα is without parallel. (Greek idiom will not admit 'An apparition (of Helen) will seem to rule the house, by reason of his (Menelaus') longing for her (Helen) who is overseas', where the πόθος is that of a person other than the subject of the main verb, and the same person is the subject both of the main verb and of the subordinate ὑπερποντίας.)   **ὑπερποντίας**: one would have expected the def. art. τᾶς (cf. E. *Hel.* 1306 πόθῳ τᾶς ἀποιχομένας); see 429 n. below.   **δόξει**: the future is uncomfortable among the present tenses, especially with πάρεισι δόξαι, resuming the present theme, following so soon.

416. κολοσσῶν: images, of whatever material or size; the idea of *abnormal magnitude* starts from the 'Colossus' at Rhodes, third century B.C. See Rumpf, *Archäologie* II (1956) 18 ff. Presumably statues *of Helen* are meant; it is easy to supply her name from the preceding sentence, and the idea is appropriate. Some edd. interpret 'of women in general', an idea both less appropriate in itself and less easily supplied from the context, since κολοσσοί does not in itself mean or imply (even with εὔμορφοι) 'statues *of women*'.

418–19. The rare and obscure word ἀχηνία is glossed ἀπορία, πενία, in the lexicographers; its meaning here may be inferred from *Cho.* 301 χρημάτων ἀχηνία, Aristophanes fr. 20 K. φίλων ἀχηνία: 'lack, want, shortage', not having something, or not having enough of it. There is no authority for taking ὀμμάτων ἀχηνίαι to mean anything but 'lack of eyes', not having eyes; neither the usage of ἀχηνία nor its relation to the genitive in ὀμμάτων can be reconciled with the rendering 'in the *starvation* of his (Menelaus') eyes'. '*In the lack of eyes*, all charm of love is lost': what is the poet's meaning? The phrase in itself would most naturally mean 'in the lack of *Helen's* eyes', but the preceding clause suggests that this thought was expressed in terms of the eyes of *statues* of Helen: the sight of beautiful statues of Helen is hateful to him; *the eyes* are the seat and source of love, the beauty of Helen shines in her eyes (cf. 742); but the eyes are the most unlifelike part of a statue—'*because they have no eyes*, they have lost all charm of love'. (It would be difficult to account for the plural ἀχηνίαις except by reference to the plurality of κολοσσοί: it is conceivable that the sole purpose of the plural form was to obviate the illicit interlinear hiatus, but of course it would have been easy to avoid using a verb beginning with a vowel.)

420. πενθήμονες: Helen appears in his dream not as she is, happily mated with Paris, but as Menelaus would have her, sorrowful, returning in tears to her lost husband and home; and that is gratifying (χάριν), however unreal (ματαίαν).

421. δόξαι: 'imaginings', 'fancies', the dream-visions of Helen.

423. It is probably a fatal objection to the MS. text, that εὖτ' ἄν has no verb (1511 below is most untrustworthy evidence; see note). The alleged anacoluthon is of a type without parallel: Fraenkel, who accepts it, further says that 'after the sentence has been interrupted, μάταν is no longer taken into account': the one anacoluthon is harsh enough, a second would reduce the words to frantic incoherence. A simple remedy is at hand: omission of Θ before Ο would give δοκοῦν ὁρᾶι for δοκοῦνθ' ὁρᾶι, and the 'correction' to δοκῶν ὁρᾶν was then very easy. 'When one sees what seems to be desirable', a phantom of the desirable. The usage of ἐσθλός here is abnormal, like that in *Pers.* 222 where the Chorus tell Atossa to pray Darius ἐσθλὰ ... πέμπειν ἔνερθεν; ἐσθλῶν in 350 above is similar.

424. παραλλάξασα: 'deviating from the straight course', here 'slipping aside'; LSJ s.v. II. 5, 6.

425 f. μεθύστερον means 'afterwards' (not 'in a moment', i.e. immediately, as LSJ and several edd. would have it). The incoherence of what follows in the MSS. is abolished by the simple change of ὀπαδοῖς to ὀπαδοῦσ': '(The vision is gone,) not afterwards accompanying on wings the paths of Sleep', i.e. it is gone and does not return, cannot be recalled. (Fraenkel objects (1) that ὀπαδεῖν is not found in Tragedy, though ὀπαδός is: evidently not a matter of importance; (2) that one would expect a future participle: but the futurity is sufficiently indicated by the adverb μεθύστερον (see Wackernagel, *Synt.* i. 158); (3) that according to regular practice ὀπαδεῖν should govern the thing or person accompanied, not the *path* of the person: so easy an extension of usage needs no defence.)

427 ff. Here a transition is made from the past to the present, not without some abruptness: τὰ μὲν ... τάδ' ἐστί refers to what precedes, 'such is the grief at home (when Helen departed)'; the present tense, ἐστί, is used of that past time, but the following present tenses, πρέπει, θιγγάνει, ἀφικνεῖται, refer to a much later time, the time when the war was in progress, when sorrow for bereavement had already afflicted many homes. **ὑπερβατώτερα:** -βατος compounds are usually passive; here active, 'surpassing'.

429. τὸ πᾶν: 'in general', as opposed to any *one* house (that of Menelaus in particular); an abnormal usage, for τὸ πᾶν, like ἐς τὸ πᾶν, as a rule means 'totally', 'utterly', not 'universally'. One would have expected the definite article with **συνορμένοισι:** cf. 414 above, K.–G. i. 608 f.

429 f. It is likely that a syllable is missing between συνορμένοις (codd.) and πένθεια: συνορμένοισι is obviously acceptable, provided that πένθεια stands.—Most feminine substantives in -ειᾰ are either (1) fem. counterparts of masc. in -εύς (type βασιλεύς, βασίλεια), or (2) abstracts related to adjectives in -ής (type ἀληθής, ἀλήθεια). πένθεια could not be a mere alternative to πένθος, but as a feminine counterpart to *πενθεύς, 'a mourner', it would be a formation similar to βασίλεια, ἱέρεια. Hence Murray suggests that Aeschylus here wished to speak of a 'female mourner'; if so, it is possible that he might coin the noun πένθεια, even though the masc. counterpart, *πενθεύς, is familiar only as a proper name. Euripides, having the same need, coined the equally isolated but less obvious πενθήτρια (*Hipp.* 805). The sense of πένθεια, 'a (female) mourner', is certainly appropriate to the context; and though the form is unexpected and must always remain under suspicion, it is what the MSS. offer, and it is at least very doubtful whether there is any other possible explanation of the text. The conjecture ἀπένθεια (Blass, supported by Fraenkel) is wholly unacceptable. In suitable contexts bereaved persons are often exhorted to suffer 'without visible signs of mourning', and occasionally they are actually said to do so. But the context here is of a type fundamentally different from those quoted by Fraenkel in *Hermes* lxviii (1933) 242 ff.: here the whole emphasis falls on the *unhappiness* caused by bereavement, and nothing could be more inconsequent than to stress the stoical *concealment* of that unhappiness, as if one should say 'these, and worse, are the sorrows in Menelaus' house; and, in general, for those who went forth with him from Hellas, there is manifest in the house of each *a stout-hearted absence of mourning*'— the whole point here is that the bereaved persons *do* show their grief, though they endure it patiently (τλησικάρδιος). στένουσι in 445 adds the final proof, if it were needed: they openly lament and complain.

431. δόμων codd.: the genitive is inexplicable, and the change to δόμοις gives no account of it. **δόμῳ 'ν** is clearly right: aphaeresis in ἐν is attested for Aeschylus by *PV* 741 μηδέπω 'ν προοιμίοις (where the ἐν is indispensable, unlike that in E. *Hec.* 1195).

432. Cf. S. *Ajax* 938 χωρεῖ πρὸς ἧπαρ, οἶδα, γενναία δύη.

433 ff. Instead of the person whom one knew, unrecognizable ashes come home.   **τεύχη**: 'urns', not 'armour'; there seems to be no evidence that the weapons or armour of the fallen were sent home with their ashes after battles overseas (see Fraenkel).   **ἑκάστου δόμους**: 431 δόμῳ 'ν ἑκάστου, see 362 n.

Attention has often been drawn to the significance of these lines in the light of the terrible losses suffered by Athens in the campaigns of the previous year, 459 B.C.: see Tod, *Gk. Hist. Inscriptions* i, no. 26 (177 deaths in the tribe Erechtheis alone in the military operations of a single year).

437 f. Lit. 'Ares, the gold-changer of corpses, holding his scales in the battle of spears.' See Headlam: as the 'gold-changer' gives gold-dust in exchange for bulkier goods, so the War-God sets up his scales in battle and gives dust (ashes) in exchange for bodies; ἀντὶ φωτῶν τεύχη καὶ σποδός.

441–2. βαρὺ ψῆγμα: cf. E. *Suppl.* 1125 βάρος μὲν οὐκ ἀβριθές, in a similar context. The image of the gold-changer is continued in ψῆγμα, commonly used of gold-dust.

443–4. γεμίζων: a stronger and grimmer term than 'filling'.

444. λέβητας: of cinerary urns, *Cho.* 686, S. *El.* 1401.   **εὐθέτου**: scribes habitually assimilate to each other adjacent case-endings; it is surprising that εὐθέτους is not offered by codd. here, but it would be much more surprising if an original -ους had been corrupted to -ου. Nor is anything gained by the change to -ους: σποδοῦ εὐθέτου = ash easily stowed in urns—'in bitter irony, because, compared with the living man, they are so small in bulk and so easily disposed of,' Verrall. εὐθέτους, with λέβητας, would have to mean 'easily stowed', in the sense 'convenient for transport in ships', 'for which it is easy to find room at home', or something similar.

448 f. διαὶ γυναικός: '*because of* a woman' (cf. 1453, 1485 f.: not 'on behalf of', for διά c. gen. is not so used in classical literature; see Stevens, *CR* 1 (1936) 162 ff.).

449 f. 'Snarls someone in a whisper', Verrall. **σῖγα** of secret speech, cf. Hdt. 8. 74. 2 σιγῇ λόγον ἐποιέετο.

450 f. φθονερόν implies that the people 'grudge' the Atridae the lives of their menfolk, lost 'because of another man's wife'. There is some dispute about the meaning of **ὑπό . . . ἕρπει** and the construction of **Ἀτρείδαις**: (1) Verbs of motion commonly govern the dative of the person approached, and though the rare verb ὑφέρπειν is very seldom elsewhere so used (cf. Eupolis, *Demoi, Greek Literary Papyri*, p. 208, v. 27, ταῖς στρατηγίαις ὑφέρπει), ὑφέρπει Ἀτρείδαις would be readily understood: the resentment of the people goes out against the Atridae. (2) Others take ὑφέρπει here as in S. *OT* 786, ὑφεῖρπε γὰρ πολύ, 'goes abroad' absolutely: but what then is to be done with the dative Ἀτρείδαις? The run of the words is very unfavourable to its connexion with φθονερόν; and φθονερός c. dat. in this sense (or any other) would be highly abnormal. Some call Ἀτρείδαις 'dative of disadvantage': but though similarly isolated datives of advantage are common enough, comparable datives of disadvantage are apparently far to seek. There seems no room for doubt that Ἀτρείδαις is in fact directly governed by ὑπό . . . ἕρπει: 'resentment spreads stealthily against the sons of Atreus' (Weir Smyth).

451. προδίκοις: 'principals in the law-suit'; cf. 41 n.

452-5. For others, no funeral urn comes home; the dead are buried, 'even there, around the wall'; they have fought for possession of enemy land, and now they have it (ἔχοντας), and it hides them from sight for ever.   **εὔμορφοι**: they are dead in the prime of their beauty; thus the Achaeans θηήσαντο φυὴν καὶ εἶδος ἀγητὸν | Ἕκτορος, when he had fallen (*Il.* 22. 370 f.).

456. Lit. 'Dangerous is the citizens' talk accompanied by anger.'

457. Who is subject of **τίνει χρέος**? Agamemnon, according to Schol. vet. It is true that in this metaphor the subject of the verb of 'pay-ing' is as a rule the person who ought to make amends for a wrong done (or favour received), and here the persons who ought to 'pay' are the Atridae. But it is very hard to supply 'Agamemnon' (or 'Menelaus') here from Ἀτρείδαις above, especially since a new nominative subject has intervened. It remains to take 'the dangerous talk of the citizens' as the subject, and to understand τίνει χρέος as meaning 'pays what it owes', with special reference to the fact that the curse ratified by the people, ἀρὰ δημόκραντος, was a formal undertaking, imposing on the community a definite obligation—the duty of vengeance against the persons cursed. The 'angry talk' of the community, which is here said to be 'dangerous' to the Atridae, is a payment in discharge of the obligation incurred through the passing of a formal decree of hostility against the Atridae—it is 'the first step towards revolt', as Fraenkel says.

459 f. Lit. 'My anxious thought is waiting to hear something which is hidden in darkness.' μένω c. infin. as in *Eum.* 677 μένω δ' ἀκοῦσαι, 'I am waiting to hear'. There is no need to alter μου to μοι: the sense is the same, and the position in the sentence abnormal, whichever is read.

461. τῶν πολυκτόνων κτλ. : not only are the citizens enraged against the Atridae because of the blood shed at Troy; the gods themselves are 'not unwatchful' of those who have caused so many deaths. The expedition to Troy was approved (60 ff.) and abetted (362 ff., 748) by Zeus: but if many lives are lost, as of course they must be, Zeus will visit his displeasure on the killers' heads.

462 ff. This, as Headlam observes, is the process described in greater detail at *Eum.* 264-75. If a man has prospered (τυχηρὸν ὄντα) without regard for Justice (ἄνευ δίκας), in the end (χρόνῳ) the Erinyes intervene and reverse his fortunes (παλιντυχεῖ) causing his life to waste away (τριβᾷ, lit. *attritione*, 'by wearing out'), and making him faint and feeble (ἀμαυρόν: Hes. *op.* 325 ῥεῖα δέ μιν μαυροῦσι θεοί; *Eum.* 359); in *Eum.* they 'make him lean' (ἰσχνάνασα 267) by sucking his blood (βόσκημα δαιμόνων 302). He goes to the Unseen World (ἐν ἀίστοις, in the realm of Ἀ-ίδης) where the Great Corrector (μέγας εὔθυνος, *Eum.* 273) calls him to account; and in that trial there is none to stand by him, no defence (οὔτις ἀλκά).

462. κελαιναί : cf. [*ScT*] 977, *Eum.* 52, μέλαιναι; everything about the Erinyes is 'dark'—their sinister aspect, their garments (*Cho.* 1049, cf. *Eum.* 352), even their skin (E. *El.* 1345 χρῶτα κελαιναί).

466. τιθεῖσι = Attic τιθέασι; Epic and Ionic form, here only in Attic poetry.

467. τελέθοντος : genitive absolute.

468 f. 'It is dangerous (βαρύ, like βαρεῖα in 456) to be excessively well spoken of (εὖ κλύειν)', i.e. there is danger inherent in glory, even if it be without injustice ; the gods are jealous of men whose success and reputation overpass a certain limit. This opinion is a commonplace in fifth-century literature : Pind. *Pyth.* 10. 20 f., *Isthm.* 7. 39, Hdt. i. 32. 1 τὸ θεῖον πᾶν φθονερόν τε καὶ ταραχῶδες; it is contradicted in

750 ff. below, where the Chorus reject this παλαίφατος γέρων λόγος that wealth begets wrong-doing, asserting that disaster is to be traced back not to prosperity as such but to impious deeds of over-prosperous men.

469–70. ὅσσοις is unintelligible. To say 'the thunderbolt of Zeus is thrown against, or upon, *the eyes*' would be dithyrambic nonsense, even if βάλλεται c. dat. could bear that meaning. The alternative, 'a thunderbolt is hurled *by* (or *from*) *the eyes* of Zeus', is mere rodomontade: φθόνος may be sent *from the eyes* of Zeus, thunderbolts are not; it is not surprising that nothing similar to such an expression can be quoted in support (947 below, μή τις πρόσωθεν ὄμματος βάλοι φθόνος, provides the sharpest contrast in every relevant respect). That on which the malice or thunderbolt commonly falls is 'the house': OIICOIC might well turn into OCCOIC; οἴκοις, 'against the house'.

471. 'I approve prosperity without envy' (i.e. not so great as to be envied); but since the words could mean 'I condemn prosperity that is abundant' (the normal sense of ἄφθονος) this sentence reaches close to the limit of ambiguity.

473. ὑπ᾽ ἄλλων codd.: this would have to be taken with ἁλούς, and then βίον κατίδοιμι will be left without a predicate and without the possibility of supplying one. ὑπ᾽ ἄλλῳ seems clearly right, 'see my life under the power of another man'.

It is questionable whether there is anything in Greek Tragedy equal to this passage (385–474) in beauty and pathos. The following version is simply an adaptation, for the purpose of this edition, of the admirable translation by Richmond Lattimore (Univ. of Chicago Press: Aeschylus, *Oresteia*, 1953):

'Persuasion the persistent compels him, invincible daughter of designing Ruin. And every medicine is vain: it is not hidden, the injury she does, but blazes into evil splendour. Like base bronze, through wear and tear he is black within, when he has met with his deserts—for he is like the child who tries to catch the bird on the wing, having brought upon his people an insufferable taint of evil. No god will listen to his entreaty; whoso turns to these ways, they strike him down in his wickedness.

'Such a man was Paris: he came to the Atridae's house and stole his wife, disgracing the table of his host.

'She left for her people the turmoil of shields, the banding of warriors and arming of seamen. She took to Ilium her dowry, destruction, and stepped forth lightly between the gates, daring beyond all daring. And the spokesmen of the palace mourned aloud, saying: "Alas, alas for our palace and our princes! Alas for the marriage-bed, and the paths where a true wife went! Look at the silent dishonour of those who sit aloof unreproaching, unentreating! In longing for her who lies beyond the sea, he shall dream that a phantom is queen of his palace:

'Hateful to him is the grace of her images in their beauty; in the emptiness of their eyes all passion is faded.

'In dreams appear sorrowing phantoms, bringing vain delight only; for vain it is,—when one sees a vision of joy, the image slips through the arms' embrace, never again on wings to follow the ways of sleep." Such are the agonies in the house, at the hearthside; such, and surpassing these. And at large, for those who set forth together from Hellas, in every house is seen a woman mourning, steadfast in sorrow. Many are the things that touch to the heart:

'Those they sent forth they know: but now, in place of men, to every house come urns and ashes.

'The God of War, gold-changer who deals in corpses, holding his scales amid the battle of the spear, from the pyres at Ilium sends to their dearest only dust, heavy and hard-lamented, packing the urns with ashes, easily stowed, that once were men. They praise them through their tears: how this man knew well the craft of battle, how another went down nobly in the slaughter; and all for some strange woman. Thus they mutter in secrecy: resentful grief goes stealthily out against the Atridae, champions in the quarrel.

'And there, around the walls, the young men in their beauty keep sepulchres of Ilian soil, possessors of the hated land that hides them.

'Danger is in the city's talk with all its anger: it pays what is due to curses sworn by a people. My anxious thought is waiting to hear what the darkness hides: the gods fail not to mark those who have killed many; in time the black Furies strike feeble the man who has prospered without justice, turning his fortune round and wasting his life away; among the Unseen he lives, and there is no help for him. Glory in excess is full of danger: the thunderbolt of Zeus is hurled ⟨...⟩.

'Wealth without envy is my choice: let me not be destroyer of cities, nor be taken in turn and see my life in another's power.'

475 ff. The Chorus were at last convinced that Troy had fallen (352 ff.), and began a hymn of thanksgiving which showed that there was no longer any doubt in their minds. Halfway through their song (429) they began to dwell on the heavy price of victory, and to express misgivings about the fate in store for the Atridae when they return (450 ff.). Nowhere in their song, down to this final epode, is there the least suggestion of any lingering remnant of doubt about the fact of Troy's fall; indeed their misgivings and anxieties presuppose the impending return of Agamemnon. And now suddenly, indeed with extreme abruptness, they say 'How do we know that the tale is true? Who would be so foolish as to believe a beacon? Rumours spread by women vanish as quickly as they came.'

Fraenkel (pp. 245 ff.) rightly rejects certain 'psychological' speculations designed (with little skill and no success) to show that the total change of mind at 475 is the natural outcome of a development of ideas in the preceding stanzas. His own explanation, that there is 'a certain looseness in the psychological texture of the Chorus', of which 'Aeschylus takes full advantage', is not comforting: supposing that Aeschylus felt that he could take greater liberties with his Chorus than with his principal characters, we should still be astonished to find here (and here only) a Chorus ending with a vehement and unmotived rejection of the theme on which the whole of its song was founded. Winnington-Ingram, *CQ* n.s. iv (1954) 23 ff., has some excellent observations which bear directly upon the question at issue here: but the fact must still be faced, that there is nothing in this play or any other properly comparable with the present example, in which the foundations of a whole stasimon are undermined in the epode with sudden and total ruin.

As Fraenkel says, 'the sceptical attitude of the Chorus . . . provides a very effective foil to the speech of the Herald who finally confirms the fall of Troy': taken with what follows, the *volte face* is very effective; taken with what precedes it is completely out of joint. A momentary dramatic advantage, for those who look forward, is allowed to outweigh a serious flaw in the structure, for those who look back; we may well judge that the advantage was too dearly bought.

475-87. There is no authority for dividing these lines among *more than two* parties of choreutae (see Fraenkel, pp. 245 f.): but there is no objection to dividing them between *semichoirs* if the facts justify such division. The three consecutive asyndetic sentences (479, 483, 485) make a good prima facie case for alternation of speakers: though the sequence of ideas is not incompatible with continuity of speaker (Wilamowitz, *Verskunst*, p. 190). Division may well be right, but is not obligatory.

478. 'It is either something divinely-inspired or something false.' The adjective ψευδές is not employed by early writers, who use ψεῦδος, ψύθος instead; LSJ s.v. ψευδής init., cf. Pfeiffer on Callimachus fr. 288. 1.

479 ff. After τίς ὧδε παιδνός we expect ὥστε καμεῖν, not καμεῖν alone; and if the participle (πυρωθ.) accompanies the infinitive καμεῖν we expect it to be nom. πυρωθείς, agreeing with the subject (τίς), whether ὥστε is expressed or understood. The simplest explanation is that of Wecklein: the accus.+infin. construction, πυρωθέντα καμεῖν, depends on the *sense* ('it is a foolish thing . . .') instead of on the *syntax* ('who is so foolish . . .?') of what precedes.   **φρενῶν κεκομμένος**: lit.

'knocked from his wits' (genitive of separation). The meaning is: 'Who is so childish, so bereft of sense, as, having been inflamed in heart by sudden (or recent) tidings of the beacon, then to be afflicted at a change of story?' The slight incoherence is characteristic of the author; so is the indifference to the awkwardness of the metaphor πυρωθέντα καρδίαν in such a context as this.

483. αἰχμᾷ: unintelligible, and therefore perhaps to be marked as corrupt. *Cho.* 630 γυναικείαν ἄτολμον αἰχμάν, and *PV* 402 f. Ζεὺς . . . ὑπερήφανον θεοῖς τοῖς πάρος ἐνδείκνυσιν αἰχμάν, are often quoted as evidence that αἰχμή can mean 'rule', but in neither place is this acceptable: *Cho.* l.c. is a corrupt passage, and the most we can safely say is that γυναικείαν ἄτολμον αἰχμάν probably refers to women being *unwarlike*; in *PV* l.c. αἰχμάν means 'spear' as usual, and though this is a metaphor for 'power', it is still with a strictly *warlike* reference. There is no authority whatever for any extension of this usage into a region in which the spear, as an instrument of war, is not relevant. Nor yet is there any evidence that αἰχμή can mean 'spirit', 'temper' (LSJ): it might, in a suitable context, mean *'warlike* spirit', but that would be out of place here. There is no useful suggestion to record, unless it be ἀρχᾷ: ΑΡΧΑΙ to ΑΙΧΑΙ is an easy step, and ΑΙΧ⟨Μ⟩ΑΙ might then be written to make a Greek word.

484. χάριν ξυναινέσαι: neither the sense of αἰνεῖν nor the force of ξυν- allows the common rendering 'give thanks' or 'yield thanks'. The phrase means 'consent to, approve, thanks together (with other people)': a Queen too readily consents to a thanksgiving, i.e. agrees with her people that thanks should be given.

485 ff. The apparent meaning is, 'Too persuasive, a woman's ὅρος spreads abroad, swiftly travelling: but swiftly perishing the rumour uttered by a woman dies'.—But what then is the meaning of ὅρος? ' ὁ θῆλυς ὅρος est opinio mulieris de re quadam gesta, quam . . . definit. is ὅρος dicitur non *credulus* (ut vulgo intpp.) sed *ad persuadendum accommodatus*', Schütz. The second point, that πιθανός is active (not passive), is convincingly argued by Fraenkel. As for the first point, that ὅρος = *definitio*, here in the sense 'saying precisely what a thing is', hence 'laying down the law about a matter', it is surely much too great a strain on the language: ὁ θῆλυς ὅρος, *feminea definitio*, is to mean 'a woman's saying that a thing is such and such'; thus Clytemnestra laid down the law about the beacons, ruling that they signified the fall of Troy. We may well hesitate to acquiesce in anything so odd, crabbed, and obscure. The conjecture ἔρος (Ahrens) is ill-suited to the two adjectives, to the verb, and to the context (especially to the following clause). The rendering of ὅρος 'decree' (recorded by Hesychius) is much too far-fetched: Clytemnestra has decreed nothing, so far as we know, except perhaps the lighting of sacrificial fires. Still farther afield is Fraenkel's 'rule of conduct'; as if Clytemnestra's belief in the beacons, instituting of sacrifices, and announcement of the fall of Troy, set up a model of behaviour to which her subjects must conform—there is no evidence that ὅρος could mean this, even if it were a reasonable thing to say here.

So great is the difficulty that we are reduced to considering the possibility that both πιθανός and ἐπινέμεται are passive, and rendering with Weir Smyth 'Over-credulous, a woman's mind has boundaries open to quick encroachment' (lit., with Paley, 'Too credulous, the boundary of the female mind is encroached upon by rapid inroads'). In general, cf. *Cho.* 845–6.

488–9. τινὲς μέμφονται τῷ ποιητῇ ὅτι αὐθημερὸν ἐκ Τροίας ποιεῖ τοὺς Ἕλληνας ἥκοντας, Schol. vet.: a considerable time must in reality elapse between the first sight of the beacons and the arrival of the Greek army from Troy at Argos; Aeschylus takes no account whatever of any such interval; the two events are presented as occurring in almost immediate sequence. This lack of realism is to be regarded not as a peculiar fault in the structure of the play, but as an extreme example of an indifference to chronological probability characteristic of Tragedy. (Refutation of theories that the preceding stasimon is intended to mark the passage of time, or that the Chorus leave the scene for an interval at 488, will be found in Fraenkel's commentary.)

489 ff. The MSS. give 489–500 to Clytemnestra, 501–2 to the Chorus. Erroneous distribution of verses is common enough in better MSS. than these; but here there is a prima facie case in favour of accepting what we are offered, since (1) σοι in 496 is evidence that two persons or parties are engaged, (2) the asyndeton at 501, unusually harsh even for Aeschylus, strongly favours change of speaker. Nor is there anything in 489–500 unsuitable to Clytemnestra (with 489–92 cf. 590–2, with 498–500 cf. 349 f.). Almost all editors and commentators since Scaliger have altered the tradition and assigned 489–502 as a whole to the Chorus (a few with change of speaker at 501 because the asyndeton is so disagreeable). The principal reason for this change (indeed the only good reason) is the apparent awkwardness of leaving Clytemnestra silent on the scene from 501 to 587: it is thought incredible that the Herald should ignore her (and she him); that such conversation as there is should be between the Herald and the Chorus only; and that the Chorus, in Clytemnestra's presence, should reveal their fears and suspicions, as they do in 549–50.

It is nevertheless as certain as such things can be that Clytemnestra *is* present when the Herald arrives. Apart from the evidence of 496 and 501 (see above), we have to consider that when Clytemnestra begins her speech at 587 *she already knows that Agamemnon has arrived at Argos* (599): she could not possibly know this unless she was present when the Herald arrived, and heard at least part of what he says. It is of course possible that Aeschylus overlooked this point, or was indifferent to the fault, or hoped that we should assume that Clytemnestra had learnt the news somehow or other; but let us rather observe that neither explanation nor excuse is called for if we follow the MSS.' distribution of verses.

Professor D. S. Robertson makes the attractive suggestion that Clytemnestra might leave the scene at 537 (it is, as he says, important that she should set all her secret machinery in motion at once; in particular she must tell the news to Aegisthus without delay), thereby obviating the objection that the nature and tone of the conversation between the Herald and the Chorus make it hard to believe that the Queen is present throughout this part.

We proceed to consider whether Clytemnestra remains on the scene throughout the latter part, from 587 right down to 680. There is one strong indication that she does remain: the Herald's last speech loses much of its significance if the Queen is not present to hear one most important piece of information—that Agamemnon's is the *only* ship so far arrived, that he will come more or less alone, an easy victim, not protected by his brother, his chiefs, and his army.

The tension and power of the scenes, 503-37 and 615-80, are greatly enhanced by her presence, and particularly by her silence, throughout.

It should be noticed further that there is nothing to indicate that Clytemnestra leaves the scene at all from the time of her entry (which we presume to be at 40, or at latest 83) down to 1068; it is possible, and perhaps preferable, to imagine her as constantly present, though often in the background—θυηπολεῖς 262 gives a clue to what she might be doing during the long periods when she is in the background. Maas draws my attention to the similar example of Medea in Euripides' play: she enters the scene at *Med.* 214 and does not leave it until 1250.

489 ff. Possibly 'we shall soon know the relays of the torch-bearing lamps and of the beaconings and of the fire': but the three genitive-nouns seem clumsily joined and redundant in sense. Better to take εἰσόμεσθα as governing both the gen. λαμπάδων ('we shall soon know about the light-bearing torches') and the accus. παραλλαγάς ('the relays of beacon-watchings and fire'). So Conington, quoted by Fraenkel, who however finds it 'too laboured to be convincing'; with this judgement we may well agree, and we ought perhaps therefore to mark the text as corrupt; Wilamowitz's φρυκτωρίας (accus. plur.) is a possible remedy.

491. εἴτε ... εἴτε: *sive ... sive*, not *utrum ... an*.

493 f. In a normal situation one would infer from the Herald's olive-wreath the bringing of good news (S. *Tr.* 178 f., Chaeremon fr. 6). Here things are not so simple: the olive-wreath may signify that the war is happily ended, but we are anxious to know further whether Agamemnon and Menelaus are safely home.

494 f. κάσις πηλοῦ . . . κόνις: perilously close to the ludicrous; *ScT* 494, λιγνὺν μέλαιναν, αἰόλην πυρὸς κάσιν, is much more successful. Similar expressions are found, where indeed they are more at home, in the language of Hipponax, frr. 38, viii. 10 Diehl, fr. 37 Knox.

495. ξύνουρος: what is meant by saying that dust 'shares a boundary with, is a neighbour of, mud'? *quia ibi est pulvis, ubi desinit luti humor*, Klausen: i.e. simply because the two are commonly found side by side; perhaps so, if πηλός means *dried* mud. Or perhaps mud is called 'sister and neighbour of dust' for the reason that mud (on one's clothes, for example) may turn to dust when dry; it is thus 'related to' and 'not far removed from' dust.

496. The reader may well agree with Maas that this 'ethic' **σοι**, even if spoken by Clytemnestra, 'specializes awkwardly and unnecessarily'; he suggests οὔτε τωι (indef.) δαίων φλόγα. οὗτος οὐ λαίων conj. Wilamowitz.

496 f. The dust 'bears witness' that the Herald has come a long journey; he will not be a 'voiceless' messenger, merely lighting beacon-fires, but will speak out his message, whatever it may be.

498. ἐκβάξει λέγων is clearly antithetic to ἄναυδος . . . σημανεῖ καπνῷ πυρός, and the general sense is that the Herald will explicitly confirm the message of the beacons; but it is quite uncertain how the words should be taken. 'Either by his words express more clearly the joyful news . . .', Fraenkel: but **τὸ χαίρειν** should mean 'the activity of rejoicing' (*Eum.* 301, 423, S. *Ant.* 1170, *Ajax* 555), not 'the joyful news', and that is not a very convincing object for ἐκβάξει, 'will speak out'. Some render ἐκβάξει in effect 'command' ('he will bid us rejoice'; for the def. art. with the infin. cf. S. *El.* 467), but it is by no means certain that ἐκβάζειν could signify or imply *command* (though λέγων could, cf. 925 below and elsewhere). Nor is the reference of **μᾶλλον** perfectly clear: some take it with ἐκβάξει, 'he will declare more fully (than the beacons did)'; others with τὸ χαίρειν, 'he will bid us rejoice the more' (i.e. more than we have done hitherto)—the former of these alternatives is strongly suggested by πρὸς εὖ φανεῖσι (the message of the beacons) προσθήκη (the addition made by the messenger) πέλοι, as Maas observes.

499. ἀποστέργω: 'I am out of love with . . . .'

500. εὖ φανεῖσι alludes to the beacons. The **προσθήκη**, 'addition', is the contribution which the Herald's message will make. εὖ πέλοι προσθήκη is like εὖ πέλοιτο πρᾶξις in 255 above. Lit. 'To what has appeared favourably, let addition come to pass favourably.'

504. δεκάτῳ codd.: the meaning would then be 'in this tenth light of the year', and could signify nothing whatever but 'on the tenth day of the year'. What the Herald says must be 'on this day of the tenth year'. Erroneous assimilation of the cases of adjacent noun and adjective, as so often in MSS. ('The words of the MSS. mean "with (or "in") this tenth year's light"', Fraenkel: that is translating δεκά-του, not δεκάτῳ. Nothing analogous to the alleged phraseology can be quoted; E. *Ion* 1486, δεκάτῳ μηνὸς ἐν κύκλῳ, 'in the moon's tenth cycle' (= after ten months) is entirely irrelevant, for μηνὸς-κύκλος is a natural combination whereas ἔτους-φέγγος is not: φέγγος is regularly applied to *day*, not year, cf. 602, 1577 below, S. *Ajax* 673, E. *Hec.* 32, *Tro.* 850, etc.)

505. ῥαγεισῶν: a very rare metaphorical usage of this verb. The Scholiast (presumably guessing) says it refers to the breaking of mooring-cables.

507. For the construction see LSJ s.v. μετέχω I. 2.

509. For ὕπατος χώρας see 51 n.

510. Though χαῖρε is only formally an imperative, it makes it easy to give ἰάπτων μηκέτι the required imperative force, 'and shoot no longer . . .'.

511. Cf. *Il.* 1. 43–52.

512. 'Now on the contrary . . .'; LSJ s.v. αὖτε II. 2.

513. τούς τ' ἀγωνίους θεούς: ἀγωνίους has been variously interpreted, (1) οἱ τῶν ἀγώνων προεστῶτες (Hesychius): but this seems an unsuitable context for such stress on the gods who presided at the Games; (2) ἀγωνίους θεοὺς Αἰσχύλος τοὺς ἀγοραίους (Schol. BT on *Il.* 24. 1), cf. 90 above τῶν τ' ἀγοραίων: but in *Suppl.* 189, 242, 333, 355, where the same expression recurs, it is clear that the ἀγώνιοι θεοί are located *outside* Argos, not in its market-place; (3) ἀγώνιοι θεοί = θεῖος ἀγών, in the Homeric sense, 'divine *assembly*', 'gathering of the gods'; not 'gods *of the* Assembly' but 'gods *in* assembly': it is, however, questionable whether this sense would not demand the order of words καὶ θεοὺς ἀγωνίους; i.e. ἀγωνίους, between article and noun, would be expected to signify some attribute or function of the gods. On the whole, (2) seems the least improbable: 'gods of the Assembly', identical with the θεοὶ ἀγοραῖοι of 90 above.

514. τόν τ' ἐμὸν τιμάορον: 'my *protector*', lit. one who watches over my office, τιμήν; see Fraenkel.

516. When Cyrus' army crossed the borders of Persia into Media, they prayed to the gods and 'heroes' of Persia ἵλεως καὶ εὐμενεῖς πέμπειν σφᾶς, and to those of Media ἵλεως καὶ εὐμενεῖς δέχεσθαι αὐτούς (Xen. *Cyr.* 2. 1. 1, quoted by Headlam). Elsewhere 'heroes' are said to accompany an army in the form of images: Hdt. 5. 80 f., 8. 64. 2, 83. 2, the Aeacidae.

519. θᾶκοι: stone seats in front of the palace; cf. *Od.* 3. 404 ff., where Nestor and his sons sit in family conference ἐπὶ ξεστοῖσι λίθοισι | οἵ οἱ ἔσαν προπάροιθε θυράων . . . .   δαίμονές τ' ἀντήλιοι: the identity of these 'Divinities facing the Sun' is unknown; see Fraenkel' discussion.

520. εἴ που: this conjectural reading is not altogether satisfactory. The local sense of που, 'anywhere', is not appropriate here; the alleged temporal sense, as if εἴ που could stand for εἴ ποτε, is unparalleled. It remains to take που merely as a particle ('if at all', 'if in any circumstances'; cf. *Suppl.* 400), which is not quite what is wanted here. It is hard to be sure whether εἴ πω might stand here: it would make better sense, and would not be harder to defend, than εἴ που.

520. τοισίδε: the form is rare in Tragedy and specially liable to corruption where it does occur. (Here and perhaps *PV* 234 only in Aeschylus, in Sophocles only *Phil.* 956; in Euripides more frequently—*Alc.* 199, *Med.* 1295 (prob.), *Hkld.* 145, 251, 965, *Hipp.* 400, 1393, *H.* 499, *Ion* 314, *IT* 35, 747, *Hel.* 313, 444, 488, *Or.* 1125, *IA* 435, 813; in all except the fifth and eighth of these places there is some confusion in the principal MSS.) If τοισίδ' is correct here, the use of ὅδε, to denote some part or feature of a thing or person addressed by the speaker, is peculiar.   **φαιδροῖσι** is predicative, 'with brightness in these eyes of yours' (the adj. is purely metaphorical: we are under no compulsion to believe that the statues' eyes are, or are deemed to be, conveniently lit up by the morning sunshine).

521. κόσμῳ: adverbially, 'in a becoming manner'.   **πολλῷ χρόνῳ**: 'after a long time'.

522. ὑμῖν: the subjects addressed in 518 f. (not the Chorus, who are included in τοῖσδ' ἅπασι 523). In 524 the subject of ἀσπάσασθε is still the same; the Chorus is not addressed throughout this speech.   **φῶς κτλ.**: cf. Heracleitus fr. 26 ἐν εὐφρόνῃ φάος.

525. σκάπτειν is 'to dig', κατα- intensifies the action as in κατακτείνω, κατακόπτω. Thus κατασκάπτειν metaph. = 'to dig thoroughly', to make Troy look like a ploughed field.

526. μακέλλῃ: a pick, used for breaking up the ground.   **τῇ**: the article used as a relative pronoun; cf. 642   **κατείργασται**: 'wherewith the ground has been *thoroughly worked*' (Fraenkel).

527. Some have rejected this line as an interpolation, on the grounds that (1) it interrupts the metaphor begun in 526 and continued in 528 (σπέρμα); (2) it resembles a line found elsewhere in Aeschylus (*Pers.* 811 βωμοὶ δ' ἄιστοι δαιμόνων θ' ἱδρύματα); (3) the Herald ought not to boast of an action so shocking to the religious feelings of the Hellenes: 'to the poet and his contemporaries the destruction of holy places by the enemy seemed an unparalleled atrocity' (Fraenkel). Of these arguments the third alone seems considerable. It must, however, be observed that Clytemnestra made it clear (338 ff.) that there was reason to fear that the army might commit just this kind of sacrilege: and here we are told that they did commit it. Without this line, the question raised by 338 ff. would be nowhere answered. Moreover it seems unlikely that the poet would allow his Herald to exaggerate so grossly as to say that the land was utterly devastated, reduced to a ploughed field, no seed left in the soil, without referring to the fact (if it was one) that the temples, altars, shrines, and the like were left intact. If nothing whatever is said about the holy places, the strength of the Herald's language is such that the Chorus is bound to infer (and so are we, who have wanted an answer to the question raised in 338 ff.) that they are included in the tale of total ruin.

530. εὐδαίμων ἀνήρ: possibly to be taken with ἧκει, semi-adverbially.

532. ἀπὸ κοινοῦ τὸ οὔτε, Schol.   συντελής: either 'who shares (with Paris) payment of the bill', or simply metaph. 'associated with (Paris)'.

533. 'Boasts that the deed was greater than the suffering'; cf. *Pers.* 813 f.

534. Strictly, ἁρπάζειν = 'take by violence', κλέπτειν = 'take by stealth'; 'robbery', and 'theft'. Many edd. take both words to refer to the rape of Helen: perhaps rightly, for κλοπή is so used above (402), and ἁρπαγή is loosely applied elsewhere to voluntary elopements, cf. Hdt. 2. 118. 2 Ἑλένης ἁρπαγήν, 1. 2. 3 ἁρπάσαι . . . Μηδείην; in that case there will be some laxity and redundance in the language, κλοπῆς following weakly after ἁρπαγῆς, the stronger term. Others refer ἁρπαγή here to the rape of Helen, κλοπή to the theft of property from Menelaus' palace (Paris' theft of such property was a commonplace in the Epic, cf. *Il.* 3. 70, 91, 282, 285, 458, 7. 350, 22. 114, etc.; Proclus' summary of the *Cypria*, p. 103, 9–10 Allen; cf. Hdt. 2. 114, 118–19).

535. ῥυσίου: another loosely employed legal term. ῥύσιον signifies *stolen property forcibly recovered by its owner* (or other property forcibly seized in compensation for stolen property). If *A* steals *B*'s cattle, then what *B* seizes in return, whether his own cattle or something else in compensation, is τὸ ῥύσιον. Here the word means no more than 'plunder' in general; Paris' seizure of Helen (who is the property denoted by τὸ ῥύσιον here) was not an act in compensation for property stolen from him by Menelaus.

536. θερίζω is 'mow down', 'reap as a harvest'; the form θρίζω occurs here only, except in the compound ἀπέθρισεν E. *Or.* 128, ἀπέθρισας *Hel.* 1188. ἔθρισεν is anomalous in another way, being one of some fourteen examples in Tragedy of the lengthening of the syllabic augment before mute+liquid or nasal consonants (A. *Suppl.* 624, *Pers.* 395, *Agam.* 536, E. *Hkld.* 646, H. 150, *Hel.* 1188, *Or.* 12, 128, Anonymous in *Gk. Lit. Papyri*, no. 33, v. 19; add κέκλησθαι S. *El.* 366, fr. 86 P., E. fr. 833, Adesp. fr. 181).

αὐτόχθονον = αὐτῇ τῇ χθονί, 'ground and all'.

537. διπλᾶ: 'twofold', with a double meaning—(1) he has lost Helen, and his home has been destroyed; (2) double damages for theft were a common penalty in Greek law. See Fraenkel.

τὰ ἁμάρτια = τὸν μισθὸν τῆς ἁμαρτίας, Schol.

538. A blend of 'Herald from the army' and 'Herald of those in the army' produces 'Herald of those from the army'. There is a similar imperfect blend in 797–8 and 1244 below.

539. Cod. F has this line in a mutilated shape. Triclinius has applied a promising remedy to οὐκ ἀντερῶ, but τεθνάναι (an impossible form) demands further treatment. χαίρω ⟨γε⟩, τεθνάναι will not serve, for γε is seldom if ever used in this way (see Headlam ad loc., and *Gk. Particles*, p. 131: E. *Alc.* 420 is a clear case if codd. LP are to be trusted; E. *Rhes.* 219 is not similar enough); moreover τεθνάναι δ' οὐκέτ' ἀντερῶ could not mean 'I will no longer refuse to die' (it is indeed difficult to think of anything that it might mean). Schneidewin's supplement, ⟨τὸ⟩ τεθνάναι, has, as Headlam said, a certain plausibility: 'as to dying, I will no longer say no to the gods'; for the loosely attached article+infin. cf. S. *Phil.* 1252 πείθομαι τὸ δρᾶν, and *Ant.* 1105 f., καρδίας ἐξίσταμαι | τὸ δρᾶν, where καρδ. ἐξίστ., like οὐκέτ' ἀντερῶ here, means in effect 'I consent'. For the tense of τεθνάναι see Burnet on Plato, *Phaedo* 62ᵃ5.

540. The position of πατρῴας *before* τῆσδε gives it emphasis; similarly in 542 τερπνῆς τῆσδε νόσου, 520 above φαιδροῖσι τοισίδ' ὄμμασιν. **ἐγύμνασεν:** 'wore out', 'harassed', LSJ s.v. II.

541. ἐνδακρύειν ὄμμασιν: an odd expression, about which most of the commentators are silent or vague. 'Weep in, or with, my eyes', LSJ: but it may be not quite so odd as that, for the force of the preverb ἐν- may be 'I *begin to* weep'.

542. Lit. 'Sweet then was this malady of which you were in possession.'

543. διδαχθείς: emphatic by its early position, 'not until you have taught me shall I be master of your story'.

544 f. 'Smitten with longing for those that returned your love.'—'You mean that this land yearned for the army, while the army yearned for it?'

547. Since στρατῷ (codd.) here could only mean 'the army', the chain of thought is incoherent ('The people were gloomy *about the army.*'—'Whence came that gloom *upon the army*?'). The punctuation πόθεν τὸ δύσφρον; τοῦτ' ἐπῆν στύγος στρατῷ, 'Whence your gloom? That hateful mood was (not on you, but) on the army', would be possible only if στρατῷ στύγος were written for στύγος στρατῷ, since στρατῷ, the word to be stressed, could not bear the required emphasis if it stood last in its clause. **στρατοῦ** is the best of the conjectures, provided that δύσφρον στύγος (like φρενῶν στύγος in 1308 below) can be regarded as equivalent to στυγερὰ φροντίς, 'hateful care', governing a normal objective genitive, 'care *about* the army'.

550. τὸ σὸν δή: in parenthesis, 'to quote your own words', as in Plato, *Symp.* 221ᵇ, *Soph.* 233ᵇ; cf. also *Gorg.* 522ᶜ τὸ ὑμέτερον δὴ τοῦτο, ' ὦ ἄνδρες δικασταί ' (Maas). The Herald takes the Chorus to mean

'So that I, like you, could now die happy'; he therefore replies 'Yes, for things have turned out well.' What the Chorus really meant was 'My fears were, and are, of such a nature that I would rather not live to see the outcome.'

551 ff. If the MSS. are to be trusted, Aeschylus has to a certain extent adapted style to character here. The Herald's speech is lively and lucid, but here and there unpolished and disjointed.

551. ταὐτὰ serves its purpose of introducing τὰ μέν, τὰ δέ: it has no other function to perform, and no further account is taken of it; cf. 558 n.

552. εὐπετῶς ἔχειν = εὖ πεπτωκέναι (cf. 32); elsewhere εὐπετής = 'easy'.

553. δ' αὖτε: 512 n.; cf. 558.

554. χρόνος = time in general, αἰών = time relative to a man's life, often 'lifetime'; Wilamowitz on E. *H.* 669.

555 ff. What dwells in the Herald's memory is not the occasional dangers, so much as the perpetual discomforts, of war.   εἰ λέγοιμι: the apodosis never comes; in 563 he starts afresh, εἰ λέγοι τις, and again the sentence runs out uncompleted.   δυσαυλίας: hard lodging, uncomfortable quarters.

556. σπαρνάς: this very rare adjective is explained by Hesychius as 'scanty', 'slender', or 'scattered'; of these three meanings the second ('narrow') is most suitable here.   παρήξεις (unique; nor is ῆξις found): explained by Schol. vet. as meaning the παραδρομαί on a ship's deck (= gangways extending along either side; Torr, *Ancient Ships*, pp. 49 f.; full discussion in Fraenkel). The general sense seems to be that the men had to sleep in narrow gangways on the ships.

556–7. Prima facie the words suggest 'what not lamenting, (what) not having got as the day's portion?' The sense is perfectly appropriate, and it is not certain that there is any fault to find with the words. There is no great difficulty in carrying τί over from the first οὐ-phrase to the second; and ἤματος μέρος, 'the day's portion', runs easily in a context in which the *daytime's* share of hardship is being put along-side the *night's* discomforts (555 f.). The difference of participial tenses corresponds to the sense (κακὰ καθ' ἡμέραν λαχόντες ἐστένομεν, we were constantly lamenting, having got nothing but hardship in the day time).

558. τὰ δ' αὖτε χέρσῳ: 'and then again, on dry land . . .'; this little clause discharges its duty of introducing a new theme, and is not resumed hereafter.   καί emphasizes what follows, especially πλέον.

560–1. λειμώνιαι δρόσοι: the dew in the meadows where they lie is regarded as partly falling from the sky, partly arising from the earth.

561–2. ἐσθημάτων may depend on either σίνος or τρίχα.   ἔνθηρον: 'with animal-life in it', verminous.

τιθέντες: δρόσος, feminine a moment ago (560 λειμωνίαι), now suddenly becomes masculine. Elsewhere it is invariably fem., one of a small class of feminine o-stems (cf. νόσος ὁδός κόπρος ταφρός). See 119 n. We have to accept here an almost, perhaps quite, unparalleled aberration of language; perhaps an intentional soloecism, as Prof. Dover suggests—the Herald's talk is in other respects from time to time incoherent (cf. 647 f. ἥκοντα . . . συμμείξω), though there is nothing else so abnormal as this. (There is nothing specially to suggest MS. corruption here; and the possibility of a lacuna is as remote as it can well be.)

564. οἶον, 'of what kind', is explained by ἄφερτον, 'insufferable', cf. *Il.* 11. 653 f. οἷος ἐκεῖνος δεινὸς ἀνήρ, and often in the Epic.

565 f. Lit. 'when the sea fell and slept waveless in its windless midday-couch'; κοίταις: 'couches', not *condicio iacendi*.

568 f. τοῖσι . . . τεθνηκόσι is governed by μέλειν, which is an explanatory or consecutive infinitive: '(it has passed,) so that the dead care not even to rise ever again'. The dead have given up all thought of return to the world above (a matter not often mentioned in early literature, but cf. *Il.* 21. 56 f., Pearson on Sophocles fr. 557, Headlam on Herodas 1. 42); they are now settled in Hades, resigned to their fate.

570 f. Provided that no great exactitude and neatness are postulated for the Herald's speech, the chain of thought is coherent enough; but there is intolerable harshness in the linguistic connexions formed (1) by δέ in 573, which responds easily if it follows τοῖσι μὲν . . . μέλειν, but very ill if 570-2 intervene; (2) by καί in 572, following the rhetorical question in 570-1. (Here the matter is complicated by the difficulty of interpreting 572 as a whole: the most natural sense is 'I think fit to rejoice greatly at what has happened'; the alternative, 'so to adversity I bid farewell' (Headlam) involves an unexampled use of καταξιῶ.) It is doubtful whether this δέ and καί will yield to emendation; and the theory that 570-2 are a 'parallel passage' transferred from margin to text is, as often, unconvincing. The obvious course is to transfer 570-2 so that they follow 574 (so Elberling); the whole passage then runs well: 'It is past, so that the dead care not even to rise ever again, whereas for us who are left of the Argive army the gain prevails and the grief does not counterbalance it.' Now follows a word about the nature of this 'grief' and its want of power to outweigh the 'gain'—'Why should one count the number of lives spent, why should the living repine at malignant fortune? I think it proper actually (καί) to *rejoice* at what has happened, since we have the right to boast (that we are the victors of Troy etc.).'

575. τάδ' (for τῷδ') Weil, perhaps rightly.

576. ποτωμένοις (sc. ἡμῖν, governed by εἰκός, cf. E. *Suppl.* 40 f.) should not be altered τὸ ποτώμενα: a man's fame is said to 'fly' over land and sea (Pind. *Nem.* 6. 48 f.), and sometimes he himself is said to do so, Theognis 237 f. σοὶ μὲν ἐγὼ πτέρ' ἔδωκα σὺν οἷς ἐπ' ἀπείρονα πόντον | πωτήσῃ καὶ γῆν πᾶσαν ἀειράμενος; Pearson, *CR* xl (1926) 184. 'Since it is fitting for us, borne on wings over land and sea, to boast to this light of the sun . . . .'

577. Τροίην cod. F: the Homeric form may be correct in this context; see Björck, *Das Alpha Impurum* (1950) 161, 233.

577–8. ποτέ and ἀρχαῖον are correctly explained by Verrall: 'the praise is worded as it will be spoken a long time hereafter'; a normal feature of dedicatory inscriptions, see Wade-Gery, *JHS* liii (1933) 72 ff.

581–2. 'And so honour shall be done to the favour of Zeus which accomplished these things.'

583. Lit. 'I do not shun being conquered by what you say', i.e. I am not sorry to be convinced. Goodwin, *MT*, § 881, E. *H.* 1235, quoted by Fraenkel.

584. The MSS. offer the choice of two abnormal constructions: (1) ἡβᾷ impersonal, with the infinitive, 'it is always youth-time for old men to learn a lesson well', i.e. one is never too old to learn; (2) μαθεῖν as subject of ἡβᾷ: the construction may have a parallel in 181 above, if σωφρονεῖν is subject of ἦλθε; but the expression 'to be teachable (is a thing that) remains always young' (Fraenkel, with εὐμαθεῖν) is disagreeably artificial. The former alternative is to be preferred; though Margoliouth's ἥβη (sc. ἐστί) may be correct. εὖ μαθεῖν (codd.) would naturally mean 'to comprehend perfectly' or the like (S. *OT* 308 μαθόντες εὖ = *accurate edocti*): εὐμαθεῖν, 'to be a good learner', is superior in sense here; cf. *Cho.* 225, δυσμαθεῖς = 'you are slow to learn'.

589. Ἰλίου: to be taken with both nouns.

590. φρυκτωρῶν: either 'beacons' or 'beacon-watchers'; see Fraenkel.

594. ἔθυον: first person.   γυναικείῳ νόμῳ: *more muliebri*, because the ὀλολυγμός was specially a woman's cry (28 n.).

597. κοιμῶντες: they heap incense (cf. θυηφάγον, εὐώδη) on the fire, thus 'putting to sleep' the *flame* (and creating *smoke* instead).

598. τὰ μάσσω: 'the further tale'; for the def. art. τά see Platnauer on E. *IT* 1233. One might have expected μοι rather than ἐμοί; such examples are quite common.

600–1. ὅπως . . . ἄριστα: naturally taken together, like ὅπως τάχιστα in 605, simply 'in the best possible way'. Some take ὅπως with σπεύσω, as an example of the idiom illustrated by Porson on E. *Hec.* 398; but that is against the run of the words here. (ὅπως c. fut. indic., without a governing clause, expresses exhortation or warning, occasionally fear. It is most often found with 2nd person verb, since one usually exhorts or warns a second person, not oneself. Occasionally with 1st pers. plur. (E. *IT* 321, *Or.* 1060, Ar. *Eccl.* 296), which of course includes a 'second person'. Sometimes with 3rd pers. It is natural that it should be very rare with 1st pers. *singular*, since one usually exhorts or warns others, not oneself: the only apparent examples are E. *Hec.* 398, *Tro.* 147 f.; Antiphanes fr. 177 K. is doubtful in the absence of context.)

601–4. 'What day is sweeter for a woman to behold than this—to open the gates when a god has saved her husband from the campaign?' The infin. ἀνοῖξαι stands in apposition to τούτου and elucidates it. Fraenkel compares Plato, *Gorg.* 519ᵈ καὶ τούτου τοῦ λόγου τί ἂν ἀλογώτερον εἴη πρᾶγμα, ἀνθρώπους . . . ἀδικεῖν;

604–5. ταῦτ' ἀπάγγειλον: 'Report back what I have just said'; ἥκειν is dependent on the idea of 'telling' in ἀπάγγειλον, 'report this back to him (and tell him) to come . . .' (Weil's ἥκειν δ' would be an improvement).   ἐράσμιον: 'darling' (Headlam), an undignified and almost offensive word here, as Fraenkel shows.

606. πιστήν is predicative.   εὕροι expresses a wish. Not 'may he find a faithful wife at home' (as if the matter was open to doubt in anyone's mind), but 'let him discover that the wife in his house is a faithful one'; so Fraenkel, comparing *Suppl.* 952 f., *Pers.* 472 ff., for this use of εὑρίσκειν, 'discover that something is indeed the case'.

609. τἄλλ' ὁμοίαν πάντα: either 'the same (i.e. unchanged) in all other respects', or 'and similar (i.e. similarly loyal) in all etc.'   σημαντήριον: σφραγῖδα τῆς πρὸς ἄνδρα εὐνῆς, interlinear gloss in cod. Tr. The word 'includes the seal of chastity', as Headlam says; cf. his note on Herodas 1. 55 ἄθικτος ἐς Κυθηρίην σφρηγίς. The following lines (611 ff.) are prompted by the theme insinuated here. The surface meaning refers to the practice of sealing up store-rooms etc. during the master's absence (Plato, *Laws* 954ᵃᵇ).

611–12. ἐπίψογον φάτιν might mean 'blameworthy speech'. 'I know of pleasure or scandalous address from any other man no more than . . .' (Verrall). Alternatively, and more probably, 'censorious rumour'; in that case ἄλλου πρὸς ἀνδρός has a double reference.—'From no other man have I known pleasure; from no other man censorious rumour.'

χαλκοῦ βαφάς: iron is hardened, bronze softened (which is what 'tempered' should mean) and made more dilatable, by rapid cooling (e.g. by immersion in cold water after heating). Clytemnestra may be using χαλκός inaccurately for σίδηρος (so Schol. vet.); or she may be referring to the tempering of bronze. What one needs to know is well set out by Schliemann in *Troja*, ed. New York 1884, pp. 101 ff.

613 f. The MSS.' ascription to the Herald is obviously wrong; decisive arguments in Fraenkel's commentary, pp. 305 f.   τῆς ἀληθείας γέμων elucidates τοιόσδε, 'such is my boast—one full of truth'. οὐκ αἰσχρὸς . . . λακεῖν adds a further point, 'not disgraceful for a noble lady to utter'.   ὡς γυναικὶ γενναίᾳ: see Headlam, *CR* xvii (1903) 242 f.: the nuance in this idiom is normally 'that allowance

must be made for such a person'; Thuc. iv. 84. 2 οὐδὲ ἀδύνατος, ὡς
Λακεδαιμόνιος, εἰπεῖν, 'a capable speaker, *for a Spartan*'. Here, as in
S. *Ajax* 395, the note of condescension is wanting, and the meaning
is that, although in general it is disgraceful to boast, in this case you
must make allowance for the fact that the speaker is 'noble' and
what she says is 'full of truth'.

615-16: it is not possible to offer more than a makeshift text and
translation here. Fraenkel renders 'Thus she has spoken, a speech
which, if thou understandest it through clear interpreters, looks
fair', (similarly Verrall): i.e. μανθάνοντί σοι τοροῖσιν ἑρμηνεῦσιν = ἐὰν
μανθάνῃς διὰ τορῶν ἑρμηνέων. But, apart from the clumsy and obscure
arrangement and use of the dative cases, the sense of this is unsatisfactory—what is the Herald to make of it? That he needs the help
of 'clear interpreters' to observe that it is a *seemly* speech? Clearly
not. That if he reads between the lines he will observe that it is only
a *fair-seeming* speech? That, put in this form, is unsuitably outspoken.

As Schütz says, the general sense indicated is a contrast between
what the Herald understands and what the 'clear interpreters' understand; and indeed the second line says clearly enough 'to clear
interpreters a fair-seeming speech', though the slight change of
τοροῖσιν to τοροῖσι δ' may be thought an improvement, and εὐπρεπῆ
λόγον, however improbable the alleged corruption, would be much
more normal language than εὐπρεπῶς λόγον (since λόγον λέγειν, εἰπεῖν,
sim. is never found in Tragedy without some qualification of λόγον;
Fraenkel, p. 307). The difficulty lies in μανθάνοντι σοί, which cannot
mean 'to thy listening ear' (Sidgwick) or 'for thy schooling' (Weir
Smyth). οὕτως εἶπε μανθάνοντι σοί should mean 'thus she has spoken
to you understanding her', and that will not do since the whole point
is that the Herald did *not* understand. Since οὕτως εἶπε is not a
Tragic locution (Fraenkel, pp. 308 f.), it is possible that οὕτως should
be taken not with εἶπε but with μανθάνοντι, 'she spoke, and you
understand her *thus*' (LSJ s.v. οὕτως IV, 'offhand', 'just like that';
Plato, *Euthyphr.* 3ᵇ ὡς οὕτω γ' ἀκοῦσαι, 'at first hearing', cf. *Ly.* 216ᵃ),
'(but) to clear interpreters a fair-*seeming* utterance'.

620-3. The language is heavy and laboured. Lit. (620-1) 'I could not
speak of what is false so as to be fair, for my friends to enjoy for the
long time ahead', i.e. I cannot tell lies in such a way that they will be
fine stories, to give lasting pleasure; καλά is the predicate, καρποῦσθαι
explanatory infinitive. The reply is (622-3): 'Would then that you
might rightly tell (εἰπὼν τύχοις, 'hit the mark saying . . .') the *truth*
so as to be good; when these (viz. the true and the good) are sundered,
they are not easily hidden' (i.e. it is hard to hide the fact); κεδνά
predicative.

626 ff. This version of the story, according to which Agamemnon and

Menelaus sailed home from Troy together, recurs in Sappho, fr. 17; the Epic gave a different account, *Od.* 3. 136 ff.

630–1. Lit. 'Was rumour about him as living, or as dead, spoken of by the other sailors?' On φάτις c. gen. see Paley on *Suppl.* 478.

633. χθονὸς φύσιν: an unusual phrase, apparently = τὰ ἐν τῇ χθονὶ φυόμενα; cf. S. *Ant.* 345 πόντου εἰναλίαν φύσιν, 'a brood living in the waters of the sea' (Jebb).

635. κότῳ with ἐλθεῖν only, τελευτῆσαί τε being more or less parenthetic.

637. χωρὶς ἡ τιμὴ θεῶν: 'apart (is) the honour of the gods' (or 'honour due to . . .', 'worship of', or the like), i.e. the honour of (or due to) the gods stands aloof from, is kept distinct from, inauspicious utterances of the kind to which the preceding clause refers. ἡ τιμὴ θεῶν = ἡ θεῶν τιμή, or ἡ τιμὴ ἡ τῶν θεῶν, a rare usage but not unexampled in Aeschylus and the other Tragedians: *Eum.* 1029 τὸ φέγγος . . . πυρός; *Niobe, Greek Literary Papyri* (Loeb) i, fr. 1. 5 τοὐπιτέρμιον γάμου, a probable example; *Pers.* 604 τἀνταῖα . . . θεῶν, another probable example; Sophocles *OC* 1721 τὸ τέλος . . . βίου; Euripides *El.* 368 αἱ φύσεις βροτῶν, *IA* 72 ὁ μῦθος Ἀργείων. (All these examples are quoted by Fraenkel, whose statement on p. 316, that there is 'no real parallel to the supposed ἡ τιμὴ θεῶν', is modified on p. 317, where the parallels are said to be 'to say the least, extremely scanty'. The interpretation which he favours involves taking ἡ τιμή to mean 'the honour done *to the Erinyes* (and suchlike powers) by him who utters inauspicious words'; then θεῶν has to mean 'heavenly' gods, contrasted with these Erinyes or the like (who have not yet been mentioned); i.e. χωρὶς ἡ τιμὴ θεῶν = 'That celebration (viz. that which consists in uttering inauspicious words) stands apart from the gods' (viz. from the heavenly as contrasted with the underworld gods). The obscurity of this—especially in respect of the sense assigned to ἡ τιμή—appears an insuperable objection.)

639. Hesychius has the entry σμοιῷ προσώπῳ· φοβερῷ ἢ στυγνῷ, σκυθρωπῷ, whence M. Schmidt conjectured σμοιῷ for στυγνῷ in the text here: a long but by no means unlikely shot.

640 ff. The Herald's Greek becomes incoherent here, if the MSS. are to be believed. It may be mistaken in theory, as it is impossible in practice, to treat it according to the rules of normal grammar. He intends an antithesis between the city as a whole and the fate of individual homes; and this he expresses as follows: '(The messenger brings the bad news) that a wound has befallen the city—*one* wound, affecting the community (τὸ δήμιον)'—then, instead of continuing 'and a *second* wound, desolating the homes of many individuals', he goes on '*and that* many persons having been taken from many homes . . .', a sentence which lacks a main verb; or we might say that the verb of speaking implied in 638–9 governs first an infinitive (τυχεῖν)

and then a participle (ἐξαγισθέντας). The incoherence may be intentional, but Blomfield's conjecture τυχόν would be an improvement, both participles being governed by the ἀγγέλλειν implicit in 638–9.
ἐξαγισθέντας: the meaning can only be guessed; perhaps 'sacrificed (or 'taken as victims') from many homes'. ἐξ- must govern δόμων, hence no help is forthcoming from the adj. ἐξάγιστος, in which ἐξ- has a different function (either 'put *outside* the bounds of the holy', 'excommunicated', or '*very* holy'; cf. S. *OC* 1526 and ἐξοσιούσθω in E. *Ba.* 70). -αγισθέντας is probably to be referred to the verb ἁγίζω, though none of its known meanings is applicable here. (Headlam referred it to the root of ἄγος, 'pollution', equating ἐξαγισθέντας with ἀγηλατηθέντας, 'driven out as accursed'; but the essential 'drive' element is wanting in the alleged verb ἁγίζω.)

642. διπλῆ: cf. S. *Ajax* 242 μάστιγι διπλῆ. The reference may be to the double use (whip and goad), or to the two points in which the μάστιξ ended: but the threefold stress on its doubleness suggests that the adj. here is not merely picturesque—it is called first 'double', then, 'two-pointed bane', finally the two points are called a 'sanguinary couple' (both the latter phrases are in apposition to τήν, which refers to the μάστιξ). Probably, as Headlam and others say, the *double* scourge refers back to the *double* harm—public and private—of which the Herald made so much a moment ago.

644. The previous sentence being now confused beyond hope of recovery the Herald begins afresh: 'Well, when a man has a load of troubles like *that* . . . .'

645. τόνδε: referring to the 'paean of the Erinyes' implicit in κακαγγέλῳ γλώσσῃ μιαίνειν above; 638–43 are in effect a sketch of such a 'paean'. See 57 n.   **παιᾶνα . . . Ἐρινύων**: a 'blasphemous paradox', as Fraenkel says; the paean was the opposite of the type of song associated with the Erinyes.

646 ff. The Herald loses the thread again; εὐάγγελον ἥκοντα never acquires a governing verb, the sentence starting afresh at πῶς . . . συμμείξω.

648. In this context, 'mix evil with the good' is what he means; he has said 'mix good with the evil'.

649. The MS. text is unintelligible, and the common solution, to transpose the terminations of Ἀχαιῶν and θεοῖς (cf. *Suppl.* 369, S. *Phil.* 324), is not attractive; it is doubtful whether Ἀχαιοῖς οὐκ ἀμήνιτον θεῶν could mean 'not without wrath on the part of the gods against the Achaeans', and the alleged parallels quoted in support seem remarkably wide of the mark. Ἀχαιοῖς τ᾽ οὐκ ἀμήνιτον θεόν, 'and that the god was enraged against the Achaeans', is what we might have hoped for, but it is not nearly what the MSS. offer.

650. The 'enmity' of fire and water was proverbial; see Headlam.

651. τὰ πιστά as in *Eum.* 673, 'their good faith'.

653. For the postponement of δέ see *Gk. Particles*, pp. 187 f. ὠρώρει is a Homeric type of pluperfect (cf. *Od.* 5. 294 ὀρώρει δ' οὐρανόθεν νύξ), not, as in Attic, of time anterior to the main action, but carrying on the narrative; see Fraenkel.

654. The feminine dative plural -ῃσι (seldom -ῃσι) is the norm in Attic inscriptions up to *c.* 420 B.C.; see Meisterhans, *Grammatik der attischen Inschriften* (third edition), pp. 120 f. The form (whether -ῃσι or -ῃσι) appears in a dozen places in MSS. of Aeschylus, and may be original (cod. M at *PV* 727, *Pers.* 189, *ScT* 460, 603, *Cho.* 569, *Eum.* 703); seldom in Sophocles; in Euripides, 23 examples in the six principal MSS.

655. κεροτυπούμεναι (here only) = 'being rammed'.

656. σύν: with both χειμῶνι and ζάλῃ. For the usage of σύν, cf. *Pers.* 775 f. τὸν δὲ σὺν δόλῳ | Ἀρταφρένης ἔκτεινεν, [*ScT*] 877 δόμους ἑλόντες... σὺν ἀλκᾷ; in effect an instrumental use (Dindorf, *Lex. Aesch.* p. 341, § 3). ζάλῃ means, or refers to, rain: hence ὀμβροκτύπῳ, 'with beating showers'; the relation of the two parts of the compound is similar to that in ἁλίκτυπον (κῦμα), E. *Hipp.* 754, κυμόκτυπος (Αἰγαῖος), E. *Hypsipyle* 3 (1) ii. 28.

657. The ships are like a flock of sheep thrown into confusion by an 'evil shepherd' (the storm). στρόβῳ: a whirling-round; cf. *Cho.* 202 f. οἷοισιν ἐν χειμῶσι ναυτίλων δίκην | στροβοῦμεθ'.

659. ἀνθοῦν ... νεκροῖς: '*blossoming* with corpses', an exceptionally incongruous metaphor; E. *IT* 300, ὡς αἱματηρὸν πέλαγος ἐξανθεῖν ἁλός, conveys an entirely different image, since ἐξανθεῖν is a medical term (of eruption, efflorescence) appropriate to the context.

661. Either 'ship unharmed in hull (σκάφος)', or ἀκήρατον σκάφος in apposition to ναῦν.

662. ἐξῃτήσατο: as Apollo, for example, 'begged off' Admetus from death.

664. σωτήρ: the use of masc. forms of agent-nouns adjectivally with fem. substantives is quite common; cf. 111 above, χερὶ πράκτορι, S. *OT* 80 f. τύχῃ σωτῆρι. θέλουσα: a commonplace in the language of prayer, illustrated by Fraenkel (*Cho.* 19, *Suppl.* 144, Pind. *Isthm.* 6. 42 f.).

665. If they try to ride out the storm at anchor they may be swamped (κύματος ζάλην ἔχειν); if they do not anchor, they may be driven ashore (666).

667 ff. 'Then, being free from death at sea, in the white daylight (cf. *Pers.* 301), not trusting in fortune (i.e. not thinking that ill-fortune was at an end), we pondered in anxious thought our recent suffering.'

670. The difference in tenses indicates that the fleet *suffered* (in the night) and *is still being* 'cruelly pounded' (in the morning).

672. τί μήν: 'what else?', i.e. 'of course'; *Gk. Particles*, p. 333.

673. τὰ αὐτὰ ἔχειν: 'to be in the same state'; LSJ s.v. ἔχω A 1. 8.

674. γὰρ οὖν signifies that *Menelaus'* safety is the essential point; it is the matter about which the Chorus had specially asked (617).

674 ff.: among the unsolved problems. προσδόκα c. aor. inf. μολεῖν would normally mean 'expect that he *arrived*': but then the sequel, 'If, then, he is still alive, there is *some hope* that he *will* arrive', seems absurd, and it is no help to suppose that μολεῖν = 'has landed somewhere in Greece' whereas ἥξειν πρὸς δόμους = 'reach his home in Argos'; for if he has reached Hellas, there is nothing whatever to stop him reaching Argos, and no sense in continuing 'in that case there is *some hope* that he will reach Argos'.

The least unpromising lines of approach are:

(1) To suppose that μολεῖν in 675 has been substituted for θανεῖν (through a mistaken conception of the sense, like μολεῖν for λαβεῖν in S. *Phil.* 47). The Herald having said 'each party thinks that the other has perished', it seemed natural to continue 'our first expectation must therefore be that Menelaus *did not survive*'. εἰ δ' οὖν then follows well, introducing as often a thesis believed to be false but stated for the sake of argument. (*Gk. Particles*, p. 465: S. *El.* 577 'He acted involuntarily; but even supposing he acted voluntarily . . . ; *OT* 851 'He cannot retract; but even supposing he does . . .'; Ar. *Equ.* 423 'Nobody saw me; but if anyone should . . .'. Paley's treatment of εἰ δ' οὖν on *Agam.* 1009 (= 1042) below is seriously at fault; the kind of ellipse which he postulates here (676) is foreign to the use of this idiom.) The sense will then be: 'Your first expectation must be that Menelaus died; but if it should happen that he did survive, there is no reason to despair of his getting home.' The great objection to this is the drastic nature of the alteration made in the text.

(2) To take προσδόκα μολεῖν in the sense 'expect that he *will* arrive', cf. *ScT* 367 ἐλπίς ἐστι . . . μολεῖν (Goodwin, *MT* § 127; Pearson on fr. 339). εἰ δ' οὖν will then be continuative, or illustrative, as often (*Agam.* 1042, *Cho.* 571, E. *Hkld.* 310, *H.* 213, *Rhes.* 572): 'if, then, some beam of the sun knows of him alive and open-eyed, . . . there is some hope that he will reach home again'. The chain of thought is: 'Each party thinks the other dead; since they are mistaken in this, so may we be; therefore our first expectation should be that Menelaus will arrive safely, as we have done. If, then (i.e. taking that assumption) he *is* still alive somewhere, having survived the storm, there is no reason to despair of his getting home again.' The form of expression is not perfect, but it remains doubtful whether the case for alteration of the text is strong enough.

676. ἱστορεῖ: 'knows', an abnormal usage; cf. *Pers.* 454, *Eum.* 455.

677. χλωρόν τε καὶ βλέποντα· ἀντὶ τοῦ ζῶντα, Hesychius: as in 639, so here, it is likely that the quotation comes from this play and that the easier word has replaced the harder in our text.

677–8. μηχαναῖς ... γένος could, but less naturally, be taken with what follows.

683. μή τις: not necessarily expecting a negative answer, cf. *Suppl.* 295, *PV* 247 (Fraenkel).

685. ἐν τύχᾳ: 'successfully', 'accurately', an apparently unique adverbial phrase, analogous to ἐν δίκᾳ = ἐνδίκως.

686 f. Perhaps as Robertson suggests, *CR* li (1937) 162, τὰν δορίγαμβρον ἀμφινεικῆ τε is the direct object of ὠνόμαζεν, and Ἑλέναν the predicate: 'Who was it that named the bride "Helen"?'   **δορίγαμβρον**: a unique compound, of loosely related elements, meaning that her γάμβρος (bridegroom) or γάμβροι (kinsmen by marriage) had to do with the spear. Not 'bride of battle', as given by LSJ, since γαμβρ- is not used of the female.   **ἀμφινεικῆ**: ἀμφι- implies *two* sides; 'a cause of dispute between two lovers' (Paley), or rather between two parties, Greeks and Trojans. Cf. S. *Tr.* 104.

688. ἑλέναυς Blomfield, perhaps rightly; but ἑλένας makes the point clearly enough (and incidentally gives a form of which the accus. would be ἑλέναν, 687).

690. ἁβροτίμων codd., perhaps rightly, 'delicate and costly', like ἁβρόπλουτος in E. *IT* 1148; but -πήνων is a considerable gain at slight cost.

691. προκαλυμμάτων: more probably curtains of the bed-chamber or of the bed itself (Pollux iii. 37) than curtains at the palace-door (so Headlam, after Athenaeus iv 145ᵇ τοῦ προκαλύμματος τοῦ ἐπὶ τῇ θύρᾳ).

692. γίγαντος: an extraordinary epithet for Zephyrus in this context. The entry in Hesychius, γίγαντος· μεγάλου, ἰσχυροῦ, ὑπερφυοῦς, may relate to this passage, but if so it adds nothing to our knowledge except the guesses of the ancients in a difficult place. Zephyrus was in fact a 'Giant', i.e. of the race of the Titans (Hes. *theog.* 378 f.), but it is hard to see why Aeschylus should have thought it appropriate to say so here.

693. πολύανδροι = πολλοὶ ἄνδρες ὄντες, 'numerous'. Perhaps δέ (Stanley) for τε.

696 ff. Text and metre are uncertain here. Many edd. take the subjects of κελσάντων (codd.) to be Helen and Paris: '(on the track) of them who had landed', or gen. absol. 'after they had landed'. It is then necessary to understand ἔπλευσαν (from 691) as the main verb for κυναγοί, a disagreeably harsh procedure. An easy sentence is made with **κέλσαν** (= ἔκελσαν) followed by τάς for -των, 'the hunters landed on to the shores of Simois'. For the rest, ἀεξι- (Triclinius) for ἀξι- is attractive, giving good sense and easy metre. See, however, 715 ff. n.

698. διά c. accus. here may be either (1) of cause, 'through the work of Strife', or (2) of purpose, 'for the sake of strife', cf. Thuc. iv. 40. 2 δι' ἀχθηδόνα, 'with the object of inflicting pain', Lysias xii. 31 διὰ τὴν ἑαυτῶν σωτηρίαν, 'in order to preserve themselves'; LSJ s.v. διά B III. 3, K.–G. i. 485. The former seems the more poetical.

699. Ἰλίῳ: apparently dependent on κῆδος, 'a bond for Ilium', since ἐλαύνω c. dat. meaning 'drive to (or against)' would be abnormal.

699–700. ὀρθώνυμον: 'rightly-named', for κῆδος may mean 'bond' either of marriage or of sorrow. For ἤλασεν, 'set in motion', see Fraenkel.

701 ff. πρασσομένα with double accusative, LSJ s.v. VI: 'in aftertime exacting requital *for* the dishonouring of the table and of Zeus, god of the common hearth, *from* those who loudly celebrated the song in honour of the bride, the marriage-hymn which at that time fell to the bridegroom's kin to sing'.   ἐκφάτως here only, probably 'outspokenly'; not in silent condonation but in loud approval of Paris' deed.

710. γεραιά: probably conventional, cf. S. *El.* 4 παλαιὸν Ἄργος, Hor. *Od.* i. 15. 8 *regnum Priami uetus*; possibly 'old though she is, she must yet unlearn . . .' (so Fraenkel).

711. πολύθρηνον: with ὕμνον, 'learning instead a song of much lamentation'.

713. τὸν αἰνόλεκτρον: for this use of the definite article where the actual words used by somebody are reported, see E. *Med.* 207 n.

714–16. The strophe at this point was corrupt enough (see 696 ff.); here corruption goes deeper, it is hard to determine how deep. **παμπορθῆ** (Seidler) is a likely correction of παμπρόσθη; and the fact that πολύθρηνον occurred a moment ago is not a fatal argument against its occurrence here (see 362 n.). The real difficulty lies in the word ἀμφί: for unless the strophe is more seriously corrupt than it appears, we need – – ∪ ∪ – where we now have – – – ∪ (αἰὼν᾿ ἀμφί); moreover it is very doubtful whether ἀμφί gives a suitable meaning— LSJ illustrate the sense 'for the sake of . . .', but their examples are not really like the present place, where anyway the meaning should be 'because of'. αἰῶνα διαί (Emperius) for αἰὼν᾿ ἀμφί would do all that is necessary to sense and metre ('having endured a lamentable life of utter destruction because of the piteous bloodshed of her citizens'); but it is impossible to explain how διαί should ever have been corrupted into ἀμφί. There has been no other likely approach to a solution.

717 ff. 'Just so (οὕτως) a man reared a lion's cub in his house, robbed of its mother's milk and longing for the breast, tame in the prelude of its life, a good friend to children and a delight to elders.'   ἔθρεψεν: a real aorist, not a 'gnomic' one, is naturally used in recounting a fable or story of this kind.   δέ is unexpected: perhaps similar to its use in opening a speech, cf. Xen. *Cyr.* 7. 1. 21 πρὸς τοῦτον ἔλεξεν· ἐγὼ δὲ ἔρχομαι; *Gk. Particles*, pp. 172 f.   ἴνιν: elsewhere only of human or divine offspring; cf. παίδων in 50.   οὕτως: the common word for starting a fable, cf. Ar. *Vesp.* 1182 οὕτω ποτ᾽ ἦν μῦς καὶ γαλῆ (Schol.: τῶν μύθων προέταττον 'οὕτω', οἷον· ἦν οὕτω γέρων καὶ γραῦς); since the fable is introduced to illustrate a given theme, it is natural to begin 'Just so . . .'. (But the word here comes unduly late in the sentence, and ἀγάλακτον αὕτως, cf. Epic νήπιον αὕτως, would be a great improvement.)

720. βιότου προτελείοις: see 65 n.

722. γεραροῖς: the word implies both age and the dignified behaviour appropriate to age.

723. 'And many a thing it got . . .': 'The pretty tricks of the beast made everyone pet it and feed it', Verrall. πολέα δ᾽ ἔσκ᾽ conj. Casaul on, 'and often it was (in their arms)': but the MSS.' text needs no change, and is supported by what follows (ποτὶ χεῖρα, γαστρὸς ἀνάγκαις).

725 f. 'With its bright eye turned toward his hand, and fawning under compulsion of its belly's need', Weir Smyth.

727 ff. Lit. 'In the fulness of time it showed the temper it had from its parents. Repaying thanks to those who reared it, unbidden it made a feast, together with ruinous slaughter of flocks, and the house was defiled with blood, for the housefolk an anguish without defence, a great havoc of many murderings; by divine will it had been reared, a new (προσ-) inmate for the house, to be a sacrificer in the service of destruction.'

The poet presumably means something more than that a lot of *sheep* (μηλοφόνοισι) were killed. From 732 onwards one has the impression that *men* too are being killed: but, if so, the fact is not stated, and the transition from animal to human victims is made with the utmost brusqueness.

737. πάραυτα· παραχρῆμα, εὐθέως, παραυτίκα, Hesychius, 'at once': but 'at once, immediately' does not suit the context here. More promising is 'at that time', 'on the very occasion', which is clearly the sense in Euripides fr. 1079. 5 πάραυτα δ᾽ ἡσθεὶς ὕστερον στένει διπλᾶ. What is required is something like 'at first': perhaps that is in effect the meaning, lit. 'at the time of the events themselves', i.e. when Paris and Helen first eloped from Sparta to Troy.

739–40. Lit. 'a disposition (spirit, mentality) of windless calm', a temper of unruffled calm. This descriptive genitive is of a type abnormal in Greek: K.–G. i. 264 ('adjectival genitives') quote a few similar examples, S. *Ajax* 1003 ὄμμα . . . τόλμης πικρᾶς, 616 f. ἔργα . . . μεγίστας ἀρετᾶς, *El.* 19 ἄστρων εὐφρόνη, E. *Ba.* 389 ὁ τᾶς ἡσυχίας βίοτος; cf. 1535–6 below.

741. ἄκασκα· ἡσύχως, μαλακῶς, βραδέως, Hesychius. The meaning is uncertain, perhaps 'gentle', 'peaceful'. ἄγαλμα πλούτου: 'ornament of wealth', i.e. something which adds adornment to wealth (conceivably but less probably 'thing in which wealth delights', ᾧ πλοῦτος ἀγάλλεται). The supplement δ' is demanded by metre and by the μέν of 740 alike (this μέν could not possibly be answered by the δέ of 745; to do so it would have to stand *outside* the coherent phrase φρόνημα νηνέμου γαλάνας).

744 ff. These lines have been generally misunderstood, as if the lion-cub were a symbol for Helen herself. That is clearly not so: what is being compared is *the lion-cub's career as a whole* with *the whole set of circumstances for which Helen was responsible*, not specifically *the lion-cub* with *Helen herself*. The poet himself misled us into thinking at first that there was going to be a close comparison between her and the lion-cub: but it was never very apt, and now it breaks down completely, and the poet unobtrusively shifts his ground. Helen did not, as the lion-cub did, change her nature and turn against her Trojan benefactors: what wrong she did was done before ever she came to Troy; she owed the Trojans no debt for her upbringing, and she made no attack upon them thereafter. To say that Helen herself, after her arrival at Troy, 'swerved aside' (παρακλίνασα), would be plainly untrue; and there are other reasons why it is impossible to take *Helen* as the subject of 744–9, identifying her with the Erinys— (1) It would be ridiculous to say that she went to Troy πομπᾷ Διὸς ξενίου, by the sending or escorting of the deity most offended by her going thither (cf. 61 f., 401 f.): it is of course the Fiend of Wrath, Ἐρινύς, who was sent by Zeus Xenios in pursuit of Helen. (2) She who was just said to have gone to Troy as a 'spirit of windless calm' cannot now be said to have gone there δύσεδρος καὶ δυσόμιλος.

It is certain that the Erinys here is the Erinys, not a personification of Helen.   **παρακλίνασα**, transitive as usual, governs γάμου τελευτάς jointly with the main verb, 'she turned from its course, and accomplished a bitter end of, the marriage'.   **νυμφόκλαυτος**, unintelligible if Helen herself is the Erinys, may now mean as it should 'bewept by the bride', i.e. by Helen. In the fable of the lion-cub, the animal itself could be, and was, the 'Priest of Ruin': in the tale of Helen this identification was ruled out by the facts, and the poet moves away from Helen to the Erinys who, in her story, is to be the ἱερεύς τις ἄτας. The common attempt to *identify* Helen with the Erinys here reduces the stanza to falsity as a whole and to unintelligibility in some of its details (particularly παρακλίνασα and νυμφόκλαυτος); the lack of balance between the two halves of the comparison is very like that in 50 ff. above.

751–2. μέγαν τελεσθέντα: 'when it has come to full growth'.

754. Fraenkel draws attention to the peculiarity of μηδέ here, where οὐδέ would be expected. The usage is as inexplicable as that in Thuc. i. 118. 2, ὄντες μὲν καὶ πρὸ τοῦ μὴ ταχεῖς ἰέναι ἐς τοὺς πολέμους, where οὐ seems imperatively demanded.

755 f. 'From good fortune there grows insatiable misery for the race.'

757–62. In the religious and ethical thought of the sixth and fifth centuries B.C. κόρος–ὕβρις–ἄτη are often linked together as successive elements in the downfall of man. κόρος is the state in which a man has *too much* prosperity—too much either absolutely or relatively to his condition and character. κόρος leads to ὕβρις, the state of being arrogantly proud, self-willed, contemptuous of duty towards gods and men. And ὕβρις is followed by ἄτη, which may signify either ruin or a ruinously sinful action (or disposition). Thus Solon fr. 3. 7–9 οἷσιν ἑτοῖμον | ὕβριος ἐκ μεγάλης ἄλγεα πολλὰ παθεῖν· | οὐ γὰρ ἐπίστανται κατέχειν κόρον: those who cannot control κόρος are driven by ὕβρις to ἄτη (ἄλγεα πολλά). Solon fr. 5. 9–10 τίκτει γὰρ κόρος ὕβριν, ὅταν πολὺς ὄλβος ἔπηται | ἀνθρώποισιν, ὅσοις μὴ νόος ἄρτιος ᾖ (cf. Theognis 153 f.) : the ὄλβος would not in itself be fatal, if the man had νόος ἄρτιος. Pind. *Ol.* 1. 55–56 (Tantalus) καταπέψαι μέγαν ὄλβον οὐκ ἐδυνάσθη, κόρῳ δ᾽ ἕλεν ἄταν: he could not 'digest' his prosperity, and κόρος led him to ἄτη. Solon fr. 1. 7–16: righteously acquired wealth endures, but ill-gotten wealth is transient and leads to ἄτη. Cf. Solon fr. 3. 34–35, Theognis 229–31, Pind. *Pyth.* 2. 28. Exceptionally, as in Pind. *Ol.* 13. 10 and the Herodotean oracle 8. 77. 1, the relationship is reversed, and ὕβρις is said to be the *parent* of κόρος : that is an opposite point of view of the same circumstances—you may say that it is excess of worldly goods which leads to arrogance of character, but you may also say that it is the man whose character is given to arrogance who allows his prosperity to pass the limits of moderation.

The opinion which the Chorus here advances as an exceptional and personal one (δίχα δ᾽ ἄλλων μονόφρων εἰμί) was not in fact at all novel : the idea that the blame falls not on prosperity in itself, but on the sinful acts of over-prosperous men, had been clearly enough expressed by Solon a very long time ago (frr. 1. 9 ff., 5. 9–10), as many a member of the audience must have recalled.

758–9. 'For it is the impious act (not prosperity) that begets a progeny of still more impious acts after it, children alike to their parents.'

761. γάρ: it is the impious act, not prosperity, that is at fault; *this is shown by the fact that* the righteous man prospers enduringly; a common use of γάρ.

762. καλλίπαις πότμος: the impious deed begets impious children (758 f.), the righteous house has 'destiny consisting in fair offspring'; the 'children' of Justice are contrasted with those of Impiety. This is the normal sense of καλλίπαις, εὔπαις, 'having good (or beautiful) children'.

766–79. Only a makeshift text can be reconstructed from the meagre and corrupt tradition. The principal difficulties are (1) 766 ὅτᾶν, against the metre (– or ‿ required); (2) 767 νεαρὰ φάους κότον is unmetrical nonsense ; (3) 768 τέ τόν, against the metre (‿ – required); (4) 770–1 εἰδομέναν can only agree with δαίμονα (fem., cf. E. *Alc.*

1003, al.); and that is very awkward, since noun and participle are separated by a weighty phrase; (5) 776 ἐσθλά needs some correction; (6) 778 προσέβᾱ τοῦ, against the metre (∪∪∪∪ required) and against the sense. The first and fifth of these problems can be simply (though not necessarily correctly) solved by ὅτε for ὅταν and by ἐδεθλα for ἐσθλά. For the second, no better suggestion is available than φάος τόκου, an attractive conjecture, νεαρά being expelled as a gloss on νεάζουσαν (for νεαρός as a gloss-word see Hesych. s.v. καινός): this involves dropping βίον from 775 as a gloss on τὸν ἐναίσιμον; its loss will not be felt, but of course our confidence is reduced if one conjecture is found to necessitate another. The third and fourth problems would be solved by the easy changes of τόν to τάν and of εἰδομέναν to -μένας: old Hybris begets both new Hybris (763–4) and also Atê (770); it is improbable that δαίμονα (768) is to stand in apposition to Ὕβριν (766), as if the Hybris and the Atê were the same thing. Then either μελαίνας . . . ἄτας εἰδομένας (genitive) or μέλαιναν . . . ἄταν εἰδομέναν (accusative, in apposition to θράσος), or (better) μελαίνας . . . ἄτας (genitive, after ἀνίερον θράσος) εἰδομένας (accus., covering both Ὕβρις and Ἄτη). The sixth problem is insoluble unless the unique form προσέβατο (for -έβη; cf. ἔφατο beside ἔφη) is admitted: the popular conjecture προσέμολε is mere rewriting (Fraenkel says that 'confusion between β and μ is very common in minuscules, and then the further corruption is easily explained'—but how is it explained? προσέβολε would lead to nothing but προσέβαλε; nobody would misunderstand or alter -έβολε to -έβα του).

The makeshift text runs literally: 'Old Insolence is like to breed young Insolence, among men that are evil, sooner or later, when the appointed day of birth arrives, together with that daimon irresistible, unconquerable, unholy boldness of black Ruin for the house—children like to their parents. But Justice shines in smoky dwellings; the righteous man she honours. From gold-bespangled mansions, where the hands are foul, she departs with eyes turned backward, and approaches the god-fearing, without respect for the power of wealth falsely stamped with man's approval. All things toward their goal she guides.'

765. κακοῖς: neuter or masc., preferably the latter.

769. ἀνίερον: better with θράσος than with δαίμονα; it does not make a good mate for the two practically synonymous adjectives which precede.

776. σὺν πίνῳ χερῶν: contrast καθαρὰς χεῖρας, *Eum.* 313.   σύν implies that the material splendours of the wealthy house are *accompanied by* hands unclean; see Fraenkel on 456 above.

780. The 'power of wealth' is said to be 'falsely stamped with praise'; it bears the hallmark, which it does not deserve, of men's approval.

782. Enter Agamemnon, with Cassandra, in a chariot. There is nothing

to indicate at what point Clytemnestra enters: Agamemnon shows
no awareness of her presence during 810–54; but neither does she
address him at 855—her first recognition of his presence is marked
incidentally in the word σῶν at 878. Perhaps Clytemnestra enters at
854–5; or perhaps she has been in the background for a long time
(there is nothing in the text to indicate that she actually leaves the
scene from her first appearance, early in the play, up to 1068; see
489 ff. n.).

783–809. The Chorus combine their greeting with a warning against
insincere persons who conceal malevolence behind a mask of friendship. The boldness of their speech is remarkable. They may (and do)
lose their nerve in the crisis (1343 ff.), but here they show high
courage. Resentment against Agamemnon is rife at Argos (447 ff.):
the Chorus, who now assert perfect loyalty, admit that they themselves strongly disapproved of him at the beginning of the war. They
warn him plainly that he has enemies at home, and that not all that
he will hear is to be trusted. There is no clear hint that danger is
specially to be expected from Clytemnestra: at 1025–9, as Wecklein
observes, they regret not having spoken still more plainly.

785. σεβίξω: the aorist subjunctive, and the form with ξ, are successfully defended by Fraenkel.

786. ὑπεράρας: 'overpassing'.   ὑποκάμψας: 'falling short of'. See
Fraenkel, who compares the similar phrase in Plato, *Laws* 717ᵈ μήτε
ὑπεραίροντα τῶν εἰθισμένων ὄγκων μήτ' ἐλλείποντα . . . .

787. καιρόν: the mark, target, exactly defined point.   χάριτος:
as often, it is hard to tell whether the reference is to the *service* given
by him who thanks, to the intrinsic *grace* of gratitude, or to the
pleasure of him who is thanked.

788–9. 'honour Seeming-to-be in preference (to Being)'.   παρα-
βάντες: the aorist implies that you *first* cross the line which divides
right from wrong, and *then* go chasing false ideals.

790. δ': perhaps better τ' (Hermann).

793–4. The case in favour of a lacuna is strong but not absolutely
compelling: (1) the interlinear hiatus βιαζόμενοι· | ὅστις has no
parallel in Aeschylus, and is foreign to the nature of this metre; but
possibly the pause in the sense might justify it; (2) in 793 one would
greatly prefer to take ξυγχαίρουσιν as dative of the participle,
governed by ὁμοιοπρεπεῖς ('like in appearance to those who share
another's gladness'): then a lacuna must be postulated to accommodate the main verb of the sentence. It remains possible that ξυγχαίρουσιν is third person plural of the present tense, and that the
meaning was 'they rejoice together with him, assuming a like
appearance (viz. of joy)'.

795. προβατογνώμων: 'judge of his flock'; metaph. as in the Epic
ποιμένα λαῶν.

796. ὄμματα φωτός: subject, not object, of λαθεῖν; 'it is not possible that a person's eyes should escape his (the 'good shepherd's') notice'. The phraseology is rough, the simple οὐκ ἂν λάθοι being replaced by οὐκ ἔστι λαθεῖν, equivalent in sense but stronger in emphasis.

797–8. τὰ δοκοῦντα κτλ. defines what kind of ὄμματα are meant, just as in 833, φίλον τὸν εὐτυχοῦντα, the article+participle defines what kind of φίλος is meant. Lit. 'those which seem from a loyal mind to fawn upon him with watery friendship'. There is, as Paley said, 'a little confusion' in the phrasing: the sentence begins 'those which seem from a loyal heart . . .', but instead of continuing '. . . to welcome him (or the like)' it goes on with words which make the true nature of the welcome explicit, '. . . to fawn upon him etc.' (Fraenkel accepts Casaubon's conjecture σαίνει: but then (1) τά has to be taken as a relative pronoun, subject of σαίνει, a harsh procedure; (2) δοκοῦντα must be taken with εὔφρονος ἐκ διανοίας, as if it could mean 'seeming *to come* from a loyal mind', a usage which would require some defence.)

800. οὐκ ἐπικεύσω: a common Epic phrase, never used with a pronoun-object (till Ap. Rhod. iii. 332 οὔ σ' ἐπικεύσω). The pronoun is one of two blemishes in Musgrave's οὐ γάρ σ' ἐπικεύσω, the other being the irregularity of the division within the anapaest, which might how ever be defended by reference to *PV* 293, *Pers.* 47; see 1521–9 n. below.

801. Lit. 'you were pictured very inartistically'; I drew an ugly picture of you in my mind.

803–4. The notion that θάρσος ἑκούσιον (F Tr) could mean *audaciam voluntariam* (Weil), in the sense 'a willing wanton' (Verrall), sc. Helen, is to be rejected absolutely. θάρσος is never used (as θράσος is) in a bad sense (in *Il.* 17. 570, 21. 395, quoted by LSJ, θάρσος has no moral colour at all); still more decisive is the objection that if θάρσος here could stand for 'bold Helen', ἑκούσιον would be an impossible adjective—a *person* cannot be described as voluntary or involuntary; 'it is not her nature but her action that is ἑκούσιον', as Fraenkel says.

It is likely that the primary fault lies in ἑκούσιον. Ahrens's conjecture ἐκ θυσιῶν (ΕΚΘΥϹΙΟΝ for ΕΚΟΥϹΙΟΝ) is very attractive: a suitably cryptic reference to Iphigeneia's sacrifice is very much in place here, for it might be expected that the Chorus would give this as the reason why they disapproved of Agamemnon at the start of the war (they have already given a general reason, in Ἑλένης ἕνεκα: but the sacrifice of Iphigeneia is much in their minds, and nothing could be more natural than that they should specify it). Then ἀνδράσι θνήσκουσι κομίζων will have to mean 'restoring (courage through sacrifices) to dying men', referring to the men dying of famine at Aulis (188 f.), whose sufferings (197: κατέξαινον is a strong term) were terminated by the sacrifice of Iphigeneia. Opinions have

differed, and will continue to differ, about the merits of this ingenious
interpretation.

Note that θνῄσκουσι could not mean 'doomed to die' or 'about to
die' (viz. at Troy) in such a context as this.

805. 'But now sincerely, and like a true friend . . .': οὐκ ἀφίλως is a
stronger term than φίλως.

806. 'I am no longer ill-disposed to those who have brought their labour
to a happy end.' This is a simple restoration of the corrupt tradition.
Headlam, Fraenkel, and others assume a lacuna to accommodate
some 'proverbial' expression, ἡδὺς πόνος εὖ τελέσασιν or the like.

808-9. πόλιν οἰκουροῦντα: simply 'staying at home in the city'.—'A
clear hint at Aegisthus: he is ἀκαίρως οἰκουρῶν, misusing his remain-
ing at home for shameful acts. In contrast with him stand the old
men, δικαίως οἰκουροῦντες, since they are long past the age for service
and also because they have kept their loyalty', Fraenkel. Cf. [Demo.]
in Neaeram 86, δικαίως οἰκουρεῖν.

810 f. θεοὺς . . . τοὺς ἐμοὶ μεταιτίους: it is a debatable question
whether Aeschylus intended this phrase to testify to arrogance in
the speaker—'the gods, who share with me the credit for success'.
Fraenkel, who denies that intention, quotes numerous passages in
which mortals pray gods for aid and alliance, or gods render aid and
alliance to mortals, or gods and mortals are said to work in partnership; but none of his quotations (except perhaps Ar. Equ. 586 ff.;
Prof. Dover adds [Herodes], π. Πολ. 3 ὑμᾶς αὐτοὺς τῶν ὑμετέρων ἀγαθῶν
αἰτίους εἶναι μετὰ τῶν θεῶν, where edd. commonly alter to μετὰ τοὺς
θεούς) touches the singularity of the present passage, in which the
mortal, in thanking the gods for success, calls the gods co-partners
without confessing his own part to be secondary (contrast E. El.
890 ff., Xen. Anab. 7. 7. 22, [A.] ScT 1074 f.). The question does not
admit of a certain answer, and is not of much importance, since the
arrogance of Agamemnon is clearly enough exposed in the sequel.

813 ff. Lit. 'having heard pleas not from the tongue (i.e. not spoken
but asserted by arms in battle), the gods, with no dissentient voice,
put into the urn of blood their murderous Ilium-destroying votes'.
Possibly Ἰλίου φθορᾶς (Dobree), governed by ψήφους, 'votes for the
destruction of Ilium'.

815. The vessel for condemnatory votes was called κάδος θανάτου, that
for acquittal κάδος ἐλέου.

816 f. All that approached the 'opposite urn' (the urn of Mercy) was,
not a hand to drop a vote in it, but only the 'hope of a hand'; and
nothing ever did come to fill it.

819-20. συνθνῄσκουσα codd.: but there is great obscurity in (1) the
apparent antithesis of ζῶσι and -θνῄσκουσα: if the 'stormwinds of
Ruin' are alive, this is not the moment to say that the 'embers' are

dying; (2) the meaning of συν-: it has to be referred to something outside the antithetic words (e.g. σὺν τῇ πόλει), an artificial and perhaps impossible procedure. Both difficulties were eliminated long ago by Enger's δυσθνήσκουσα 'dying hard', i.e. struggling against death, being kept alive by the θύελλαι.

821. πολύμνηστον: in 1459 = 'much-remembered', and that may be the meaning here; 'to pay a much-remembered debt of gratitude' = to remember (or make mention of) one's debt of gratitude on many occasions.

822 f. There is no certain choice between (1) παγὰς . . . ἐφραξάμεσθα (better ἐφαρξ-), cf. 1376 f. ἀρκύστατ᾽ ἂν φάρξειεν; (2) χάρπαγὰς . . . ἐπραξάμεσθα, cf. Hdt. 5. 94. 2, *P.Oxy.* xx 2253 (a) 4 f. (from an unidentified play by Aeschylus) Με]νέλεω τὴν βίαιον ἁρπαγὴν ᾱ [   ] πράσσουσι Πριαμίδην Πάριν. (Fraenkel's argument from the double καί is mistaken: the first καί goes with ἐπείπερ, 'since in fact . . .'; *Gk. Particles*, 296 ff.) With (2) ὑπερκόπους is a necessary conjecture, with (1) preferable but not absolutely necessary.

825. Corruption following on the metathesis of -ηφορος to -ηροφος.

826. The 'setting of the Pleiads' regularly denotes a particular season of the year, early November, but in this context (*a*) the information, *what season of the year it was* when Troy fell, seems exceptionally gratuitous and arid; (*b*) less important, but still puzzling enough— the season stated is contrary to the common tradition, viz. that Troy fell in the early summer (Robert, *Gr. Heldens*. 1289). It would have been much more to the point, if the words could signify *what hour of the night it was* (traditionally midnight: *Ilias Parva* fr. xii Allen, νὺξ μὲν ἔην μέσση . . ., E. *Hec.* 914 μεσονύκτιος), but of course the setting of stars cannot mark a *fixed* hour; we should have to suppose that the poet indulges in what Fraenkel elsewhere calls a 'vague lyricism', telling us that, as it happened (by way of picturesque detail), the Pleiads were setting about the time when the Wooden Horse did its work—that tells us that it was night-time, but conveys no information whatever about the *hour* of night; and most unfortunately it is expressed in words which instantly suggested to every mind *a particular season of the year* (autumn), not night-time, let alone hour of the night.

(The problem is unsolved, and seems insoluble. No good comes of quoting in this connexion the well-known lines of unknown date and authorship, δέδυκε μὲν ἁ σελάνα | καὶ Πληιάδες, μέσαι δὲ | νύκτες, παρὰ δ᾽ ἔρχεθ᾽ ὤρα: here no indication of *hour* of night is given until μέσαι νύκτες; the setting of moon and Pleiads, which of course cannot mark any fixed hour, are merely picturesque details. If one wanted to see where such merely picturesque details are and are not at home, one could hardly do better than contrast this little poem with Aeschylus' line.)

828. τυραννικοῦ: Agamemnon, like other kings in Tragedy, is anxious to show himself as different from the oriental despot; at 844 ff. he will convene Assembly like an honest constitutional monarch; at 918 f. he rejects oriental obeisances; at 935 f. he speaks contemptuously of the vainglory of Priam. Yet he will walk on the purple vestments which Clytemnestra spreads before him.

830. τὰ δ' ἐς τὸ σὸν φρόνημα: a prosaic formula of transition, introducing a new theme but not grammatically fitted into it; illustrations in Fraenkel.

833. φθόνου Triclinius, a bad guess, for the alleged corruption is exactly the reverse of what is probable, and the plural is protected by Plato, *Laws* 801ᵉ νόμος ἄνευ φθόνων εὐθὺς γίγνοιτ' ἂν ὅδε. The fact that it is the singular φθόνου which is preserved in Stobaeus' anthology is of no critical importance.

834. καρδίᾳ conj. Casaubon: but the accusative has support in *Suppl.* 189, E. *Hec.* 935, cf. *Od.* 22. 334 f., *PV* 276 πρὸς ἄλλοτ' ἄλλον πημονὴ προσιζάνει.

834–7. The 'owner of the disease' (sc. of envy) suffers both from sorrows of his own (especially the lack of that which he envies in others) and from the sight of his neighbours' better fortune. This is more detail than we need in the present context; the effect (which may or may not have been intended by the poet) is to make the speaker seem dull and sententious.

838–40. The meaning here is obscured by the ambiguity of ὁμιλίας κάτοπτρον, for to speak of Society as a 'mirror' might have either of two contrary implications—the image seen in a mirror is (a) a *true* reflection of the real thing, (b) nevertheless only a *reflection*, as opposed to the reality: which of these two aspects, the truth or the falsity, did the poet intend to portray here? In favour of (a) is the normal use of κάτοπτρον in Greek figurative language (see Headlam and Fraenkel); in favour of (b) is the immediate juxtaposition of terms denoting 'unreality', εἴδωλον σκιᾶς.

If (a) were correct, the general sense (leaving room for variety of opinion about the detail) would be: 'From experience I would say—having seen men's true natures reflected in Society's mirror—that those who seem most gracious to me are the image of a shadow.' This is far from satisfactory, since δοκοῦντας urgently needs the definite article τούς, and the singular εἴδωλον as predicate to the plural δοκοῦντας is almost intolerable; on this interpretation εἰδώλων σκιὰς (Keck) should be read.

If (b) were correct, it would perhaps be best (though not necessary) to take εἴδωλον and δοκοῦντας in apposition to ὁμ. κάτ., explaining its content, and to give the general sense as in Verrall's translation: 'I may speak with knowledge, having learnt thoroughly that mirror of friendship [rather, 'society'], —image of a shadow, the hypocrite's semblance of devotion to me.' A variation of this view is proposed by Stanford in *CR* n.s. iv (1954) 82 ff.: Plutarch (*How to tell a Flatterer from a Friend*, ch. 8) describes a flatterer as 'receiving images of other people's feelings, lives and movements, as if he were a mirror', δίκην κατόπτρου: so ὁμιλίας κάτοπτρον here might imply that the king in society sees nothing but flatterers aping himself; εἴδωλον σκιᾶς, 'the reflection of a shadow', then follows well, for the flatterers are *shadows* of the king, and what he sees in Society's mirror is merely the reflection of those 'shadows'; δοκοῦντας κτλ. stands in apposition, and clarifies what is meant by κάτοπτρον and εἴδωλον σκιᾶς.

A decision here is impossible so long as the primary question, whether appearance or reality is stressed in ὁμιλίας κάτοπτρον, admits of no certain answer.

841 f.: What had Agamemnon to complain of in Nestor, Diomede, and many others? Perhaps the answer is to be found in Proclus, on the Νόστοι of Agias, p. 108 Allen (Lloyd-Jones). On Odysseus' reluctance to go to Troy see Pearson, *Fragments of Sophocles* ii, pp. 115 f.

842. σειραφόρος: 1640 n.

844. τὰ δ' ἄλλα: like τὰ δέ in 830, a formula of transition standing outside the structure of the sentence. ἄλλα is clarified by πρὸς πόλιν, 'As for the rest, concerning the city and gods . . .'.

845. ἀγῶνας: in the Epic sense, 'assemblies'.

846–7. Lit. 'That which is well, we must plan how, continuing (χρονίζον, cf. Plato, *Phaedr.* 255ᵇ), it shall remain well.'

849. εὐφρόνως looks either forward, or back, or both. The meaning is 'in the manner in which a sensible (εὔφρων) person would act'; so also in 351 above.

850. ἀποστρέψαι: 'turn back', i.e. put to flight; ἀποτρέψαι, as Fraenkel says, would have done well here (though ἀπό- τρ. is abnormal prosody in Tragedy).

851. δόμους ἐφεστίους: an odd expression, since the 'house' is not 'at (or 'on') the hearth'; apparently 'house with its hearth'. The conjecture ἐφέστιος would be attractive, if the same phrase did not recur at *ScT* 73.

852. δεξιώσομαι elsewhere governs the accus. and means 'clasp hands with a person', or simply 'greet'. An odd word to use of greeting *the gods*: LSJ suggest 'raise one's right hand to the gods', an equally unexampled sense and construction.

854–5. Clytemnestra comes forward (or possibly enters; but see 489 ff. n., 783 n.). It is remarkable that she should address her speech to the Chorus, not to the husband whom she now sees for the first time in ten years—he is οὗτος in 860, ἀνὴρ ὅδε in 867. Remarkable too is her theme: she suspects that Agamemnon has heard, or will soon hear, rumours of her infidelity: she therefore at once enters upon her defence to a charge which has not yet been made—otherwise

Agamemnon may be reluctant to enter the palace alone and un-
armed. Before turning to him (which she does at last, in the most
indirect manner possible, at 877) she takes the extraordinary course
of stressing her honour as a wife, addressing herself *to the Chorus* in
her husband's presence. The Chorus knows, or at least suspects, the
truth about her amour with Aegisthus: she is anxious to prevent
them from conveying their suspicions to Agamemnon, and here she
tries to win their sympathy, or at least to disarm their hostility, by
professing her innocence and dwelling on the hardships which she
has undergone.

858 ff. οὐκ ἄλλων πάρα: i.e. we have just heard 'from others' (the
Herald) of the army's sufferings at Troy; but the lot of a wife left
at home has hardships of its own, and that is a tale I can tell of my
own knowledge.

861. τὸ μέν and πρῶτον are to be taken together; for the word-order
Fraenkel compares S. *Ajax* 311 καὶ τὸν μὲν ἧστο πλεῖστον ἄφθογγος
χρόνον. One expects an ἔπειτα δέ (or equivalent), but it never comes,
the sentence taking a different turn. (Ahrens, followed by Fraenkel,
interprets καί in 864 as equivalent to ἔπειτα δέ: he must then delete
863 on the ground that it anticipates a topic—rumours of Agamemnon's death—which is not introduced before this καί-clause; the
recurrence of κληδόνων παλιγκότων is thought to support the condemnation of 863. Much stronger arguments would be needed to
justify the conclusion.)

864 f. Clear in meaning, confused in expression: she means τὸν μὲν
ἥκειν κακὸν πῆμα λάσκοντα δόμοις, τὸν δὲ κάκιον ἄλλο πῆμα ἐπεισφέρειν
(λάσκοντα δόμοις καὶ τοῦτον). The phrase τὸν μὲν ἥκειν is left uncompleted, but all that is necessary to complete it is immediately supplied
in what follows; then, because *two* persons have now been mentioned,
λάσκοντας appears instead of that which would have made the
grammar (but not the sense) clearer, viz. λάσκοντα.

866 ff. 'And of wounds, if he was getting as many as rumour came
pouring (lit. 'was led in conduits') into the house, he has now more
holes to count in him than a net.' 'The cold-blooded phrase suits
Klytaemnestra', as Sidgwick says.

869. Perhaps rather 'if his deaths had been as numerous as the stories'
(Headlam) than 'if he had died, as stories were prevalent'.

870 ff. 'Three-bodied Geryon the second, he might have boasted that
he had got a threefold cloak of earth, having died once in each
several shape.' This ludicrous conceit is, and is meant to be, distasteful to Agamemnon; still grosser exaggerations are to come
(896 ff.).

Geryon, a three-bodied (sometimes said to be only three-headed)
herdsman, was killed and robbed by Heracles in the far West: his
death is depicted on the metopes of the Athenian Treasury at Delphi

and the temple of Zeus at Olympia.   ὁ δεύτερος : the definite article is abnormal in this idiom (illustrated by Headlam : ὁ δεύτερος also in *Anth. Pal.* 12. 55. 3, a poem of unknown date and authorship). The 'cloak of earth' worn by the dead man is a common image, earliest in Alcaeus fr. 129. 17 γᾶν ἐπιέμμενοι (*Il.* 3. 56 f., λάϊνον ἔσσο χιτῶνα, is not relevant).   λαβών : λαβεῖν conj. Paley ; but since there is no objection in principle to the participle, the change to apparent normality is hazardous.

So far there is no difficulty : but now what of 871 ? The 'threefold cloak of earth' is said to be 'ample above him, not to mention that which lies under him' ; i.e. being trebly buried he would have, in comparison with ordinary mortals, a large mantle of earth above him and a still more disproportionate amount below him (this idea, that a huge amount of earth lies beneath the buried man, is expressed also in *ScT* 949–50, of Eteocles and Polynices, ὑπὸ δὲ σώματι γᾶς πλοῦτος ἄβυσσος ἔσται).

The objection to the line is not that there is anything amiss in language or sense ; it is simply that we are very unwilling to believe, what the tradition asserts, that Aeschylus wrote such rodomontade. (The repetition of πολλὰς ἄνωθεν in 875 is an insufficient ground for suspecting interpolation here.) The notion that this remarkable thought entered the mind of some later person, who thought it worth adding to Aeschylus' text, seems as far-fetched as a notion can be. It is hard to see what better course can be adopted than to hand on the tradition with a note of strongest disapproval and suspicion.

876. πρὸς βίαν λελημμένης : λελημμένης signifies that hands had been laid upon her in the act of suicide. The tense indicates that the freeing of the noose took place while she was thus held by her rescuers, who laid hands on her and did not let go ; πρὸς βίαν signifies that she resisted this treatment. 'Many nooses, up aloft, were loosed from my neck by others while they held me in their grip perforce.' For other interpretations see Fraenkel.

877. ἐκ τῶνδε : 'for these reasons'. Orestes must be sent away because his mother might at any moment succeed in hanging herself.— Clytemnestra is treading on delicate ground here : she knows that Agamemnon will be astonished (879) and highly displeased to learn that his son and heir is not at home to greet him on this most important occasion. It is an extremely serious, and suspicious, matter ; she deals with it most skilfully.

878. κύριος πιστωμάτων : Orestes is regarded as the holder of pledges between husband and wife, as a security for their continued affection ; the interests of the son and heir protect the bond of loyalty between the parents.

881. ἀμφίλεκτα : 'of which people speak on two sides' (ἀμφι-), i.e. in two ways; the two matters in question are defined in τόν θ᾽ ὑπ᾽ ᾽Ιλίῳ σέθεν κίνδυνον and εἴ τε δημόθρους ἀναρχία κτλ.

883–4. The most natural interpretation of these ambiguous words, 'and if popular clamorous lawlessness should overthrow the Council' may well be the correct one: (1) ἀναρχία in this sense is attested elsewhere as early as S. *Ant.* 672, cf. [*ScT*] 1030. (2) βουλή in the sense 'Council' is not found elsewhere in Tragedy: but (*a*) there is not much opportunity for its use in that sense, and (*b*) nobody will suppose that an Athenian audience would be in doubt about its meaning in a place where it is the object of such a phrase as ἀναρχία καταρρίψειεν; and since we have just heard that a Council-assembly is to be held even after Agamemnon's return (845 f. ἐν πανηγύρει βουλευσόμεσθα, 847 βουλευτέον), we are ready to hear that some sort of βουλή existed during his absence; cf. [*ScT*] 1006. (Fraenkel objects: 'Nowhere in the whole play . . . has the poet given the slightest indication that the Chorus of Old Men was to be regarded as representing an advisory body': but why must *the Chorus* be brought into the picture? Clytemnestra says simply 'Council', leaving its membership wholly indefinite.) (3) δημόθρους, as an adjective for ἀναρχία, means 'associated with popular clamour', a common type of freedom in the relation of compound adjectives to their nouns (1511–12 n.).

Scaliger's conjecture βουλὴν καταρράψειεν, 'devise a plan against us', has the merit of giving βουλή here its normal Aeschylean sense of 'plan', to which the verb adds the required sinister colour. (Fraenkel renders: 'If the ruler's absence (ἀναρχία), asserted noisily by the people, should overthrow (quiet) deliberation'. This is unconvincing in respect of (*a*) the sense given to δημόθρους ἀναρχία, which could surely not mean 'lack of a ruler, spoken about by the people'; (*b*) the phrase 'overthrow (quiet) deliberation', surely a most improbable expression in the Greek, at least in this context; moreover βουλή means 'plan' (result of deliberation), not 'deliberation', always in Aeschylus and normally in the other Tragedians and elsewhere.)

884. ὥστε codd.: causal ὥστε is not found elsewhere in Tragedy (*CR* xlvii (1933) 163 f.); ὥς τε is possible ('*and* saying that . . .'), but the sense required is causal, '*since* it is natural to kick people when they are down', and the slight change of τε to τι is a great improvement.

886. *et haec quidem excusatio mea omni dolo vacat*, Schütz: 'now *that* is a plea which brings no guile with it'; she is anxious to show that her removal of Orestes from the scene was thoroughly justified.

889. i.e. 'with watching late mine eyes are sore' (Verrall).

890. Lit. 'bewailing the beacons concerning you that were ever neglected', i.e. lamenting that the beacons remained so long unlit. αγπτ ηρουχίας: 'holdings of lamps', probably abstract for concrete;

the places where the beacons are piled, the 'beacon-holders', were uncared-for, nobody was busy about them.

891 ff. 'And during my dreams I would be awakened by the light rapid movement of a gnat trumpeting' (the last word is directly borrowed from Fraenkel, q.v.). ὑπαί is best taken as governing λεπταῖς ... ῥιπαῖσι, not κώνωπος; a rare usage of ὑπό c. dat. causal or instrumental, cf. 1164 below, *Cho.* 28, Bacchylides 3. 17, *Il.* 13. 667.

893 f. Lit. 'sufferings greater in quantity than the time that shared my sleep', i.e. more than could be suffered in the time I was asleep. With ξυνεύδων χρόνος edd. compare Pind. *Pyth.* 9. 23 f. τὸν σύγκοιτον ... ὕπνον, S. *OC* 7 ὁ χρόνος ξυνών, al.

896. τῶν σταθμῶν: probably 'of our stables' (or, more broadly, 'farmsteads'). It is unlikely that σταθμῶν here is merely a synonym for 'house', since it is the practice of Tragedy not to add the definite article to δόμος δῶμα οἶκος στέγη etc. unless there is a particular reason for doing so; here δωμάτων (cf. 607) would have served if that had been the meaning desired.

897. 'Saviour fore-stay of the ship.'

898. ποδήρη: lit. 'foot-fixed', i.e. with its base firmly fixed.

899-902. The text is exposed to grave suspicion at three points. As it stands, the meaning is 'And land made manifest to sailors contrary to expectation; day most fair to look upon after storm; to thirsting wayfarer the stream of a spring; and pleasant it is to escape all stress of need'. There is nothing wholly impossible in this, but (1) καί in 899 is hardly tenable: though the last two members of an asyndetic series may be coupled by καί, δέ, τε, it is very unusual so to couple a pair *within* such a series (for a few examples in prose, see Denniston, *Greek Prose Style*, p. 105). Hence γαῖαν for καὶ γῆν, Blomfield, just as γαίας has to be written for καὶ γῆς in *Eum.* 755; see further E. *El.* 678 n. (2) 900: there is much force in the opinion of Headlam, reinforced by Fraenkel, that this line has been interpolated from some other context, in which κάλλιστον was not an adjective but a predicate: '*fairest (is)* the sight of day after storm'. (3) Connected with this is the question of 902: this line, in its present place, is flat and feeble; and its form—τερπνόν being a predicate—is the same as that of the suspected line 900, '*fairest is* daylight . . ., *pleasant is* escape . . . '. The suggestion is that these two lines have found their way into the text from the margin, having been quoted from some source of a common type represented by Theognis 255 f., **κάλλιστον** τὸ δικαιότατον, λῷστον δ' ὑγιαίνειν, | πρᾶγμα δὲ **τερπνότατον** τοῦ τις ἐρᾷ τὸ τυχεῖν.

Rejection of 900, 902 may be the correct treatment. We cannot, however, rule out the possibility that 901 should be transposed to follow 898 (Bothe): καὶ γῆν in 899 will then need no change, καί coupling the last two members of a series. The sequence of comparisons will then end at 899, and there will follow a couple of

conventional maxims, 'Fairest is the sight of day after storm, pleasant is escape from all stress of need.' We may still judge that the
passage runs much better without these two maxims, but there will
no longer be any compelling objective argument for deletion.

903. 'With such addresses do I honour him'; ἀξιῶ c. accus. as in E.
Hkld. 918, cf. *Hec.* 319, *Or.* 1210.

904. φθόνος δ' ἀπέστω: to make sure that φθόνος is *not* absent is of
course her principal object here and in what follows.

904-5. γάρ: envy ought to be withheld, *for* this moment of triumph is
nothing in comparison with our past sufferings.

908. αἷς ἐπέσταλται τέλος: the servants know what they have to do;
it has all been arranged long beforehand.

909. πετάσμασιν: things spread out. The question, what these objects
are, is answered in 921, 960, 963: they are εἵματα, 'garments'. They
are not (what they have sometimes been called) *carpets*, but fabrics
which are, or resemble, *clothing* (this is the only sense of εἷμα: LSJ
erroneously quote S. *Ajax* 1145 for εἷμα in the sense 'rug'). They are
woven (949) and dyed (946, 957) and variegated (923, 926, 936). It is
of the first importance to understand that these garments are, and
are known by Agamemnon to be, 'things wherewith *the gods* ought to
be honoured' (923): whether or not they were actually dedicated to
the gods (cf. E. *Ion* 1141 ff., Pausanias v. 12. 4), Agamemnon is well
aware that no godfearing and right-minded mortal indulges in such
antics, and that he is likely to incur the jealousy of gods (946 f.) and
men (939) if he treads on these πετάσματα; and yet he does it. (The
term 'carpets' should not be used. It is worth noticing that floor-
carpets were not common articles of furniture in Greece till the time
of Alexander the Great. Grohmann, *Pauly–Wissowa* s.v. 'tapes',
notes that in Xen. *Cyr.* 8. 8. 16 carpets are regarded as a sign of
oriental effeminacy; but does not note that τάπης in Ar. *Plut.* 542
is clearly a rug or carpet and is there spoken of as a normal sort of
luxury; cf. also LSJ s.v. δάπις.)

911. The hidden meaning is: 'that Retribution (for Iphigeneia) may
lead him to a home far different from the one he expected'; the
surface meaning, 'that Justice may lead him to the home he never
expected to see again'.—Agamemnon went to Troy to exact a rightful
claim (41, 812 f.): he will be pleased to hear that it is Δίκη who escorts
him home (cf. *ScT* 646 ff.).

912-13. Lit. 'What remains, careful thought not overcome by sleep
shall arrange in just manner, with the gods' help, what is fated.' It
is a commonplace in Greek thought that the gods (and men too) can
assist and guide an action to its predestined end.   θείμαρμένα =
τὰ εἱμαρμένα; similar examples of unusual crasis (537 above, θἀμάρτια)
in K.–B. i. 220 f., e.g. S. *Ant.* 397 θοὔρμαιον, E. *Tro.* 384 τἀσχρά, S.
Ajax 756 (prob.) and *OT* 1283 θἠμέρᾳ. Here the definite article seems

indispensable, whether εἱμαρμένα is taken in apposition to τὰ ἄλλα or as the direct object of θήσει (τὰ δ' ἄλλα then being introductory, standing outside the main structure, as in 844).

915 ff. i.e. 'your speech was like my absence, a very long one; and I shall have enough praise from others, so yours is not required.' This does not seem to us a gracious, let alone cordial, way to address the wife whom he has not seen for ten years: to the Athenian audience, however, these sentiments may have seemed so conventional as to be entirely without offence. The point is of no importance, for we have not to wait a moment before the coldness, indeed the hostility, of Agamemnon's demeanour is openly avowed; his words become rougher as his speech proceeds (919–20, 926). His annoyance is natural enough: at the climax of his triumphant return his wife proposes to him a course which (glad though he would be to follow it) outrages the feelings of decent men and insults the gods. Moreover she has evidently seen him at once for what he is: with oriental luxuriance of language (896 ff.), and with grovelling prostrations abominated by the Greeks (919 f.), she sets him in a most unfavourable light. He might recover much of his lost ground by refusing to walk on the purple vestments: but to refuse is (as she had guessed) just what he cannot bring himself to do.

918 ff. 'For the rest, do not pamper me like a woman; nor, as if I were a barbarian, gape grovelling acclaims at me; nor, by spreading my path with vestments, make it the object of jealousy: it is the gods whom one should honour with such things.' γυναικὸς ἐν τρόποις and βαρβάρου φωτὸς δίκην are both better taken to refer not to the manner in which Clytemnestra acts but to the effect of her acts on Agamemnon. Fraenkel compares *Eum.* 26 λαγὼ δίκην Πενθεῖ καταρράψας μόρον, where λαγὼ δίκην refers to the effect on Pentheus, not to the action of the subject of the verb.

920. βόαμα: a kind of cognate accus. with προσχάνῃς. **χαμαιπετές,** 'fallen on the ground', suggests that the poet thought of his Clytemnestra as actually prostrating herself, with oriental προσκύνησις, in Agamemnon's path.

The phraseology of this line is meant to be very offensive to Clytemnestra: προσχάνῃς is an insulting word, cf. χανεῖν in S. *Ajax* 1227, Ar. *Vesp.* 341.

924. ἐμοὶ μέν: *Gk. Particles,* p. 381; whatever others may do, *he* is correctly religious.

926 f. 'Fame shouts aloud, without footwipers and embroideries', i.e. my fame speaks for itself, needs no external pomp. The sequence of thought is: 'Respect me as man, not god: my glory needs no such embroideries; and a modest mind is Heaven's best gift.'

(Fraenkel, following Blass, renders 'Different is the ring of the words "footmats" and "embroideries"', i.e. footmats are one thing, embroideries another, and a man should not use the latter as if they were the former. If this were correct, the language would be obscure and ambiguous in the highest degree; but it is surely not correct, for (1) αὐτεῖ would be an unsuitable verb, and κληδών a particularly ambiguous noun (very seldom 'name' of a thing; but cf. *Eum.* 418); (2) whether χωρὶς αὐτεῖν could mean 'sound separately' in the sense required is at least very doubtful; (3) finally, if the point lies in the *distinction* between ποδοψήστρων and τῶν ποικίλων, they could not have been *coupled*, as they are, by τε καί. (Opposition or contrast can be expressed by τε καὶ οὐ, as is natural, e.g. βίᾳ τε κοὐχ ἑκών, *Gk. Particles*, p. 512; but not by τε καί as alleged here.))

928-9. For this common sentiment, 'call no man happy until he is dead without disaster,' cf. Hdt. 1. 32, S. *OT* 1528 ff., *Tr.* 1 ff., fr. 646 P., E. *Andr.* 100 ff., *Tro.* 509 f., and the lines quoted by Schol. on *Andr.* l.c. μήποτέ τις ⟨βροτὸν⟩ ἄνδρα πανόλβιον αὐδήσειεν, | πρίν ⟨κεν⟩ ἴδῃ πῶς κεῖνος ἔχοι ποτὲ πότμον ἀπήμων.

930. 'If I should in all circumstances behave thus, I have no misgivings.' The text is sound, unless πράσσοιμεν should be written for πράσσοιμ' ἄν; but not even this change is necessary. The MSS. offer the earliest example of an idiom later common enough, better defined and explained by K.–G. ii. 482 than by Goodwin, *MT* § 506, or Wyse on Isaeus, p. 451: a potential optative with ἄν may be used within a conditional clause, where it is desired to stress the probability of the condition. Thus χρήματα ἄν προοῖντο, 'they may very likely squander money', is a potential clause which may now be included in a conditional clause: εἰ χρήματα ἄν προοῖντο = 'if, as is likely, they should squander money'; without ἄν, the clause εἰ χρήματα προοῖντο is a mere hypothesis, 'if they were to squander money'. This is a relatively common (though not the only) implication of the optative with ἄν in conditional clauses. So here: πάντα ὡς πράσσοιμ' ἄν is a positive assertion in a potential form, 'I am likely to do all things thus', and this is included in an εἰ-clause, 'If, as is to be expected, I should do all things thus'. The idiom is not at present attested elsewhere earlier than Xenophon and Plato: a fact which has led many to acquiesce in a wooden conjecture, εἶπον τάδ' ὡς πράσσοιμι ἄν εὐθ. ἐγώ, '*I have said how* I would do these things with good confidence'; a much inferior sentence to that offered by the MSS. If change were required, πράσσοιμεν for -οιμ' ἄν would be both simpler and better. (2) **ὥς**= οὕτως: modern editors are strangely reluctant to admit this, though ὥς in this sense occurs in both poetry and prose (*a*) in certain set phrases: ἀλλ' ὡς γενέσθω (E. *Hec.* 888, *Tro.* 726, *IT* 603), οὐδ' ὥς (S. *Ant.* 1042, Thuc. i. 132. 5, Xen. *Anab.* 1. 8. 21, al.), καὶ ὥς (Thuc. i. 44. 2, vii. 74. 1), ὡς δέ (usually followed by καί, cf. Ar. *Lys.* 804; seventeen times in Hdt.); ὡς πράσσειν may be regarded as one of these stereotypes, cf. ὡς ποιεῖν in Plato, *Prot.* 338ᵃ, Thuc. iii. 37. 5;

(b) occasionally in a less stereotyped form: E. *Hec.* 441 f. ὡς τὴν
Λάκαιναν . . . ἴδοιμι (where ἔχουσαν, πάσχουσαν, or the like must be
supplied with ὡς); Hdt. 9. 18. 2 ὡς γὰρ ἐνετείλατο; in A. *Suppl.* 622
ἔκραν᾽ ἄνευ κλητῆρος ὡς εἶναι τάδε, ὡς is obviously probable, though
ὡς εἶναι cannot be ruled out.

931 ff. This scene, and in some degree the whole play, reaches its
climax here. Agamemnon yields to Clytemnestra's will and treads
the path of purple vestments; he enters the palace, and we are sure
that he will not be seen alive again. Clytemnestra's conduct is consistent throughout: she wishes to alienate sympathy from him, to
expose him as arrogant and sacrilegious, an orientalized despot, a
victim deserving of his fate. Hence the fantastically fulsome flatteries
(896 ff.); the barbaric prostrations (919 f.); the insistence that,
although he knows it to be an offence against gods and men, he
should tread a path strown with costly vestments. Up to 930 Agamemnon's response is rudely negative. He knows that it would be a
grievous error to yield, and he rebuffs Clytemnestra with harsh
words of disapproval. And then, in a few moments (between 930,
where he is still firmly refusing, and 944, where he consents) his resolve is broken, and he commits the act of ὕβρις which he knows to
be sacrilegious (922, 925), the sort of thing an oriental despot might
do (936). His change of mind is most unexpectedly rapid. Clytemnestra uses in effect only two arguments: the bubble is pricked by a
couple of extraordinarily shrewd and penetrating questions. (1) His
religious scruples are shown to be illogical, for he must admit that the
deed which he declines is one which, in certain circumstances, might
actually have been a religious *duty* (933–4).—Agamemnon does not
notice that the circumstances do not really apply to his case (ibid.,
n. below). (2) His *moral* or *social* scruples are indefensible and without
substance: she shows him that what he fears is nothing in the nature
of the action, but only the criticism of his fellow men; and that, in
his position, he can afford to ignore (935–9).—Agamemnon has
nothing to argue against this, except that women ought not to be
so quarrelsome.

The truth is that he needed no more than this easy allaying of his
religious and social scruples: there is no conceivable reason why he
should now suddenly change his mind—unless he secretly wishes to
do so. The fallacies in Clytemnestra's arguments are obvious enough;
but Agamemnon is easily satisfied. It is not because he is too tired
to consider or argue the matter, and certainly not because he cannot
say no to a lady: it is simply because he is at the mercy of his own
vanity and arrogance, instantly ready to do this scandalous act the
moment his personal fears of divine retribution and human censure
are, by whatever sophistry, allayed. Of course he puts the blame on

Clytemnestra: εἰ δοκεῖ σοι ταῦτα, 'just to please you'; notice too the absurdly strong expression in 956 κατέστραμμαι, 'I have been *subdued* by you'—in truth he had yielded in a few seconds, and there had been nothing to prevent him continuing to refuse, as he had done up to 930.

(Details of the controversial views held about 931–4 are now omitted here, since reference can be made to Fraenkel's very full discussion. The interpretation of 933–4 in particular is extremely uncertain: the following notes offer, almost without argument, what is considered to be the most probable text and meaning; but it is admitted that, for these two lines especially, no more than a speculative result is attainable.)

931–2. 'Come now, tell me this, not contrary to your true opinion.'— 'As for my true opinion, rest assured that I shall not corrupt *that*.' διαφθείρειν is an unusual word in such a connexion; there is some similarity in E. *Hipp.* 388 f.

933–4. 'You would have vowed to the gods, in a moment of terror, to act thus?' (i.e. to tread on purple vestments).—'Yes, if anyone with full knowledge had proclaimed this duty.' Cf. 963 f., where Clytemnestra says that she would have 'vowed to tread vestments underfoot in abundance, *if an oracle had ordered it*': so here she allays the religious scruples of Agamemnon by forcing him to admit that there might have been circumstances in which he would actually have vowed to do what he now refuses to do, and that he might actually have been ordered by oracle or priest to make such a vow. True, he had had no such order: but he *might* have had one; the occasion for it must often enough have arisen, and the vow may be deemed to have been made. The underlying notion is that a man in a moment of distress or danger might vow—or be ordered by the priests to vow— that, if delivered from peril, he would humble himself before the gods by destroying or otherwise disposing of some of his valuable possessions at home (cf. 1573: Clytemnestra will give up almost all her property, if the daimon will now at last leave her in peace; the story of Polycrates' Ring is a species of the same genus). Agamemnon conveniently overlooks the fact that what *he* is being invited to do is not at all the kind of thing a man in distress might vow: whoever yet vowed, or was ordered to vow, that if released from peril *he would make a triumphal entry into his palace, stepping on purple vestments, as if he were not a mortal but a god* (922, 925)?

On the abnormal position of ἄν in 933, see Fraenkel.   **ἔρδειν**: ἔρξειν conj. Headlam; the future would be normal, but is not absolutely indispensable.   **εἴπερ** usually introduces a fact or probability in conditional form; there are some other exceptions, e.g. S. *El.* 312.   **εἰδὼς εὖ**: of the religious expert, θεοπροπίων εὖ εἰδώς. τέλος: 'duty', *munus*, rather than 'ritual' (for which τάδε . . . τέλη would be expected).

935–8. If Agamemnon were not purblind in his pride, the question in 935 would strongly confirm him in his resolution not to yield. Treading on purple, as Clytemnestra says, is just the kind of thing you would expect a Priam to do: and he agrees. But now she tempts him to consider that what Priam can do, he can do—there is no other objection to it than the fear of what people will *say* (937); and surely a man in his position can afford to ignore that (939: you cannot have an enviable position without being exposed to uncharitable comment).

942. ἦ καί: introducing a surprised question, 'do you really . . .?'; *Gk. Particles*, pp. 285, 316. (Not καὶ σύ, 'You too', as some would have it). νίκην τήνδε δήριος: 'this victory of strife' seems an odd expression, and it would be reasonable to prefer τῆσδε (Auratus), 'victory in this . . .'.

943. The MSS.' text seems untenable. μέντοι . . . γε is regularly adversative (*Gk. Particles*, p. 409), and it is hard to see what room there is for opposition or contrast between πιθοῦ and κράτος κτλ.: the order of the words, particularly the unemphatic position of ἑκών, can hardly be reconciled with the suggestion that the general sense was 'yield, *but* do so *willingly*'. Possibly κρατεῖς (Weil) μέντοι παρεὶς (Bothe: γ' del. Wecklein) ἑκὼν ἐμοί, 'you are the *winner*, you know (μέντοι emphatic, *Gk. Particles*, pp. 399 f.), if you concede it to me of your own free will'; cf. S. *Ajax* 1353 παῦσαι· κρατεῖς τοι τῶν φίλων νικώμενος.

944 f. ὑπαί with λύοι, ὑπολύειν being the normal term for undoing footwear.

945. πρόδουλον ἔμβασιν ποδός: ἐμβάς is common Greek for a slipper or shoe; ἔμβασιν ποδός is a grandiloquent paraphrase, 'what the foot steps into', simply 'footgear'; πρόδουλον signifies that his shoes are his feet's *slaves*, a grotesque metaphor.

946. ἁλουργέσιν: '*wrought in* or *by the sea*, always in sense *sea-purple*, i.e. *genuine purple dye*', LSJ; here 'purple vestments'. θεῶν: with ἁλουργέσιν; these vestments belong to the worship of the gods, 922. It could not well be taken with what follows, for there would not be sufficient justification for the exceptionally heavy emphasis which would arise from its position as first word of its clause, preceding even the μή.

947. 'Let no eye's envy strike me from afar.' πρόσωθεν = οὐρανόθεν.

948. πολλὴ (sc. ἐστίν) αἰδώς governs accus.+infin., as e.g. αἰσχρόν ἐστι might.

948–9. -φθορεῖν . . . φθείροντα: see 362 n.

950. τούτων μὲν οὕτω: 'so much for that'; a variation of the normal idiom, in which the genitive (τούτων) is not used; contrast *PV* 500 τοιαῦτα μὲν δὴ ταῦτα, and other examples quoted by Fraenkel.

950. The first reference to Cassandra. 954–5 make it clear to the audience (if they have not already guessed) who she is: 'the chosen flower of many treasures, the army's gift·to me'. The King's first acts on returning home are to trample on purple vestments and to command a gracious reception for his concubine: Clytemnestra could not possibly have hoped for more, or indeed so much.

958–72. Agamemnon walks slowly along the purple-strown path to the palace. He disappears inside at 972. The purple vestments must be removed by the attendants after Agamemnon has trodden them: Clytemnestra must not tread them when her turn comes to leave the scene.

958–62. i.e. there is no danger that the sources of sea-purple will dry up; and the house has a plentiful supply in store.

958. κατασβέσει: the metaphor as in 888 above, *ScT* 584.

959–60. πορφύρας ἰσάργυρον κηκῖδα: 'juice of purple (dye), worth its weight in silver'; edd. quote Theopompus, *FGH* 115 F 117, 'purple for dyes fetched its weight in silver at Colophon'. **παγκαίνιστον:** 'wholly renewable', 'of the supply of purple constantly renewing itself in the inexhaustible sea', as Fraenkel says.

961. οἶκος ὑπάρχει: οἴκοις conj. Porson; but cf. Theocr. 22. 222 ἐμὸς οἶκος ὑπάρχει, *domus suppeditat*, contrary to normal idiom. If the text is correct, ἔχειν is explanatory infinitive, 'so that one may have . . .', and τῶνδε is partitive, 'to have *of these things*'. Such a sentence (particularly the alleged partitive genitive) is an unsatisfactory muddle, and ought perhaps to be marked as corrupt.

963–4. 'I would have vowed the trampling of many vestments, if it had been proposed (LSJ s.v. προφέρω I. 5) to our house in oracular responses' (LSJ s.v. χρηστήριον I. 2; or 'at the seats of oracles'). **προυνεχθέντος:** the impersonal genitive absolute in the singular number is very rare; Thuc. i. 74. 1, vi. 58. 1, K.–G. ii. 81–82, 90.

965. κόμιστρα: 'means of recovering'. The γάρ in 966 shows that *Agamemnon's* life is meant by ψυχῆς τῆσδε here: but it is most abnormal to use the pronoun ὅδε with reference to a person who is actually being addressed (ἄναξ 961) and present on the scene; the harshness is intensified by the use of the second person (σοῦ 968) in the vicinity. **μηχανωμένη:** governed by προυνεχθέντος, 'if it had been proposed *to me* devising etc.'. Since δόμοισι must also be governed by προυνεχθέντος, the sentence runs a little awkwardly; but a genitive -μένης would be clumsy, and a nominative -μένη would not satisfy since this line coheres in sense with 964 not with 963.

966 ff. 'For just as, while the root exists (i.e. while the tree is alive), leafage comes to the house, having spread shade overhead against the dogstar, so, now that you have come back to hearth and home, warmth signals its coming in winter-time; and when Zeus makes wine from the unripe grape (i.e. in the heat of summer), then at once there is cool in the house, when the lord and master moves about it.' Codd. have σοῦ μολόντος . . . σημαίνεις μολών, pitiable writing, even if an example or two of comparably incoherent syntax can be gleaned elsewhere. But whatever the true reading may be in that place, the sentence as a whole is inelegant enough ('Just as a tree provides *shade in summer*, so the lord and master provides *warmth in winter* and coolness in summer.').

Notice the indifference to repetition: 961 οἶκος, 962 δόμος, 964 ~~See Jones~~ δόμοισι, 966 δόμους, 968 δωματῖτιν, 971 δόμους, 972 δῶμα (cf. *Od.* 6. 296 δώματα, 297 δώματα, 299 δώματα, 302 δώματα and δόμος, 303 δόμοι).

972. **τελείου**: of the man who has the final authority in the house, cf. *Cho.* 663 ἐξελθέτω τις δωμάτων τελεσφόρος.   **ἐπιστρωφωμένου**: cf. *ScT* 648, Polynices when restored to Thebes will have δωμάτων ἐπιστροφάς, freedom to move about as he will in his own house.

973. **τέλειε**: it is for the sake of this contrast that the expression ἀνδρὸς τελείου was chosen in 972; it is Zeus, not Agamemnon, who will decide the issue here.

974. 'Take thought for whatsoever you intend to fulfil', i.e. do what you have decided to do.   τῶνπερ = ἐκείνων, ἅπερ.

975–83. Lit. 'Why does this terror persistently hover in front of my divining heart? It plays the prophet, my song, though none has bidden or hired it. Nor yet, to reject it (viz. the terror) like dreams of doubtful import, does confidence persuasive sit on the throne of my thought.'   ἀποπτύσαι is governed by the content of οὐδὲ . . . θάρσος ἵζει, as if it were οὐ θαρρῶ (ἀποπτύσας cod. F: an incoherent nominative participle of excessive awkwardness, in a tense which is hard to reconcile with the context).   **φίλον**: the Homeric use, 'my own'; LSJ s.v. I. 2 c.

984–7. Hopelessly corrupt. The general sense may have been: 'Why am I so frightened (975–83)? A long time has passed since the army went to Troy, and now they are safely home again, and nothing disastrous has occurred.' But there remain unsolved problems in the detail: (1) ξυνεμβόλοις is not a known word; perhaps ξυνεμβολαῖς or ξὺν ἐμβολαῖς, 'together with the casting-in' (of the πρυμνήσια, mooring-cables). (2) ψαμμίας ἀκάτα (cod. F) is nonsense, and no cure has been found. (Wilamowitz's ψάμμος ἄμπτα is to be rejected absolutely: sand does not 'fly up' when mooring-cables are 'thrown in'; the deficiency of sense is as great as the disregard of palaeographical probabilities.) (3) It is not clear whether χρόνος παρήβησεν εὖτε means 'Time passed its prime when . . .' or 'Time has passed its prime since . . .' (for the quasi-perfect aorist see Wackernagel, *Stud. z. Perf.* (1904) 6 ff.; for εὖτε = ἐξ οὗ cf. S. *El.* 508). (4) It is not even certain that χρόνος was the subject of παρήβησεν: if it was, it is unlikely that a verb for ἐπεί can be found; ἐπεί too has therefore come under suspicion (δέ τοι for δ' ἐπεί Hermann; δ' ἐπί Triclinius, but ἐπῑ πρ- is a licence of prosody unexampled in Aeschylus, though it would cause no comment in Soph. or Eur.).

The likeliest account of ψαμμίας ἀκάτα is that ΨΑΜΜΙΑCΑΤΑ (where ψαμμίας was being corrected to ψαμμίαις, presumably to agree with -βολαῖς) was misunderstood, the suprascript AIC being added to the text (between ΑC and ΑΤΑ), making -ΑCΑΚΑΤΑ = -ας ἀκάτα. If so, the suggested reading was πρυμνησίων ξὺν ἐμβολαῖς ψαμμίαις ἄτα παρήβησεν, 'Ruin passed her prime together with (= at the time of) the casting of the cables into the sand (lit. 'sandy in-throwings of cables'), when the naval host went to Troy.' But then χρόνος δ' ἐπεί ... would have to mean 'it is a long time since ...' (as Ahrens took it), and χρόνος is not—nor would one expect it to be—elsewhere so used without some attribute such as πολύς, παλαιός.

990. τὸν δ' ἄνευ λύρας: cf. E. *Hel*. 185 ἄλυρον ἔλεγον (θρῆνον codd. LP, from a gloss), *IT* 146 ἀλύροις ἐλέγοις (= θρήνοις, 144), *Eum*. 331 f. ὕμνος ἀφόρμικτος. 'Lyreless' in these contexts means in effect 'gloomy', for dirges were regularly sung not to the lyre but to the *flute*, an instrument deemed most suitable to songs of lamentation; see *Greek Poetry and Life*: *Essays presented to Gilbert Murray* (1936) 206 n. 1, 211 n. 2.

991. ὕμνῳδεῖ: a vowel short by nature is very seldom allowed to remain short if followed by μν. Tragedy offers a few exceptions to the rule, allowing a vowel at the end of one word to remain short before μν at the beginning of another word: E. *IA* 68 θυγατρῖ μνηστήρων, 847 δεινά· μνηστεύω, cf. *Eum*. 383 where τἒ μνήμονες is almost certainly intended; also Callim. fr. 61 Pf., quoted by Hephaestion, π. κοινῆς 8 (p. 6 Consbruch), who further quotes an isolated example *within* a word, εὕμνος from Epicharmus (fr. 91 Kaibel). We should not accept ὕμν- here, superior though it is rhythmically to ῡμν- (which would involve the change of ποτᾶται to πωτ- in the strophe), if Aeschylus did not himself offer the necessary parallel in *Pers*. 287, μἒμνῆσθαι τοι παρα = 281 δύσαιανη βοαν (the idea that ∪ – – could stand in correspondence with – – – in such a line is not supported by anything in Aeschylus; *ScT* 356 = 368 is notoriously problematical).

992. αὐτοδίδακτος: i.e. spontaneous; so in 979 the song is ἀκέλευστος ἄμισθος, it comes unbidden, unhired, self-taught.

993 f. Lit. 'Not at all having the welcome confidence of hope.'

995-8. The language is very strained. Omitting for the moment πρὸς ἐνδίκοις φρεσὶν τελεσφόροις, it runs: 'My innermost feelings (σπλάγχνα, cf. *Cho*. 413) tell no idle tale', (then κέαρ in apposition to σπλάγχνα) '—my heart which goes round and round in revolutions.' κυκλούμενον and δίναις, both of which imply circular or rotatory movement, are apparently used here of the recurrent throbbing of the heart. τελεσφόροις, 'bringing fulfilment', could be taken either with φρεσίν or with δίναις (preferably the latter); in either case it is contrasted with οὔτοι ματάζει, 'not in idle panic, but with a purpose to be fulfilled'.   πρὸς ἐνδίκοις φρεσίν could be taken either (preferably) with what precedes or with what follows; in either case the meaning is in effect 'in the vicinity of my mind' (or 'midriff': but the adj. ἐνδίκοις favours the non-physical sense); πρός c. dat. of location, without attachment to the verb (or anything else), as in S. *Tr.* 371 f. and elsewhere.   ἐνδίκοις is obscure: perhaps simply 'just' or 'in which justice dwells'; the Chorus's agitation of mind arises from their consciousness that the claims of justice have yet to be settled.

998–1000. Lit. 'I pray that (these things?) may fall out of my expectation, as falsehoods, into non-fulfilment.'   ψύθη is clearly predicative, but it is most awkward that the context supplies nothing as subject of πεσεῖν ('these things'): εὔχομαι ⟨τά⟩δ' ἐξ ἐμᾶς (Blomfield) is plausible, especially since the strophe strongly suggests that this line is here a syllable short.

1001 ff. First, health and wealth are compared in respect of the dangers of excess; secondly, excessive wealth and famine are contrasted with bloodshed in respect of remediability. There is a point at which health, cultivated to excess, turns to ill-health (1001–3); and so with property, the man who has too much will come to grief (1005–7). Now excess of wealth is remediable, for the overladen ship can be lightened by jettison (1008–14); remediable too is famine, by god's gift of an abundant harvest (1015–17). But remedy there is none for blood once shed (1018–21): τί γὰρ λύτρον πεσόντος αἵματος πέδοι; (*Cho.* 48).

1001–6. Incurably corrupt. Strophe and antistrophe do not correspond at the beginning, and a whole line ($- \cup \cup - \cup \cup -$) is wanting before or after 1005. μάλα γέ τοι τὸ μεγάλας ὑγίας (after Paley: for υγιΐ- see Herodas 4. 94 and K.–B. ii. 276 f.) is a barely respectable makeshift for the beginning. The sense seems to be: 'Great good health has a boundary (τέρμα, a point where health ends and disease begins), and disease is its next-door neighbour'; but ἀκόρεστον, 'insatiable', seems the wrong word, unless 'the limit of health is never satisfied' may mean 'men are never satisfied with any limit of health they may reach'; whatever limit they reach, they are not content with it— but then γάρ does not follow easily, and anyway the language seems tortured.

1004. ὁμότοιχος ἐρείδει: lit. 'sharing a party-wall, presses upon it', i.e. thrusts against it and is likely to break it down, invading the home of Health. For the idea that health can be over-cultivated, edd. quote the Hippocratic *Aphorisms* i. 3, 'good condition at its peak is dangerous, if it has gone to extremes'.

1005 ff. 'A man's destiny, travelling a straight course, strikes an unseen reef'; this is the apparent sense in general, though the detail may be much affected by the contents of the missing line.

1008 ff. Lit. 'Caution, hurling a part, in defence of properties acquired, from a sling of proper measure—the whole house does not founder, overburdened with repletion, nor does it sink the vessel.' The construction is incoherent: τὸ μέν ('a part') is not followed by τὸ δέ, and βαλών is left in the air. The sentence starts afresh at οὐκ ἔδυ πρόπας δόμος, and it is then hard to say just what or who is the subject of ἐπόντισε.   βαλὼν σφενδόνας ἀπ' εὐμέτρου: 'having thrown from a sling of proper measure', i.e. throwing overboard, by means of rope-tackle which may be called a 'sling'; εὐμέτρου, because just the right measure, neither more nor less, should be jettisoned. For σφενδόνας see Wyse, *CR* xiv (1900) 5: σφενδόνη was the name given to a device for unloading vessels from the dockside; here in Aeschylus the same metaphorical name, 'a sling', is applied to an essentially similar device—a rope slung round an object is naturally called σφενδόνη, a sling, whether with reference to a fixed device in harbour or, as here, an extemporized device on deck at sea. For the sense and metaphor in general see *ScT* 767 ff. (The rendering '*by* a well-measured *throw*' is contrary to the uses of both σφενδόνη and ἀπό, despite Fraenkel, p. 455.)

1012. πλησμονᾶς is a very doubtful conjecture. πημονᾶς (cf. codd.) may be right, though what the ship is too full of, and what must be diminished by jettison, is not 'woe' but 'wealth', 'surfeit of goods'. Housman, *J. Phil.* xvi (1888) 274, suggested παμονᾶς, 'property' (related to πάομαι); but the word does not exist in Greek, and there is no reason why it should have been invented here, where e.g. κτημάτων lay ready to hand.

The aorists throughout 1006–17 are gnomic.

1015–17. τοι is odd here, for this is simply a further illustration of the same theme ('shipwreck may be averted by jettison, famine by a good harvest'); perhaps τ' αὖ.

Lit. 'Great bounty from Zeus, abundant and proceeding from the annual furrows, destroys the plague of famine'; i.e. the dangers of famine may be countered by a good harvest.

1018 ff. 'But the dark blood, once fallen in death on the ground at a man's feet, who shall call up again by incantation?'   πρόπαρ ἀνδρός: 'in front of a man'; the rare word πρόπαρ is so used by Hesiod, *theog.* 518; at E. *Ph.* 120 it is adverbial, 'in front', at A. *Suppl.* 791 it is used of time, 'sooner'.

1022–4. The reference is to Asclepius (son of Apollo and Coronis), who restored Hippolytus to life; Zeus therefore slew him with a thunderbolt (Hesiod fr. 125, Pind. *Pyth.* 3. 54 ff., E. *Alc.* 3 f., 122 ff., Virgil *Aen.* 7. 765 ff.). Lit. 'Not even him who knew aright how to bring (men) up from the dead did Zeus restrain in harmless manner' (lit. 'on terms of not-harming', cf. E. *Hipp*. 511 f. οὔτ' ἐπὶ βλάβῃ . . . παύσει, 'on terms of injuring'), i.e. Zeus put an end to Asclepius' activities in no gentle fashion; even this benevolent healer, son of Apollo, was punished in the severest manner. This is what the context suggests, or even demands; but ὀρθοδαής c. infin. is very bold. τῶν φθιμένων is genitive of separation.

1025–33. 'And had not, by divine decree, one appointed lot prevented another from getting more than its share, my heart anticipating my tongue would be pouring these things forth; but, as it is, it mutters in the dark, in grief of spirit, and not expecting ever to accomplish anything opportune, while my mind is aflame.' Such is apparently the drift of this obscure phrasing.   εἰ δὲ μὴ κτλ. means 'to speak out now would be useless; it is impossible to alter the divinely appointed succession of events; the chain of destiny is forged beforehand, and each link comes in its turn'—one link is not allowed to encroach upon or anticipate another; each μοῖρα must wait for its own turn.   ἐκ θεῶν: with εἷργε, 'prevented by divine decree'. προφθάσασα καρδία γλῶσσαν: it is the tongue which controls, or should control, man's utterance; when his emotions are too strong for that control, it may be said that his heart outruns, or anticipates, his tongue.   ἐκτολυπεύσειν: 'unravel', LSJ s.v. τολυπεύω II. 1. ζωπυρουμένας φρενός: gen. absol. (not governed by ἐκ-τολυπ.).

1035 ff. Clytemnestra begins by using persuasion and feigning magnanimity; it was a good omen, if the victim approached the altar voluntarily, and anyway the use of force is excluded here. At the same time she gives herself the satisfaction of humiliating the daughter of Priam, the concubine of Agamemnon: 'You will have the privilege of attending family worship; we have a great many slaves like you, and you will find us humane masters.' There is something ironical, almost contemptuous, in the futile consolation of 1040–1, 'Don't think yourself too good for your position: cheer yourself up with the example of Heracles in bondage to Omphale.' Although Clytemnestra knows that Cassandra will not live to undergo these humiliations for a single hour, yet it gives her great satisfaction to dwell on them. All is said in terms of apparent kindness, in order that her primary object may be accomplished.

1036. ἀμηνίτως qualifies the act of Zeus in sending Cassandra to such a good home: 'kindly', 'of his mercy'.   δόμοις: with κοινωνόν.

1036–8. It is clear from numerous passages in literature that slaves were normally admitted to participation in domestic worship; in Isaeus 8. 16 it is stated as something exceptional that a certain person did not admit slaves and ἐλευθέρους ὀθνείους when sacrificing to Ζεὺς

Κτήσιος. It is not implied here that Clytemnestra is offering any special privilege to Cassandra.

1037. πολλῶν μέτα: Clytemnestra misses no opportunity of wounding her victim; let Cassandra understand that she is now just one among a herd of slaves.

1038. κτησίου βωμοῦ: see Farnell, *Cults* i. 56, 'The image of Zeus *Κτήσιος* stood in the store-rooms of houses, and his symbol was commonly an urn containing a mixture called *ἀμβροσία*, compounded of water, honey, and various fruits'; Cook, *Zeus* ii. 1067, 'As a rule Zeus Ktesios was a homely power content with worship in a small way—he never has a temple or a statue, but puts up with a jar or a hearth or at most a trumpery altar.'

Clytemnestra, having told Cassandra that the amenities of her life include admission to the worship of *Ζεὺς Κτήσιος*, goes on (1056 f.) to invite her indoors to attend a sacrifice at a *ἑστία μεσόμφαλος*, 'central hearth'. Though there is nothing to prove that the same cult is referred to in both places, one would naturally suppose that it was the same; and though there is nothing in the words *ἑστίας μεσομφάλου* irreconcilable with the cult of *Ζεὺς Κτήσιος*, the peculiar adjective (properly used of the site of Delphic Apollo's shrine) and the nature of the rites would naturally be taken to indicate something more important than the 'trumpery altar' in a store-room. The poet's intention is obscure: perhaps it was that Clytemnestra should first tell Cassandra that she is free to join in the routine domestic worship of *Ζεὺς Κτήσιος*, and then go on to invite her to certain special rites at a hearth in the centre of the palace, celebrating the Master's return.

1040. Both *τοι* and *καὶ γάρ* are commonly used to introduce proverbs, maxims, illustrations, and the like: the combination of the two, *καὶ γὰρ . . . τοι*, is extremely rare (except, in other senses, in the Attic orators; *Gk. Particles*, p. 113).

1041. There is an irreconcilable conflict of MS. evidence. (*a*) cod. F has *δουλείας μάζης βία*: this might represent either (1) *δουλίας μάζης βίον* (Blomfield; for the type of genitive see 1535–6 n.; for the phrase, [Archilochus] 79. 6 *δούλιον ἄρτον*, Hipponax 39. 6 *δούλιον χόρτον*), or (2) *δουλίας μάζης βίαν* (Thiersch: 'endured the compulsion of the bread of servitude', where again *δουλία μᾶζα* is a periphrasis for *δουλεία*—there is no particular stress on the 'coarse diet' of slavery). (*b*) Triclinius offers something entirely different: *καὶ ζυγῶν θίγειν βία*, which cannot be explained in relation to the text of cod. F; nor can it be ignored as a mere rewriting by Triclinius, who does not indulge in that sort of thing (moreover, as Fraenkel observes, he would not then have added a gloss to explain one of his own words, 'Tr. wrote above the *θίγειν* the gloss *ψαύειν*'; Fraenkel, p. 472, n. 1). It is clear that two irreconcilable versions of the second part of this line were to be found in the ancient tradition (as often in Euripides, very seldom in Aeschylus): there is no means of determining what the original form of one of the two versions ((a) above) was, let alone which of the two was authentic.

1042. δ' οὖν: 'slavery is a bad thing; but if one *must* be a slave . . .'; *Gk. Particles*, p. 465.

1043. The meaning of χάρις with a dependent genitive is often hard to define: here apparently 'much cause for gratitude belongs to masters whose wealth is of long standing', i.e. there is much to be grateful for in having masters who are not *nouveaux riches*.

1044–6. As it stands, the meaning must be: 'They who, never having expected it, have reaped a fine harvest, ⟨are⟩ cruel to their slaves in everything and with strict exactness—you have heard from us what is customary.' Hartung, followed by Fraenkel, rightly inferred that a line (or more) must have dropped out of the text after 1045, saying what it is that the *nouveaux riches* do παρὰ στάθμην, 'according to strict rule' (this seems to be the only attested sense of the phrase: *ad amussim*, as Pearson says on S. fr. 474. 4 f.; Theognis 543 χρή με παρὰ στάθμην καὶ γνώμονα τήνδε δικάσσαι, | Κύρνε, δίκην ἴσόν τ' ἀμφοτέροισι δόμεν, and 945, where παρὰ στάθμην and ὀρθὴν ὁδόν are nearly synonymous metaphors. There is no authority in literature for Schol.'s explanation here, ἀντὶ τοῦ παρὰ τὸ πρέπον, 'contrary to what is proper'). The only way of evading this inference is to treat the adverbial phrase παρὰ στάθμην as if it were an adjective, coupled (by τε . . . καί) with ὠμοί, 'they are cruel and according-to-rule (i.e. strict) with their slaves': to this unlikely procedure Thomson, who doubtfully accepted it, could find no adequate parallel (S. *El.* 521 f., *OT* 929 f., which he admits to be inexact analogies, appear essentially different). Conjectural emendation has, as so often, failed signally.

1046. ἔχεις means, in this context, 'you have *heard* . . .'; for this sense of ἔχειν, especially at the end of a speech, cf. E. *Ph.* 953 τὰ μὲν παρ' ἡμῶν πάντ' ἔχεις, *Ion* 1367 f., ἐξ ἡμῶν δ' ἔχεις ἅπαντα (quoted by Fraenkel).

1047. Cassandra makes no reply, and the Chorus prompt her: **σοί τοι**, 'it's *you* she is speaking to, you know'.

1049. πείθοι' ἄν, εἰ πείθοιο is an indirect way of saying πιθοῦ, εἰ πείσῃ, 'obey, if you are going to obey'; the direct way is seen in E. *IA* 817 δρᾶ γ', εἴ τι δράσεις, Plato *Rep.* 350ᵉ εἴπερ τοῦτο ποιήσεις, ποίει (quoted by Headlam), and 1059 below. The optative with ἄν in place of the imperative (often used for the sake of courtesy; contrast S. *El.* 1491, *Ant.* 444) attracts the subordinate verb, πείσῃ, into the same mood. Cf. 1394 χαίροιτ' ἄν εἰ χαίροιτε = χαίρετε εἰ χαιρήσετε, 'rejoice, if that is what you intend to do'. **ἀπειθοίης**: supply ἄν from what precedes; cf. S. *OT* 937 ἥδοιο μέν, πῶς δ' οὐκ ἄν; ἀσχάλλοις (supply ἄν) δ' ἴσως.

1050. χελιδόνος δίκην: see LSJ svv. χελιδονίζω, χελιδών.

1052. Aeschylus is much given to elliptical expression, but it is very doubtful whether even he could have said ἔσω φρενῶν λέγουσα meaning 'speaking ⟨so as to reach⟩ inside someone's mind'. ἔσω φρενῶν must be taken with πείθω νιν (Il. 9. 587 τοῦ θυμὸν ἐνὶ στήθεσσιν ἔπειθον), 'I persuade her within her mind.' λέγουσα . . . λόγῳ seems very feeble, but we must tolerate it unless we are prepared to alter the text in Sophocles also, Phil. 55 ὅπως λόγοισιν ἐκκλέψεις λέγων.

1053. τὰ λῷστα τῶν παρεστώτων here could mean 'the best of the things that are at hand'; but PV 216 f., Ar. Equ. 30, where τῶν παρεστώτων, τῶν παρόντων occur with κράτιστα without the article, suggest that τῶν παρ. has become a stereotyped genitive absolute, 'things being as they are'.

1055. θυραίαν τήνδ' codd. There is more than one possibility here: (1) supply τριβήν as a cognate accusative from τρίβειν, 'I have (πάρα = πάρεστι) no leisure to waste this time out of doors'; this, as Sidgwick says, seems 'sufficiently improbable'; (2) θυραίαν might be interpreted as a substantival adjective of the type of τροπαίαν in 219 above; this seems still more improbable; (3) a simple sentence can be restored by the easy changes θυραίᾳ (sc. ἐμοί) τῇδ' (= 'here'), 'I have no leisure to loiter here out of doors' (or 'at the door'). τρίβειν in the sense 'waste time' is abnormal, but διατρίβειν is so used, and the use of simple instead of compound verb is in general not uncommon in poetry.

1056–7. A good deal of guesswork would be required to put these lines in order. (1) **ἑστίας μεσομφάλου**: on what does the genitive depend? 'A loose local gen. . . . vaguely indicating the *region*', Sidgwick: it would take more than a few isolated abnormalities such as Il. 9. 218 f. ἷζεν . . . τοίχου τοῦ ἑτέροιο to create confidence in this approach. Musgrave conjectured πάρος (for πυρός) at the end of the next line, to govern ἑστίας: but the preposition seems too widely separated from its noun (cf., however, the separation of θυρῶν from ἔνδον in S. El. 78–79). One might simply alter genitive to dative, ἑστίᾳ μεσομφάλῳ: but then why was it changed to the genitive? What is needed is πρὸ μὲν γὰρ . . . in place of τὰ μὲν γὰρ . . . (Bamberger): but the corruption is not a common one (cf., however, Ar. Equ. 272 τό cod. R, πρός rell., and E. IT 335, where Housman held that the impossible τε of the MSS arose from a contraction of πρός). It is to be noticed that τά here is in itself suspect: 'article separated from substantive [sc. μῆλα], really a usage from Epic poetry, where the article is still a demonstrative or pronoun: "they, the sheep",' Sidgwick; it is doubtful whether there is any other such example in the iambics of Tragedy, except where the subject is (or means) a *person*. (2) Fraenkel justly demands evidence that **ἕστηκε πρὸς σφαγάς** could mean 'stand *for* (meaning 'ready for', 'looking toward') slaughter'. Further (3) σφαγαὶ πυρός should imply that *fire slaughters* (or *is slaughtered*; if that made any sense); but it is not the fire that slaughters the victims. Sense could be restored by postulating the form προσφαγαί, equivalent to προσφάγματα, 'victims' (see 1278 ff. n.) of the fire, προσφαγαὶ πυρός. But all is darkness here.

1058. Fraenkel follows Wilamowitz and others in deleting this line: (1) 'The Queen is in a very great hurry . . . the addition of an emotional flourish is intolerable'; (2) 'Clytemnestra has now no reason for making any further display of gratitude or pleasure for the benefit of Cassandra or the Chorus'; (3) the 'repetition' of οὔποτ' ἐλπίσασι after οὔποτ' ἐλπίσαντες in 1044 is judged to be offensive. These are singularly unconvincing arguments. The true nature of the impending 'sacrifice' is obvious, and Clytemnestra is not to be denied her sinister jubilation: she 'never expected to have this pleasure'.

1060. μὴ δέχῃ: 'If, not knowing Greek, you do not *receive* my speech', i.e. if my speech stops outside, instead of being received into, your comprehension; not 'if you do not understand the meaning of my words'. So Fraenkel.

1060–1. Clytemnestra says in effect: 'If, not knowing Greek, you find my words convey nothing to you, then explain yourself by a gesture instead of by speech.' This has been called an 'absurdity'; but some of those who have attacked or defended it seem to have overlooked the most likely meaning. She is not saying 'If you do not understand me, *signify as much* by a gesture' (Fraenkel ad loc.: 'she could . . . make clear καρβάνῳ χερί her lack of understanding'). That would indeed be ludicrous, and beyond excuse. What she means is surely 'if, not knowing Greek, you do not take in my words, at least you might *signify your answer to my question* (whether you will accompany me indoors) with a gesture'.—'No doubt you remain silent because you cannot understand or speak my language: but surely you can make some gesture in response to my obvious insistence that you should leave the chariot and go indoors.'—That is illogical enough, but at least not absurd: Clytemnestra has become more and more impatient; she is losing her temper, and is determined to get *some* response from her victim—it is intolerable that the girl should sit there and make no motion; even a benighted barbarian could surely understand that she is being urged to enter the palace, and could surely say Yes or No by a gesture. It is not necessary to postulate any elaborate by-play: it is hard to imagine the scene so played that Clytemnestra's desire to take Cassandra indoors is not quite obvious apart from the words she uses, and the minimum of gesture by Clytemnestra to Cassandra would clarify well enough what she means by φράζε καρβάνῳ χερί.

The position then is that Clytemnestra, assuming that Cassandra must at least understand that she is being invited to get down from

the chariot and enter the palace, says in effect 'Even though you do
not understand my words, yet you must surely perceive what is
required of you, and you might at least signify your answer by a
gesture.'

1061. δέ in the apodosis, without change of subject, is not uncommon;
Gk. Particles, pp. 180 f.　　　With **φράζε ... χερί** cf. Hdt. 4. 113 (the
amour of an Amazon and a Scythian) καὶ φωνῆσαι μὲν οὐκ εἶχε, οὐ γὰρ
συνίεσαν ἀλλήλων, τῇ δὲ χειρὶ ἔφραζε ἐς τὴν ὑστεραίαν ἐλθεῖν.　　**καρβάνῳ**: this very rare word (twice in *Suppl.*), evidently meaning something like 'barbarian', here reflects the speaker's anger and contempt.

1063. 'Her manner is that of a creature newly caught': Cassandra,
then, is not sitting immobile, apparently insensible of her position;
if she is 'like a wild beast newly caught', she is either cowering in
terror or furiously agitated (probably the latter: 1066 f. 'she knows
not how to endure the bridle, *before foaming her spirit away in blood*').

1065. νεαίρετον: 1063 νεαιρέτου, see 362 n.

1067. αἱματηρόν: predicative.　　**ἐξαφρίζεσθαι**: better middle than
passive.

1068. πλέω ῥίψασα: 'throwing away', i.e. wasting, more words.

1071. ἑκοῦσ᾽ (codd.) ἀνάγκης τῆσδε (Casaubon) is as likely to be the
correct reading.

The Cassandra-Scene, 1072–1330.

This scene is composed of two parts, the former mainly sung (1072–
1177), the latter spoken (1178–1330).

I. 1072–1177. Cassandra's visions (1090–1129) and the prophecy
which follows them (1136–72) form a continuous series of events.
Cause and effect, the crime of Atreus and the murder of Agamemnon,
are revealed to her stage by stage in a stream of visions, past and
future in orderly sequence. These visions she describes as she sees
them developing: 1090–92: The house to which she has come she sees
as a place of murder. 1095–97: The vision of murder takes definite
form: she sees the children of Thyestes, whom Atreus killed and
served to their father at the banquet-table. 1100–4: The vision progresses; the crime of Atreus against Thyestes leads at once to its
consequence, the murder of the former's by the latter's son. The
house is again revealed as a place of Death. 1107–11: As before, the
vision of murder takes definite shape: she sees a wife attending her
husband at the bath, with murderous intent. The end is near.
Already the woman's hands reach out, one after the other,—for
what purpose? 1114–18: Again the vision makes plain what was
dimly seen: the woman's hands, reaching out, are seen to be casting
a Net of Death—the robe in which Clytemnestra entangled Agamemnon. But further: the vision becomes clearer still, and shows not only
a net flung over the man, but the woman too engaged with him,

enfolding him, fastening him in the net. The net, and the woman who entangles him in it, are for the moment fused into one: 'No, to say "Net of Death" is not enough; what entangles him is she who shares his bed and shares his killing' (1115–16). Now for the first time (since 1090) Cassandra expresses her own thought about the visions: 'The end is at hand; now is the time for the Spirit of Discord to uplift its voice in triumph' (1117–18). 1125–9: The act of murder is revealed. The victim is in the toils: the woman strikes, he falls; it is done. For the first time Cassandra speaks directly to the Chorus: δολοφόνου λέβητος τύχαν σοι λέγω (1129). 1136 ff.: The visions have vanished; henceforth Cassandra expresses her own prophetic thought. She has not yet named the murderer or the murdered, but she knows well who they are (1139 ξυνθανουμένην can only mean 'to die *together with Agamemnon*'), and foresees that her own death must follow. This is the main theme of the rest of her semi-lyrical utterances, 1136–9, 1146–9, 1156–61, 1167–72; each of these ends with a clear statement of her own impending death.

It is natural, however vain, to wonder how Aeschylus himself envisaged the behaviour of Cassandra throughout this part of the scene. A few points, attested by the text itself, are worth noticing: (1) At the beginning of the visions Cassandra is not so absorbed that she cannot attend to the Chorus's comments: 1090 ff. μισόθεον **μὲν οὖν**, 1095 ff. μαρτυρίοισι **γάρ**, take the form of replies to what the Chorus has said. (Not until 1129, when the visions have gone, does she directly address the Chorus.) (2) Her expressions of grief and horror are not extravagant. Her observations and thoughts are described in singularly coherent order and for the most part in straightforward language. Even when the visions approach their climax, she is yet self-possessed enough to break off the description and express her own thought about it (1117–18). (3) In each of her utterances from 1080 onwards, at least one iambic trimeter, exhibiting none of the features of *sung* verse, is included. Whether these verses were in fact sung or not (in more than one place they form part of sentences begun in lyrical verse), their essentially non-lyrical nature indicates a note of restraint, acting as a brake on the emotions expressed in the surroundings. (4) The tempo of the scene is slowed up in the earlier part by the Choral responses. These quietly spoken and rather uninteresting couplets stand in sharpest contrast with Cassandra's impassioned revelations. At 1119 ff. the Chorus is at last infected with her dread and foreboding. From spoken iambics (1119–20) they pass into the agitated rhythm of dochmiacs, in which metre they continue henceforward to the end. But while the tempo of the Chorus is thus accelerated, in the second half of the scene, Cassandra reverses the process: each of her last four utterances ends with two full iambic trimeters of the spoken type, apparently not sung.

The general indications are that Cassandra is portrayed as greatly agitated, but still commanding throughout a considerable measure of self-control. During her visions she is not possessed or entranced, let alone in a state of Pythian frenzy. She remains aware of her surroundings, the Palace and the Chorus. She speaks not as in a dream, or as one supernaturally inspired: fully understanding what she is doing, and aware that others are listening, she describes with clarity the appalling phantoms which loom and fade before her.

II. The structure of the second part (1178–1330) is sharply defined in three phases concluded by a brief epilogue. All three phases have the same inner structure: a speech by Cassandra, followed by a dialogue with the Chorus; but the length of Cassandra's speeches grows progressively greater (20 lines–28–39), and her mood more and more agitated.

1178–1213: Her first speech is calm and strictly reasonable. She wishes to convince the Chorus, and employs the common argument that the truth of her visions of the past should prove the truth of her prophecies about the future. She even carries the revelation of her knowledge a step back beyond her recent visions, so far as the πρώταρχος ἄτη, the adultery of Thyestes with Atreus' wife, the reason for Atreus' crime against Thyestes. Then in dialogue with the Chorus she seeks further to convince them of her truth, reluctantly disclosing the source of her prophetic power and the circumstances in which it was conferred upon her.

1214–55: From the beginning of her second speech, all is suddenly changed. She begins with a cry of anguish: the vision of Thyestes' butchered children looms again before her—'cannot the Chorus *see* them?' (1217 ff.). She furiously abuses Aegisthus and Clytemnestra, her language becoming more and more violent. In dialogue with the Chorus she at last states in unambiguous language what impends: Ἀγαμέμνονός σέ φημ' ἐπόψεσθαι μόρον (1246).

1256–94: In her third speech, the grief and fury of the second are strung to a still higher pitch: her theme is now her own misery, her own humiliation and dread of death. And here, at the climax of the whole scene, she takes a step into the future: hitherto she has re-traced the ground of her visions and prophecy—the crime of Atreus, the impending murder of Agamemnon, her own death; now for the first time she prophesies the next event in the inevitable sequence—the murder of Clytemnestra by her son Orestes (1280 ff.). All is now revealed, and told, and believed; nothing remains but despair and extremity of suffering. In the short concluding passage (1313–30) the intensity of emotion is as great as ever, the violence of the language abates; 'unfathomable misery speaks in a low voice' (Fraenkel, p. 627).

1072. δᾶ: an exclamation of horror (the old view that it is 'Doric' δᾶ = γᾶ, γῆ, is to be rejected; see Fraenkel).

1075. οὐ γὰρ τοιοῦτος κτλ.: mournful songs were inappropriate to the cult of Apollo; Stesichorus fr. 22 παιγμοσύνας τε φιλεῖ μολπάς τ' Ἀπόλλων, κάδεα δὲ στοναχάς τ' Ἀίδας ἔλαχεν.

1078. Most of the modern editors print ἡ δ', but this use of article for pronoun is abnormal in such a context, and ἥδ', 'this woman here', is preferable in itself.

1079. οὐδὲν προσήκοντα = ᾧ οὐδὲν προσήκει, a usage illustrated by LSJ s.v. III. 3 b.

1080. ἀγυιᾶτα: Cassandra sees and addresses the symbol of Apollo standing at the palace gates. See Farnell, *Cults* iv, pp. 148 ff., Cook, *Zeus* ii, pp. 160 ff.: the function of 'Apollo of the Street' seems to have been to protect the passage to and from men's houses. Originally his symbol was a block of stone, cone-shaped or with a rounded top; its representation on the scene of Attic Tragedy is quite often attested, cf. S. *El.* 637, 645, 1376, *OT* 919, E. *Ph.* 631, Ar. *Vesp.* 875 with scholia.

1081 f. ἀπόλλων . . . ἀπώλεσας: the play on the name was, at least later, a commonplace; E. fr. 781. 11 f. Ἥλι' ὥς μ' ἀπώλεσας | καὶ τόνδ', Ἀπόλλων δ' ἐν βροτοῖς ὀρθῶς καλῇ, Plato, *Cratylus* 404ᵈ.

1082. οὐ μόλις: 'easily' (there is no proof of the meaning 'utterly' given by some edd. and by LSJ for this passage and for *Eum.* 864, E. *Hel.* 334. μόλις means *aegre*, not *parum*, always meaning or implying 'with difficulty', and *haud aegre*, not *non parum*, is the meaning of οὐ μόλις wherever it occurs). **τὸ δεύτερον**: the *first* occasion is described in 1202 ff.

1084. The 'day of slavery which takes from a man half his excellence' (*Od.* 17. 322 f.) has not robbed Cassandra of her gift of prophecy (which is all that τὸ θεῖον means here).

1087. Cassandra knows perfectly well where she is: the question conveys her feeling of horror and foreboding, '*What manner of house is this . . .?*' The Chorus's reply, especially the second line, is very dull.

1090. μισόθεον: this word should mean 'hating the gods' (a sense which must not be toned down to a vague 'ungodly'), not 'hated by the gods'. **συνίστορα**: the adjective retains sufficient verbal force to allow it to govern the following accusatives; the house '*has on its conscience* many guilty secrets of kindred-murder . . . .'

1091. Triclinius' text, with κἀρτάνας, brings the apparent tradition into line with the demands of syntax, but is still doubly exposed to objection: (1) if, as seems certain, cod. M has the right reading in 1096, 1091 lacks one short syllable after αὐτόφονα; (2) ἀρτάναι, 'ropes for hanging', suggesting *suicides*, have no place in the story in question. The popular conjecture καρατόμα (Kayser) is too long a shot palaeographically; and, as Rose observes (*CR* lvi (1942) 71), 'behead-ings' are not much less irrelevant to Cassandra's vision than 'suicides' would be. κρεαρτόμα (Weil), or κρεάρταμα, would do justice to the sense. (Headlam conj. κἆι ἄρταμα, an illicit hiatus and shortening in this place of the iambic metron, viz. between the *anceps* and the cretic.)

1092. ἀνδρὸς σφαγεῖον is much less likely than the compound word, for ἀνδρός, which must refer to *somebody*, could only be understood as alluding to *Agamemnon*; and that would be wholly premature, for we are at this time farther back in the past, about to witness a vision of the mutilation of Thyestes' children. The choice between πέδον ῥαντήριον and πεδορραντήριον is harder: formations in -τήριον often have *prepositional* prefixes (type περιρραντήριον), but are never until Byzantine Greek compounded with *substantives* (type ψυχοσωτήριον); moreover the meaning of πεδορρ., 'floor-besprinkler', is not much in its favour. πέδον ῥαντήριον makes a slightly inferior mate for the compound ἀνδροσφαγεῖον, but presents no intrinsic difficulty ('ground sprinkled (with blood)': ῥαντήριον passive as in περιρραντήρια ap. Aeschines 1. 21; LSJ s.v. II. 8). Perhaps γάπεδον ῥαντήριον, in apposition to ἀνδροσφαγεῖον (γαπεδ- for καὶ πέδ- conj. Franz).

1094. Lit. 'She is seeking the blood of those whose blood she shall find.'

1095. γάρ: '(Yes, I shall find it), *for* here is the evidence . . . .'

1096. The accusatives σφαγάς and σάρκας are governed by κλαιόμενα: but what are the case and construction of τάδε βρέφη? Most edd., with a semi-colon after ἐπιπείθομαι, take βρέφη as a nominative, and take τάδε 'deictically', understanding ἐστί, '*These here* (are) infants bewailing etc.' This is surely ruled out by the position of τάδε in the sentence, standing as it does together with its noun *between* the participle and the words governed by the participle. Not less un-likely is the suggestion that μαρτυρεῖ, or ὁρῶσα, or the like, could be supplied from the context to govern the accusatives. We must surely remove the stop after ἐπιπείθομαι and take κλαιόμενα τάδε βρέφη σφαγάς as directly governed by that verb: πείθεσθαί τινί τι = 'believe someone in respect of something', as in Hdt. 2. 12. 1 τὰ περὶ Αἴγυπτον . . . τοῖσι λέγουσι αὐτὰ πείθομαι, 'I take the facts about Egypt on trust from my informants'. The construction here is the same, though the meaning emerges less clearly: 'these witnesses (viz. the ἀνδροσφαγεῖον and πέδον ῥαντήριον) I believe in respect of these children bewailing murder', i.e. the 'witnesses' give reliable evidence that the children's protestations are truth. Obscurity arises here from the extension of a simple construction of πείθομαι.

1098 f. There is nothing demonstrably wrong in the text indicated by the tradition, viz. ἦ μήν in 1098, ἦμεν in 1099. ἦ μήν in Attic 'intro-duces a strong and confident asseveration' (*Gk. Particles*, pp. 350 f.; not always so in the Epic, e.g. *Il.* 13. 354, 17. 429): here the Chorus very much dislikes being reminded of the horrors of the house of Atreus—'I assure you that we are fully informed of your prophetic fame; but we are not looking for any display of such powers at the moment.' The use of the plural in προφήτας οὕτινας makes their reply the more emphatic (οὕτινες is a very rare plural), thus repeating the nuance of ἦ μήν. Headlam's conjecture, τὸ μὲν κλέος . . ., is not called for by any demonstrable fault in the tradition.   μαντικόν . . . προφήτας: a common contrast between the *divination* and the *pronouncement* of what is revealed thereby.

1100. μήδεται: the subject of the verb is the woman (Clytemnestra) who becomes clearer to Cassandra as the vision unfolds itself (1107 ff.).

1104. 'Help stands far away': the Scholia mistakenly suppose an allusion to Orestes, the potential rescuer.

1106. ἐκεῖνα: the fate of Thyestes' children (1096 f.).

1107. γάρ gives the reason for the exclamation (*Gk. Particles*, p. 80).

1109. πῶς φράσω τέλος: 'the sentence ought to end with κτενεῖς', as Sidgwick says. It is obvious from the context (ἰὼ τάλαινα, τόδε γὰρ τελεῖς;) that Cassandra guesses what the τέλος was, but she does not actually mention the killing until its turn comes to be revealed in the vision (1128 τύπτει). She could not say πῶς φράσω τέλος unless she had a good general idea of what the τέλος was : cf. E. *Tro.* 713 ἔδοξε τόνδε παῖδα, πῶς εἴπω λόγον;

1110. τόδε: sc. τὸ τέλος.   γάρ: ('I speak thus of a τέλος) *because* there will soon be one.'

1110 f. Lit. 'She stretches forth hand after hand, reaching them out.' τοῖς ὀρέγμασι τῶν χειρῶν Schol., by which Hermann was prompted to alter the text from ὀρεγομένα to ὀρέγματα (with χείρ nominative 'hand after hand stretches forth its reach'); as a corruption, unlikely; as a change, unnecessary.

As the vision develops Cassandra sees the woman stretch forth first one hand, then the other, toward her victim—her *purpose* is not revealed until her next utterance, when the vision has made it clear. (It is thus unnecessary, as well as impossible, to believe with Fraenkel that 'the sentence προτείνει κτλ. describes nothing but the movements of Clytemnestra as she is attending her husband in his bath'.)

1112–13. Obscure and ambiguous. (1) 'For now, after riddles, I am bewildered by dark oracles' (Weir Smyth, after Hermann): but there is not much point here in such a distinction between 'riddles' and 'oracles', αἰνίγματα and θέσφατα—a distinction certainly not made elsewhere in this context (the enigmatic sayings of 1100-4 were called μαντεύματα in 1105). (2) Perhaps ἐξ αἰνιγμάτων gives the source of her ἀμηχανία (ἐκ of cause or means, LSJ s.v. III. 6), 'I am bewildered by obscure sayings'; to this is attached a causal dative, ἐπαργ. θεσφάτοις, 'by reason of dark prophecies'. (3) A further possibility is to take ἐπαργέμοισι closely with ἐξ αἰνιγμάτων, 'I am bewildered by prophecies which arise darkly from obscure sayings'; so Schütz. The second of these choices is perhaps the least objectionable.

1115. ἤ ... γε: a very rare combination of particles (E. *Cycl.* 207 ἤ πρός γε μαστοῖς ἐστι, where however τε for γε may be correct) except where γε signifies assent to a preceding affirmation (1064 ἤ μαίνεταί γε, 'yes, she is indeed out of her mind').

It is uncertain whether this phrase is a statement or a question; preferably the latter.

1116. Lit. '(Is it a net of Death?) No, rather it is his own wife who is the snare . . . .' To call it a 'net of Death' is only half the truth: it is his own wife who entangles him; she and the snare are one.

ξύνευνος ... ξυναιτία: she who shares his bed shares also his murdering. The general sense is plain enough, the detail (naturally, in this context) somewhat cryptic: it is not clear whether ξυναιτία means 'sharing the guilt' *with the net*, or *with Aegisthus*.

Normally in such a phrase as ἄρκυς ἡ ξύνευνος, ἄρκυς would be a predicate: here the preceding δίκτυον Ἅιδου rules that possibility out.

1117. στάσις: spirit of discord.   **γένει**: better with ἀκόρετος than with κατολολ.

1118. θύματος: it is natural that *Clytemnestra* (1054) should refer to the murder of Agamemnon as a 'sacrifice', as if it were a religious duty; on *Cassandra's* lips the word is pure metaphor. Cf. E. *Andr.* 506, where the killing of Astyanax is called θῦμα δάιον not by the killer but by the mother herself.   **λευσίμου**: an uncommonly free use; a 'stoning sacrifice' has to mean something like 'a sacrifice connected with stoning'; cf. 1616, where λευσίμους ἀράς means 'curses of (curses which threaten) stoning'.

1119. ποίαν: cf. 1087; with surprise and disgust, 'What sort of an Erinys is this . . .?'

1121–2. ἐπὶ ... σταγών: the 'saffron-dyed drop' means *blood*, as Schol. cod. M says. The blood, in moments of great terror, was said to run to the heart: Aristotle fr. 243 (Rose), (τὸ αἷμα) τοῖς φοβηθεῖσιν συντρέχει εἰς τὴν καρδίαν, ὥστε ἐκλείπειν ἐκ τῶν ἄλλων μερῶν (cit. Headlam). 'Saffron-dyed', because *yellow* is the colour of the complexion associated with the emotion of fear (χλωρὸν δέος).

1122–3. Most modern attempts at restoration assume, improbably enough, that καὶ δορία (cod. M) represents a combination of καὶ δορί and καιρία: it is doubtful whether either would yield acceptable sense.—(1) ἅτε καιρία πτώσιμος will not do, for though καιρία might mean either 'at the fatal time' or 'in the fatal place', πτώσιμος is an impossible adjective for the blood in this context, which is not concerned with blood *falling* (which could only mean *falling to the ground*). καιρία πτωσίμοις (Enger) is worth consideration only if πτωσίμοις be taken with αὐγαῖς, 'blood which at the fatal hour

(καιρία) reaches its goal together with the falling rays of life's sunset':
but πίπτειν (and its cognates) of the setting of the sun or its rays is
abnormal and unnatural language. (2) ἄτε καὶ δορὶ πτωσίμοις (Casaubon) is not less unsatisfactory. The meaning would be 'blood flows to
my heart, the blood which, for those too who fall by the spear,
reaches its goal together with the rays of their life's sunset': but (a)
ἄτε must then stand for οἷα τε, 'of a kind which . . .' (the one which . . .'
would be an absurdity), and that would be contrary to Tragic (and
Epic) practice; (b) the general sense would presumably be that
extremity of terror, and the moment of death, are alike marked by
the same symptom, viz. the flow of blood to the heart: but then it
would appear impossible to attach any meaning to the specific reference to death by the spear, death in battle—indeed the blood of those
who die by the spear is likelier to flow to the ground than to the
heart. The problems here remain unsolved.

1124. ταχεῖα δ' ἄτα πέλει: better general ('calamity loses no time in
coming') than more closely attached to what precedes ('(when the
sun of life sets) and doom comes swiftly').

1125–6. ἄπεχε τῆς βοὸς τὸν ταῦρον: 'Keep the bull away from the cow'
at once suggests the meaning 'protect the cow from the bull':
Aeschylus of course meant 'protect the bull from the cow', a reversal
of the order of nature which would have been effective enough if only
he had reversed the phraseology accordingly.

1126–8. Clytemnestra has entangled Agamemnon in a robe (the 'net'
of 1115; cf. *Eum.* 634 f.), and now she strikes, and he falls.

The detail presents a difficult problem. It seems certain that
μηχανήματι cannot be left unqualified by an adjective, so μελαγκέρῳ
must be preferred to -κερων despite the MS. evidence. But can we
now take μελαγκέρῳ . . . μηχανήματι with τύπτει, λαβοῦσα with ἐν
πέπλοισι? If we can, all is very simple and clear: 'having caught him
in the robes, she smites him with a black-horned device (i.e. with a
deadly instrument, her sword or axe; -κέρῳ continues the picture
begun in βοός . . . ταῦρον). But Fraenkel states that the mingling of
the two clauses is 'linguistically unsound'; and this is a very important matter here, since (as may be seen from his and other commentaries) μελαγκέρῳ λαβοῦσα μηχανήματι, if these words must be
taken together, defies all reasonable interpretation (Wecklein: 'having
caught him by means of a black-horned device' means that she
advances to the attack holding out the 'robe' on arms extended in
front of her *like the horns of a cow*. Fraenkel: 'with black contrivance
of the horned one', paraphrased as 'with the contrivance which
secretly works black mischief, the contrivance of the horned animal
which uses its horns to attack'). The advantage on the one side and
the loss on the other are so great that it is legitimate to question
whether Fraenkel's objection is sufficiently well founded.

In fact examples of closely similar type are occasionally to be found elsewhere; what is alleged here is of the same kind as, and not more extreme than, for example, S. *Ajax* 286-7 ἄμφηκες λαβὼν | ἐμαίετ' ἔγχος ἐξόδους ἔρπειν κενάς, where ἔγχος, the object of the participial clause, is inserted into the ἐμαίετο–ἔρπειν clause; Ar. *Ach.* 672 f. οὕτω σοβαρὸν ἐλθὲ μέλος εὔτονον ἀγροικοτόνον ὡς ἐμὲ λαβοῦσα τὸν δημότην, where the main and participial clauses are wonderfully interlaced; E. *Hel.* 718 f. νῦν δ' ἔχει | αὐτόματα πράξας τἀγάθ' εὐτυ-χέστατα, where again the participle has moved into the main clause; species of the same genus as S. *Ajax* 723 f. πρόσωθεν αὐτὸν ἐν κύκλῳ | μαθόντες ἀμφέστησαν, where the interruption of αὐτὸν ἐν κύκλῳ ἀμφέστησαν by the participle μαθόντες, which belongs to πρόσω-θεν, is very harsh; E. *Or.* 506 αὐτὸς κακίων μητέρ' ἐγένετο κτανών, where a very proper feeling against the mingling of main and parti-cipial clauses has brought about the reversal of the order of μητέρα and ἐγένετο in all our MSS.; cf. further S. *Ant.* 960 f. Even the Epic, in which eccentricity of word-order of this type is very rare, provides such aberrations as *Il.* 16. 511 f. ὁ δή μιν Τεῦκρος ἐπεσσύμενον βάλεν ἰῷ | τείχεος ὑψηλοῖο, where ἐπεσσύμενον, which governs τείχεος, has invaded and rudely interrupted the main clause; cf. 11. 326 f. Ἀχαιοὶ | ἀσπασίως φεύγοντες ἀνέπνεον Ἕκτορα δῖον, a similar example; 9. 567 πόλλ' ἀχέουσ' ἠρᾶτο κασιγνήτοιο φόνοιο, where ἀχέουσα goes with κασιγν. φόν.; in *Il.* 8. 455 f. the whole participial clause is most un-comfortably located in the middle of the main clause, οὐκ ἂν ἐφ' ὑμετέρων ὀχέων πληγέντε κεραυνῷ | ἂψ ἐς Ὄλυμπον ἵκεσθον, where the meaning is 'you would not have returned to Olympus, because you would have been smitten by a thunderbolt'. Cf. Solon 25. 7 (Diehl).

Evidently there can be no question of 'linguistic unsoundness': the poets do from time to time allow themselves liberties of the kind alleged here, or even worse. We are free to choose this possibility in preference to a course which reduces the greatest simplicity to the darkest confusion.

1129. λέβητος: the bath (δροίτη in 1539 f.) in which Agamemnon stood when she attacked him. The word normally denotes a much smaller washing-vessel. **λέβητος τύχαν**: an unusual expression, per-haps meaning 'what happened in the bath', or possibly 'what the murderous treacherous bath brought to pass', analogous to the com-mon δαίμονος τύχη, 'the daimon's doing' (LSJ s.v. τύχη init.).

1130 ff. The general sense is: I do not understand what she is saying, but she speaks as a prophetess, and it is therefore safe to assume that what she forecasts is evil, not good.—'For from oracles what message of *good* for men is sent? It is through *misfortunes* (διαί c. gen. of the instrument, or means) that the wordy arts of prophets bring a tale of *terror* for men to learn.' Some take κακῶν διαί to mean 'by means of ill-omened *words*' (cf. S. *Tr.* 1131); but the point is not so much that

prophets express themselves in gloomy terms as that the subject of
their pronouncements is invariably bad news.

1137. ἐπεγχέασα codd., a syllable too long for the line. ἐπεγχέαι, an
epexegetic infinitive, 'so as to pour it on top (of the πάθος of Agamemnon)', may be right, perhaps altered to the participial form
to ease the syntax. Headlam suggested ἐπεγχύδαν, supposing the
adverb (cf. *Cho.* 67, *Eum.* 553) to have been replaced by a participial
gloss; but one would not have expected the participle here to be in
the aorist tense.

1138. ποῖ must not be replaced by Heimsoeth's conjecture τί. The
meaning (with ποῖ) is not 'what is the name of this place to which you
have brought me?' but 'to what end, for what purpose, have you
brought me hither?', exactly as in E. *IT* 77, where Orestes says ποῖ μ'
αὖ τήνδ' ἐς ἄρκυν ἤγαγες, although he knows perfectly well what the
place is at which he has arrived (69 ff.: Orestes, like Cassandra, knows
where he is, though he has never been there before, *IT* 93 f.). The
question is presumably addressed to Apollo (not, as some have
thought to Agamemnon).

1139. 'only to share another's death'.   τί γάρ; = 'of course', *Gk.
Particles*, p. 85.

1142. ξουθά: it is disputed whether the reference is to *colour* or to
sound. Contrast Fraenkel (following Blomfield and Wilamowitz), 'in
the fifth century the word was always taken to refer to colour', with
Rutherford (on Babrius cxviii. 1), 'in none of these passages is there
any necessity to understand the word as referring to colour'. In most
of the fifth century examples colour and sound have more or less
equal claim to recognition, and in none of them is the choice un-
mistakably dictated by the context. The most helpful passages lie
outside that time-limit: Hom. *Hymn.* 33. 13 (cf. Bacchyl. 5. 16 ff.)
ξουθῆσι πτερύγεσσι (of the Dioscuri), where *colour* is very improbable,
and Chaeremon fr. 1. 7 ξουθοῖσιν ἀνέμοις, where *colour* is out of the
question.

1143. The MS. evidence points to original φεῦ ταλαίναις φρεσίν. ταλαίναις
was glossed φιλοίκτοις (used as a glossword elsewhere, e.g. Schol. B
on *Iliad* 22. 88), hence the text of cod. F.

1144 ff. The root of the difficulty lies in 1146 ff. The general sense is
clear enough: 'the nightingale was more fortunate than I, for she was
given life, with nothing to cry for, whereas I am to be given death in
a brutal form.' But nobody has yet made sense of the MSS.' ἰὼ ἰὼ
λιγείας ἀηδόνος μόρον.

Before we consider the question whether the end of 1146 should be
altered to ἀηδοῦς μόρον or μόρον ἀηδόνος, we must ask what could be
meant by the 'death of a nightingale' in this context, starting from
the position that μόρος in Aeschylus elsewhere always means 'death',
not 'destiny' or 'portion'. The gods rescued Procne from death at the

hand of Tereus, and turned her into a nightingale destined to mourn eternally her dead son Itys: that is the story to which Aeschylus here alludes; and clearly it has nothing to say about the 'death of a nightingale'. Procne might be said to 'die' at the moment of transformation into a nightingale, but there is no story about a *nightingale's death* (and, if there were, it could not possibly be fitted into this context). The fact must be faced that there is no place here for the '*death* of a nightingale'.

But further: the accusative μόρον is unintelligible. Exclamations do not 'govern' accusatives in Greek, as they so often do in Latin. There is indeed not a single certain or probable example of an accus. governed by an exclamation in Greek literature before the Hellenistic era (even then it is very rare: Asclepiades, *Anth. Pal.* 13. 23. 5, Duris (3rd cent.) ibid. 9. 424. 6, Meleager ibid. 7. 468. 6, Philip of Thessalonica ibid. 7. 554. 3. In Callim. *Lav.* 89 ἐμὲ δειλάν is presumably governed by ἐπράξαο below. In E. *Tro.* 138 the correct reading is given by cod. V. There is nothing else but a ritual cry (not a grammatical sentence), ὦ τὸν Ἄδωνιν, ascribed to Sappho (cf. Ar. *Lys.* 393, Bion *Adon.* 28, 32) which should not be used as evidence of grammatical usage).

Finally, the sense requires that the fate of the nightingale should appear to Cassandra as enviable in comparison with her own: but, unless the context dictates otherwise, anybody who says 'Oh, the death of the nightingale!' will be understood to utter a cry of grief or compassion (as in 1136, 1146, 1167).

If only μόρος could mean 'portion' (as it does seldom but sometimes in the Epic, e.g. *Od.* 11. 618), and if only μόρος were in the text instead of μόρον, something could be done: for there is the possibility that this phrase was followed by an *adversative* particle. It is much easier to substitute -βαλον γάρ οἱ for -βάλοντο γάρ οἱ than to show how the alleged corruption could have arisen. An original -βαλον δέ οἱ (with hiatus before οἱ as in S. *Tr.* 650) might well be variously corrupted to -βάλοντο δ' οἱ and -βαλον γάρ οἱ; and -βάλοντο γάρ οἱ might arise from combination of the two. We might then say that Cassandra, having begun 'Alas, unhappy nightingale!', at once corrects herself— 'but, after all, she had a happier lot than mine' (δέ strongly adversative, *Gk. Particles*, pp. 166 f.). It remains, however, impossible to acquiesce in so abnormal a sense of μόρος; and we should still not have explained the accusative case.

If we now look back to what precedes, we find it hardly less obscure: ἴτυν ἴτυν στένουσ᾽ ἀμφιθαλῆ κακοῖς ἀηδὼν βίον.—what is the construction of βίον, and what is meant by ἀμφιθαλῆ κακοῖς βίον? Most edd. take βίον as accusative of *duration*, 'mourning Itys *throughout* her life . . .': that would be harsh enough in itself, but it is the sense rather than the grammar which rules it out. Apart from the abuse of the word ἀμφιθαλής, which would have to be stripped of its proper meaning and reduced to something like 'rich', 'flourishing', there is no sense here in talking about the *nightingale's 'life rich in evils'* : her *life* is, as Cassandra at once says, 'a sweet life with nothing to cry for'; she must bemoan the past, the death of Itys, but her *life* is free from further troubles. To call the *lifetime* of the nightingale 'rich in evils' would be false in any context and absurd in this one, where the blunt contradiction γλυκὺν αἰῶνα κλαυμάτων ἄτερ follows at once. The same fatal objection applies to the alternative interpretation, according to which ἴτυν-στένουσα forms a single concept directly governing βίον, 'bewails, with "Itys, Itys", her life that has woe flourishing on either side' (Fraenkel). *What the nightingale bemoans is the death of Itys, not her own life as a nightingale; what was ἀμφιθαλὴς κακοῖς was not her life but her son's death.*

All explains itself so soon as these simple facts are recognized: what we need in 1145 is μόρον, not βίον, and what we need in 1146 is βίος, not μόρος—'mourning "Itys, Itys", his death rich in evils on both father's and mother's sides'. 'O the life of the tuneful nightingale! The gods dressed her in feathered shape, and gave her sweet life with nothing to cry for; whereas for me . . .'.

βίον (1145) was written in error, under the influence of βίος immediately below (cf. E. *Rhes.* 776 πλάθειν cod. V, for πελάζεσθαι, from πλάθειν in the line below; the same sort of thing happened at *Agam.* 1216, 1324, S. *Ant.* 606 f. (-γήρως), E. *Tro.* 1243, *Rhes.* 208, al.). μόρον, the correct reading, was added in the margin, and became wrongly attached to the end of the next line, whence βίος was accordingly expelled. The process is less elaborate than it sounds; and it allows us for the first time to understand several things: (1) why μόρον is in the accus. case (see above), hitherto unexplained; (2) why it is at the end of the line, not as we should expect in the middle (μόρον ἀηδόϊ̈ός corresponding exactly to 1136, 1156, 1167); (3) what is meant by ἀμφιθαλῆ: this can now at last refer to Itys, as it obviously should, not to his mother—the term is semi-technical, signifying a child who has both parents living: the death of Itys is excellently described as ἀμφιθαλὴς κακοῖς, 'beset with evils on both parents' sides', for his mother killed him and his father ate his flesh; if ever a child's death was, in precise terms, ἀμφιθαλής in evil, that child was surely Itys. Cf. *Suppl.* 65, where παιδὸς μόρον is the object of the nightingale's song.

The construction is similar to that in 1191 f., ὕμνουσι δ' ὕμνον . . . πρώταρχον ἄτην, where the theme of the song, πρώταρχον ἄτην, stands in apposition to the cognate accusative ὕμνον; so here ἀμφιθαλῆ κακοῖς μόρον, the theme of the song, is in apposition to ἴτυν ἴτυν, 'her Itys song'.

κλαυμάτων ἄτερ: since the nightingale was a byword for the melancholy of her song, and since this fact was stressed only a moment ago, it would be ludicrous to say here that the gods gave her 'sweet life *without lamentations'*. It does not help to translate, as Fraenkel does, 'without cries of woe'; the nightingale's song was one continuous lament for her dead son, and no useful distinction can be drawn in such a context between *lamentations* and *cries of woe*. Nor can we take κλ. ἄτερ with περέβαλον.

The sense surely is 'a sweet life *without troubles*, without anything to cry for': though she must lament the past, yet the present, her life-time (αἰών) as a nightingale, is free from further troubles. The sense of κλαύματα is just what it is in S. *Phil.* 1260 ἐκτὸς κλαυμάτων, *Ant.* 931 f. τοῖσιν ἄγουσιν κλαύμαθ' ('something to cry for') ὑπάρξει.

1149. δορί not 'spear', as the adjective shows; apparently 'weapon', a looseness of usage unexampled elsewhere.

1150. Some edd. delete τ', without sufficient cause: the first two adjectives, being coherent in sense, are connected by τε; the third, being of a different quality, follows without a connecting particle.

1152–3. Lit. 'Why do you mould to melody these dreadful things, with ill-omened din, together with piercing strains?'   **δυσφάτῳ**: probably = δυσφήμῳ, meaning much the same thing as κακορρή-μονας below; possibly = ἀσαφεῖ, αἰνιγματώδει (Schol.).   **κλαγγᾷ**: elsewhere almost confined to the voices of animals; of human beings also S. *Tr.* 207 f., cf. 156 above ἀπέκλαγξεν (also of a seer).   **ὁμοῦ**: *vehementer languet*, as Hermann says; it is doubtful whether the text is sound.

1154–5. Lit. 'Whence have you the ominous boundaries of your prophetic path?', i.e. who marked out for you the ill-omened path which your prophecy follows?   **θεσπεσίας ὁδοῦ**: cf. Ar. *Equ.* 1015 λογίων ὁδόν, E. *Ph.* 911 θεσφάτων . . . ὁδόν, Pind. *Ol.* 9. 47 οἶμον ἐπέων. On the meaning of θεσπέσιος see Fraenkel.

1157. ὀλέθριοι φίλων: cf. Hdt. 2. 74 ἀνθρώπων δηλήμονες; K.–G. i. 371, n. 19.   **ποτόν**: of a river, Theocr. 13. 46 with Gow's note.

1159. ἠνυτόμαν: ηὐξόμην, Schol., 'I grew up', an unique usage.

1164. The δῆγμα ('bite', 'sting') is regarded as that which causes the effect denoted by the verb πέπληγμαι: for this rare use of ὑπό c. dat. see 891 ff. n.

1165. δυσαλγεῖ τύχᾳ: causally with μινυρὰ θρεομένας. Weir Smyth gives the sense well: 'I am smitten with a deadly pain, the while, by reason of thy cruel fortune, thou criest aloud thy piteous plaint that breaks my heart to hear.'

1166. θραύματα: an uncommon metaphor, cf. Ar. *Av.* 466 θραύσει ψυχήν, E. *Hipp.* 765 f. φρένας . . . κατεκλάσθη, and the Odyssean κατεκλάσθη φίλον ἦτορ; but here the lack of a word meaning 'heart' makes a difference.

1168. πρόπυργοι: a formation analogous to πρόδομος, πρόναος; more probably 'in front of the towers' than 'on behalf of the towers'.

1169. 'prodigal in slaughter of the grazing flock', Fraenkel.

1169–71. 'They supplied no cure to prevent the city suffering as it was ordained.' On the use of μή, where μὴ οὐ would be expected (Goodwin *MT*, § 811), see A. C. Moorhouse in *CQ* xxxiv (1940) 70 ff. (Fraenkel, p. 533 n. 3, does not mention the decisive point: Moorhouse shows that all four dramatists have *unemendable* examples of μή for μὴ οὐ; there is therefore no linguistic necessity to insert the οὐ in emendable examples, though of course such insertion *might* be right.)   ἐχρῆν: cod. F's ἔχειν is unintelligible; Triclinius' ἔχει (probably his own conjecture) makes an unnatural phrase (one said πάσχω ἃ πάσχω, ἔχω ἃ ἔχω, but not πάσχω ἃ ἔχω). The form ἐχρῆν (for χρῆν) is not demonstrable in Tragedy until E. *Med.*, but occurs elsewhere as early as Pindar, *Nem.* 7. 44.

1172. The general sense was apparently 'and I, Cassandra, shall soon die', the detail perhaps something like 'I shall soon let fall my warm blood on the ground'; but the text is hopelessly corrupt. The harshness of the change in construction, τὸ μὴ πόλιν μὲν πα θεῖν, ἐγὼ δὲ βαλῶ, has analogies elsewhere, e.g. *ScT* 815 πόλιν μὲν . . ., οἱ δ' ἐπιστάται; and the words ἐγὼ δὲ . . . τάχ' ἐμ πέδῳ βαλῶ, 'I shall soon let (something) fall on the ground', seem particularly apt. The main difficulty lies in θερμόνους: Cassandra cannot in this context say 'I, *with impassioned mind* (or the like), shall shed my blood'; and somewhere in θερμόνους must lurk the object required by βαλῶ (which is not intransitive, despite *Eum.* 751). But there is no conjecture worth recording.

1173. Perhaps προτέροις τάδ' ⟨ἐπ⟩εφημίσω (Paley).

1174 ff. For τιθέναι with accus.+infin., 'to make someone do something', see LSJ s.v. B. I. 4, E. *Med.* 718 n.

1176. γοερὰ θανατηφόρα (Triclinius) creates a dochmiac of the shape ⏑ ⏑⏑ ⏑⏑ – ⏑⏑, unexampled in Aeschylus and Sophocles, very rare in Euripides (only *H.* 888 and perhaps *Tro.* 269; corrupt in *Hel.* 687 codd., very doubtful in *Or.* 1501).

1178. καὶ μήν marks the transition to Cassandra's more explicit prophecies (*Gk. Particles*, pp. 351 f.; this example should not have been included among those on p. 355).

1180–3. Lit. 'Bright it is likely to arrive, like a wind (πνέων), at the sun's uprising, so that a far greater woe than this shall surge, like a wave, toward the rays' (or, with κλύζειν transitive, 'so as to wash toward the rays, like a wave, a far greater woe than this'). The 'oracle' (χρησμός, = her powers of divination) is likened to a wind which blows toward the rising sun and drives the waves to a point where they may be clearly seen (cf. Catullus 64. 269 ff.): the calamity to be revealed by the oracle is likened to the waves thus exposed in the light; i.e. just as the wind drives the waves toward the light of the sun's early rays, so the oracle brings the calamity to revelation. Image and reality are confused, as often in Aeschylus.

λαμπρός : keen or fresh, of the wind; clear, of the oracle; LSJ s.v.
I. 5.   ἔοικεν : ἔοικε with future infin. usually expresses a *probability* (1161 above); here abnormally a *certainty*.   ἐσήξειν codd. :
as Fraenkel says, 'there is no certain instance of εἰσήκειν, at any
rate not in literary language, before the time of the Empire'; and
much the same is to be said of Bothe's popular conjecture ἐσάξειν (Ar.
Nub. 543 only; its meaning, 'rush in', is not very apt here). ἐφήξειν
is an easy change and a suitable verb (S. *Ajax* 34, *El.* 304, *Ant.* 1257).
τοῦδε πήματος πολὺ μεῖζον : what are the two πήματα thus compared?
The great impending calamity is in fact the murder of Agamemnon;
and the principal revelation made by Cassandra in accordance with
her promise here is the unambiguous statement in 1246, Ἀγαμέμνονός
σέ φημ' ἐπόψεσθαι μόρον—clearly the πῆμα πολὺ μεῖζον cannot be
anything but the murder of Agamemnon. What τοῦδε πήματος refers to is less easily definable: probably the present calamitous
state of affairs in general, perhaps with special reference to her
own δυσαλγὴς τύχα (1165), the subject of so much of the preceding
strophes.

1184. συνδρόμως : with ῥινηλατούσῃ.

1187. 'chanting in unison, but unmelodious; for it telleth not of good'
(Weir Smyth).

1190. συγγόνων : the 'kindred' Erinyes are the Erinyes who seek vengeance for the deaths of members of this family (Atreus, Thyestes);
the Erinys is more or less identified with the ghost of the dead man
demanding revenge (Rohde, *Rh. Mus.* 50 (1895) 10 ff.).

1191. προσήμεναι : 'besieging'. The Furies sit in the court besieging the
house (δώμασιν : this does not really clash with ἐν δόμοις 1189, which
denotes 'the residence' in its broadest sense).

1192. πρώταρχον ἄτην : in apposition to ὕμνον, giving the content or
theme thereof.   ἐν μέρει : 'in turn', one after another.

1192–3. ἀπέπτυσαν κτλ. : 'expressed their loathing for a brother's bed,
with enmity toward him who trampled thereon'. 'Brother's bed'
stands for 'crime against a brother's bed' (Thyestes' adultery with the
wife of Atreus); πατοῦντι, as usual, implies 'defiled'; δυσμενεῖς is
nominative (not accus. with εὐνάς).

1194. No known sense of τηρῶ satisfies here. Canter's θηρῶ is attractive (this verb almost invariably means 'hunt', not 'catch', but
Aeschylus has the middle θηρῶμαι in the sense required here, *PV*
109 f. θηρῶμαι πυρὸς πηγὴν κλοπαίαν, 'I *catch* a stolen fount of fire', not
'I go chasing after etc.' Also S. *Ant.* 433). Most of the modern edd.
approve Ahrens's conjecture κυρῶ, but it is not easy to see why this
should have been turned into τηρῶ.

1195. θυροκόπος φλέδων : lit. 'door-rapping talker of nonsense'; cf.
Plato *Rep.* 364ᵇ ἀγύρται ... καὶ μάντεις ἐπὶ πλουσίων θύρας ἰόντες.

1196–7. Having summoned the Chorus to act as witnesses of her powers in 1184 f., and having then displayed those powers in 1186–92, Cassandra concludes (ἐκμαρτύρησον referring back to μαρτυρεῖτε), 'Bear witness under oath that I do know the ancient sins of this house.' A more careful writer might have avoided adding λόγῳ to παλαιάς, foreseeing the scholarly objection that if the sins were ancient *in story*, Cassandra might have heard of them *in story*; they would not then be good evidence of her prophetic powers (cf. *PV* 824 ff., 842 f.). All she meant was that the events of which she has shown knowledge belong to the distant past: they are events now known to many of the natives only by hearsay—indeed she is saying no more than the Chorus themselves told her in 1106, πᾶσα γὰρ πόλις βοᾷ.

(There is no other difficulty in the MSS. Fraenkel objects that τό with infinitive, without a negative, elsewhere in Aeschylus occurs only 'in the simplest form, i.e. with the unexpanded infinitive as the object of the verb, as, for example, *Ag.* 498 τὸ χαίρειν μᾶλλον ἐκβάξει λέγων ': but the required construction is common enough in Sophocles. The translation (with μὴ εἰδέναι) runs: 'Bear witness that thou hast not heard, and dost not know, the ancient wrongdoings of this house' presumably this implies 'I defy you to disclaim knowledge', this being a tortuous way of saying 'you must surely admit that you know the story [and can therefore testify that what I say is true]'. The awkwardness of λόγῳ seems a trifle compared with this.)

1198–9. καὶ πῶς here introduces a 'rhetorical' question (*Gk. Particles*, pp. 310 f.): 'How could an honestly given oath give relief?' = 'An honestly given oath could not possibly give relief.' Cassandra has challenged the Chorus to swear, from their knowledge of the facts, that her visions are true. It would be a great relief if they could honestly swear the contrary: but this they cannot do. They avoid the issue, saying 'The truthful oath would work no cure', i.e. the true answer, if we gave it, would not make things any better. **γεν-ναίως παγέν** does not mean '*if*, or *however*, honestly compacted': this defining phrase is essential to the meaning, which is not 'how could *an* oath help?' but 'how could *a truly-given* oath (i.e. how could the *truth*) help?' The emphasis corresponds to that of Cassandra's ἐκμαρτύρησον πρωμόσας, 'let me have your testimony *under oath*', i.e. your true and honest opinion.

1200–1. κυρεῖν λέγουσαν: 'hit the mark in speaking', as in *Suppl.* 588 f. τόδ᾽ ἂν γένος λέγων ἐξ Ἐπάφου κυρήσαις. If the text is sound, πόλιν is directly governed by λέγουσαν, a most uncommon usage: λέγειν πάθη, τύχας, simm., 'to recount, tell the tale of . . .', is one thing; quite another is πόλιν ἀλλόθρουν λέγειν, 'speak about, describe, a foreign city'. The gap is at least partly bridged by such usages as 648 f. λέγων χειμῶνα, 'telling the tale of the storm', *Cho.* 594 f. ὑπέρ-τολμον ἀνδρὸς φρόνημα τίς λέγοι, 'who could *describe* etc.'

1204. As Wecklein says, the question is a natural one, for Apollo was known to confer oracular powers on his favourites (Linus, Daphne, others).

1205. 'Everyone feels greater delicacy when in prosperity' (Paley); the implication is 'your present position leaves no room for coy reticence'.

1206. παλαιστής: Love is sometimes described as a boxer (Anacreon fr. 27. 2, S. *Tr.* 442 f.), very seldom as a wrestler (cf. S. fr. 941. 13; Παλαιστώ is the name of an hetaera on a vase by Euphronios quoted by Kretschmer, *Gr. Vaseninschriften*, p. 209). It is hard to catch the nuance of this word here: it is anything but a faded metaphor, and its apparent meaning is at variance with the conventions of reticence in Tragedy and with the facts of the case.

1207. νόμῳ codd.: the Chorus, their interest aroused by what Cassandra has just said, ask in surprise, 'Were you really *lovers*?' The addition of νόμῳ, 'according to use and wont', however applicable to a wedding-ceremony, would be ludicrous in the circumstances: there could be no question of Apollo *marrying* Cassandra. On the form ἠλθέτην see K.–B. ii. 69.

1209. ἠρημένη: the divine arts are said to 'gain possession' of her, she is 'taken captive'.

1212. ὡς: temporal, = ἐξ οὗ.

1213. γε μὲν δή: strongly adversative (*Gk. Particles*, p. 395), 'but, for all that, *we* believe you'. .

1215 f. ὑπό in tmesis with στροβεῖ, the gap between them being unusually wide, as in *PV* 878–9 ὑπό μ' αὖ σφάκελος καὶ φρενοπληγεῖς μανίαι θάλπουσι (cf. also S. *Ant.* 601 f.). Both there and here ὑπό signifies 'inwardly', 'deep inside me'.

1216. After φροιμίοις the MSS. repeat ἐφημένοις from the end of the line above; Hermann's is much the likeliest stop-gap.

1217. δόμοις ἐφημένους: sitting at, i.e. just outside, the house; *Cho.* 501.

1219. ὡσπερεὶ πρὸς τῶν φίλων: Hermann's objection to ὡσπερεὶ κτλ., viz. that there is something absurd in saying 'I have a vision of children murdered—*they look as though their own kindred had killed them*' ('in occisis non apparet a quibus sint occisi'), is over-scrupulous. The content of the following lines shows that the children are recognizable as having died a violent death, and their position at the door suggests that they are at home here and must have been killed here; it is a natural presumption that they were killed by persons belonging to the house, πρὸς τῶν φίλων. It is, however, perhaps imprudent to reason so narrowly about such matters: as Mr. Barrett suggests, ὡσπερεί here may be merely the expression of a normal 'mantic' vagueness (cf. Dodds, *CQ* n.s. iii (1953) 12 f.).

Fraenkel objects further that elsewhere in Tragedy (and in 13 out of 14 places in Aristophanes) the word ὡσπερεί introduces a true comparison between two objects; in that respect this passage is abnormal.

The force of this observation seems diminished by the facts (1) that the generalization for Tragedy is based on very few examples (only two each for Aesch. and Soph., not counting hypothetical clauses of the type of *Agam.* 1201); (2) that Ar. *Av.* 51, ἄνω κέχηνεν ὡσπερεὶ δεικνύς τί μοι, shows the usage in question to be intelligible Attic speech.

1220. πλήθοντες : intransitive ; χέρας is accus. of respect. 'Having their hands full.'   οἰκείας βορᾶς : from time to time Aeschylus strains language, or even tortures it ; here 'their own food' means 'their own flesh, served to others as food'.

1221. The σπλάγχνα are the heart, lungs, liver, and kidneys, which were eaten at sacrifices ; the ἔντερα are primarily the intestines, which were not as a rule eaten. It is an added touch of horror, that both should have been served up together at that hideous feast.   τε joins πλήθοντες and ἔχοντες.

1224. λέοντα, applied to Aegisthus, is most unexpected, particularly since the same metaphor is applied to *Agamemnon* in 1259; and the phrase as a whole, 'a cowardly lion', is so unlikely that corruption of the text may well be suspected here (λύκον, λέοντος for λ. ἄναλκιν conj. Maas : that is what we need, but there is great difficulty in accounting for such a corruption). If the text is sound, we must stress the fact that the lion symbolizes *savagery* (cf. 717, 827, *Cho.* 938, *Eum.* 193), not as a rule *courage* : Aegisthus here is called a 'savage brute', and also a coward, ἄναλκιν. There may be a reminiscence of *Od.* 4. 333 f. κρατερόφρονος ἀνδρὸς ἐν εὐνῇ | ἤθελον εὐνηθῆναι ἀνάλκιδες.   ἐν λέχει : sc. τοῦ Ἀγαμέμνονος.   στρωφώμενον : lit. 'going to and fro', hence (as LSJ says) 'moving freely', i.e. making himself at home there.

1225. οἴμοι codd. : but (1) οἴμοι in mid-verse and mid-sentence does not occur elsewhere in Aeschylus and is extremely rare in Sophocles (*Phil.* 363) and Eur. (*Med.* 1371) ; (2) there is nothing in the context here to justify such an exclamation ; (3) the dative τῷ δεσπότῃ is unintelligible unless something is provided to govern it (οἰκουρός cannot do so (see Fraenkel) ; and ποινὰς βουλεύειν is much too far away). Simplest ὠμόν for οἴμοι (ᾤμοι).

1226. This feeble line is very offensive to our taste : see esp. A. Y. Campbell, *CQ* xxix (1935) 27 f., and Fraenkel, pp. 562 f. It must, however, be admitted that it contains no fault of sense, syntax, metre, or style, and that we can give no good reason why it should have been interpolated. (Fraenkel follows Campbell in supposing that 'ἐμῷ was first added as a gloss and then extended to a trimeter' : but no such gloss was needed, or even suggested ; and the idea that a gloss ἐμῷ might be expanded to a trimeter is not strengthened by reference to such purely speculative examples as *Il.* 8. 183, *Agam.* 7, *Cho.* 562, S. *OT* 827.)

182 COMMENTARY

1227. ἄπαρχος: the very unsatisfactory treatment of this word in LSJ is corrected by Fraenkel, pp. 565 f.

1228–30. With κἀκτείνασα for καὶ κτείνασα (and with οἴα, not οἷα) it becomes possible to say what the words mean as they stand; and it is not certain there is any serious fault to find.—Lit. 'He does not know what kind of detestable bitch's tongue, having spoken and with cheerful disposition prolonged her plea, shall strike by evil chance the target of secret destruction', i.e. he (Agamemnon) does not know that she (Clytemnestra), despite her long submissive speech and expression of friendly intentions, is aiming at his secret destruction and will in fact hit her target. **λέξασα καὶ ἐκτείνασα δίκην** refers to Clytemnestra's lengthy self-justification, 855 ff. (cf. 916 μακρὰν γὰρ ἐξέτεινας: δίκην λέγειν as in LSJ s.v. δίκη IV. 2 b; δίκη in the sense 'plea', or more broadly a party's 'case' at law, recurs in *Eum.* 492.) **φαιδρόνους** (cf. *Cho.* 565 φαιδρᾷ φρενί): here and in the next line the real subject is the μισητὴ κύων, Clytemnestra; the fact that the syntactical subject is still γλῶσσα is forgotten. **τεύ-ξεται**: future of τυγχάνω, 'shall hit', governing ἄτης; the usage as in LSJ s.v. B 1.

1231. τοιάδε (cod. F) τόλμα would mean 'such is recklessness' (or 'daring'); without the definite article it could not possibly mean 'such is *her* daring' (τοιάδε ἡ τόλμα). **τοιαῦτα** is what we may expect to find in a good MS. of this play; whoever wrote τοιάδε supposed, erroneously, that τόλμα represented the noun, not the verb.

1232. Enclitic ἐστί, unless it is the first word of its clause, does not elsewhere begin a line in Aeschylus. But since an example occurs in Sophocles (*OC* 1168, cf. *OT* 89) and an example in Euripides (*H.* 1293), we are not justified in altering the text when offered an example in Aeschylus. Cf. also *Od.* 12. 321: in all these four places there is more or less heavy punctuation after the initial ἐστί.

1232 f. Lit. 'giving her the name of what loathsome monster should I hit the mark?'

1233. ἀμφίσβαιναν: other references to this horrific monster are assembled by Demiańczuk, *Supplementum Comicum*, p. 16; Photius Berol. 103. 22 ἀμφίσβαινα: ὄφις ὁ καὶ ἐπὶ τῆς οὐρᾶς κεφαλὴν ἔχων· Ἀριστοφάνης Πελαργοῖς.

1235. Since there is no adjective formed from Ἅιδης, the genitive of the noun is used to signify 'hellish', as in E. *Cycl.* 397 Ἅιδου μαγείρῳ, *H.* 1119 Ἅιδου βάκχος, *IT* 286 Ἅιδου δράκαιναν; and so Ἅιδου μητέρα here is usually taken to mean 'hellish mother'. But why *mother*? Cassandra is preoccupied with the impending murder of Agamemnon, and we are not specially expecting an allusion to Clytemnestra's relation to her *children* here. Some have thought that the meaning is 'mother of death' in the sense *'necis auctor'*: the murderess may well be called 'she who gives birth to death'—'a bold imaginative name', said

Sidgwick; perhaps too much so. A. Y. Campbell in *CR* xxix (1935) 33, n. 2 and Fraenkel approve Karsten's assertion that μήτηρ *metaphorical* should not be used of one who is *actually* a 'mother': but it is hard to see why it should not be so used.

Perhaps it is likeliest, as Mazon suggests, that Clytemnestra is here called a 'raging hellish *mother*' because the murdering of Agamemnon is directly motived by the death of her *daughter*: the allusion comes in a little obscurely, but it is not as if there were any fault to find with the fact or with its relevance—it was indeed the injury done to Clytemnestra as a mother that turned her into a fiend of vengeance. τ' joins θύουσαν and πνέουσαν, 'raging, and breathing relentless war against her dearest'.

1236. ὡς seems to be exclamatory, 'And how she cried in triumph...!', presumably referring to the exultant prayer at 973 f.

1239. ὁμοῖον: 'it is *all the same* if you disbelieve me'; cf. 1404 below.

1241. γ': exclamatory, transferred to reported speech (*Gk. Particles*, p. 130), 'You will cry "too true a prophetess!"'

1242–5. The story of the Thyestean banquet has been told plainly enough, though no names have been mentioned. The prophecy of Agamemnon's murder by Clytemnestra has indeed been conveyed in terms hardly less plain. But an allusion to the known past is more easily caught than one to the unknown future; and Cassandra's language, despite her promise (1183), has left much in obscurity. The Chorus have some excuse for refusing to understand what they are unwilling to believe.

1244. Since κλυόντ' ἀληθῶς, if taken together, could not mean anything but 'truly hearing', as opposed to 'pretendedly hearing' (not 'hearing *a truly told tale*', 'hearing *a tale in terms of reality*', or anything else of that sort), it is necessary to take the object of κλυόντα to be a blend of οὐδὲν ἐξηκασμένα and ἀληθῶς εἰρημένα. Cf. 538 n., 797–8 n., 1470–1 n., for examples of similar imperfect blend.

1245. The metaphor as in 1185: like a hound that loses the scent and 'runs out of the track'.

1246. Here at last in unambiguous words Cassandra reveals what is to be: this is the first time that she has named *Agamemnon*.

1248. Since the verb εὐφημεῖν is used of the utterance of the cry ἰὴ παιών, or more generally of the kind of song or prayer called a Paean (Aesch. fr. 350. 4 παιῶν' ἐπευφήμησεν, E. *IA* 1467 f. ἐπευφημήσατε ... παιᾶνα), Cassandra may well retort to the command εὐφήμει that 'this is no occasion for a Paean': but the connexion of thought is obscure, for (1) the detail of her sentence shows that παιών here plays on the double sense of 'Paean, the song', and 'Paeon (Apollo), the god of healing'—lit. 'The Healing-god (to whom the εὐφημία of the Paean appertains) is not the director of this speech of mine'; (2) εὐφημεῖν means both to utter propitious speech and to keep silence in order to avoid unpropitious speech: the verb κοίμησον shows that the Chorus meant the latter, 'Hush your voice to auspicious *silence*'; Cassandra's reply would be more appropriate if they had recommended auspicious *speech*.

1249. ἔσται: the subject is 'Agamemnon's death', supplied from the context, esp. 1246.

1250. κατεύχῃ: perhaps 'pray *against* it', a sense applicable in *ScT* 633 (cf. 709); but, as Fraenkel observes, this is not the usual meaning in Aeschylus (*Eum.* 921, of a prayer *in favour*, cf. *Eum.* 1021, *Cho.* 88, 139).

1252. ΚΑΡΤΑΡΑΝ (codd.) may be derived from an attempt to make sense of **ΚΑΡΤΑΝΑΝ**, which should have been articulated ΚΑΡΤΑ-ΛΙΑΝ, κάρτα λίαν. παρακοπῆναι ('knocked off the track') is not elsewhere so used, but cf. the glossary edited by Bekker, *Anecd.* i. 428. 25 f. ἀποκοπῆναι τῶν ἰχνῶν τὴν κύνα λέγουσιν ὅταν μηκέτι εὑρίσκῃ τὰ ἴχνη, sim. Hesych. s.v. ἀποκοπῆναι (quoted by Headlam). The metaphor refers back to 1245, ἐκ δρόμου πεσὼν τρέχω.

1253. The sequence of thought is: 1251 'who is to be the murderer?'— 1252 'If you can still ask, you must have wholly failed to understand me'.—1253 'Yes, I did so fail, for I could see no means (μηχανήν) in the murderer's power', i.e. I did not see how the doer was to set about the deed. The Chorus suspect that *Aegisthus* is to be the killer (1251 ἀνδρός shows that they are not thinking of a *woman*); now, in 1251, they invite Cassandra to do what she has not yet done—to name the killer, as she at last named the victim in 1246. She accuses them of stupidity: they admit the charge, but also explain the reason—they cannot see *how* Aegisthus or anyone else can get the better of Agamemnon in his own house surrounded by his own people.

(The conjecture τοὺς γὰρ τελοῦντας give the dullest repetition of the sense of 1251, and reduces μηχανήν to a useless and unnatural appendage.)

1256–7. There is no substance in the points which led Wilamowitz to make drastic alteration and rearrangement here. He began Cassandra's speech thus (creating a phenomenon without parallel in Tragedy): παπαῖ· | οἷον τὸ πῦρ ἐπέρχεται· | ὀτοτοῖ· | Λύκει' Ἄπολλον, οἲ ἐγώ |. The reasons given for this procedure carry no conviction: (1) objection is taken to the prosody of οἶον, despite ποῖον elsewhere in Aeschylus (*Suppl.* 911: 'rudioris artis signum', Wilamowitz; at that time, but not today, a reasonable comment, however unconvincing); (2) the hiatus in παπαῖ οἷον and in ἐγὼ ἐγώ is condemned: but hiatus within or after exclamations is a normal feature of Greek prosody; all that is unusual here is that the metre is the iambic dialogue of Tragedy, and in that respect there are analogies (S. *Phil.* 759) which should serve as a warning against dogmatism; (3) ὀτοτοῖ is not elsewhere found in the iambic dialogue of Tragedy: but must we then reject ὠή in *Eum.* 94 on the ground that it is not found elsewhere in Aesch. or Soph. (or, except at the beginning of the line, in Eur.)? Or πόπαξ in *Eum.* 143 on the ground that it is unique in dochmiacs (or indeed anywhere else)? (4) It is further alleged that ἐπέρχεται δέ μοι is 'lame, not to say childish', following οἶον τὸ πῦρ: it seems unlikely that many will concur in this judgement.

1256. πῦρ: in effect = πυρετός (LSJ s.v. πῦρ I. 7), the fever which possesses her.

1260–1. Image and reality are sometimes rather confused than blent in Aeschylean metaphors, but the expression 'preparing a drug, she will insert requital for me also *into her anger*' seems an unusually harsh example. ποτῷ (Auratus) would be an improvement. **μισθὸν ἐμοῦ**: 'a paying-out of me', giving me my due wages (μισθός as in S. *Ant.* 221, E. *Hipp.* 1050), or 'a paying-out (of Agamemnon) for me'.

1262–3. 'While whetting the sword against the man, she boasts that she will exact death as requital for *my* having been brought': the implied object of ἀντιτείσεσθαι φόνον is Cassandra herself, not Agamemnon. The meaning is not 'she claims that in killing Agamemnon she is exacting vengeance for his having brought me', but 'she boasts, while preparing to kill Agamemnon, that she will kill me too for having been brought hither'; but there remains some ambiguity in the expression (see further Barrett ap. Fraenkel, Addenda, p. 831).

1264 ff. Since she is to die, and Apollo has long ago turned against her, she has nothing more to fear from man or god, and there is nothing to deter her from wreaking such feeble vengeance on Apollo as she may by destroying the symbols of his worship.

καταγέλωτα: predicate, in apposition to the following pronoun and nouns; 'why do I keep these things to mock myself?' This is one of the few places in Tragedy where the meaning of the words is obscure without visual aid; and it is not clear what stage-directions should be supplied—τάδε must be something other than the σκῆπτρα and στέφη (for one could not say τάδε καὶ σκῆπτρα καὶ στέφη, meaning τάδε σκῆπτρα καὶ στέφη), possibly her robe, the χρηστηρίαν ἐσθῆτα of 1270. **σκῆπτρα**: the prophetess's staff (plural as in E. *Ion* 217, cf. K.–G. i. 18); *Il.* 1. 14 f., Hesychius s.v. ἰθυντήριον· ὃ φέρουσιν οἱ μάντεις σκῆπτρον ἀπὸ δάφνης. **στέφη**: woollen bands worn round the neck.

1266. σέ: perhaps the σκῆπτρον or στέφος; probably not (as some say) the robes, for 1270 ff. indicate that their turn comes later. But the obscurity is great, and the intervention of the singular number between 1265 and ἴτε 1267 is disagreeable; Meineke's athetesis of 1266 greatly improves the passage, if only we could account for the interpolation.

1267. The text is corrupt. The makeshift restoration assumes that Cassandra accompanies her words by some action, e.g. trampling ('*thus* I pay you out').

1268. ἄτην is (despite Verrall) meaningless here; **ἄτης** seems the obvious correction, though the genitive with πλουτίζειν is abnormal, and there is no apparent reason why a normal dative, ἄταις, should not have been written. If ἄτης is correct, it may represent ἄτη(ι)σ', dat. pl.

1269 ff. She takes off the prophetess's robe, and her imagination pictures the hand of Apollo at work.

1270–2. The continuation ἐποπτεύσας δέ με demands a finite verb in the sequel: 'and having watched me being greatly mocked by friends who are enemies . . .', *what* did he do? Mere anacoluthon seems improbable here: but the most important fact is that nothing whatever can be made of the words οὐ διχορρόπως μάτην, or at least of μάτην. (We must surely reject as impossible the interpretation 'not-ambiguously foolishly', meaning 'obviously foolishly'—my enemy-friends mock me, and are clearly foolish to do so.) It looks as though μάτην may conceal some quite different word, presumably a finite verb; or else a line is missing from the text after 1272. οὐ διχορρόπως may go with what precedes, 'mocked *unanimously*', or with whatever underlies μάτην (or a lost sequel thereof).

1273–4. 'Like one wandering from house to house (φοιτάς) in search of alms (ἀγύρτρια), I endured being called "beggar", poor wretch, and "starveling".' τάλαινα, thus taken as a piece of self-commiseration in parenthesis, is a little awkwardly placed; the alternative, to take it together with the other terms of abuse, is legitimate but not more attractive.

1275. Elsewhere in Aeschylus ἐκπράσσω regularly means 'carry out', 'accomplish', 'finish' a business: *ScT* 840, *Pers.* 723, *Agam.* 582, *Suppl.* 102 (another sense is possible but not necessary in *Suppl.* 472). Here the usage is extended and metaphorical: 'the seer, having *finished the business* of the seeress', exactly as in S. *OC* 1659, E. *Hec.* 515; in these two places the implication is 'killed', whereas here it is less extreme, 'ruined'—it cannot imply 'killed' here, for the time of the aorist participle is anterior to that of the main verb ἀπήγαγε; you could not say 'having killed me, he brought me here to die like this'. Fraenkel and others take ἐκπράξας here to mean 'having exacted as his due' ('Cassandra herself is the debt owed to the god: he has now called in (*exegit*) her person and her life'): this seems obscurer.

1276. ἀπήγαγε: 'led off *under arrest*'; LSJ s.v. IV. 1.

1277. ἀντί very seldom follows what it governs, as here; *Ilias Parva* fr. 6. 4, Hesiod, *theog.* 893. ἐπίξηνον: a butcher's block.

1278. κοπείσης: since the butchery is still to come, in the future, the aorist tense seems odd (Miss Lorimer, *CR* xlv (1931) 211 f. compares δαμέντα in *Il.* 16. 852 ff.; cf. also Pseudo-Eur. *IA* 1503 θανοῦσα δ' οὐκ ἀναίνομαι); but, as Prof. Dover observes, the aorist here gives the right temporal sequence in relation to φοίνιον προσφάγματι (on which the genitive κοπείσης depends).

See Miss Lorimer, l.c.: 'The πρόσφαγμα is the libation of blood offered to the dead as the preliminary rite of a Greek funeral in the heroic age . . . . The meaning of προ- is purely temporal . . . . By an easy transference πρόσφαγμα acquires the meaning of the victim which supplied the blood . . . . Cassandra then alludes in grim parody to the obsequies which Clytemnestra will provide for Agamemnon: the πρόσφαγμα at least he shall have in her blood. This is not all. There is no executioner's block in Greece: ἐπίξηνον, as Hesychius tells us, is ξύλον ἐφ' οὗ τὰ κρέα τιθέντες ἔκοπτον. The victim furnishes the δεῖπνον as well.'

1279. ἄτιμοι: here apparently in effect 'unavenged', LSJ s.v. II. **τε- θνήξομεν**: herself and Agamemnon.

1280. ἄλλος: somebody else, one with whom the murderers have not reckoned.

1283. 'To put a coping-stone on these deeds of ruin'; cf. E. *H.* 1280 δῶμα θριγκῶσαι κακοῖς, *Tro.* 489 θριγκὸς ἀθλίων κακῶν.

1284 ff. Something is amiss in the text hereabout: (1) 1290 is impossibly placed in the MSS. (2) 1284, the infinitive ἄξειν (cod. F) is unintelligible, and the asyndeton if we read ἄξει (Tr) is very offensive. Hermann's transposition is a simple and effective remedy: 'For a great oath has been sworn of the gods, that his father's body lying supine shall bring him (sc. Orestes).' **ὑπτίασμα**: that which is, or that which renders, supine; elsewhere only in *PV* 1005 ὑπτιάσμασιν χερῶν, *manuum resupinatione*, i.e. with hands raised palm uppermost, in supplication (a very odd phrase: and though χερῶν ὑπτ. there is strained far enough to signify 'supplication', ὑπτίασμα *without* χερῶν could surely not do so, especially in conjunction with κειμένου). ὑπτίασμα κειμένου πατρός is nothing but a poetical variation of πατὴρ ὕπτιος κείμενος; unless perhaps (but less probably) ὑπτίασμα means '*rendering* supine', i.e. simply 'overthrow'.

(Fraenkel objects against Hermann (*a*) that we are not elsewhere told of an *oath* of the gods; *Od.* 1. 37 ff. gives the promise of the gods, ἐκ γὰρ 'Ορέσταο τίσις ἔσσεται, but not an *oath*: but the distinction between an oath and a promise or threat is unimportant here; nor is it necessary that the oath must be found elsewhere before it can be recognized here; (*b*) that what the Homeric gods promise is that Orestes shall avenge his father, whereas the Aeschylean gods are alleged to swear that he shall be summoned by his father's corpse: surely a slight objection; (*c*) 'that the run of the poet's sentence 1280–4 clearly shows that there is no room before 1284 for Hermann's proposed insertion': this contention is supported by very disputable arguments (p. 601); and it is a further weakness of the case, that the MSS.' reading ἄξειν must be rejected in favour of the much easier, and presumably conjectural, ἄξει.)

1285. κάτοικτος: not found elsewhere, and not an altogether convincing correction of κάτοικος.

1286. ἐπεὶ τὸ πρῶτον: 'having once seen...'; LSJ s.v. πρότερος B III. 3 e.

1287. εἶχον codd., but we need a reference to the *takers* of the city.

1289. πράξω is meaningless here; attempts to defend it are summarized and refuted by Fraenkel. The slightest change of the letters gives ΙΟΥΣΑΠΑΡΖΩ for ΙΟΥΣΑΠΡΑΖΩ: ἰοῦσ᾽ ἀπάρξω, 'I will go and *lead off*', i.e. start off the proceedings. The active form of this verb is very rare: for the sense cf. *Anth. Pal.* 9. 189. 3 f. (anonymous, probably of Alexandrian date) ὔμμι δ᾽ ἀπάρξει | Σαπφώ, 'Sappho shall lead off for you'.

(In Pind. *Nem.* 4. 46 and the Theban inscription ap. Schwyzer, *Dial. graec. exempla epigraphica* 440. 11, ἀπάρχειν is more or less synonymous with ἡγεμονεύειν. In Bacchylides 12 (11). 6, ἐς γὰρ ὀλβίαν ξείνοισί με πότνια Νίκα νᾶσον Αἰγίνας ἀπάρχει ἐλθόντα κοσμῆσαι . . . πόλιν, the usage is peculiar, apparently 'shall lead me off to the island . . .'. See further Fraenkel on 1227 above.)

1291. 'I address these (gates) as the gates of Hades.'

1293. αἱμάτων: as in *Eum.* 253, the plural though only one person's blood is meant. Elsewhere in Aeschylus (and Sophocles: *Ant.* 121 only) when the plural of αἷμα in the sense 'blood' is used, more than one person's blood is or may be meant; the same is generally true of Euripides, but there are exceptions (*El.* 1172, *IA* 1485).

1297. θεηλάτου: driven not by the hand of man, therefore presumably by the will of god. It was proper that the victim should appear to approach the altar voluntarily.

1299–1300. The general sense suggested is: 'There is no escape for any further time.'—'But the last remnant of one's time is the most valued.' χρόνῳ πλέω(ι), the reading of codd. in 1299, is intractable as it stands: far the simplest remedy is Hermann's χρόνον πλέω (supposing χρόνον assimilated to the apparent termination of its adjective, a very common class of error, though one might rather have expected χρόνον πλέον, cf. *Eum.* 226 πόνον πλέον codd., for πλέω).—'There is no escape, no, my friends, for any further time.' The sequence of thought is then just what it should be. The Chorus pick up the word χρόνον, 'You say you have come to the end of your time: but it is just the last remnant of one's time (such as you now have) that is held most precious.' **ὁ ὕστατος τοῦ χρόνου**: this seems, but is not, odd phraseology, cf. Xen. *Resp. Lac.* 1. 5 τὸν πρῶτον τοῦ χρόνου, Demo. 15. 16 τὸν λοιπὸν τοῦ χρόνου; K.–G. i. 279ᶜ. **πρεσβεύεται**: *primum locum obtinet*, as Dindorf puts it; cf. *Cho.* 631 κακῶν δὲ πρεσβεύεται τὸ Λήμνιον ('among disasters, the Lemnian is pre-eminent').

1302–3. Lit. 'Be assured that you are steadfast from a bold heart.'— 'None of the happy is so spoken of' (**ἀκούει** as in LSJ s.v. III. 4).

1304. What **εὐκλεῶς κατθανεῖν** means may be seen in *Pers.* 328, *Il.* 22. 110 ὀλέσθαι εὐκλειῶς: here there is no question of Cassandra's dying εὐκλεῶς, '*gloriously*', 'so that men shall sing her praises'; even the

Chorus understood (1296 ff.) that she is to be cut down like a cow at the·altar. Wilamowitz saw this point: the victim, he says, is 'Cassandra, cui turpissima mors imminet nec quisquam eius meminerit'; hence an over-bold conjecture in the text. The fact must be faced that εὐκλεῶς κατθανεῖν is quite out of place here, a cliché used without sufficient regard for the context; we need 'bravely', not 'gloriously'.

1305. Cassandra ignores what the Chorus had said. Moving toward the palace-doors she stops, turns round (1306 ἀποστρέφει), and calls in agony of heart upon the father and brothers whom she is soon to join.

1307–8. Since φεῦ normally expresses either (a) grief or (b) astonishment or admiration, and the sequel shows that what Cassandra uttered was a cry of *disgust*, it is quite probable that φῦ φῦ and ἔφυξας (Heyse) should be written here (cf. Ar. *Thesm.* 245 φεῦ cod., φῦ Dindorf); but perhaps the freer use of φεῦ is sufficiently defended by such examples as *PV* 124, 687.

1308. Lit. 'unless (it is) some loathsome thing belonging to your imagination', i.e. 'unless there be some horror in your soul' (Weir Smyth). The Chorus think that Cassandra may be seeing visions again.

1310. καὶ πῶς: 'surely not!' The Chorus point out that there is a simple explanation for the smell of blood—there are victims slaughtered on the hearth-altar; no need to suspect murder (φόνον). Cassandra retorts: 'It is like a vapour from a tomb.' The Chorus, still marvellously matter-of-fact, rejoin: 'It is of no Syrian splendour (i.e. splendour of Syrian incense) for the house that you speak', i.e. what you describe is something different from what *we* perceive, viz. the odour of incense from sacrificial rites.   **δώμασιν** with ἀγλάισμα, 'adornment for the house'.

1314. 'Let life suffice' = I have had enough of life.

1315. ἰὼ ξένοι: a cry of appeal to the bystanders to bear witness (1317 μαρτυρῆτε) to her ill-treatment. See Schulze, *Kleine Schriften*, pp. 160 ff., and Fraenkel, p. 614, 'The principle of Attic law, that only if . . . the cry of distress has been raised, can evidence of the deed of violence be later laid before a court of law', is frequently reflected in Tragedy; A. *Suppl.* 905, E. *Tro.* 998 ff.

1316. The accusative **θάμνον** is indefensible unless it is governed by δυσοίζει, supplied from δυσοίζω, which must therefore be capable of transitive usage. (Fraenkel suggests that θάμνον ὡς ὄρνις may stand alone, as a proverbial type of phrase, like ὁ νεβρὸς τὸν λέοντα, ὄνος λύρας; but such phrases are never admitted in Tragedy—E. *H.* 510 ὥσπερ πτερὸν πρὸς αἰθέρα, 869 ταῦρος ὣς ἐς ἐμβολήν, *Or.* 45 πῶλος ὣς ὑπὸ ζυγοῦ, S. *Tr.* 441 f. πύκτης ὅπως ἐς χεῖρας, are all of a different type, having preposition+noun, with a verb easily supplied from the context, none having an incoherent accusative of the type alleged.)

Apollonius Dyscolus (*adv.* 128. 7 Schneider) suggests that οἴζω was derived from the cry οἰοί: but the verb οἴζειν is not in fact found

anywhere in use (though an οἴζομαι appears in the papyrus-text of
Sophocles' *Inachus*), and it is a mere guess that δυσοίζω is related to
it: the prefix δυσ- tells strongly against the relationship—we do not
(and do not expect to) find δυσοιμώζειν δυσαιάζειν δυσφεύζειν and the
like (an *adjective* such as δυσβάνκτος, on the other hand, is both
expected and found). δυσ-οίζω is presumably related to something
entirely different—to the stem which provides οἴσω, οἴσομαι, the
forms used as a future of φέρω: the sense will then be 'to bear things
hard'; and of the definitions in Hesychius δυσοίζει· δυσχεραίνει
(Hermann: δυσχερει cod.) comes nearest to the truth; cf. Schol. vet.
here, οὐ δυσχεραίνω φησί. In the only other places where δυσοίζειν
occurs, E. *Rhes.* 724 and 805, the sense 'bear hard' is perfectly apt.
Thus Cassandra, having uttered her cry of appeal, explains what she
has done by saying 'I am not *taking it hard*, as one frightened: I am
only summoning you to act as witnesses of my ill-treatment.' δυσοίζειν may, like δυσχεραίνειν, be used both with and without an object:
'I am not *making a fuss*, like a bird *making a fuss* about the bush'.
θάμνον: not merely 'bush', but specifically the place where traps
are set.

1320. ἐπιξενοῦμαι: the meaning is uncertain; see Pearson on S. fr. 146
and Fraenkel, pp. 615 f. The preceding cry ἰὼ ξένοι suggests that
ἐπιξενοῦμαι ταῦτα signifies 'I call upon you thus, as guest upon host',
'I make this claim as due from one stranger to another', or something
similar.

1322–3. 'I wish to utter once more a speech, or dirge, my own': her ῥῆσις,
she thinks, might as aptly be called a θρῆνος—spoken by herself still
alive instead of by others when she is dead. ζῶσα γόοις με τιμῶ, *Suppl.*
116 (Wecklein).

1324. πρὸς ὕστατον φῶς: '(I pray to the sun), towards its latest light';
πρός signifies the direction taken by her prayer.

1324–5. The general sense appears to be: 'I pray that my death, as well
as Agamemnon's, shall be avenged.' The words are incurably corrupt: the sense would be satisfied by something like δεσπότου
τιμαόροις | ἐχθροὺς φόνευσιν τὴν ἐμὴν τίνειν ὁμοῦ, '(I pray) to those who
avenge my master that they should pay out our enemies for my
killing as well' (δεσπότου M. Schmidt, φόνευσιν Bothe, τὴν ἐμὴν
Heller); but there are other plausible possibilities. It looks as though
the trouble arose primarily from misunderstanding φόνευσιν as
φονεῦσι(ν), dat. pl. of φονεύς; hence τοῖς ἐμοῖς for τὴν ἐμήν, then τοῖς
ἐμοῖς invaded the line above, ousting some other word, a process
exemplified by E. *Tro.* 1243, *Rhes.* 208.

(Wackernagel is quoted by Fraenkel, p. 618, n. 1, as saying that
the word φόνευσις is impossible for Aeschylus: the statement is
invalidated by the exactly parallel formation χόρευσις in Pindar
Paean 6. 9.)

1326. εὐμαροῦς χειρώματος : χείρωμα may be passive, 'thing overcome', 'an easily-effected conquest' ; or active, 'an easy subduing' (in apposition to the thought underlying δούλης θανούσης).

1327–30 'Alas, for man's dealings : while they prosper, one might compare them to a shadow ; and if they prosper not, the wet sponge with its strokes makes an end of the picture.'

The meaning of εἰ δὲ δυστυχῇ κτλ. is that if man's affairs meet with adversity, they (the men, or their affairs) are obliterated, wiped out (ὤλεσεν is 'gnomic' aorist). That seems an absurd thing to say, as it stands ('if man suffers misfortune, he (or his πράγματα) is wiped out, annihilated') : yet it is in fact said here, and it remains to consider what may have been meant by it. Of those who have seen and faced the difficulty, Conington is perhaps the most plausible. Aeschylus meant, 'Prosperity is in constant danger of a reverse ; adversity is next-door to annihilation'—when prosperous, a man remains always on the verge of a disastrous change of fortune ; when reduced to adversity, he is defenceless against the lightest blow, a touch is enough to push him down to destruction. (This interpretation does not necessarily involve reading into 1329 the idea of *speed* or *ease* : Fraenkel maintains that βολαῖς 'suggests the notion of a movement swift as lightning' ; the context may suggest something of the sort, but there is no such implication in the word itself.) An alternative interpretation is suggested by Wecklein : 'When a man is afflicted by misfortune, then everything is at once lost and forgotten—splendour, fame, gratitude and love disappear at a stroke ; not only present and future but also the past appears all at once destroyed'—i.e., in effect, there is no misfortune but total misfortune ; a considerable exaggeration, but a true reflection on Cassandra's own fate. It should be noticed that the difference between εὐτυχοῦντα μὲν κτλ. and εἰ δὲ δυστυχῇ κτλ. corresponds exactly to the difference between the present positions of Agamemnon and Cassandra : he is the one whose apparent εὐτυχία is a mere shadow, she is the person upon whom δυστυχία has already come with total ruin.

It remains very uncertain what Aeschylus meant here ; and 1330 adds to the obscurity—what are ταῦτα and ἐκείνων? According to Conington, 'This last change (from adversity to annihilation) I deplore much more than that former one (from prosperity to adversity).' This seems likely enough, though it remains possible that Aeschylus meant 'This (universal misery of man) I deplore much more than that (which I was speaking of before, the particular case of Agamemnon and myself).'

In 1328 the text suggested by the MSS. σκιά τις ἂν τρέψειεν, with its unhappy τις and feeble verb ('turn', in the sense 'alter' ; not '*over-turn*', as Fraenkel shows) is easily corrected by a very simple change, σκιᾶ(ι) and πρέψειεν, cf. Photius πρέψαι· τὸ ὁμοιῶσαι. Αἰσχύλος

(= Fr. 439 Nauck). δυστυχῇ (codd.) is not impossible, but probably represents the subjunctive δυστυχῇ; εἰ c. subj. is quite common in poetry, K.-G. ii. 474, n. 1.

1331–42. The Chorus now clearly recognize the likelihood that Agamemnon will fall. It is to him, their king, that their thoughts are turned; they bid no farewell to Cassandra, and pass no comment here on her fate.

'Men never have their fill of prosperity: nobody says 'No' (ἀπειπών and bars it from palaces that are pointed at (i.e. already enviable enough), saying "Enter no more!".' For the tense of ἀπειπών cf. *Il.* 7. 225 ἀπειλήσας δὲ προσηύδα, and similar aorists, K.-G. i. 197 f. The popular punctuation in 1334 which divorces τάδε from μηκέτ᾽ ἐσέλθῃς and attaches it to φωνῶν seems highly artificial here; it is not supported by such passages as *Cho.* 313 f., where the structure of the sentence is quite different.

1335. καὶ τῷδε: introducing an illustration of the general rule.

1338–40. The future tenses of the MSS. are best in accord with the sense, but it seems impossible to accept the prosody of ἐπικρᾱνεῖ (Apollonius Dyscolus, *adv.* 187. 26, testifies to φᾶνω as future of φαίνω, and in E. *Ba.* 528 ἀναφᾶνω is the tradition, cf. Ar. *Equ.* 300 φᾶνω codd., φαίνω edd.; in *Eum.* 950 M² offers -κρᾱνεῖ, but the sense supports -κραίνει; and *Cho.* 1075 is a clear example of κρᾱνεῖ). The change to either optative or subjunctive is prudent; and of these the former is practically ruled out by the context, which demands that the condition should be expressed as being as likely as possible.

The text is in other respects probably sound, though not clearly phrased. προτέρων αἷμα must refer to the killing of Thyestes' children: then θανοῦσι...θανὼν...θανάτων presumably refer to the three principal stages in the development of the story—the children of Thyestes—Agamemnon—Clytemnestra and Aegisthus. 'If he is now to pay for the blood of those who have gone before, and, for the benefit of those already dead (Thyestes' children), by dying himself (Agamemnon) should bring to pass retribution consisting in yet other deaths (of Clytemnestra and Aegisthus), then what mortal could boast that he was born with scatheless fortune, hearing such a tale?' (Many edd. take προτέρων αἷμα and τοῖσι θανοῦσι to refer to the killing of *Iphigeneia*: this may be possible, but it is not what the phraseology, especially προτέρων, suggests.)

The principal weakness of this rendering is the sense given to ποινὰς θανάτων, which would naturally mean 'penalty *for* deaths', not 'penalty *consisting in* deaths': but this latter type of genitive is in general very common, and the freedom seems pardonable enough if no more is required to make the sentence intelligible and indeed very powerful.

1341. K omitted by haplography after IC, TICAN for TICICAN.

1343. ἔσω: Paley quotes E. *Ion* 766 f. ἔτυπεν ὀδύνα με πλευμόνων τῶνδ' ἔσω, *El.* 1222 ff. φασγάνῳ κατηρξάμαν ματέρος ἔσω δέρας μεθείς, *Hel.* 354 ff. ξιφοκτόνον δίωγμα . . . αὐτοσίδαρον ἔσω πελάσω διὰ σαρκὸς ἄμιλλαν, *Rhes.* 750 f. φονίου τραύματος εἴσω; but in all these (and other) passages ἔσω is assisted by the genitive which it governs or by the verb of motion which accompanies it. The isolated ἔσω here is very unusual.

1344. πληγήν apparently governed by ἀντεῖ, the accusative giving the gist of, or an extract from, the words actually used by the subject of ἀντεῖ; cf. βοᾷ μὲν ὅρκους, E. *Med.* 21 n. The order of the words is against taking πληγήν as cognate accus. with οὐτασμένος.

1345. οἴμοι . . . πεπληγμένος: the expression is of the type of οἴμοι τάλαινα and the like; εἰμί is not to be supplied (Fraenkel).

1346. οἰμώγμασιν: instrumental dative, of the means by which the supposition (δοκεῖ μοι) was reached; such loosely attached datives, half causal and half instrumental, are not uncommon, cf. Thuc. iii. 98. 5 τοῖς πεπραγμένοις φοβούμενος τοὺς Ἀθηναίους, 'afraid of the Athenians *because of* what had been done'; K.–G. i. 439, Jebb on S. *Ant.* 391.

1347. 'Let us take counsel together, to see if our plans may somehow be safe': this is not a very satisfactory makeshift in a corrupt place; ἤν for ἐάν in Aeschylus could not be more weakly attested (*ScT* 1027, probably the work of a later hand; *Pers.* 708, a play which has numerous non-recurrent Ionic features, cf. Headlam in *CR* xii (1898) 189 f.).

1348. γνώμην: perhaps rather 'proposal' than 'opinion'.

1349. Lit. 'To proclaim to the citizens rescue toward the house hither': πρὸς δῶμα is governed by βοήν; 'rescue to the palace' is what the κήρυκες are to cry.

1350. δὲ . . . γε: here as usual introducing an *objection* to what precedes.

1351. 'To prove the deed together with the fresh-flowing sword', i.e. to catch the guilty person in the act, while the sword is still flowing with blood. The expression 'a *fresh-flowing* sword' has given offence to some, who have therefore preferred to derive -ρύτῳ from ἐρύω, 'freshly-*drawn* sword': surely an unnecessary and improbable idea, for the Chorus are already too late for the moment when the sword is freshly-*drawn*; but they may now catch the murderer at the moment when it is freshly-*flowing*. (The Chorus cannot mean *their own* swords; not only because they have no swords (1650–3 n. below), but also for other reasons given by Fraenkel.) S. *Ajax* 30, ξὺν νεορράντῳ ξίφει, is less boldly phrased.

1352. γνώματος = γνώμης; cf. E. *Hkld.* 407.

1353. Most edd. overlook the fact that whereas ἀκμὴ μὴ μέλλειν is normal Greek, ἀκμὴ τὸ μὴ μέλλειν is not. The text is easily corrected.

1354. The object of ὁρᾶν is, as Paley says, 'their intentions'.

1354–5. φροιμιάζονται κτλ.: 'their prelude is that of people whose actions betoken tyranny'. On the position of ὧς at the end of the line, and on the sense of the word τυραννίς here, see Fraenkel.

1355. γάρ: a common elliptic use, '(Yes, they are getting ahead with their plans), *because* we are wasting time.'

1355–6. If the text is correctly restored, the expression is odd and obscure. Paley interprets: 'trampling underfoot the *report* (κλέος as in 487 above) of delay', i.e. they will not have it said of them that they wasted any time. But **πέδον πατοῦντες** ought to govern a *good* object, something that ought not to be trampled on: if τῆς μελλοῦς κλέος means 'the reputation of being procrastinators', the normal metaphorical usage of πατεῖν will not apply here. Sense of a kind can be made if we suppose that Delay, looking before you leap, is assumed by the Chorus to be in all circumstances a proper and honest course: we, they say, are taking our time, as befits a grave occasion; our opponents have no respect for the honourable name of Delay, they trample it underfoot. This is substantially the view of Headlam and Fraenkel, who, however, go too far in referring to a 'proverb in praise of *cunctari*', for no such proverb is known; and none is necessary here. (Both H. and F. quote Antiphilus, *App. Planud.* iv. 136 ἀρκεῖ δ' ἁ μέλλησις, ἔφα σοφός: but that has nothing to do with 'delay' or 'looking before you leap'; ἁ μέλλησις means 'her *intention*'.—'Do not ask to see Medea *in action*: the portrait of her *being about to act* is sufficient.') This interpretation seems rather forced in itself, and the idea from which it starts, that Delay may be assumed to be a good thing, is hardly tenable in the light of 1353 μὴ μέλλειν δ' ἀκμή. In particular κλέος seems a most unnatural word, and it may be that the grammarian Trypho, to whom we owe the reading μελλοῦς, has preserved the end of the line correctly, viz. χάριν instead of κλέος— either 'trampling on the favour of delay' (the courtesy or favour of a breathing-space which one might expect to be granted); or 'the graciousness of delay' (they are in an altogether indecent hurry). **πέδον πατοῦντες**: as in *Cho.* 643, Callim. *h. Del.* 227, almost as a compound verb; but πέδοι (Hermann) may be correct.

1359. πέρι codd., ill supported by *Cho.* 849 f. οὐδὲν ἀγγέλων σθένος | ὡς αὐτὸς αὐτὸν ἄνδρα πεύθεσθαι πέρι, which is in other respects obscure and surely corrupt.

Good sense would follow if πέρι were here, as often, a corruption of πάρα: for ΠΑΡΑ and ΤΙΔΡΑ might very easily be confused; τί δρᾷ is exactly what the sense requires: 'the man who acts must also plan *what his action is to be*', i.e. it is no good acting without a plan of action. Demand for action is the last definite proposal so far made (1353). The speaker in 1358–9 comments: 'But I cannot think of any *plan*, and he who would act must first plan what his action is to be.' The following speaker continues (1360–1): 'I agree (that we must have a plan); mere words will not resurrect the dead.'

1362. 'dragging out our lives', E. *Med.* 670 n.

1363. ἡγουμένοις: quasi-predicative, 'as rulers'.

1365. πεπαιτέρα: 'riper', i.e. 'softer'.

1366–7. τἀνδρὸς ὡς ὀλωλότος: gen. absolute, the idiom as in Xen. *Cyr.*
3. 1. 13 αἱ γυναῖκες ἀναβοήσασαι ἐδρύπτοντο ὡς οἰχομένου τοῦ πατρὸς καὶ
ἀπολωλότων σφῶν ἤδη (K.–G. ii. 93).

1370. πάντοθεν πληθύνομαι: the meaning is uncertain. πληθύνειν, causal
counterpart to πληθύειν ('to be full'), would be expected to mean 'to
make full' or 'to make numerous', 'multiply'; the latter is the meaning in Aristotle, *hist. anim.* 587ᵇ20 (τὸ γάλα πληθύνεται, 'the milk
becomes abundant'), the earliest appearance of the verb after the
present passage. Assistance is commonly sought from (1) *Suppl.* 604,
where the text is corrupt and the sense doubtful: δήμου κρατοῦσα
χειροπληθύεται cod., perhaps χεὶρ ὅπῃ (Dobree) πληθύνεται (Hermann),
'in what direction the people's winning hand is multiplied', i.e. on
what side the hands are raised in a victorious majority. If this is the
meaning, it does nothing to help explain πληθύνομαι here. (2) Hdt. 7.
220. 2 (cf. 1. 120. 4) ταύτῃ καὶ μᾶλλον τὴν γνώμην πλεῖστός εἰμι: but
there γνώμην is 'accus. of respect', πλεῖστος is superlative of πολύς,
and ταύτῃ πλεῖστός εἰμι is an idiom of the type of πολλὸς ἦν ... ἐν τοῖσι
λόγοισι (Hdt. 8. 59); it is entirely irrelevant to πάντοθεν πληθύνομαι.

If πληθύνομαι is not being used in some extraordinary sense, the
meaning should be either (1) 'I am being filled from all sides' (with
votes, as if he were a voting-urn) 'to approve that proposal'; so
Tucker on *Suppl.* l. c. (his 587).—I, like a voting-urn, am being filled
with votes from every quarter; or (2) 'I am being *multiplied* from
every quarter, to approve' etc. i.e. many voters come over to my
side, my party is being made more numerous. Both usages seem
strained; the former less so, and perhaps not beyond the limits of
normal Aeschylean brachylogy.

1371. 'to know clearly how the son of Atreus is faring': **κυροῦντα ὅπως**
for ὅπως κυρεῖ is an incoherence of language without parallel or
proper explanation. Maas, who would obelize εἰδέναι κυροῦνθ' ὅπως,
observes that εἰδέναι is out of place here: we need a verb signifying
'to find out', or the like, e.g. ἐκμαθεῖν.

Fraenkel rightly observes that there is no support whatever in the
text for the modern notion that the old men run or march to the
rescue at this point: there is no indication that they do anything but
stand and discuss their policy. It is clear enough in 1370–1 that a
decision is taken—they will find out what has happened to Agamemnon; but there is nothing to show how they propose to do so, or that
they proceed to do so, before the appearance of Clytemnestra interrupts them.

1372. Clytemnestra appears, standing over the bodies of her victims.
The nature of the stage-mechanism (if any) is disputable: the question

of the 'eccyclema' is fully considered by Pickard-Cambridge, *The Theatre of Dionysus in Athens*, pp. 100 ff.; see esp. pp. 106 f., on the present passage: 'Clytemnestra's words are sufficiently true if she is shown standing over the bodies now exposed side by side in the doorway, where it was the early Greek custom to lay the dead. Some kind of ἐκκύκλημα (in a wide sense) *may* have been used; certainly some sort of bier would be necessary, and this may have been on wheels; but the conditions of the text would be satisfied by the display of the bodies in a moderately wide doorway, on a very simple and unobtrusive vehicle.'

1372. καιρίως: 'to suit the moment'.

1374. πῶς γάρ: (I am not ashamed of my duplicity), *for how else* could I have overcome my enemy?

1374–5. ἐχθροῖς ... φίλοις δοκοῦσιν εἶναι: 'enemies who *pretended* to be friends'; i.e. my duplicity is matched by that of my opponents.

1375–6. '(How else) could one fence the nets of harm (i.e. build net-obstacles, to injure one's enemies), a height greater than outleaping (i.e. too high to leap out of)?'   ὕψος is in apposition, more or less predicatively, to ἀρκύστατα, 'build a snare-fence, (to be) a height too great etc.'.

1377–8. ἀγὼν ὅδε ... νείκης παλαιᾶς: 'this conflict of a long-standing quarrel', i.e. this occasion when a long-standing quarrel comes to its decisive point. The form νείκη (equivalent in sense to νεῖκος) is attested for the fifth century only in one place—by cod. M in E. *Or.* 1679.

Clytemnestra has reason to emphasize the long duration of the feud, but the repetition in πάλαι νείκης παλαιᾶς is more than usually inelegant. Perhaps νίκης τελείας (Karsten) or δίκης (Pauw) τελείας; cf. 1432 below.   γε μήν: 'but still it *did* come'.   ἦλθε goes with both clauses.

1382. ἀμφίβληστρον: also *Cho.* 492. Specifically a fishing-net, used in Tragedy in a more general sense immediately derived from ἀμφιβάλλεσθαι, 'a wrapping', cf. *PV* 81, E. *IT* 96, *Hel.* 1079. Here ὥσπερ ἰχθύων shows that 'fishing-net' is meant.   ἄπειρον: ὃ πέρας οὐκ ἔχει, 'without an end'. This may mean either 'immensely large' or 'having no terminal point'. ἀριθμὸς ἄπειρος = 'very large number', but ἄπειρα δίκτυα (Ibycus fr. 7. 3 f.) = 'nets which have no terminus (πέρας)', and therefore no egress. Here as often the word is ambiguous, though 'without egress' suggests itself; cf. *Eum.* 634 f. ἀτέρμονι . . πέπλῳ, E. *Or.* 25 πόσιν ἀπείρῳ περιβαλοῦσ' ὑφάσματι, Sophocles fr. 526 P. χιτών σ' ἄπειρος ἐνδυτήριος κακῶν, A. *PV* 1078 ἀπέραντον (s.v.l.) δίκτυον ἄτης. There is nothing to indicate that Aeschylus intended the robe in question to be a garment 'having no opening for head or hand' as it is described by Schol. on E. *Or.* and others; see Fraenkel, p. 649.

1383. περιστιχίζω: a unique verb-form, related to στίχα as the normal

-στοιχίζω to στοῖχος. 'The many instances of the present tense from here to 1390 βάλλει are noticeable; they probably serve to enliven the recital. . . . Clytemnestra lives and acts the whole story again while she tells it. Miming gestures are likely to have supported the vivid description of each stage', Fraenkel, p. 650.   πλοῦτον εἵματος κακόν: 'fatal *splendour* of garb', Sidgwick; '*rich* robe deadly dyed', Verrall; but the implication of πλοῦτος is probably simply that there was a lot of it—it was a very large robe, as *Cho.* 983 ff. shows (cf. Fraenkel, p. 649). Xen. *Anab.* 7. 7. 42, πλουτεῖ μὲν ὄντων φίλων πολλῶν, he is 'rich' because of the *number* (not the quality) of his friends.

1384. ἐν: while ἐν is sometimes used of *means* (S. *Phil.* 102 ἐν δόλῳ . . . ἄγειν, K.-G. i. 466), its apparent use here of *accompanying circumstances* is highly abnormal: E. *Ba.* 1165–7 ὁρμωμένην . . . ἐν διαστρόφοις ὄσσοις, *Suppl.* 593 καινὸς ἐν καινῷ δορί, come close to it. Perhaps, as Plüss suggested, ἐν here signifies *duration* (K.-G. ibid.), 'within the space of two groans'.

1385. αὐτοῦ: 'on the spot'.

1386–7. Ἅιδου codd.: but while there is much point in calling Hades the 'Zeus of the Underworld' (cf. *Suppl.* 156 ff., 230 f., Eur. fr. 912), it seems dull to call him 'the Hades of the Underworld'. Probably Διός has been ousted by an explanatory gloss, Ἅιδου. It remains just possible that the MSS. are correct, the sense being 'him of the Underworld—Hades, saviour of corpses'.

The third libation was made to *Zeus Soter*: Aeschylus, fr. 55. 4 τρίτην Διὸς σωτῆρος εὐκταίαν λίβα. Similar to the present passage is *Cho.* 577 f. φόνου δ' Ἐρινὺς οὐχ ὑπεσπανισμένη | ἄκρατον αἷμα πίεται τρίτην πόσιν.   νεκρῶν σωτήρος: Hades, like Zeus, is σωτήρ—he holds the dead safe in his keeping; cf. S. *Ajax* 660 ἀλλ' αὐτὸ νὺξ Ἅιδης τε σῳζόντων κάτω.   εὐκταίαν χάριν: the interpretation favoured by Fraenkel, 'the welcome gift that accompanies a prayer', throws a heavy burden on the language—a 'blow' is described as a 'libation', and that is now to be called a *gift* or *service* accompanying *prayer*. Better simply 'votive rendering-of-thanks', i.e. thanksgiving in fulfilment of past prayers or vows. (In fr. 55, quoted above, the context does not suffice to show what εὐκταίαν means.)

1388. θυμὸν †ὁρμαίνει†: the post-Homeric usages of this verb differ markedly from the Homeric ('ponder' only), and among the few examples of a later transitive use is Aeschylus' *Dictyulci*, P. Oxy. 2161 ii. 24 στείχωμεν ὅπως γάμον ὁρμαίνωμεν, presumably 'let us go to set in motion the marriage', but γάμον ὁρμαίνειν is an altogether inadequate parallel to θυμὸν ὁρμαίνειν in respect of sense, and without better evidence it would be imprudent to acquiesce in the MS. tradition here. Hermann's conjecture ὀρυγάνει ('vomits': Hesych. ὀρυγάνει· ἐρεύγεται, from an unknown source) has found much favour, but it would be equally imprudent to admit to the text a word of which the source and associations are wholly unknown.

1387. ὀξεῖαν: here presumably 'swift'. αἵματος σφαγήν: 'breathing out a swift *slaughter* of blood', or '*wounding* of blood' seems a confusion of language beyond the pale of poetry. Yet it has an exact parallel in E. *Rhes.* 790 f. (quoted by Headlam), θερμὸς δὲ κρουνὸς δεσπότου πάρα σφαγαῖς | βάλλει με δυσθνῄσκοντος αἵματος νέου, where αἵματος must be taken with σφαγαῖς (not with the distant κρουνός), 'a hot stream, issuing from my master, strikes me with woundings (or whatever σφαγαῖς does mean) of fresh blood, while he struggles against death' (the alternative, to join δεσπότου with παρὰ σφαγαῖς and αἵματος with κρουνός, is surely to be rejected absolutely). It is noticeable that in these two passages the situation is essentially the same : the one party is being splashed by the blood of the other, and the blood is in both contexts called σφαγὴ αἵματος. (The alternative courses are either to admit that Aeschylus has strained his language beyond breaking-point, or to condemn the text as corrupt: but if αἵματος is hard to explain, it is still harder to explain away. σφυγήν (Wilamowitz), a word which, if it existed, could have no meaning apt to this context ; ῥαγήν (Fraenkel), a word attested only twice, in technical medical writings, both probably of a much later era ; αἱμάδα σφαγῆς (A. Y. Campbell) would give good sense but does not account satisfactorily for the MS. tradition. The apparent imitation in S. *Ant.* 1238 φυσιῶν ὀξεῖαν ἐκβάλλει ῥοήν is unhelpful, for it does not include the one word, σφαγήν, which causes difficulty here.)

1391–2. 'rejoicing no less than the crop (rejoices) in the gladness given by Zeus, during the birth-pangs of the sheath'. διὸς νότῳ γᾶν εἰ codd. : Porson's conjecture is little if at all superior to Lloyd-Jones's, Διὸς νότῳ γαθεῖ, 'rejoices in the rain-bearing wind of Zeus' ; γαθεῖν seems a certain conjecture in *PV* 760, cf. *Cho.* 772. ἐν λοχεύμασιν: ἐν of space of time within which a thing occurs, cf. 1384 above. κάλυξ is the sheath, outer covering, which may be said to suffer λοχεύματα, pangs of travail, when the fruit or grain swells inside. In general cf. *Il.* 23. 597 ff. τοῖο δὲ θυμὸς | ἰάνθη ὡς εἴ τε περὶ σταχύεσσιν ἐέρση | ληΐου ἀλδήσκοντος ὅτε φρίσσουσιν ἄρουραι.

1393–4. The polite phrases are spoken ironically. ἐγὼ δ' ἐπεύχομαι: 'I exult', or 'I utter imprecations', probably the latter. Even if she was justified in killing her husband, this behaviour violates the code of Hellenic morality as reflected in the *Odyssey* 22. 412, οὐχ ὁσίη κταμένοισιν ἐπ' ἀνδράσιν εὐχετάασθαι, and Archilochus, fr. 65 οὐ γὰρ ἐσθλὰ κατθανοῦσι κερτομεῖν ἐπ' ἀνδράσι, cf. E. *El.* 900 ff.

1395–8. The sense is : 'had it been possible to pour a libation on the corpse *in a manner befitting*, it would have been right or more than right (to pour) *these things*', (viz. my curses, from ἐπεύχομαι), 'for he has filled a bowl at home so full of evils fit for cursing, and drained it himself at his homecoming' (the italic words are those rendered specially emphatic by position in their clauses).

Clytemnestra reflects that no ordinary libation would be suitable to such a case as this: if it were possible to make the libation fit the corpse, it would be a libation of exultant curses (τάδε, referring to ἐπεύχομαι, more fully elucidated later by ἀραίων). πρεπόντως is explained by the content of 1397–8: what is so *fitting* about such a libation is that it may be poured from a bowl which the dead man himself has filled (as he has also drained it, ἐκπίνει, hypercriticism may object that nothing is left for a libation). Thus justice is done to the connexion of thought between 1395–6 and 1397–8—a connexion welcomed in this context by τοσῶνδε in 1397, which implies an antecedent correlative, ὅσων or the like, expressed or implicit, in 1395–6. (Beware of renderings of the type 'If it were proper to pour libations over the corpse . . .': in fact it *was* proper to do so, a ritual act essential to the funeral ceremony; Pernice, *Privatleben* 62; Blümner, *Privataltertümer* 368; Baumeister, *Denkmäler* i. 307 f.; *RE* s.v. *Bestattung* 341.)

The above is essentially the explanation of Headlam: Fraenkel objects (1) 'the sentence which begins with τοσῶνδε clearly starts afresh'—but if τοσῶνδε starts the last sentence of a speech, its correlative ὅσων (or equivalent) is likely to be found in what precedes; (2) 'τάδε, "this here", must refer to what Clytemnestra is doing, and cannot point forward to τοσῶνδε κτλ.'—but there is no question of its pointing forward; its meaning is explained by what she says she is doing (ἐπεύχομαι), and later more fully elucidated by ἀραίων.

For the construction ἦν . . . ὥστε c. infin., 'it is possible to' (better perhaps 'the situation is such that one can . . .') cf. S. *Phil.* 656 ἔστιν ὥστε . . . λαβεῖν, E. *Hipp.* 705 ἔστι . . . ὥστε σωθῆναι. The choice between πρεπόντων (codd.) and πρεπόντως cannot be made with certainty: the partitive genitive (choose a libation from among things suitable to the occasion) is defensible, and the absence of the definite article τῶν is natural in this context.

1399–1400. The dominant feeling in the minds of the Chorus is at first amazement at the murderess's effrontery; expression of horror at the nature of the crime comes later (1407 ff.).

1403. i.e. εἴτε αἰνεῖν εἴτε ψέγειν; *Gk. Particles*, pp. 507 f.

1404–6. This seems the easiest and most effective punctuation. Some put a comma after χερός, but the phrase νεκρὸς τῆσδε δεξιᾶς χερός, in the sense 'a corpse slain by my right hand', is at least doubtful. Others have no punctuation between νεκρός and ἔργον, a device acceptable only if ἐστί is understood, 'the corpse (is) the work of . . . .'

1407–1576. On the structure see the full discussion by Fraenkel, pp. 660–1.

1407 ff. So extraordinary a deed, and so extraordinary a demeanour

after it, argue madness, and the madness must surely have been
induced by poison: E. *Ba.* 326 f., with Dodds's note; Ar. *Thesm.*
533 f. οὔ τοι . . . εὖ φρονεῖτε, ἀλλ' ἢ πεφάρμαχθ' ἢ κακόν τι μέγα πεπόνθατ'
ἄλλο (quoted by Fraenkel). The distinction between drugs to eat and
drugs to drink is a commonplace: *PV* 479 f., E. *Suppl.* 1110, Longus
2. 7 (quoted by Headlam); so is the reference to 'earth and sea' as
their sources: Ap. Rhod. iii. 530, Ovid *Fasti* v. 243 f. (quoted by
Headlam). Aeschylus, with more neatness than reason, combines the
two ideas, deriving the edible from earth and the potable from sea.

1408. πασαμένα: 'having tasted' (πατέομαι).

1409–10. Sense, and therefore punctuation, are uncertain: '. . . you
have taken upon yourself this sacrifice, and cast away and cut away
the execrations of the public voice; but away from the city shall you
go, a burden of hatred to your people.'   **θύος**: 'sacrifice', here
(see 1118 n.) = 'murderous killing'.   **ἐπέθου**: for the use of
τίθεσθαι see Dodds on E. *Ba.* 837.   **ἀράς** should be taken with
ἀπέδικες (= ἀπέρριψας), for otherwise it will make an awkward couple
with θύος, and ἀπέδ. ἀπέτ. will be left without any conceivable object.

1412. The Chorus threaten banishment, the penalty expected by
Orestes in E. *El.* 1191 ff. (cf. *Il.* 24. 481, *Od.* 13. 259, 15. 224, 23. 118 ff.).
By 1430 they have seen that this is not enough: blood must be
avenged with blood.

1413. μῖσος and **ἀράς**: probably both governed by ἔχειν, though both
(or the former only) might be governed by δικάζεις.

1414. τότε: in the days at Aulis; she attacks the Chorus for not having
opposed the resolve to sacrifice Iphigeneia.

1415 f. μόρον is governed by οὐ προτιμῶν (cf. E. *Hipp.* 48 f.), 'caring
not (for her death), as if it were the death of a beast'.   **μήλων
φλεόντων κτλ.**: not with special reference to Agamemnon, but 'caring
no more than one would care for the death of one beast out of a large
herd'.

1418. A spell to bind the contrary winds blowing from Thrace (cf. 193
above).

1421–5. Lit. 'I tell you to utter such threats on the understanding that
I am prepared on equal terms—that if one conquer me by force, he
rules; but if Heaven ordains the opposite, you shall learn discretion,
late though the lesson be.' The accus.+infin. clause νικήσαντα . . .
ἄρχειν (σέ is better not supplied, the reference being general) gives
the first half of the *terms* implied in ἐκ τῶν ὁμοίων; the second half
('but if *I* conquer *you*') follows in a fresh construction, ἐὰν δὲ κτλ.
ἐκ τῶν ὁμοίων: 'on equal terms', *starting from* conditions equal to both
sides. The accus.+infin. construction giving the content of the terms
is normal after such expressions as ἐπὶ τοῖσδε, 'on the following conditions . . .' (Thuc. ii. 70. 3), and the extension of usage to ἐκ τῶν
ὁμοίων here is easy.

1426. μεγαλόμητις: 'of high design', 'ambitious'. περίφρονα = ὑπέρφρονα, 'haughty', as in *Suppl.* 757, cf. Thuc. i. 25. 4, Ar. *Nub.* 225 f. (Fraenkel). ὥσπερ οὖν: this must look forward, not backward; it is inconsequent to say 'your words are proud, *just as* your mind is mad'; παράφρονα (Musgrave) would be needed to connect the phrases logically. The connexion of ὥσπερ οὖν with what follows, on the other hand, is immediately seen: 'Just as your mind is mad by reason of this deed of blood, so your eyes are bloodshot'; what is connected with her being mad (through bloodshed) is the fact that her eyes are bloodshot (see the evidence assembled by Fraenkel on this point).

1428. λίπος codd.: but this means 'fat' (or some fatty substance), an impossible sense here. λίβος (*Cho.* 448; presumably = λιβάς) would most naturally mean 'stream', 'trickle', and we might then be tempted to suppose that a *bloodstain* was visible *on the eyes* (ἐπ' ὀμμάτων) of Clytemnestra. It is, however, much likelier (see Verrall, Fraenkel) that *bloodshot eyes* are meant, and λίβος will then signify the vein, thin stream, of blood on the eyeball. The repetition φονολιβεῖ–λίβος αἵματος is presumably intentional: the *stream of blood* from the deed of murder is reflected in the *stream of blood* in the murderess's eyes. εὖ πρέπει codd.: εὖ is meaningless here. εὐπρεπτος in *Suppl.* 722, so far from offering an exact parallel (Fraenkel), is clearly opposed to εὖ here, since the context there supports, or even requires, the expected *complimentary* statement.

1429. ἄντιτον: though far from certain, this gives the best account of the MS. tradition. It represents ἀντί-τιτον, as ξύλοχος represents ξυλόλοχος, ἀμφορεύς ἀμφι-φορεύς. Elsewhere only in *Od.* 17. 51 = 60, αἴ κέ ποθι Ζεὺς ἄντιτα ἔργα τελέσσῃ (LSJ add *Il.* 24. 213, where ἄν τιτά is generally read, and Callim. *Iamb.* i. 160 Mair, which is no longer relevant; see Pfeiffer on Callim. fr. 192. 4). In *Od.* the apparent meaning is 'deeds of paying-back', 'deeds done in requital'. If correct here, the word presumably means 'paid back', agreeing with σέ: 'you must be paid out, deprived of friends you must yet pay for blow with blow.' (ἄντιτον is not well taken with τύμμα, for τύμμα denotes the blow with which Clytemnestra struck Agamemnon; the blow which she must receive in requital is expressed by τύμματι: 'to pay for a blow—τύμμα, her striking Agamemnon—with a blow'.) στερο-μέναν φίλων: this suggests to Clytemnestra her retort in 1435 ff.— 'Not while *Aegisthus* is beside me!'

1431. ἀκούεις: the imperative is (despite Hermann and Fraenkel) urgently required here; but it is imprudent to write ἄκουσον, ἀκούσαθ', or other forms which give no satisfactory account of the MS. tradition. The best that can be said for ἀκούεις here is that it is 'inaccurate and irregular, though perhaps not impossible' (Verrall).

ὁρκίων . . . θέμιν is an obscure expression: 'sanctity, solemnity, sanction, of oaths' are the common renderings, but it is not easy to find any other place where θέμις, 'what is prescribed by custom', 'what is right and proper', has acquired such a meaning as 'sanctity'. E. *Med.* 208 ὁρκίαν Θέμιν and similar passages, where Themis is personified, do not help. More probably the meaning is 'propriety', 'justness': Clytemnestra deliberately insists that it is right and proper for her, placed as she is, to swear by such sinister demons as Atê and Erinys; the expression is equivalent to θεμιτὰ ἀκούεις ὅρκια, 'you hear my right and proper oaths'.

1432. τέλειος Δίκη (personified) would naturally mean 'Justice that accomplishes' (cf. 973 Ζεῦ τέλειε): the context here suggests rather 'Justice *that is accomplished* for my child'.

1432–3. θ': see *Gk. Particles*, p. 501 (with Fraenkel's comments and additions, p. 675).

1434. φόβου must be taken with μέλαθρον (not with ἐλπίς; see Fraenkel): 'for me, expectation treads not in the house of fear', i.e. my hopes are far removed from, not attended by, misgivings. Similar, but much simpler, E. *Hkld.* 996 μὴ συνοικοίην φόβῳ, 'share the house with fear'; cf. also 1003 above, where ὑγίεια and νόσος are called 'neighbours sharing a party-wall'.

1435. 'In ascribing to Aegisthus the αἴθειν πῦρ ἐφ' ἑστίας ἐμῆς, Clytemnestra assigns to him the position of the legitimate lord of the house', Fraenkel. (It is not, however, necessary to agree that Clytemnestra is now for the first time 'conscious of a whisper of fear in her heart': there is no indication whatever that this is so; her confidence is not necessarily shaken because she states the grounds on which it is based.)

1438. '*The* ravager' would have to be ὁ λυμαντήριος (or -τήρ), so we cannot translate (with no comma after κεῖται) 'the ravager of me is lying . . .', but only (with the comma) 'he lies, ravager of me'. This makes the asyndeton and change of subject (from Aegisthus 1437 to Agamemnon 1438) disagreeably abrupt. The very slight change of τῆσδε to τῆσδ' ὁ is a great improvement. (Fraenkel's alleged parallels to λυμαντήριος without the article are all, with one apparent exception, examples in which words of this formation are either accompanied by article or pronoun or in agreement with substantival words: *ScT* 710 f. ὄψεις δατήριοι, S. *OT* 327 οἶδ' ἱκτήριοι, Ar. *Equ.* 445 τῶν ἀλιτηρίων, Menander *Epitr.* 574 ὁ ἀλιτήριος; the apparent exception is pseudo-Epicharmus fr. 44ᵃ (Diels–Kranz, *Vorsokratiker*⁶ i, p. 205) ἁδοναὶ δ' εἰσὶν βροτοῖσιν ἀνόσιοι λαστήριοι, a line of unknown date and authorship.)

1439. For the contemptuous plural Χρυσηίδων cf. E. *Rhes.* 866 οὐκ οἶδα τοὺς σοὺς οὓς λέγεις Ὀδυσσέας. μείλιγμα: normally 'that which soothes', cf. *Eum.* 886 μ. καὶ θελκτήριον; here therefore perhaps not 'darling of . . .' but 'one to soften the hearts of . . .'.

1440–2. Clytemnestra stresses the charge that Cassandra is both prophetess and concubine. The best punctuation is that implied by
cod. F, in which the sense of τερασκόπος καὶ κοινόλεκτρος is repeated
in the apposed words θεσφατηλόγος . . . ξύνευνος.

1443. ἱστοτρίβης codd.: ναυτίλων σελμάτων -τρίβης, 'wearing out the
ship's benches', is suitable to this context, but the first part of the
compound, ἱστο-, seems meaningless. The attractive conjecture
ἰσοτρίβης, where ἰσο- means 'equally (with Agamemnon)', may well
be right, though Fraenkel has shown that it is exposed to the objection that a *verbal* compound in ἰσο- is almost without example in
classical Greek; it is imprudent to introduce such a novelty as a
conjecture, though it could have been defended as a reading. A
further objection, that ὁμο- would have been expected instead of ἰσο-,
has much less force: ἰσώνυμος in Pind. *Ol.* 9. 64 (quoted by Fraenkel
on 1470 f.) is indistinguishable in sense from ὁμώνυμος.

ἄτιμα δ' οὐκ ἐπραξάτην: 'they have fared after their deserts',
Fraenkel; 'they have met their deserts', LSJ; 'they deserved their
fate', Sidgwick; 'not undeservedly', Paley; 'both have their deserts',
Headlam; 'no undeserved fate', Weir Smyth; and so others. But
ἄτιμα means not 'undeserved' or 'unpunished' but 'without honour',
'without privilege'. The context shows that this is the meaning here:
Clytemnestra sarcastically observes 'their fate is not without its
privilege—in death too the lovers lie side by side'. Cf. *Cho.* 894–5
(Orestes to Clytemnestra) φιλεῖς τὸν ἄνδρα; τοιγὰρ ἐν ταὐτῷ τάφῳ |
κείσῃ.

1444. οὕτως: sc. κεῖται, for which we have to wait until the δέ-clause
comes; 'as you see', viz. side by side with Cassandra.   κύκνου
δίκην κτλ.: presumably referring to the scene from 1072 onwards,
though Clytemnestra was then absent; indifference to fact in such
matters is characteristic of Tragedy (cf. 1035: how does Clytemnestra
know her name?).

1446. φιλήτωρ: agent-noun from φιλεῖν (nothing to do with ἦτορ),
= ἐραστής; see further Headlam–Thomson on 1445–8.

1446–7. The text and the detail of the meaning remain uncertain.
There are two primary difficulties: (1) The subject of ἐπήγαγεν may
be either Agamemnon (easily introduced by τοῦδε) or Cassandra: the
latter is favoured by the run of the words, the former by the sense
('he brought her in above me'—ἐπάγω as in S. *Ajax* 1296, *Tr.* 378—
'as an added relish to my bed'. Musgrave's χλιδῇ is perhaps the least
unlikely of the conjectures, 'added relish to the luxury of my bed';
but the order of the words, especially the position of τῆς ἐμῆς and of
χλιδῇ, tells against it). (2) The pair of genitives εὐνῆς and χλιδῆς defies
interpretation: yet χλιδ-, whatever the form, is surely not corrupt,
and the reference to εὐνή is indispensable to the context (the meaning
and metaphor are illustrated by Aristophanes fr. 187, quoted by

Blomfield, πάσαις γυναιξὶν ἐξ ἑνός γέ του τρόπου | ὥσπερ παροψὶς μοιχὸς
ἐσκευασμένος, and it is probably no mere coincidence that Ar. *Eccl.*
225 μοιχοὺς ἔχουσιν ἔνδον ὥσπερ καὶ πρὸ τοῦ is followed by 226 αὐταῖς
παροψωνοῦσιν ὥσπερ καὶ πρὸ τοῦ). εὐνῆς and χλιδῆς have proved so
intractable that we ought to consider whether the fault may lie in
παροψώνημα: the word is not found elsewhere, its duty being done by
παροψίς in the fifth century and by παρόψημα later. Though *πάροψον
is not found, εὐνῆς πάροψον, ὄμμα τῆς ἐμῆς χλιδῆς (ὄμμα = 'brightest
object', LSJ s.v. III, A. *Eum.* 1025) would remove the difficulties and
at the same time account for the corruption (ΠΑΡΟΨΟΝΟΜΜΑ
to -OMA is an easy step, and -HMA would readily follow).

1448–51. τίς ἂν ... μόλοι ... μοῖρα: 'would that some fate might
come ...'. They pray for death, provided it be swift in coming, not
very painful, and not preceded by long illness; a remarkable quantity of irrelevant detail.   δεμνιοτήρης is best taken to mean '(a
fate) which involves watching over the patient's bedside', i.e. a *long*
illness; τηρεῖν connotes *careful* watching, guarding, not merely
'keeping' one's bed.

   φέρουσ' ἐν ἡμῖν: cf. the rare use of ἐν with verbs of giving, E. *Med.*
424 f. ἐν ἀμετέρᾳ γνώμᾳ λύρας ὤπασε θέσπιν ἀοιδάν; *Od.* 24. 201 codd.
The change of ἐν to ἂν (Emperius: it would be most oddly placed in
the sentence) is not attractive.

1451–3. Here, as at 1489–91, the Chorus reveal their affection for
Agamemnon, their 'most kindly guardian'—unlike the 'tyrants'
(1355) who will now be their rulers.   [καί] was inserted to connect
the two participles, δαμέντος and τλάντος, a function much better left
unperformed. In the antistrophe the position of μοι, between the
coherent δίκαν and κόρακος, is so abnormal (E. *Tro.* 511 ἀμφί μοι ῎Ιλιον
is not parallel) and so bad that μοι may confidently be expelled (presumably inserted to balance καί in the strophe).   πολλά: corresponding metrically to κόρακος in the antistrophe, − ∪ = ∪∪∪;
since the correspondence of a long to two short syllables, though
found in the lyrical iambics of other Aeschylean plays, is not certainly
to be found in *The Oresteia* (see 408 n.), the conjecture πολέα has
found much favour. One would prefer a stronger argument for altering the MSS.   γυναικὸς διαί: 'by the agency of a woman', 'a
woman being the cause'; see Stevens, *CR* l (1936) 162 ff.

1458–61. There is some corruption in the text, and the general sense is
by no means clear. ἐπηνθίσω should mean 'you have adorned yourself' (the metaphorical sense indicated here has good parallels in *ScT*
951 f. πολλοῖς ἐπανθίσαντες πόνοισι γενεάν, '*adorning* the race with
many labours', *Cho.* 150 ὑμᾶς δὲ κωκυτοῖς ἐπανθίζειν νόμος (sc. τὰς
χοάς), 'to *adorn* the libations with moans'), and we expect to be told
with what she has adorned herself. The modern edd. (Weir Smyth,
Murray, Mazon, Fraenkel) accept Wilamowitz's conjecture νῦν τελέαν

πολύμν. κτλ., 'you have adorned yourself with a perfect (or 'final') adornment, long memorable', τελέαν being taken as a substantival feminine adjective of the type of *Cho.* 640 διανταίαν . . . οὐτᾷ (see E. H. 681 with Wilamowitz's note): this is no more than a makeshift; the use of τελέαν is not found elsewhere, and has very few analogies.

δι' αἷμ' ἄνιπτον: 'by means of (or possibly 'by reason of') blood not washed away'; Helen is apparently said to have adorned herself with a 'final garland', viz. the death of Agamemnon, *through* (or *because of*) *blood not washed away*. That is hard to understand except as a reference to the death of Iphigeneia: Helen's elopement was the first cause of the events which culminated in Agamemnon's murder; but the means by which that end was attained is to be found in the unexpiated sacrifice of Iphigeneia. This is allusive and obscure: but **τότε**, drawing our attention to some particular occasion in the past, suggests that ἄνιπτον αἷμα does indeed refer to Iphigeneia's death: the thought of 'blood not washed away' leads at once to the reflection 'Truly *at that time* (*what* time, if not the time of Iphigeneia's death; and *whose* αἷμα ἄνιπτον suggests reference to a particular time in the past, if not hers?) there was a Spirit of Strife in the house . . ..' Possibly, however, the reference is to Thyestes' children.

ἐρίδματος (here only): (1) from δεμ-, 'strongly-built', or from δαμ-, 'strongly-subdued' or 'strongly-subduing'; (2) nom., with Ἔρις or οἰζύς, or gen. with ἀνδρός. 'Strong-built' seems an unlikely epithet for Strife or Misery (being a novel formation, it cannot be toned down to 'firmly-established', 'immovable', or the like). There is no means of telling what the poet intended: perhaps either (*a*) nom. ἐρίδματος governing ἀνδρός, 'domitrix viri' (Hermann), 'Strife, the sorrow that subdues a man'; or (*b*) gen. ἐριδμᾶτος, 'of a man subdued'.

1467. ἀξύστατον: 'that will not stand together', i.e. uncohesive, not compact or solid. The context here suggests '*uncongealed* pain', the pain of a wound that will not close up. A striking example of the condensed phraseology typical of Aeschylus.

1468 f. διφυίοισι Τανταλίδαισιν: 'either Atreus and Thyestes or Agamemnon and Menelaus', Schol.: the context suggests the latter pair, whose wives are the principal theme at the moment.

1470–1. κράτος τ' ἰσόψυχον ἐκ γυναικῶν . . . κρατύνεις: the adjective is simply transferred from γυναικῶν to κράτος: 'you wield power through women like-minded', i.e. through two women (Helen and Clytemnestra) of equally disastrous temperament. ἐκ γυναικῶν, for the power of the daimon is seen *proceeding from* them. The expression is a blend of κράτος ἰσόψυχων γυναικῶν and κράτος ἰσοψύχων ἐκ γυναικῶν.

ἰσόψυχον: Fraenkel shows that ἰσο- compounds are normally of two main types—(1) type ἰσόθεος = ἴσος θεοῖς, (2) type ἰσόψηφος = ἴσοις ψήφοις, ἰσο- denoting 'equal in quantity, measure, weight' or the like. Neither type covers ἰσόψυχον here, which must be classed with such examples as ἰσοκεφάλους (Ibycus fr. 2. 3), 'equal-headed', of the twin sons of Molion, or ἰσοδαίμονα (Pind. *Nem.* 4. 84), 'equal in happiness'.

1472–4. σταθεῖσα or **σταθείς?** The choice is between two evils: with σταθείς we have to understand ὁ δαίμων, who a moment ago was in the vocative case; with σταθεῖσα we must understand 'Clytemnestra', an abrupt change of subject. Perhaps the most helpful consideration is the fact that the phrase 'like a crow, standing over the body', exactly describes what *Clytemnestra* is at this moment doing, for all to see, on the scene; and ἐπεύχεται may remind us of ἐπεύχομαι in 1394. Moreover the abruptness of the change of subject is less offensive than the change of person from κρατύνεις 2nd pers. to ἐπεύχεται 3rd pers. **ἐκνόμως:** 'out of tune'; the harsh voice of the crow was proverbial (and so was its nature as a bird of carrion). **ὕμνον ὑμνεῖν ἐπεύχεται:** two syllables are missing, probably from the end of the line. It would be hard to justify the rendering 'glories in singing' (let alone 'boasts that she will sing', Schütz); ἐπεύχεται c. pres. infin. should mean 'boasts that she is singing' (cf. *Hom. Hymn. Ven.* 286, ἐπεύχ. c. aor. infin., 'you boast that you did . . .', though there ἐπεύξεαι is assisted by ἐξείπῃς), but whether that would suit the context here depends on the unknown factor—the missing word, which may well have been an epithet for ὕμνον. ὑμνοῦσ' conj. Herwerden.

1476. τριπάχυντον: τρι- may be intensive (cf. *Cho.* 314 τριγέρων), but is perhaps better taken to be numerical (referring to the activity of the daimon through three generations).

1477–80. Text (and punctuation) uncertain. Apparently 'Through him it is that the lust for lapping blood is fostered in the belly: before the old pain has ceased, ⟨comes⟩ fresh suppuration.' The mention of the 'belly' is unusual in such contexts, but here τριπάχυντον leads up to it. **νείρᾳ:** this is very doubtful. Hesychius s.v. νείραι· κατώταται. οἱ δὲ κοιλίας τὰ κατώτατα. The form is a great rarity in two respects: (1) νειρ- for νειαιρ- in this word occurs very seldom (E. *Rhes.* 794 (conj.), Lycophron 896, Hesychius, l.c.); (2) its normal use is adjectival; the pro-substantival use alleged here is almost unexampled (Callim. fr. 43. 15 with Pfeiffer's note; Hesych.). It must be added that if νείρᾳ is correct there seems no reason why the MSS. should offer νείρει, and that the ellipse of the main verb in the following clause is of an unusual type (hence Housman conj. τρέφεται καὶ νᾷ, for τρέφεται νείρει; Margoliouth τείρει· τρέφεται, ingeniously). **ἰχώρ:** see Headlam, Fraenkel, and Dumortier, *Le vocabulaire médic. d'Éschyle*, p. 53; not 'blood' but 'pus', a reflection of contemporary medical usage.

1481–8. The Chorus continue their train of thought.—Yes, the Spirit of the House, whose sinister quality Clytemnestra has so powerfully described, is the cause of all. And then comes the cry of surprise—if the Spirit is the immediate cause, the final cause must be Zeus himself, the cause and author of all things. This, then, is what Zeus, whose heartfelt worship was the only source of peace and comfort for men (161 ff.), wills to do with them; what resource is now left?

1481. οἴκοις τοῖσδε (codd.) may be a gloss (wholly or in part) which has ousted the word or words which it explained. Supplements of the type of οἰκοσινῆ ('house-destroying', Wilamowitz; the word is his own invention) are merely speculative. It is possible that οἴκοις was part of the original text (correspondence with 1515 is easily effected by adding σύ after εἰ there), and the solution may lie in the region of Weil's ἦ μέγαν ⟨ἦ μέγαν⟩ οἴκοις.

1481–4. Clytemnestra has described the daimon which causes an unending series of troubles; the Chorus comment: 'Great, and heavy in wrath, is this daimon whose praises you tell—an evil tale of calamity (ἀτηρὰ τύχη) insatiable.' Todt's conjecture ἀκόρεστον, on which τύχας will be dependent, may be correct but is not called for by any definable fault in the tradition.

1485. διαὶ Διός: see 1453 n.

1488. θεόκραντον: '*ordained* by the gods' (Fraenkel; not, as in LSJ, *accomplished* or *wrought*).

1489–96. The Chorus are roused from their brooding over human destiny by the thought and sight of the body of their murdered king: whatever the theological implications may be, this crime is the work of a human hand, and human responsibility cannot be evaded.

1493. ἐκπνέων: the synizesis of -εων is unparalleled in Tragedy, and the present tense is unintelligible; ἐκπνεύσας (Hartung) would do all that is needed, but is too drastic a change.

1494. κοίταν: internal accus. with κεῖσαι.

1495–6. 'Subdued *by hand* in a treacherous death by a two-edged weapon': it seems at first sight necessary to say whose, or what kind of, hand; hence δαμεὶς ⟨δάμαρτος⟩ suppl. Enger, but the isolated ἐκ χερός here is fully protected by S. *Ajax* 25 ff., ἐφθαρμένας γὰρ ἀρτίως εὑρίσκομεν | λείας ἁπάσας καὶ κατηναρισμένας | ἐκ χειρός, where ἐκ χ. is similarly unqualified; in both passages there may be a suggestion that the deaths are not 'natural' or accidental, but *by hand*, i.e. some human being is responsible for them.

1497. αὐχεῖς: 'You confidently assert'; see Fraenkel's note on the meaning and construction of this verb.

1498–1500. The text is unintelligible at one point and very obscure at two others: (1) On μηδ' ἐπιλεχθῆς see Fraenkel, pp. 708 ff. It is doubtful enough whether the middle usage of the passive ἐπιλεχθῆς is justifiable ('do not think, consider, imagine'; so Schol. and most edd.). Much more serious is the fact, established by Fraenkel, that μηδέ *connective*, 'and . . . not', *without a preceding negative* (or equivalent) is unexampled and therefore surely impermissible. Thus the common interpretations, starting from '*And do not* (think me . . .)' are ruled out at once. (2) The context imperatively demands something like Paley's paraphrase: 'you insist that this deed is *mine*; I tell you, it was not *I* who did it, but the evil genius of the family in my form and shape'. But how can the phrase Ἀγαμεμνονίαν εἶναί μ' ἄλοχον, 'that I am Agamemnon's wife', be reconciled with this requirement of the context? Only if the meaning is: 'you wrongly think that what you see in me is simply the wife of Agamemnon; in truth I embody a Spirit of Vengeance'. Since the negative form of command with μηδέ is impossible (see above), we may do well to read τῆδ' ἐπιλεχθείς, κτλ., '(You assert that the deed is mine), reckoning thus— that I am the wife of Agamemnon; but in fact what you see in me is the embodiment of a Spirit of Vengeance'. ἐπιλεχθείς conj. Scaliger. For τῆδε cf. such phrases as ὅρα τῆδε, σκόπει τῆδε, 'consider in the following way', Plato, *Phaedo* 79ᵉ, *Rep.* 433ᵉ. (3) **φανταζόμενος δὲ γυναικὶ νεκροῦ**: this would normally mean 'making himself manifest to the wife . . .'. The context here appears to rule that out, and we have to accept a remarkable abuse of language, φαντ. γυναικί being here treated as equivalent to εἰδόμενος γυναικί, 'in the semblance of the wife . . .'. We must tolerate also some obscurity in the thought, for one would naturally take the words to imply that there were *two* 'bodies', Clytemnestra and her ghostly double, of whom the latter did the deed while the former looked on. It is, however, certain that this is not intended. Clytemnestra is not saying (what would be patently false) that it was not her hand which did the deed, but only that the Alastor worked *through* her; there was only one person engaged—the Alastor embodied in Clytemnestra.

1501 f. 'The deed now appears to her so frightful that, at least at this moment, she is convinced that only the Spirit of Vengeance, Alastor, can have done it; he has maliciously borrowed her shape', (Fraenkel): but there is nothing in the text to suggest that Clytemnestra is suddenly aware of the horror of her deed, and looking round for an excuse or explanation. She coldly tells what she consistently supposes to be the truth—that her killing of Agamemnon is not an act of individual impulse, but the working out of the rule of divine vengeance, of which she is the minister; Agamemnon's death is just, and she is the willing instrument of that justice.   **χαλεποῦ θοινα-τῆρος**: 'cruel feaster', referring to Atreus' serving the bodies of Thyestes' children for their father to eat.

1503–4. τόνδ' ἀπέτεισεν τέλεον κτλ.: lit. 'offered this man (Agamemnon) as payment (for the sins of his father Atreus), having sacrificed a grown man (Agamemnon) on top of young ones (the children of Thyestes)'. Or 'rendered this full-grown man as payment to the young, a crowning sacrifice' (Fraenkel).

1505–12. The Chorus refuse to accept wholly the plea which they themselves had suggested (1468–74), that Clytemnestra is the instrument of divine justice. But still they admit that supernatural powers 'might have had a hand in it' (1508).

1507. πῶ πῶ = πόθεν, in the idiomatic sense 'how can that be?', LSJ s.v. ποθεν I. 4. The adverb in -ω, elsewhere confined to the Western Greek dialects, is surprising here, but very unlikely to be the result of corruption. The obvious conjectures πῶς πῶς, ποῦ ποῦ, do not really suit the sense. **πατρόθεν**: vengeance *proceeding from his father* (Atreus).

1509–11. 'The black Spirit of Slaughter' (for Ares in such contexts cf. *Cho.* 461, *Eum.* 355 f., S. *El.* 1384 f.) 'acts with violence' (βιάζεται as in *PV* 1010) 'with fresh (ἐπι-) streams of kindred blood'. **ὁμοσπόροις**: a striking example of the 'transferred' epithet.

1511–12. ὅποι δὲ καὶ προβαίνων (προ- for προσ- conj. Canter) codd.: i.e. a relative adverb introducing a participle but not followed by a main verb; there is no adequate parallel to this (423 above being suspected, if not convicted, of corruption). And there is the further difficulty that παρέξει is left without an object, and πάχνᾳ κουρ. without anything to govern the dative case (πάχναν κουροβόρον, Auratus, would solve both these problems: but the change from dat. to accus. here is in the highest degree improbable). **δίκαν** removes all difficulty.

κουροβόρῳ: in this context, which has been so much concerned with the crimes of the past, and specifically with the devouring of the sons of Thyestes (1501), it is impossible to understand this adjective as referring to anything but that event, the 'Thyestean feast'. **πάχνᾳ**: something frozen, solidified, congealed; here 'clotted blood' (so LSJ and many edd., rightly; cf. *Cho.* 67 τίτας φόνος πέπηγεν οὐ διαρρύδαν, *ScT* 737 μελαμπαγὲς αἷμα). The point is that the blood cannot be washed away, is inexpiable. The adj. κουροβόρῳ is of the common brachylogic type, 'related to the devouring of children': cf. *Eum.* 281 μητροκτόνον μίασμα, 283 καθαρμοῖς . . . χοιροκτόνοις, and others quoted by Wecklein on 735 above. Ares is said to force his way 'to the point where, in his advance, he shall provide justice for the clotted blood of children devoured'.

1521–9. Clytemnestra's reply, which was evidently addressed to the Chorus's words at 1518–20, is gravely corrupt. Starting from the position that there is no metrical correspondence between 1521 ff. and 1497 ff., we note as follows:

I. (1) 1521 **οὔτε** 'neither', demands a following 'nor' (or equivalent), which is not to be found in the text (οὐδέ in 1523 will not serve; see below). (2) 1522–3 γενέσθαι | οὔτε offers a hiatus which is not permissible in anapaests. (3) 1523–4 **οὐδὲ γὰρ οὗτος δολίαν ἄτην κτλ.** demands, what is not in the text, a preceding reference to the Chorus's accusation that *she* used deceit.

The first and third points prove that something has fallen out of
the text, the second indicates the location of the gap—between
γενέσθαι and οὐδέ. The general sense would be given by: . . . γενέσθαι·
⟨δολίαις δὲ τέχναις | ἐμὲ χρησαμένην οὐκ εὖ μέμφεσθ'·⟩ | οὐδὲ γὰρ . . .,
i.e. 'nor am I to blame for using deceit, for did not he too . . .?'
II. Whether the text is seriously in error at 1526 ff. is much less
certain. (1) In πολύκλαυτόν τ' Ἰφιγένειαν the τε is almost if not quite
indefensible (see Fraenkel on this point); but -κλαύτην Ἰφιγένειαν
(Porson) would be an easy correction (cf. Suppl. 62, where κιρκηλάτου
τ' ἀηδόνος, similarly an appositional phrase, must be altered to -ηλάτας
ἀηδ.). (2) It has been too readily assumed that the place at which
word-division occurs in the anapaestic dimeter Ἰφιγένειαν ἀν|άξια
δράσας condemns the text at this point: it is indeed anomalous, but
anomaly does not automatically prove corruption; and here the
wholly dactylic run of the line frees the rhythm from all awkwardness
(contrast the less fluent rhythm of the anomalous divisions in PV 293
γνώσῃ δὲ τάδ' | ὡς ἔτυμ', Pers. 47 δίρρυμά τε | καὶ τρίρρυμα τέλη; in
1555 below, ἀλλ' Ἰφιγένειά νιν | ἀσπασίως, the line runs smoothly
despite the anomalous division). (3) The sense requires what the
MSS. have, Ἰφιγένειαν ἀνάξια δράσας ἄξια πάσχων, 'suffering what he
deserves, having done to Iphigeneia what she did not deserve'.
Hermann's conjecture ἄξια δράσας ἄξια πάσχων ('suffering deservedly,
having done what deserved those sufferings') might stand only if
it stood independently: it is impossible if ἄξια δράσας governs
Ἰφιγένειαν; so also Fraenkel, 'it is obvious that Ἰφιγένειαν ἄξια
δράσας is nonsense'. (There is no authority for Ἰφιγενείᾶν.)

1523. οὐδὲ γὰρ οὗτος = οὐ γὰρ καὶ οὗτος, 'did not he too . . .?'

1525. ἀλλά: (Is he innocent of deceit?) No, his dealings with Iphigeneia show the contrary.   ἐμὸν ἐκ τοῦδ' ἔρνος ἀερθέν: we have
to choose between several more or less equally unfamiliar senses of
the verb ἀείρομαι. (1) Most edd. have taken ἔρνος ἀερθέν as 'shoot
(of a plant) risen up', i.e. simply 'grown up'; but there is no reason
to suppose that the verb could mean this. (2) A. C. Pearson suggested
'my branch begotten of him, her whom I upreared': this seems the
least unlikely, ἀείρεσθαι being used as in Nicander fr. 108. 3 κακὸν γόνον
ἤρατο βούτεω (Herodas 9. 13 is unreliable evidence). (3) Schütz trans-
lates susceptam, 'conceived from him'; there is no other certain
evidence for this use of the verb.

1528. μεγαλαυχείτω: he had better not give himself airs in the underworld as the mighty and blameless king of the Achaeans. Cf. Od. 11.
484 f. (Odysseus to Achilles) πρὶν μὲν γάρ σε ζωὸν ἐτίομεν ἶσα θεοῖσιν |
Ἀργεῖοι· νῦν αὖτε μέγα κρατέεις νεκύεσσιν. The same primitive notion,
that the king on earth remains king in Hades, recurs in Pers. 691,
Cho. 354 ff., S. El. 840 ff., al.

1529. 'Having paid, by his death, for what he began': Agamemnon was the aggressor; it is an essential part of Clytemnestra's defence that *he* began the shedding of blood. Cf. Trag. adesp. 490 τιμωρίαν ἔτεισεν ὧν ἦρξεν κακῶν, E. H. 1169 τίνων ἀμοιβὰς ὧν ὑπῆρξεν Ἡρακλῆς. (Housman, *J. Phil.* xvi (1888) 284). ἔρξεν (Spanheim) makes no important difference to the general sense; it may be right, but is certainly not necessary.

1530 f. Lit. 'I am at a loss, which way to turn, deprived of thought's resourceful care.'

1533–4. 'I am frightened by the beating of this (τόν) *rainstorm* of blood that shakes the house; for the *shower* is ceasing'—the point apparently lies in the contrast between ψακάς and ὄμβρος: 'the *shower* ceases, a *torrent* is upon us'; ψακὰς δὲ λήγει stands paratactically, equivalent to ψακάδος ληγούσης, ἐπεὶ λήγει ψακάς. Up to the murder of Agamemnon there had been nothing but a 'drizzle', ψακάς, of foreboding: now the deed is done, and a heavy downpour shakes the house. This is not entirely satisfactory, but it is hard to see what else the words could mean.

1535–6. 'Justice is being sharpened, for another deed of injury, on other whetstones of Destiny.' Or, with δίκαν (Auratus), θηγάνει (Hermann), and μοῖρα, 'Destiny is sharpening (her sword of) Justice . . .'. Cf. *Cho.* 646 f. Δίκας δ' ἐρείδεται πυθμήν, προχαλκεύει δ' Αἶσα φασγανουργός; S. *Ajax* 1034 Ἐρινὺς τοῦτ' ἐχάλκευσε ξίφος.   **πρᾶγμα . . . βλάβης**: an uncommon genitive of quality, very like ἔργα . . . ἀρετᾶς in S. *Ajax* 616 f.; see 739–40 n. above.

1539–40. For the 'silver-walled' bath cf. *Od.* 4. 128 δύ' ἀργυρέας ἀσαμίνθους.   **χάμευναν**: a humble sort of couch, no fit place for a king's body; κοίταν ἀνελεύθερον, as the Chorus said just now.

1541–50. It is assumed that Agamemnon will have a decent burial: but who is to bury him? And who is to deliver the customary lament and tale of praise? That is the business of relatives, and here the nearest relative is the murderess herself. In the event (*Cho.* 429 ff.) he is buried without lamentation, and the citizens are forbidden to attend; Electra is shut up indoors (*Cho.* 444 ff.) 'like a dangerous dog'. But there is a further horror, which the Chorus cannot foresee—the dead body is *mutilated* (*Cho.* 439 ἐμασχαλίσθη).

1545 f. ψυχῇ . . . ἐπικρᾶναι: 'and wrongfully to fulfil for his ghost an ungrateful grace in recompense for mighty deeds'.   **ἄχαριν χάριν**: the tribute, coming from Clytemnestra, would be no tribute but an insult: cf. *Cho.* 43.   **ἀδίκως**: such fulfilment would be contrary to what is right and proper.

1547–8. The MSS. have assimilated the case-endings of ἐπιτύμβ. αἶν. to that of the preceding nom. τίς, a very common sort of error.   **θείῳ**: the Homeric epithet seems specially apt in a context concerned with the funeral-praises of the great king.

1549. ἰάπτων (governing αἶνον): usually 'sending forth', or the like, here 'emitting', meaning little more than 'uttering'.

1550. ἀληθείᾳ φρενῶν πονήσει: lit. 'shall do his work with truthfulness of mind', i.e. with sincerity. The 'work' is the making and giving of the ἐπιτύμβιος αἶνος.

1551–9. Clytemnestra's contemptuous and cynical reply shows that she has had no change of thought or emotion. She does not even shelter any longer behind the daimon: 'That is no business of yours; we who killed him are the right people to bury him. He will have to do without the tears of his household—*but no doubt a kiss and a loving embrace from his daughter Iphigeneia await him on the other side!*'

1554. ὑπό: 'to the accompaniment of'. τῶν ἐξ οἴκων: τῶν is masc., 'of the people from his home'.

1557 f. πρός c. accus., where *previous* motion is implied, LSJ s.v. C. I. 2: 'going to the πόρθμευμα and meeting him there'. **πόρθμευμα ἀχέων**: the river Acheron, cf. Licymnius fr. 2 Ἀχέρων ἄχεα πορθμεύει βροτοῖσιν; lit. 'swift-travelling ferry-stream of woes'.

1559. χεῖρε (Porson) is not necessary; cf. Simonides fr. 13. 6 ἀμφί τε Περσέι βάλλε φίλαν χέρα, E. *IT*. 799 περιβαλὼν πέπλοις χέρα.

1560–6. The Chorus are in the same mood as before, despondent and full of foreboding.—'Reproach thus meets reproach (our attack on Clytemnestra is answered by hers on Agamemnon), and it is a hard struggle to decide between them. The spoiler is despoiled, the killer pays his debt in full. *Reprisal* is the law of life; the house of Atreus is bound fast to Ruin.'

1562. φέρει: sc. τις, '(someonè) plunders him who is plundering'.

1563–4. '(the law) remains while Zeus remains on his throne: *that the sinner must suffer.*' [ἐν χρόνῳ (codd.) may be right, = ἀεί; *Eum.* 1000.]

1565. γονὰν ἀραῖον: 'the seed of curses', i.e. that from which the disasters spring. Not 'the accursed family'.

1567–76. Clytemnestra remains as before, unrepentant, clear-minded.— This 'law of Reprisal' is indeed the heart of the matter: but she, unlike the Chorus, has a practical suggestion to offer.—Let the gods count this as the last link in the chain of calamities, let them now call a halt and transfer their attentions elsewhere; they shall then hear no more complaint from her about the present sorry state of affairs in the house of Atreus. Indeed she will go farther, and strike a bargain: she will placate the gods by giving up most of her worldly goods (cf. 1008 ff.) and living in modest style. There is no suggestion of 'cold irony' (Sidgwick) or 'deep anxiety' (Fraenkel): only a cool, practical, and thoroughly sensible suggestion for solving the problem to the satisfaction of both parties.

1567 f. Perhaps ἐς τόνδ' (sc. Agamemnon) ἐνέβη . . . χρησμός (Casaubon), for παθεῖν τὸν ἔρξαντα is hardly a 'χρησμός'. If the text is sound, we must suppose that something which is θέσμιον and proceeds from Zeus might be called a χρησμός, or that χρ. here =' oracular sort of saying'.

1569. Πλεισθενιδᾶν: the place of this shadowy person, Pleisthenes, in the line of Atreus is wholly uncertain; see Fraenkel, p. 740.

1569-73. Lit. 'I am willing, having made a sworn compact with the daimon of the house of Pleisthenes, to put up with these things (viz. with all that has happened so far), hard though they are to bear; and, for what remains (i.e. for the future), that the daimon should go from this house and wear out some other family with kindred-murders.' Both infinitives, στέργειν and τρίβειν, may be regarded as governed by ἐθέλω, but both are affected by the intervention of ὅρκους θεμένη, which introduces the terms on either side of the compact, assisting the change of subject from στέργειν (subject ἐμέ) to τρίβειν (subject τὸν δαίμονα).

1575. It is strange to find the word ἀπόχρη, which belongs to the language of prose and comedy, in such elevated company.   πᾶν ἀπόχρη μοι: apparently 'everything suffices me', in the sense 'I am perfectly content with anything'.

1577-8. Aegisthus enters attended by a bodyguard. He speaks in a style unlike that of any other character in Aeschylus, high or low. After a grandiose opening he lapses into a glib, leisurely flatness, enlivened by an occasional proverb or cliché (1623-4), puns (1591, 1629-30), and bombastic grandiloquence (1628, 1639 ff.). The contents are not much less ignoble than the style: with undisturbed complacency he asserts that both the grievance and its avenging were his business; he does not address Clytemnestra, indeed he does not even allude to her until he is forced to do so (1636).

1577. εὔφρον: This is one of the few places where 'welcome', 'pleasant', may be thought apter to the context than 'well-intentioned' (or 'cheerful' or 'reasonable'); but 'kindly' may well be right, the light of day being personified as in S. *Ant.* 100 ff., *El.* 201 ff., al.

1578 f. Sense and word-order are most simply satisfied by taking βροτῶν with τιμαόρους, 'avengers of mortals', and γῆς with ἄχη, 'sorrows of the earth' (cf. *Cho.* 585 f. γᾶ τρέφει ... ἄχη), ἄνωθεν being adverbial, 'from above'.

1580. ἐν πέπλοις Ἐρινύων: the fatal robe of 1126. Since 'woven' is a dull epithet for 'robes' here, Nauck conjectured πάγαις for πέπλοις, 'in the woven snares (= robe-net) of the Furies', a much better phrase than the text offers.

1582. μηχανάς: Atreus' crime against Thyestes was not an open and straightforward act, but a deceitful plot. Aegisthus, admitting that the murder of Agamemnon was performed by guile, δόλῳ, and must therefore be particularly displeasing to the gods (S. *Tr.* 274 ff.), defends himself as Clytemnestra did (1523 f.) by pleading that he used deceit in retaliation for deceit.

1585. αὑτοῦ δ' ἀδελφόν: δ' should be preferred to τ' in this idiom; *Gk. Particles*, p. 502, Elmsley on E. *Med*. 940, Fraenkel, pp. 744 f.
ἀμφίλεκτος : lit. 'spoken about on both sides', i.e. disputed, challenged ; 881 ἀμφίλεκτα πήματα = 'sorrows about which some say one thing, some another'.

The dative κράτει is perhaps of the same type as in σώμασιν ἀδύνατοι, ἀρετῇ διαφέρων, ἡλικίᾳ νέος, describing the matter or region to which the quality in question may be applied (K.–G. i. 440).

Aegisthus alludes to the story that his father, Thyestes, having seduced Aerope, wife of his brother Atreus, stole a golden lamb which was the warrant of Atreus' title to the throne.

1587. προστρόπαιος ἑστίας : 'suppliant of the hearth' ; objective genitive of the type described in K.–G. i. 371, n. 19.

1588. ηὕρετ' : 'found for himself' ; most translators render as if it were ηὗρεν. Cf. *PV* 267 θνητοῖς ἀρήγων αὐτὸς ηὑρόμην πόνους : the middle voice signifies that the speaker claims or accepts responsibility for what has happened. Thyestes found for himself a safe berth by taking the action described in προστρόπαιος ἑστίας.

1589. τὸ μή ... +consecutive infin. = 'so as not to ...'.

1590. αὑτοῦ : 'on the spot'.   ξένια : the tribrach fills the second half of the first iambic metron ; *Cho*. 1 is the only other example in Aeschylus.   τοῦδε (sc. Ἀγαμέμνονος) goes with πατήρ.

1591. προθύμως μᾶλλον ἢ φίλως : a remarkably insipid expression, though there is no fault to be found with its meaning, 'a zealous host rather than a true friend'—there was nothing amiss with Atreus' *manner*—he was only too eager to put ξένια before his guest—but all the time he was acting as an enemy, not as a friend. It is hard to believe that Aeschylus wrote all just as we have it in this region.

1592. κρεουργὸν ἦμαρ : a day for the 'working' (cutting up) of meat ; a rare occasion in classical Greece except at festivals. See further Fraenkel, p. 748, on the history of the words κρεουργία, κρεουργεῖν in the Tantalid legend.   εὐθύμως : for the repetition after προθύμως see 362 n.

1593. The fourth consecutive line with a pause after the second syllable : cf. 1403–6 (Plüss). The Tragedians are seldom so inadvertent (but even Sophocles can write three consecutive lines with only a formal caesura, *El*. 1036 ff.).

1594–6. At first sight it may seem that the serious difficulties are confined to 1595 : (1) ἀνδρακάς : in *Od*. 13. 14 (the only other example) this adverb appears to mean κατ' ἄνδρα, 'each man by himself', a plurality of men being concerned. One would have thought that it was a *distributive* word, inapplicable to an *individual*, though such abuse of language cannot be said to be uncharacteristic of Aeschylus ; thus Triclinius καθ' ἑαυτόν, 'by himself', i.e. simply 'alone'.

(2) **καθήμενος**: grammar demands that the subject should be Atreus, the context insists that it must be Thyestes.

But the presence of deeper corruption (the loss of a line or more) is strongly suggested by at least two points: (*a*) **τὰ μέν** in 1594, to which no δέ-clause responds: ἄσημα δέ will not serve the purpose, at least unless ἔθρυπτε is altered, since the objects in τὰ μὲν κτλ. were broken up to prevent recognition and were therefore just as ἄσημα as the rest. It is a natural inference, that a δέ-clause, stating what happened to the *other* parts of the body, is missing from the text. (Something may well have been said about the *heads*, which must have been *hidden*: adjacent lines beginning ἔθρυπτε—ἔκρυπτε would readily account for a lacuna. Or perhaps Aeschylus, in accord with the tradition popular later, and like Herodotus (1. 119) in the similar story of Astyages and Harpagus, said that 'the feet and hands ⟨and heads were hidden: the rest⟩ was chopped up and served'; see Platt, *CR* xi (1897) 96 f.; ἄνωθεν would then require special treatment.) (*b*) The mincing of hands and feet, though not a necessary or, so far as we know, normal feature of the story, is here described *to the exclusion of all other detail*: this want of proportion, together with the lack of a δέ-clause to answer τὰ μέν, argues loudly for a lacuna.

Granted a lacuna, scrutiny of what at present stands on its edges is likely to be vain, since the meaning may have depended on words now lost. (i) ἔθρυπτ᾽ ἄνωθεν: this might mean 'minced on top', i.e. on top of the παιδείων κρεῶν, easily supplied from the end of the preceding sentence; but it seems absurd to put just these tell-tale pieces (however finely chopped) *on top*, and it is very odd that this unusual and illogical detail should be so particularly stressed. (ii) ἀνδρακὰς καθήμενος: see above. (iii) ἄσημα δ᾽ αὐτῶν: those who retain this generally understand 'he took *the indistinguishable parts of them* (viz. of the meats)': that is quite impossible; *all* the meats served to Thyestes were (in this sense) *indistinguishable*. It is likely too that this sense would require τἄσημα (Burges) for ἄσημα.

If there is a lacuna, the problems are of course insoluble. It remains possible that slight changes in 1595–6 alone will cure the disease. The guesses of several scholars might be combined to produce something which might have been acceptable if the MSS. had offered it (it differs from them in only four letters): τὰ μὲν ποδήρη καὶ χερῶν ἄκρους κτένας | ἔκρυπτ᾽ ἄπωθεν ἀνδρακὰς καθημένους | ἄσημ᾽· ὁ δ᾽ αὐτῶν αὐτίκ᾽ ἀγνοίᾳ λαβὼν | ἔσθει, 'The feet and hands he concealed at a distance (ἄπωθεν), so that they were unperceived (ἄσημα), from the men who were sitting each by himself; and the other (Thyestes) at once partook of the meats themselves, not knowing what they were, and ate . . . .' Here τὰ μέν (the hidden portions, too recognizable to be served up) are contrasted with αὐτῶν, sc. τῶν κρεῶν (the meats which were served up to him). The point of 'each man sitting by himself' is of course that there may be no danger of the fatal dish being taken by, or shared with, somebody else; they were sitting each at a distance from another.

1597. ἄσωτον: active ('bringing destruction on the race', LSJ).

1599. ἀπὸ ... ἐρῶν: in tmesis, 'vomiting out'.

1600. Fraenkel follows Wilamowitz in deleting this line. The chief objections are: (1) The family is called both 'Pelopidae' and 'the race of Pleisthenes' in a short space. (2) 1600 is said to anticipate, and therefore to weaken, the curse uttered in 1602. (3) The line is said to interrupt the closely connected actions of ἀμπίπτει and λάκτισμα τιθείς. (4) μόρον ἄφερτον, 'intolerable death' is an unworthy expression. Of these points the first seems unimportant, the second arbitrary (one might say, with as much justification, that 1600 announces a course of action in general (ἐπεύχεται), of which the manner is defined in 1601 and the content in 1602); the third is unconvincing, for there is no need to suppose that λάκτισμα τιθείς is so closely connected with ἀμπίπτει—it is much more closely connected with the *curse* promised in 1600 and given in 1602: he kicks the table over and says '*thus* (just as this table falls over) may the downfall of the family come to pass'. The fourth point deserves greater attention. Fraenkel is surely justified (*a*) in saying that μόρον ἄφερτον here is not supported by *Cho.* 441 f., μόρον κτίσαι μωμένα | ἄφερτον αἰῶνι σῷ, for ἄφερτον there is predicative and governs αἰῶνι σῷ; (*b*) in asking 'is it appropriate to use "mortem intolerabilem", in itself a strange phrase, in this passage where, as the following words show, the speaker is concerned with the extinction of the race and not with the kind of death its individual members are to suffer?' It is indeed an odd expression, both in itself and in relation to its context: but the evidence falls a long way short of what is required to prove an interpolation. It may be that Aeschylus has used without sufficient care an adjective of which he appears particularly fond in the Oresteia: nobody else ever used it, so far as we know, but Aeschylus has it in *Agam.* 386, 395, 564, 1103, 1600, *Cho.* 442, 469, *Eum.* 146, 479.

1601. λάκτισμα with τιθείς, ξυνδίκως with ἀρᾷ, 'giving a kick to the laden board together with his imprecation' (Headlam).

1602. οὕτως: the kicking over of the table symbolizes the overthrow of the house of Atreus.

1603. ἐκ τῶνδε: as a consequence of what I have just told you.

1604. δίκαιος ... ῥαφεύς: cf. 1406, Clytemnestra's δικαίας τέκτονος.

1605. According to the MSS. Aegisthus calls himself his father's *thirteenth* child, a ludicrous multitude in this context; and we should then have to suppose that the authority of Aeschylus was ignored by the later mythographers, who give the number as only two or three. δέκ' is almost certainly corrupt.

1605–6. The narrative is not very clear. It looks as though συνεξελαύνει refers to the banishment described in 1586 ἠνδρηλάτησεν: perhaps we are meant to infer from τυτθὸν ὄντ' ἐν σπαργάνοις that Aegisthus was too small to make the return journey (1587 ff.), and that is how he escaped the fate of the rest of the children—he alone stayed in exile until he grew up (1607).

1607. ἡ δίκη: Aegisthus naturally insists on this point, cf. 1577 δικη-φόρου, 1604 δίκαιος φόνου ῥαφεύς, 1611 τῆς δίκης ἐν ἕρκεσιν. It is indeed the strength of his case: nobody could deny that the surviving son of Thyestes was bound by law, human and divine, to take the life of Atreus' son in return for the murder of Thyestes' family. His position is stronger than Clytemnestra's, whose case leaves a loophole for argument. Here as elsewhere Aeschylus goes out of his way to stress that the conflict is between right and right, not between right and wrong.

1608-9. The sense is well understood by Paley: 'though not present in the house at the time, yet I reached him, as it were, by the plot I laid'.   ἡψάμην ... συνάψας: 362 n.   δυσβουλία: here 'wicked plan'; elsewhere 'ill-advised plan', *ScT* 802, S. *Ant.* 95, 1269.

1610-11. ἐμοί is governed by καλόν: ἰδόντα agrees with the implied subject of κατθανεῖν in the accusative+infinitive construction.

1612. ὑβρίζειν codd., but οὐ σέβω ὑβρίζειν would mean (if it were a possible expression) 'I am not in awe of committing ὕβρις'; cf. *Pers.* 694 σέβομαι προσιδέσθαι. The sense 'I do not approve *that you* (or '*that one*') commit ὕβρις' is not to be extracted from the Greek (even if σέβω could mean 'approve': but it cannot. Fraenkel shows that it can mean something like 'practise (or 'celebrate') *with veneration*'; but his translation here, 'to triumph in misfortune is a thing I care not to practise', omits the essential idea of *veneration*, which indeed the context does not admit). The impossible MS. text is easily emended: 'I have no respect for one who triumphs insolently amid misfortunes.'

1613-16. The Chorus seize upon his admissions that he acted *voluntarily* (ἑκών) and that he *planned* the murder (and is therefore guilty, whether his hand performed the deed or not). They make no attempt to answer the strong point of his case—that his act was justified by the universally recognized right or duty of retaliation.

1615. ἐν δίκῃ: 'in the hour of Justice (or 'Judgement')'; cf. *Cho.* 987, Solon fr. 24. 3, quoted by Fraenkel.

1616. For the freedom in the usage of the adjectives ('curses which threaten the throwing of stones by the people's hand') see 1512 n. Stoning, in which the whole community may take part, was a proper punishment for crimes such as the murder of a king, by which the whole community was injured.

1617-24. When Aegisthus entered, and throughout his opening speech, he could not be sure what the attitude of the Chorus would be: he therefore condescended to explain himself at some length in quite civil language. Now that he is no longer in doubt about their hostility, he replies with cruel and angry threats.

1617–18. 'It is not for *you* to adopt such a tone, sitting as you do at the oar below: the *masters* of the ship are those on the steersman's seat (ζυγῷ); the position of σύ and κρατούντων gives them the required emphasis. For the sense of ζυγόν edd. quote the Homeric ὑψίζυγος (of Zeus), E. *Ph.* 74 f. ἐπεὶ δ' ἐπὶ ζυγοῖς | καθέζετ' ἀρχῆς, οὐ μεθίσταται θρόνων, *Ion* 595 τὸ πρῶτον πόλεος ... ζυγόν; in these places, however, the distinctive nature of the ζυγόν is defined (ὑψι-, ἀρχῆς, τὸ πρῶτον), whereas here it stands alone (though assisted by the sense of κρατούντων). Some special definition might seem to be needed, since there was a category of *rowers* called ζυγῖται (Schol. Ar. *Ran.* 1074), *inferior* in status to the θρανῖται.

δορός: perhaps better with κρατούντων than with ζυγῷ. For δόρυ = 'ship' cf. *Pers.* 411, E. *Hel.* 1611. **κρατούντων** is a generalizing plural (not specifically Aegisthus and Clytemnestra).

1620. εἰρημένον: accus. absolute, 'it having been ordered that ...'.

1621. δεσμόν cod. F, perhaps rightly, a neuter nominative as in 'Hesiod', *Pap. Soc. Ital.* 1935 xi 4 (see Pfeiffer, *Philol.* xcii (1937) 5, n. 9). Hesychius: δεσμόν· οὐδετέρως Ἀττικοί; neuter pl. δεσμά is common (demonstrably *masculine* singulars are rare in Tragedy; *PV* 97, Eur. *Suppl.* 32).

1621–2. We are apparently required to take **καὶ τὸ γῆρας** as object of **διδάσκειν**, 'bonds and the pangs of hunger are most excellent at teaching *even* old age'. The word-order is excessively awkward: perhaps ῥυτῆρες (straps for flogging) for τὸ γῆρας (Maas).

1623. ἰατρομάντεις: used of Apollo in *Eum.* 62 and of his 'son' Apis in *Suppl.* 263. The adj. suits Apollo (ἰατρὸς ὢν καὶ μάντις, Ar. *Plut.* 11) but it is hard to see what the element -μάντεις means here. **οὐχ ὁρᾷς ὁρῶν τάδε**; 'have you eyes, and yet cannot see this?' Cf. S. fr. 923. 2 P., οὐδ' ὁρῶντες εἰσορῶσι τἀμφανῆ, 'though they have eyes, they do not see what is apparent'; [Demo.] 25. 89 ὥστε, τὸ τῆς παροιμίας, ὁρῶντας μὴ ὁρᾶν; *PV* 447 βλέποντες ἔβλεπον μάτην.

1625–7. γύναι is addressed in contempt *to Aegisthus*; because this was not understood, αἰσχύνων was changed to the fem. participle in the MSS. Cf. *Cho.* 304 f. δυοῖν γυναικοῖν (Aegisthus and Clytemnestra) ... θήλεια γὰρ φρήν (of Aegisthus).

τοὺς ἥκοντας is, in the MSS.' text, an inexcusably incoherent accusative; it is very improbable that, in so short a sentence, mere anacoluthon is to be recognized. Casaubon's change to τοῦδ' ἥκοντος is no more than a makeshift, since we cannot explain why it should have been altered to a nonsensical accusative. It is likelier that τοὺς ἥκοντας was originally governed by a participle (μένων, Wieseler) at the end of the line: the misunderstanding of γύναι led to an easy change at αἰσχύνων, but more drastic measures would have been required to deal with a masc. participle at the end of the line.

1626. οἰκουρός as in 1225, 'stay-at-home'; cf. E. *Hkld*. 700 f. αἰσχρὸν γὰρ οἰκούρημα γίγνεται τόδε, | τοὺς μὲν μάχεσθαι τοὺς δὲ δειλίᾳ μένειν; *Od*. 3. 262 ff. ἡμεῖς μὲν γὰρ κεῖθι πολέας τελέοντες ἀέθλους | ἥμεθ', ὁ δ' (sc. Aegisthus) εὔκηλος μυχῷ Ἄργεος κτλ.

1626–7. ἀνδρός . . . ἀνδρί: see 362 n.

1628. Well rendered by Fraenkel, 'the breeders of a race of rueful cries': contrast with this (perhaps deliberate) bombast the dignity of E. *Hipp*. 881 αἰαῖ κακῶν ἀρχηγὸν ἐκφαίνεις λόγον, where the expression is apt and adequate to the emotion.

1629–32. Orpheus *led on* all that heard him, you will be *led off* to execution; *he* delighted with the charm of his voice, *you* infuriate me with your barking.

1629. δὲ γλ-: for the prosody see E. *El*. 1014 n.

1630. ἀπὸ φθογγῆς χαρᾷ: χαρᾷ is instrumental-causal, 'through delight'; ἀπό in ἀπὸ φθογγῆς gives, as often, the source from which an action or condition is derived (*source* is sometimes, as here, hardly distinguishable from *agency*). The usage is closely similar to that in 1643 f. below, ἀπὸ ψυχῆς κακῆς . . . ἠνάριζες, and to that in 1302 above τλήμων οὖσ' ἀπ' εὐτόλμου φρενός; cf. also ἀπὸ γλώσσης in Hes. *op*. 322. There is no need to change ἀπό to ὑπό (Margoliouth) or anything else (πάντα που, Rees in *CR* lxi (1947) 74, where που is wrongly placed).

1631. ἐξορίνας: sc. τὸν ἀκούοντα.

1633. ὡς δή = *quasi vero*, ironical (*Gk. Particles*, p. 229).

1634–5. οὐκ . . . οὐκ: for the redundant second negative cf. Hdt. 7. 101. 2 οὐ γὰρ . . . οὐκ ἀξιόμαχοί εἰσι, Xen. *Anab*. 3. 2. 25 δέδοικα μὴ . . . μὴ ἐπιλαθώμεθα; K.-G. ii. 205 f.

1636. The thought is clearer than the expression: the Chorus having said 'you *planned* the deed but dared not *do* it', Aegisthus replies 'Yes, because *deception* was clearly the woman's part.'—δολῶσαι does not, as the word itself would suggest, refer to the *planning*, but to the fact that the *deed* involved the use of trickery.

1637. 'I was a suspect enemy from of old.'

1638. For the position of **δέ** between preposition+article and noun, a great rarity, see *Gk. Particles*, p. 186 (to be corrected from Fraenkel, p. 776, n. 1).

1640. βαρείαις: ζεύγλαις must be supplied from ζεύξω, a most unusual sort of ellipse; none of the examples quoted by Wilamowitz on E. *H*. 681 is properly comparable.   **οὔ τι μή**: οὐ μή of vehement denial elsewhere introduces a finite tense, not as here an adjective (+adjectival participle). It is an easy extension of usage, as Sidgwick says; there is no need to alter the text (οὔ τι μοι Pauw, οὔ τι μήν Wieseler, both good in themselves).   **σειραφόρον**: the point lies in the contrast between the *yoked horse* (ζεύξω) and the *trace-horse*. The σειραφόρος, though in general it had lighter work than the yoked horses, was called upon to exert great strength in taking the chariot round the bend (S. *El.* 721 ff.; Hdt. 3. 102. 3): that is why σειραφόρος is often applied metaphorically to a person who gives help when special exertions are necessary (842 above; S. *Ant.* 140). The trace-horse is specially fed on barley (κριθαί), and is likely to be almost too high-spirited (*Il.* 6. 506, Sophocles fr. 876 P.; cf. Ar. *Nub.* 1300). Aegisthus says in effect: the disobedient man will find himself in the unenviable position of being under the *yoke*; trace-horses are too mettlesome, and he will find that he has no such privileged position— indeed he will be unlike them in another respect, viz. he will have no high feeding; hunger shall teach him discipline.

1643. ἀπό: 1630 n.

1644. σύν: Why did you not kill him with your own hand? Why must a woman, *in partnership with you* (σύν, cf. Wilamowitz on E. *H.* 832), do the killing? Cf. E. *Or.* 1089 συγκατέκτανον, said by Pylades with reference to his share in the killing of Clytemnestra. The sentence is weakened by the change (in itself unlikely) of σύν to νυν. Aegisthus has claimed the full credit for the deed: it is therefore only to be expected that the Chorus will retort 'then why did you let a woman *associate herself* with you?', even though they may think that Clytemnestra's part was much the more important.

1645. μίασμα: in apposition to γυνή simply, not to the content of the clause ἀλλὰ . . . ἔκτεινε as a whole.

1646. ἄρα is positive, not questioning; cf. the same use in a similar context in *Cho.* 435 (Maas).

1648. ἀμφοῖν τοῖνδε: 'The coryphaeus has turned away from Aegisthus, and is speaking . . . "aside" or (in terms of Aeschylean ideas) to the gods . . . . This sentence has something of the nature of a prayer', Fraenkel.   **παγκρατής**: here, as Fraenkel says, probably not 'all-powerful' but 'all-victorious'.

1649. δοκεῖς: 'you have a mind to . . .', as in 16 above.   **γνώσῃ τάχα**: a common idiom, 'you will soon learn your lesson'.

1650–3. The clue to the correct distribution of these lines is given by the one certain fact which emerges from the tangle of probables and possibles—*that the Chorus do not wear swords*: therefore 1651 must be spoken by Aegisthus, hence 1652 by the Chorus, 1653 by Aegisthus. This is a welcome sequence, for Clytemnestra's intervention at 1654, being, as it is, addressed to Aegisthus and intended to interrupt him in action, now follows naturally on a line spoken by him. Thus only 1650 is left in doubt: not a very serious doubt, for it is not very likely that Aegisthus, as portrayed by Aeschylus, would summon his bodyguard (λοχῖται, *Cho.* 768) with the adjective φίλοι. On the other hand it is natural that the Chorus should address each other in these terms (λόχος may signify the 'company' of a Chorus: *ScT* 110 f.,

ἴδετε παρθένων ἱκέσιον λόχον; *Eum.* 46, the Chorus of Furies is a
θαυμαστὸς λόχος, though there the notion 'ambush' may be present;
cf. also *Eum.* 1026. λοχῖται here probably has a military connotation,
appropriate to the present context, where they have to stand and fight.

On the crucial question, whether the Chorus wear swords, see
Thomson's note and Fraenkel's reply to it. The consequences of the
conclusion that they do wear swords would be so unfortunate that it
must be rejected absolutely. Old men did not wear swords, either in
contemporary life or in the conventions of Tragedy. Yet here we
should have to suppose that these particular old men, ἰσχὺν ἰσόπαιδα
νέμοντες ἐπὶ σκήπτροις, who cannot move without a staff to lean on,
entered (at 40 above) *with swords* as well as staves, wearing them
throughout the play solely for the sake of this very brief moment at
the end, in defiance of convention, and to the wonder and wild sur-
mise of the audience. It is inconceivable that Aeschylus should
deliberately have involved himself in so startlingly obtrusive an in-
congruity for the sake of a moment so brief, so long-postponed, and
so indecisive. (The opinion that they do wear swords may well be
thought self-refuting if it leads to the conclusion that these incongruous, unconventional, and almost if not quite unemployed objects
might have been 'practically non-existent for the minds of the spectators', as Fraenkel puts it, 'who are fully occupied in taking in what
is being offered to their eyes, their ears, and their minds'; among the
objects being offered to their eyes there is one, we must hope, which
they will not notice—the most incongruous and inexplicable of all—
the *swords* worn by the old men throughout the play, for no apparent
reason.)

1652. πρόκωπος: Aegisthus has ordered his bodyguard to prepare ξίφος
πρόκωπον, 'sword with hilt forward'; this means that the sword,
which before use hangs more or less perpendicularly, is now held
more or less horizontally with the hilt projecting forward ready for
the act of drawing. The Chorus replies 'I too am πρόκωπος, hilt-
forward', meaning that they are holding their staves at the ready as
if they were swords. Both the idea and the phraseology are odd, and
it may well be that those scholars are in the right who suppose that
some different word has been ousted by an erroneous repetition of
πρόκωπ- from the line above.

1653. δεχομένοις = 'accepting the omen'; S. *El.* 668 ἐδεξάμην τὸ ῥηθέν,
Hdt. 8. 115. 1 δεξαμένοις τὸ ῥηθέν, 9. 91. 2 δέκομαι τὸν οἰωνόν. After
θανεῖν codd. have σε: but λέγεις θανεῖν σε means 'you say that you
died' (not 'you speak of your death', referring to a *future* death).
Sense must be restored by writing γε for σε: 'we accept the omen
when you say " θανεῖν " (when you use the expression "to die")'; γε,
as often, underlines a word quoted from a previous speaker (*Gk.
Particles*, pp. 129 f.).   **τὴν τύχην δ' αἱρούμεθα:** this obscure

phrase may mean something like 'we gladly welcome (lit. 'take upon ourselves, as a matter of choice') this (τήν) hazard', i.e. we welcome what is happening (the trial of strength with the Chorus).

1655. 'Even these things (the grievous things so far suffered and done) are many to reap, a wretched harvest'; for the infinitive after πολλά cf. Thuc. vi 34. 4 τὸ δὲ πέλαγος αὐτοῖς πολὺ περαιοῦσθαι, quoted by Barrett ap. Fraenkel (Addenda, p. 832; for other renderings see Fraenkel, p. 791).

1656. Continuative δέ γε or δὲ . . . γε is very rare in Tragedy, commoner in Comedy and Prose (Gk. Particles, pp. 155 f.): hence πημονῆς ἅλις δ' ὑπάρχει Hermann, perhaps rightly.   **μηδὲν αἱματώμεθα:** if the reading is correct, = 'let us by no means stain ourselves with blood'; μηκέθ' (Auratus), 'let us no longer . . .', would be more suitable in the circumstances.

1657. στείχετε δ' οἱ codd.: Ahrens's conjecture, στείχετ' αἰδοῖοι, supposing the common ε for αι, and haplography of οι, is so neat palaeographically that we may be tempted to overlook its deficiency in sense: it is in the highest degree improbable that Clytemnestra should address her enemies by this exceptionally respectful term (αἰδοῖος in addresses is anything but a commonplace, as Fraenkel shows); that she has not modified her attitude towards the Chorus is plain from the harsh words ματαίων ὑλαγμάτων 1672. There is no attractive conjecture to record.

1657–8. πρὸς δόμους πεπρωμένους τούσδε | πρὶν παθεῖν ἔρξαντες (cod. F: -αντα Tr.) καιρὸν χρὴν τάδ' ὡς ἐπραξάμην codd. This is incurably corrupt: (1) πεπρ. τούσδε is unmetrical nonsense; deletion of τούσδε is not enough, for the 'houses' of the Chorus could not possibly be described as 'predestined'. The words have presumably replaced something very different. (2) καιρόν is unmanageable; good sense is given by πρὸς δόμους· ⟨κρεῖσσον φρονεῖν, suppl. Fraenkel⟩ | πρὶν παθεῖν ἔρξαντα· κυροῦν χρὴ τάδ' κτλ., 'better to come to one's senses before acting and suffering accordingly; these things must be confirmed as we have done them', i.e. what is done is done, and must be recognized and ratified; you will only come to harm if you rush into indiscreet action.

1659. 'If of these troubles there should be *enough*, we should welcome it': this would be a grotesque way of expressing what the context requires, 'if no further trouble occurs, we should be content' (Sidgwick). μόχθων ἅλις would be normal for 'No more troubles!', 'Enough of troubles!', i.e. 'Spare me further troubles!'; but then to include this in a conditional clause as the subject of the verb, εἰ 'μόχθων ἅλις' γένοιτο, 'if "enough of troubles!" might come to pass', is surely beyond the pale of intelligible speech. Possibly ἄκος (Donaldson).

1660. χηλῆ: the comparison of misfortune to a beast of prey, pouncing upon its victim, is quite common, cf. 1175 above, *Pers.* 515 f., *Eum.* 372 f., S. *Ant.* 1272 f., 1345 f., *OT* 263, 1300 ff., 1311.

1661. εἴ τις ἀξιοῖ μαθεῖν: these men have said contemptuous things about women : now here they are behaving like fools, and it takes a woman to bring them to their senses.

1662. There is no earlier example of the exclamatory infinitive *without the article*; also *Eum.* 837; see Stevens, *CQ* xxxi (1937) 187.

ἀπανθίσαι: another unsolved problem. '*Cull the flowers* of a foolish tongue', Sidgwick, but then ἐμοί is hard to interpret. ἀκοντίσαι (Wakefield) gives a good sense but is too far from the tradition.

1663. 'Putting their fortune to the test.'

1664. Once more, this (or any other) restoration can only be regarded as a reasonable makeshift in a hopeless situation.

1667. δαίμων γ' Headlam, which would be a slight improvement.

1668. 'To feed on hope' was a quasi-proverbial expression ; E. *Ph.* 396 αἱ δ' ἐλπίδες βόσκουσι φυγάδας, ὡς λόγος, and other illustrations in Fraenkel, p. 799.

1669. πρᾶσσε: cf. *Il.* 22. 181 ἔρδ', ἀτὰρ οὔ τοι κτλ., *PV* 939 (also S. *Ant.* 768) δράτω.   **πιαίνου:** in defiant reply to ἐλπίδας σιτουμένους, 'very well, *we* may starve : *you* go ahead and get as fat as you like, defiling Justice, since you have the opportunity' (ἐπεὶ πάρα, perhaps with the implication '*while* you have the opportunity').

1670. 'You will pay me amends, as a return for your folly', or simply 'because of your folly': χάριν as in S. *OT* 887 f. κακά νιν ἕλοιτο μοῖρα δυσπότμου χάριν χλιδᾶς. (There is no need for Wecklein's χρόνῳ (for χάριν), introduced to normalize the usage of ἄποινα, which elsewhere takes a plain genitive (cf. 1420 above), and to bring in—what is wholly superfluous—an explicit reference to the *future*.)

1672–3. The MSS. end two syllables short in both lines.   ἐγώ and καλῶς are restored from the Schol. vet. in Triclinius: ἐγώ, φησί, καὶ σὺ κρατοῦντες τῶνδε τῶν δωμάτων διαθησόμεθα τὰ καθ' αὑτοὺς καλῶς. Yet it is by no means satisfactory, as Fraenkel shows, merely to add these two words to the ends of the lines, for (1) an object for θήσομεν καλῶς would be very welcome, indeed seems almost indispensable ; (2) τῶνδε is suspect, since 'in the only two passages in Aeschylus where δώματα has a deictic pronoun attached to it, the distinction made is an indispensable one' (Fraenkel). It is a natural inference, that τῶνδε (like τούσδε in 1657 and τοῖσδε in 1481) is an intruder here, and that it has ousted an object for θήσομεν καλῶς, e.g. πάντα, τἆλλα. Unfortunately the inference would involve us in further change, for the word-order θήσομεν, κρατοῦντε, πάντα, δωμάτων, καλῶς is obviously intolerable. Hence Fraenkel expels τῶνδε and makes θήσομεν and δωμάτων change places : but that leaves us so far from our starting-point in the text that we may well prefer either to leave the whole matter in suspense or to tolerate the anomalous (but not otherwise offensive) τῶνδε and the objectless θήσομεν καλῶς.

THE METRES

Abbreviations

dact = dactyl, $-\cup\cup$ $-\cup\cup$, capable of the forms $-\cup\cup$ and $--$.

anap = anapaest, $\cup\cup-$ $\cup\cup-$, capable of the forms $\cup\cup-$, $-\cup\cup$, and $--$. Anapaestic runs may include, and generally close in, an abbreviated form of the anapaestic dimeter, called **paroemiac**, $\cup\cup-$ $\cup\cup-$ $\cup\cup-$ $-$.

ion = ionic, $\cup\cup--$ $\cup\cup--$.

anacr = anacreontic, $\cup\cup-\cup$ $-\cup--$, commonly associated with the ionic.

cr = cretic, $-\cup-$. This may be 'syncopated', to produce

sp = spondee, $--$ (i.e. $-(\underset{\cup}{)}-$).

The cretic may be accompanied by *syllaba anceps*, i.e. a syllable to whose quantity the metre is indifferent. This variable syllable may *precede* the cretic, forming

ia = iambic, $\underset{\cdot}{\smile}-\cup-$: or it may *follow* it, forming

tr = trochaic, $-\cup-\underset{\cdot}{\smile}$.

The cretic is often prolonged, to form

lec = lecythion, $-\cup-\cup-\cup-$, a conventional name for this common unit. It has an abbreviated form, cr ba $-\cup-\cup--$ (called **ithyphallicum**).

Commonly associated with these forms of the cretic is

ba = bacchiac, $\cup--$.

Closely resembling the cretic, and commonly associated with it in lyrical metres is

cho = choriambic, $-\cup\cup-$.

A very common unit in lyrical metres is one for which there is no ancient name, and unfortunately no convenient modern one, $-\cup\cup-\cup-$, a combination of choriamb and cretic. When preceded by *syllaba anceps*, this is called

tel = telesillean, $\underset{\cdot}{\smile}-\cup\cup-\cup-$, with abbreviated form $\underset{\cdot}{\smile}-\cup\cup--$ (the so-called *reizianum*; without the *anceps*, $-\cup\cup--$, the *adonius*). In early lyrical poetry (esp. Sappho and Alcaeus), the unit $-\cup\cup-\cup-$ may be preceded by two syllabae ancipites, forming

glyc = glyconic, $\underset{\cdot}{\smile}\underset{\cdot}{\smile}-\cup\cup-\cup-$: in Tragedy, the beginnings $-\cup$, $--$, $\cup-$ are much commoner than $\cup\cup$; and the first syllable is often a true long syllable, capable of resolution into two shorts,

⏑⏑–⏑⏑–⏑– (this is a different type of 'glyconic', formed by prolonging cretic to choriambic to cretic, –⏑– (⏑⏑– (⏑–, not from two *ancipites* + –⏑⏑–⏑–).

The glyconic has an abbreviated form,

pher = pherecratean, ⏓̆ ⏓ –⏑⏑–– (i.e. ⏓̆ ⏓ –⏑⏑–(⏓)–).

The telesillean and glyconic may be lengthened by one syllable, forming (*a*) ⏓–⏑⏑–⏑––, a common verse for which, in this metrical context, there is no convenient modern name, and (*b*)

hipp = hipponactean, ⏓⏓–⏑⏑–⏑––.

dochm = dochmiac, a verse of obscure origin, very seldom found outside the dramatic poets. Its scheme is ⏓⏥⏥⏓⏥, i.e. *syll. anceps*, two long syllables, *syll. anceps*, one long syllable, with 32 theoretically possible variations: but half this number occurs in practice seldom or not at all, and nearly three-quarters of the total number of extant dochmiacs take only three forms, ⏑⏥–⏑– (commonest), ⏑––⏑– (second commonest), and –⏥–⏑– (third): next commonest, but a long way behind, come ⏑⏥–––, ⏑⏥⏥⏥⏑–, ⏑⏥⏥⏥⏑⏥, –⏥–––, –––⏑–.

anapaests: 40–103

Parodos 104–257

str. 104–21 = ant. 122–39: mainly dactylic

104	–⏓̆⏓̆ –⏑⏑ –⏑⏑ –⏑⏑ –⏑⏑ ––	6 dact
	–⏑⏑ –⏑⏑ –⏑⏑ –⏑⏑ ––	5 dact
	–– –– –– –⏑⏑ ––	5 dact
	⏑–⏑– –⏑⏑ –⏑⏑ –⏑⏑ ––	ia 6 dact
110	–⏑⏑ ––	
	–– –⏑⏑ –⏑⏑ –⏓̆⏓̆	8 dact
	–⏑⏑ –– –⏑⏑ –⏑	
	–– –⏑⏑ –⏑⏑ –⏑⏑	8 dact
115	–⏑⏑ –⏑⏑ –⏑⏑ ––	
	⏑–⏑– –⏑⏑ –⏑⏑ –⏑⏑ ––	ia 4 dact
	–– –⏑⏑ –⏓̆	3 dact
	–⏑⏑ –⏑⏑ –⏑⏑ –⏑⏑ –⏑⏑ ––	6 dact
120	⏐–⏑– ⏑–⏑–	2 ia
	–⏑⏑ –⏑⏑ –⏑⏑ –– ––	5 dact

In 122 a spondee (ant.) corresponds to a dactyl (str.); in 129 = 111 the same feature is observed, unless δημιοπληθἔᾱ (O. Müller) is written for -θῇ in 129.

In 113 and 131, and again in 135, the line ends with *syllaba brevis in elemento longo*, i.e. a syllable short by prosody is counted as being long, standing at the end of the line in a place where metre requires a long syllable.

epode 140–59: mainly dactylic

140 ∪–∪– ––∪–	2 ia
∪–∪– –∪∪– ∪––	ia cho ba
–– –∪∪ –∪∪ ––	4 dact
–– –∪∪ –∪––	2 dact+clausula
	–∪––
–– –– –∪∪ ––	4 dact
145 –∪∪ –∪∪ –∪∪ –∪∪ ⟨––⟩	5 dact
∪–∪– ∪∪∪– ∪–∪	ia cr ba
–∪∪ –∪∪ –∪∪ –∪∪ –∪∪ –∪∪ ––	7 dact
150 –– –∪∪ –∪∪ –∪∪ –∪∪ –∪∪ ––	7 dact
–– –∪∪ –∪∪ ––	
–∪∪ –– –∪∪ –∪∪ –∪	} 9 dact
155 –∪∪ –∪∪ –– ––˙ –∪∪ ––	6 dact
–∪∪ –– –∪∪ –∪∪ ˙–∪∪ ––	6 dact
–∪∪ –– –∪∪ –– –∪∪ ––	6 dact
–∪∪ –∪	2 dact
–∪∪ –∪∪ –∪∪ –– ––	5 dact

143. Dactylic runs in lyrical poetry often end –∪––: see Fraenkel, *Rh. Mus.* lxxii (1918) 166 ff.

146. Scanning παιανα (the final syllable is *brevis in longo*, see note on 113 above), cf. Bacchylides 17 (16) 129 παιανιξαν.

str. 160–7 = ant. 168–75: mainly trochaic

–– –∪–∪–∪–	sp lec
–∪–∪–∪–	lec
–∪–∪–∪–	lec
–∪–∪–∪–	lec
–∪–∪–∪–	lec
–∪∪ –∪∪ –∪∪ –∪∪ ––	5 dact
–∪–∪–∪–	lec

str. 176–83 = ant. 184–91: trochaic

—∪—∪—∪—	lec
—∪—∪—∪—	lec
—∪—∪—∪—	lec
— — —∪—∪—∪—	sp lec
—∪— —∪— —∪—	3 cr
—∪—∪—∪—	lec
—∪—∪—∪— ∪— —	lec ba
—∪—∪—∪—	lec

str. 192–204 = ant. 205–17: iambic and choriambic

＼ ∪—∪— —∪— ∪— —	ia cr ba
∪—∪— —∪— ∪— —	ia cr ba
∪—∪—	ia
∪̆—∪— —∪— ∪—∪̆	ia cr ba
∪— — —∪— ∪— —	ba cr ba
∪̰—∪— —∪— ∪— —	ia cr ba
—∪—∪—∪—	lec
—∪∪— ∪— —	cho ba
—∪∪— ∪— —	cho ba
—∪∪— —∪∪—	2 cho
—∪∪— —∪∪—	2 cho
—∪∪— —∪∪—	2 cho
—∪∪— ∪— —	cho ba

208. αγαλμᾱ: *brevis in longo*, see note on 113 above.

str. 218–27 = ant. 228–37: iambic and choriambic

∪—∪— —∪— ∪— —	ia cr ba
∪—∪— —∪— ∪— —	ia cr ba
∪—∪ᴗ ∪—∪—	2 ia
∪—∪— —∪— ∪— —	ia cr ba
∪—∪— —∪— ∪— —	ia cr ba
∪—∪ᴗ ∪— — ∪— —	ia ba ba
∪— — ∪—∪—	ba ia
—∪∪— ∪—∪—	cho ia
—∪∪— ∪— —	cho ba
∪∪— ∪— —	cho ba

str. 238–46 = ant. 247–57: iambic

∪–∪– –∪– –∪–	ia cr cr
∪–∪– –∪– ∪–⏓	ia cr ba
∪–∪– –∪–	ia cr
–∪–∪–∪– ∪––	lec ba
∪–∪– –∪–∪–∪–	ia lec
∪–∪– –∪–	ia cr
∪–∪– –∪– ∪––	ia cr ba
∪–∪– –∪– –∪– –∪–	ia 3 cr
∪–∪– –∪– ∪––	ia cr ba
–∪∪– ∪––	cho ba

237. The first line of the new stanza continues and completes a sentence begun in the former one. This is rare in Tragic *stasima*; the closest parallels are *Suppl.* 581–2, *ScT* 749–50, E. *Hec.* 647–8, *Rhes.* 351, though in only one of them does the end of an antistrophe run into the beginning of a strophe. Elsewhere the new stanza, though continuing a sentence, yet possesses a much greater self-sufficiency: *Agam.* 175, *Pers.* 870, S. *Ant.* 1137, *Phil.* 690, 706, E. *Hec.* 942.

238 f. χεουσᾱ | εβαλλ': see Appendix, p. 239.

First Stasimon 355–488

355–66: anapaests

str. 367–84 = ant. 385–402: iambic, with glyconic coda

∪–– –∪– ∪––	ba cr ba
∪–– –∪– ∪––	ba cr ba
∪–∪– ∪–∪– ∪––	2 ia ba
∪–∪– –∪– –∪–	ia 2 cr
∪–∪– –∪–	ia cr
∪–∪– –∪–	ia cr
∪– – –∪–	ba cr
∪–– –∪–	ba cr
∪–– –∪– ∪––	ba cr ba
∪–– –∪– ∪––	ba cr ba
∪–∪– –∪– –∪–	ia 2 cr
–∪– ∪––	cr ba
–∪∪– ∪––	cho ba

–⏓–∪∪––	pher
–⏐–∪∪–⏓	pher
–⏓–∪∪–∪–	glyc
–∪–∪∪––	pher

The stanza ends in a clearly marked-off period of glyconic metre: cf.
416–19, 452–5 below, and *Suppl.* 638–42, 663–6, 683–7, E. *H.* 359–63,
389–93, 419–24. Note the *brevis in longo* at the end of 380, and the hiatus
at the end of 368, 377.

str. 403–19 = ant. 420–36: similar to the preceding

◡–◡– –◡– –◡–	ia 2 cr
◡–◡– –◡–	ia cr
–◡– ◡––	cr ba
◡–◡– ◡–◡– ◡–◡–	3 ia
◡–– –◡◡	ba cr
◡–◡– ◡–◡– ◡–◡–	3 ia
◡–◡– –◡– ◡––	ia cr ba
◡–◡– –◡–◡–◡–	ia lec
◡–◡– –◡–◡–◡◡̄	ia lec
◡–◡– –◡– –◡–◡–◡–	ia cr lec
–◡–◡–◡–	lec
◡–◡– –◡–	ia cr
–◡– –◡– ◡––	2 cr ba
–––◡◡–◡̄	pher
–◡–◡◡–◡̱	pher
–◡̱–◡◡–◡̱	glyc
–◡̄–◡◡––	pher

str. 437–55 = ant. 456–74: similar to the preceding

◡–◡– –◡– –◡–	ia 2 cr
–◡– –◡–◡–◡–	cr lec
◡–◡– –◡–	ia cr
◡–◡– –◡–	ia cr
–◡–◡–◡–	lec
–◡–◡–◡–	lec
–◡–◡–◡–	lec
◡–◡– ◡–◡–	2 ia
◡–◡– ◡–◡–	2 ia
◡̄–◡– ◡–◡–	2 ia
–◡◡– ◡–◡–	cho ia
–◡◡– ◡–◡–	cho ia
–◡◡– ◡–◡–	cho ia

−∪∪− ∪−−	cho ba
−−−∪∪−−	pher
−−−∪∪−−	pher
−−−∪∪−∪−	glyc
−∪−∪∪−−	pher

448–51. As good a case can be made for dividing thus: αλλοτριας διαι γυναικος | ταδε σιγα τις βαυζει | φθονερον δ' υπ' αλγος ερπει | προδικοις ατρειδαις ||, i.e. a type of hipponactean, −∪∪−∪−∪−− (see Fraenkel, p. 185), followed by two anacreontics, closed by a syncopated catalectic anacreontic, ∪∪−∪ −− = ∪∪−∪(∪̭)−(−̭).

pode 475–88: iambic

∪−∪− −∪−	ia cr
∪−∪− −∪−	ia cr
−∪−∪−∪−	lec
∪−∪− ∪−∪− ∪−∪−	3 ia
∪−∪− ∪−∪− ∪−∪−	3 ia
∪−∪− −∪−	ia cr
∪−∪− −∪−∪−∪−	ia lec
−∪−∪−∪−	lec
∪−∪− −∪−	ia cr
∪−∪− −∪−∪−∪−	ia lec
∪∪∪∪− ∪−∪∿ ∪∿∪∪−	3 ia
∪∪∪∪− ∪∪∿∪−	2 ia
∪−∪− −∪−∪−∪−	ia lec

Note the resolved long syllables in 485–6, a rare phenomenon in the lyrical iambics of Aeschylus; cf. 766 ff. below.

Second Stasimon 681–781

str. 681–98 = ant. 699–716: iambic, ionic, glyconic

−∪−∪−∪−		lec
−∪−∪−∪−		lec
−∪−∪−∪− −∪−		lec cr
−∪−∪−∪−		lec
685	−∪−∪−∪−	lec
−∪∪− ∪−∪−		cho ia
−∪∪− ∪−∪− ⊃		[see note below]
∪∪−∪ −∪∪−		[see note below]

690 ∪∪−− ∪∪−−	ion
∪∪−∪ −∪−−	anacr
∪∪−∪ −∪−−	anacr
∪∪−− ∪∪−∪ −∪−−	ion anacr
695 ∪∪−∪ −∪−−	anacr
−−−∪∪−∪−	glyc
−∪∪− ∪−−	cho ba
∪∪∪−∪∪−−	pher

688–9. On the former of these two verses, cho + ia + −, taking a 'hipponactean' form, see Fraenkel, p. 185. With the latter, ∪∪−∪ −∪∪−, compare 748 below, πομπᾳ διος ξενιον, −−∪ −∪∪−, also in an ionic context: it is to be understood as a form of anacreontic, with −∪∪− for −∪−− in the second half. There is no other example of the kind in ionic contexts in Tragedy except E. *Ph.* 1515 ∪∪−∪−∪∪− | ∪∪−− ∪∪−− κτλ. (or ∪∪−−−∪∪−|, if ορνῖc).

696–7. The metre is uncertain because of textual corruption.

str. 717–26 = ant. 727–36: mainly glyconic

∪−−∪∪−∪−	glyc
−∪−∪∪−∪−	glyc
−∪−∪∪−∪	pher
720 −∪∪−∪∪−−	⎫
−∪∪−∪∪−∪	⎬ see note below
−∪∪−∪∪−−	⎭
∪∪−∪−∪−	lec
∪∪−∪−∪∪	lec
−∪−∪∪−∪−	glyc
−∪−∪∪−−	pher

720–2. −∪∪−∪∪−+∪ is a very common unit in lyrical verse, here evidently meant to be a variation on the pherecratean, −−−∪∪−−; it would be misleading to call it 'dactylic' in this context.

str. 737–49 = ant. 750–62: iambic, ionic, with some glyc. types

∪−∪− −∪−∪−∪−	ia lec
∪−− ∪−∪−	ba ia
−∪− ∪−−	cr ba
∪−− −∪− ∪−−	ba cr ba
−∪∪− ∪−∪−	cho ia

$-\cup-\cup\cup-\cup--$	hipp
$\cup\cup--\ \ \cup\cup--$	ion
$\cup\cup-\cup\ -\cup--$	anacr
$\cup\cup--\ \ \cup\cup--$	ion
$\cup\cup--\ \ \cup\cup--$	ion
$--\cup\ -\cup\cup-$	[see note on 689]
$-\cup-\cup\cup--$	pher

str. 763–72 = ant. 773–81: iambic, choriambic

$\cup-\cup-\ -\cup-$	ia cr
$-\cup-\ -\cup-$	2 cr
$-\cup-\cup-\cup-$	lec
$\cup-\cup-\ \cup\cup\cup-$	2 ia
$\cup-\cup-\ \cup-\cup-$	2 ia
$-\cup\cup-\ \cup\cup\cup\cup$	2 ia
$\cup\cup\cup-\ \cup-\cup-$	2 ia
$-\cup\cup-\ \cup--$	cho ba
$-\cup\cup-\ \cup--$	cho ba

The text in mid-stanza is gravely corrupt. Other schemes of line-division may be adopted.

anapaests: 782–809

Third Stasimon 975–1034

str. 975–87 = ant. 988–1000: mainly trochaic

$-\cup-\cup-\cup-$	lec
$-\cup-\cup-\cup-$	lec
$-\cup-\cup-\cup-\ \cup--$	lec ba
$-\cup\cup\ -\cup\cup\ -\cup\cup\ -\cup\cup\ --$	5 dact
$-\cup-\cup-\cup-$	lec
$-\cup-\cup-\cup-$	lec
$-\cup-\ -\cup-$	2 cr
$-\cup-\cup-\cup-$	lec
$\cup-\cup-\ --\cup-\ \cup-\cup\cup$	3 ia
$-\cup-\ \langle-?\rangle\ -\cup-$	2 cr, *or* tr cr
$-\cup-\cup-\cup\underset{\smile}{\cup}$	lec
$-\cup-\cup-\cup-$	lec

990. On the prosody of ὑμνῳδει, see the Commentary.

The fourth line is not very aptly called 'dactylic', for in this context it is evidently meant to be a variation of the preceding line, lecythion+ bacchiac, with which it is identical except in having double instead of single shorts between the long syllables.

str. 1001–17 = ant. 1018–34

⏑⏑– ⏑⏑– ⏑⏑–	3 cr
⏑⏑––, ⏑⏑⏑⏑ ⏑⏑–	ion anap?
⏑⏑– ⏑⏑– ⏑⏑– –	anap (paroemiac)
–⏑⏑–⏑⏑–	hemiepes [see note]
1005 –⏑⏑–⏑⏑–	hemiepes
–⏑⏑–⏑⏑–⏑–⏑	2 dact+clausula
	–⏑––
–⏑–⏑–⏑–	lec
–⏑–⏑–⏑–	lec
–⏑–⏑–⏑–	lec
–⏑–⏑–⏑–	lec
–⏑–⏑–⏑̣–	lec
–⏑–⏑–⏑̣–	lec
–– –⏑⏑ –⏑⏑ –⏑⏑	8 dactyls
–⏑⏑ –⏑⏑ –⏑⏑ ––	
–⏑–⏑–⏑–	lec

The opening is gravely corrupt in the strophe. With the metre, compare *Cho.* 806 ff. ⏑⏑–⏑⏑–⏑⏑––, followed by ⏑⏑⏑–⏑⏑⏑–⏑⏑––; *Eum.* 328 ff. ⏑⏑–⏑⏑–⏑⏑–⏑⏑–⏑⏑–⏑⏑––.

1004. 'hemiepes' is the conventional term for –⏑⏑–⏑⏑–, 'half an Epic verse'. In 1006 the dactylic run ends in –⏑–– (see note on 143 above). The unit –⏑⏑–⏑⏑–⏑–– is common in various contexts, and is conventionally called 'the alcaic decasyllable' (last line of an alcaic stanza, *aut Lacedaemonium Tarentum*)—a description which is less appropriate in dactylic contexts than in some others, where it may represent a prolongation of the common –⏑⏑–⏑––, choriambic+ bacchiac.

Amoibaion 1072–1177

str. I. 1072–5 = ant. I. 1076–9

Cass.	⏑⏑–⏑––	cr ba
	––⏑– ––	ia sp
Cho.	2 ia trimeters	

Text and metre uncertain. 1072 perhaps ὀτοτοτοτοῖ πόποι δᾶ ∪∪∪−
∪−−, ia ba; in 1073, 1077 cod. M has ωπολλον ωπολλον, but in 1080, 1085
απολλον απολλον; codd. FTr have the latter in all four places. If απολλον
απολλον is read, it is best taken (with Schroeder) as ∪−− ∪−−, 2
bacchiacs, the final syllable of the first απολλον being long (*brevis in
longo*), a licence which would have to be justified by assuming a pause
after it.

str. II. 1080–4 = ant. II. 1085–9

Cass.	−−∪− −−	ia sp
	∪−− ∪−−∪−	ba dochm
	∪̲−∪− ∪−∪− ∪̲−∪−	3 ia
Cho.	2 ia trimeters	

str. III. 1090–4 = ant. III. 1095–9

Cass.	−∪∪−∪− −∪∪−∪∪̲	2 dochm
	−∪∪∪∪ ∪−∪−	2 ia
	−−∪− −−∪− −−∪−	3 ia
Cho.	2 ia trimeters	

Note the *brevis in longo*, accompanied by hiatus, at the end of 1090.
συνιστορᾶ | αυτοφονα. The strophe is corrupt in the latter half of 1091.

str. IV. 1100–6 = ant. IV. 1107–13

Cass.	∪−∪− ∪∪∪−∪−	ia dochm
	∪∪∪̲∪∪−∪∪̲	lec
	∪̲−∪− ∪̲−∪− ∪−∪−	3 ia
	∪−− ∪−− ∪−− ∪−−	4 ba
	∪∪∪⏑̅∪−	dochm
Cho.	2 ia trimeters	

The dochmiac responsion 1104 ∪∪∪−∪− = 1111 ∪∪∪∪∪∪− recurs
in 1121 = 1132 below (and elsewhere).

str. V. 1114–24 = ant. V. 1125–35

Cass.	∪−∪− ∪∪∪−∪−	ia dochm
	−−∪− ∪−−	ia ba
	∪̅−∪− ∪−∪− ∪−∪∪̅	3 ia

‿–‿– ‿‿–‿–	ia dochm
‿‿–‿– –‿– –‿–	dochm 2 cr
Cho. 2 ia trimeters	
‿‿–‿– ‿‿‿‿–	2 dochm
‿––‿– ‿––‿–	2 dochm
‿‿–‿– –‿––	dochm tr
‿–‿– –‿–	ia cr

str. VI. 1136–45 = ant. VI. 1146–55

Cass. ‿‿– ‿–– ‿‿–‿–	cr ba dochm
‿‿–‿– ‿‿–‿–	2 dochm
2 ia trimeters	
Cho. ‿‿–‿– ‿‿–‿–	2 dochm
‿––‿–	dochm
‿‿‿‿ –‿– ––	2 cr sp
‿‿–‿– –‿– –‿–	dochm 2 cr
‿‿–‿– –‿–‿–	2 dochm
‿––‿–	dochm

str. VII. 1156–66 = ant. VII. 1167–77

Cass. ‿–‿– ‿–‿‿ ‿‿–‿–	2 ia dochm
‿–‿– –‿–‿–	ia dochm
‿‿–‿– –‿–‿–	2 dochm
–‿–‿–	dochm
2 ia trimeters	
Cho. ‿‿‿‿‿– ‿‿–‿–	2 dochm
‿–‿‿ ‿–‿–	2 ia
‿––‿– ‿‿–‿–	2 dochm [responsion as in *ScT* 564 = 627, *Cho.* 960 = 971]
‿––‿– ‿‿‿‿‿‿	2 dochm
–‿–‿–	dochm

anapaests 1331–42

1407–1576

On the structure of this epirrhematic composition see Fraenkel
pp. 660 f.

str. 1407–11 = ant. 1426–30

Cho.	∪∪–∪–	dochm
	∪∪∪∪ ∪–∪–	2 ia
	∪∪–∪– –∪∪∪–	2 dochm
	∪∪–∪– –∪–∪–	2 dochm
	∪∪∪∪∪ ∪∪–∪–	2 dochm
	–∪–∪∪––	pher

Clytemnestra replies to both str. and ant. in ordinary dialogue-trimeters, 1412–25 and 1431–47.

str. 1448–54 = ant. 1468–74

Cho.	–∪–∪– –∪–∪–	2 dochm
	–∪–∪∪––	pher
	∪–∪– –∪– ∪––	ia cr ba
	–∪∪–∪∪–∪––	'alcaic decasyllable' [see note on 1004 above]
	∪∪–∪–∪–	lec
	∞∪– –∪– –∪–	3 cr
	–∪– –∪–∪–∪–	cr lec

After the strophe, *but not after the antistrophe*, there follows an 'ephymnium', 1455–61

	∪∪– ∪∪–	anap
	∪∪– –– –∪∪ ––	anap
	–– ∪∪– ∪∪– –	anap (paroemiac)
	†–∪∪––∪–† –∪∪–∪–	probably 2 dochm
	∪–∪– ∪–∪– ∪–∪–	3 ia
	∪∪– –∪– ∪––	2 cr ba

Clytemnestra replies in anapaests, 1462–7 and 1475–80.

str. 1481–8 = ant. 1505–12

Cho.	–∪∪–∪∪–	hemiepes ⎱ see note
	–∪∪–∪∪–∪––	2 dact+ ⎰ on 1004
		clausula –∪–– ⎰ above
	––∪∪–∪––	tel+ –
	–∪–∪∪––	pher
	∪–∪– ∪–∪–	2 ia
	∪–∪– ∪–∪–	2 ia

◡–◡– ◡–◡– ◡––	2 ia ba
◡––◡◡–◡––	hipp

The third line bears the same relation to the telesillean (◡‒◡◡–◡–)
as the hipponactean to the glyconic.

After the strophe, *and also after the antistrophe*, there follows another
'ephymnium', 1489–96

–– –– ◡◡– ◡◡–	anap
–◡◡ ––	anap
◡◡– ◡◡– ◡◡– –	anap (paroem.)
–– ◡◡– ◡◡– ◡◡–	anap
◡◡– ◡◡– ◡◡– –	anap (paroem.)
––– –––◡◡–◡–	'molossus'+glyc *or* 2 dochm
◡◡– ◡–◡–	[see note]
–◡◡–◡◡–◡––	'alcaic decasyllable' [see note on 1004 above]

In 1493 = 1517 the scansion assumed here, εκπνεῶν, is suspect; there
is no parallel in Tragedy for the synizesis of -εῶν in a present participle
of this type. In 1494 = 1518 οιμοι μοι may be *extra metrum*; if it is
within the metre, the interpretation ––––– –◡◡–◡–, 2 dochmiacs,
is possible, but not more likely than ––(◡)– –––◡◡–◡–, ia+glyc.

In 1495 = 1519 ◡◡– ◡–◡– may be compared with S. *OT* 1209,
where ◡◡– ◡–◡– is followed by –◡◡– ◡–◡– | –◡◡– ◡–◡– |
–◡◡– –◡– ◡––: i.e., ◡◡– ◡–◡– is shown by its context to be a
'decapitated' choriambic dimeter, (◡)◡◡– ◡–◡–. Similarly E. *Hipp.*
125 = 135 ◡◡– ◡–◡–, preceded by –◡◡– ◡––.

Clytemnestra replies to both str. and ant. in anapaests, 1497–1504
and 1521–9.

str. 1530–6 = ant. 1560–6

Cho.		
◡–◡– –◡– ◡––	ia cr ba
–◡◡– ◡–◡	cho ba
◡–◡– –◡– ◡––	ia cr ba
◡–◡– –◡–◡–◡–	ia lec
◡–◡– –◡– ◡––	ia cr ba
◡–◡– ◡–◡– ◡–◡–	3 ia
◡–– –◡– ◡––	ba cr ba

After the strophe, *but not after the antistrophe,* there follows another 'ephymnium', 1537–50

—— —— —⏑⏑ ——	anap
—— ⏑⏑— —⏑⏑ ——	anap
—— ⏑⏑— ⏑⏑— —	anap (paroemiac)
⏑⏑— —— ⏑⏑— ——	anap
—⏑⏑ —— —— ——	anap
—⏑⏑ —— ⏑⏑— ——	anap
—— ⏑⏑— ⏑⏑— ——	anap
⏑⏑— ⏑⏑— ⏑⏑— —	anap (paroemiac)
—⏑⏑—⏑⏑—⏑⏑—⏑——	praxilleum [see note]
—⏑⏑— ⏑——	cho ba
⏑—— —⏑— ⏑——	ba cr ba

1547. The common —⏑⏑— ⏑—— (cho ba) is often prolonged to —⏑⏑—⏑⏑—⏑—— (the so-called 'alcaic decasyllable'), and sometimes further to —⏑⏑—⏑⏑—⏑⏑—⏑——, a verse called by the ancients after the name of the poetess Praxilla (Hephaestion, p. 24. 8 Consbruch).

Clytemnestra replies to both str. and ant. in anapaests, 1551–9 and 1567–76.

APPENDIX ON *AGAM*. 239 f.

239 f. χέουσᾱ | εβαλλ᾽: the *stasima* of Tragedy are constructed in stanzas consisting of *periods* comprising *cola* (κῶλα) comprising *metra* (though (*a*) *period* and *colon*, (*b*) *colon* and *metron*, may coincide), thus:

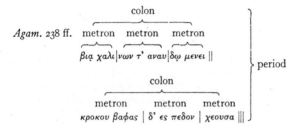

The final syllable of a *period* (but not of any lesser unit) possesses at all times the powers (*a*) of standing in hiatus with the syllable which begins the next 'line' (i.e. with the opening syllable of the following *period*); (*b*) of counting as a *long* syllable, even though it be by nature a *short* one. (This latter phenomenon is conveniently called *brevis in longo*, i.e. a short syllable standing in a 'long' place: it is to be sharply distinguished from *syllaba anceps*, which describes a syllable to the quantity of which the metre is indifferent, as in the first syllable of an 'iambic', ⏕–⏑–).

From the treatment of the final syllable of χέουσα (*brevis in longo*) in this place we must infer that χέουσα is standing at the end of a period: there is then nothing in theory abnormal about it; it is exercising both the powers inherent in the final syllable of a period.

It remains generally true that neither of these powers is often exercised except where the end of the period coincides either with (more or less) heavy punctuation, or with transition to a different metre, or both; there are nevertheless some relevant examples in Aeschylus:

(i) *brevis in longo* in lyric iambics: the iambic ends in a vowel short by nature at the end of a period without heavy punctuation or change of metre:

Pers. 136   -στα ποθῳ φιλανορῐ, ‖ τον, with light punctuation.
ScT 858   θεωριδᾰ, ‖ ταν, again with light punctuation.

Agam. 208 τεκνον δαιξω δομων αγαλμᾱ, ‖ μιαινων, again with light punctuation.

ScT 306 αφεντες ταν βαθυχθον' αιᾰν ‖ υδωρ τε, with no pause.

In *Pers.* 572 it looks as though there is an example of a very rare phenomenon, *brevis in longo* at the end of a colon within a period :

-ζου βαρυ δ' αμβοασὄν | ουρανια κτλ.

(ii) *hiatus* : in the following, a bacchiac stands in hiatus at the end of a period :

Cho. 435 πατρος δ' ατιμωσιν αρα τεισει ‖ εκατι κτλ, with no (or the lightest) punctuation,

Agam. 377 υπερφευ ‖ υπερ το βελτιστον

(iii) both *brevis in longo* and *hiatus* :

Cho. 426 επασσυτεροτριβη τα χερος ορεγματᾰ ‖ ανωθεν : here, as in χεουσᾰ ‖ εβαλλ', *both* of the vowels which stand in hiatus are by nature short, a very rare phenomenon (except where *exclamations* are involved).

PRINTED IN GREAT BRITAIN AT THE UNIVERSITY PRESS, OXFORD
BY VIVIAN RIDLER, PRINTER TO THE UNIVERSITY